THE CAMBRIDGE COMPANION TO
THE IRISH NOVEL

The Irish novel has had a distinguished history. It spans such diverse authors as James Joyce, George Moore, Maria Edgeworth, Bram Stoker, Flann O'Brien, Samuel Beckett, Lady Morgan and John Banville. Yet it has until now received less critical attention than Irish poetry and drama. This volume covers three hundred years of Irish achievement in fiction, with essays on key genres, themes and authors. It provides critiques of individual works, accounts of important novelists and histories of subgenres and allied narrative forms, establishing significant social and political contexts for dozens of novels. The varied perspectives and emphases by more than a dozen critics and literary historians ensure that the Irish novel receives due tribute for its colour, variety and linguistic verve. Each chapter features recommended further reading. This is the perfect overview for students of the Irish novel, from the romances of the seventeenth century to the present day.

JOHN WILSON FOSTER is Professor Emeritus of English at the University of British Columbia, Canada.

THE CAMBRIDGE COMPANION
TO THE IRISH NOVEL

EDITED BY
JOHN WILSON FOSTER

CAMBRIDGE
UNIVERSITY PRESS

1-25-2007
WW
≠ 29.99

CAMBRIDGE UNIVERSITY PRESS
Cambridge, New York, Melbourne, Madrid, Cape Town, Singapore, São Paulo

Cambridge University Press
The Edinburgh Building, Cambridge CB2 2RU, UK

Published in the United States of America by Cambridge University Press, New York

www.cambridge.org
Information on this title: www.cambridge.org/9780521679961

First published 2006

Printed in the United Kingdom at the University Press, Cambridge

A catalogue record for this publication is available from the British Library

ISBN-13 978-0-521-86191-5 hardback
ISBN-10 0-521-86191-8 hardback
ISBN-13 978-0-521-67996-1 paperback
ISBN-10 0-521-67996-6 paperback

CONTENTS

NOTES ON CONTRIBUTORS

TERENCE BROWN is Professor of Anglo-Irish Literature and Dean of Arts and Humanities, University of Dublin, Trinity College. He is a member of the Royal Irish Academy and Academia Europaea. His recent publications include *The Life of W. B. Yeats: A Critical Biography* (1999) and *Ireland: A Social and Cultural History 1922–2002* (2004). He was a consultant editor of *The Encyclopedia of Ireland* (2003).

MIRANDA BURGESS is Associate Professor of English at the University of British Columbia. She is the author of *British Fiction and the Production of Social Order 1740–1830* (2000).

AILEEN DOUGLAS is a member of the School of English, University of Dublin, Trinity College and has published a range of articles on eighteenth-century Irish writing in English.

ADRIAN FRAZIER is Senior Lecturer and Director of the MA programmes in Writing and Drama & Theatre Studies at the National University of Ireland, Galway. He is the author of *George Moore 1852–1933* (2000) and editor of *Playboys of the Western World: Production Histories* (2004).

ELIZABETH GRUBGELD is Professor of English at Oklahoma State University. She is the author of *George Moore and the Autogenous Self* (1994) and *Anglo-Irish Autobiography: Class, Gender and the Forms of Narrative* (2004).

ELMER KENNEDY-ANDREWS is Professor of English Literature and Head of the Research Graduate School at the University of Ulster. His books include *The Poetry of Seamus Heaney: All the Realms of Whisper* (1988), *The Art of Brian Friel* (1995) and *(De-)Constructing the North: Fiction and the Northern Ireland Troubles since 1969* (2002).

SIOBHÁN KILFEATHER is Lecturer in nineteenth-century Irish writing in the School of English, Queen's University, Belfast. She is the author of *Dublin: A Cultural and*

Literary History (2005). She is one of the editors of the *Field Day Anthology of Irish Writing*, vols. 4 and 5: *Irish Women's Writings and Traditions* (2002). She contributed the entry on 'Feminism' to the *Cambridge Companion to Modern Irish Culture* (2005).

VERA KREILKAMP is Professor of English at Pine Manor College and Visiting Professor with the Irish Studies Programme at Boston College. She is the author of *The Anglo-Irish Novel and the Big House* (1998) and co-edits *Éire-Ireland: An Interdisciplinary Journal of Irish Studies*.

JAMES H. MURPHY is Professor of English and Director of Irish Studies at DePaul University of Chicago. His recent books include *Abject Loyalty: Nationalism and Monarchy in Ireland During the Reign of Queen Victoria* (2001) and *Ireland: A Social, Cultural and Literary History 1791–1891* (2003).

EVE PATTEN is Lecturer in English at the University of Dublin, Trinity College. She is the author of *Samuel Ferguson and the Culture of Nineteenth-Century Ireland* (2004) and co-author of *Irish Studies: The Essential Glossary* (2003).

BRUCE STEWART is Lecturer in Irish literary history and bibliography at the University of Ulster. He is Literary Adviser to the Princess Grace Irish Library (Monaco) and edits the PGIL transactions. He was Assistant Editor of the *Oxford Companion to Irish Literature* (1996) and wrote the entry on James Joyce for *The New Dictionary of National Biography* (2004).

ALAN TITLEY is Head of the Irish Department of St Patrick's College, Drumcondra. Among his publications are *Eiriceachtaí agus Scéalta Eile* (1987), *A Pocket History of Gaelic Culture* (2000) and a children's novel in Irish, *Amach* (2003).

NORMAN VANCE is Professor of English at the University of Sussex. His recent publications include *Irish Literature: A Social History* (2nd edn 1999) and *Irish Literature since 1800* (2002).

ANN OWENS WEEKES is Associate Professor of English, University of Arizona. She is the author of *Irish Women Writers: An Uncharted Tradition* (1990) and *Unveiling Treasures: The Attic Guide to the Published Work of Irish Women Writers* (1993).

JOHN WILSON FOSTER was Visiting Professor, University of Toronto (2005) and Leverhulme Visiting Professor to the UK (University of Ulster, 2004–5). His recent books include *Recoveries: Neglected Episodes in Irish Cultural History 1860–1912* (2002), *The Age of* Titanic: *Cross-Currents in Anglo-American Culture* (2002), *Titanic* (ed. 1999), and *Nature in Ireland: A Scientific and Cultural History* (sen. ed. 1997).

ACKNOWLEDGMENT

Thanks are due to Dr Daniel O'Leary for compiling the chronology.

CHRONOLOGY

1641–1700

1641	Catholic rebellion in Ulster
1651–65	*Parthenissa*, Roger Boyle
1665	*The English Rogue*, Richard Head
1676	*English Adventures*, Roger Boyle
1687	*Theodora and Didymus*, Robert Boyle
1690	Victory of William of Orange over James II at the Battle of the Boyne
1691	Treaty of Limerick
1692	*Incognita*, William Congreve
1693	*Vertue Rewarded*, Anonymous
1695	Institution of anti-Catholic Penal Laws by Dublin parliament

1700–1800

1716	*Irish Tales*, Sarah Butler
1726	Dublin printing and book-selling shop opened by George Faulkner
	Gulliver's Travels, Jonathan Swift
1745	Death of Swift
1752	*The History of Jack Connor*, William Chaigneau
1756–66	*The Life and Opinions of John Buncle, Esq.*, Thomas Amory
1759–67	*The Life and Opinions of Tristram Shandy, Gentleman*, Laurence Sterne
1760–65	*Chrysal*, Charles Johnstone
1761–7	*Memoirs of Miss Sidney Bidulph*, Frances Sheridan
1762	*The Reverie*, Charles Johnstone
1765–70	*The Fool of Quality*, Henry Brooke

1766	*The Vicar of Wakefield*, Oliver Goldsmith
1767	*The History of Nourjahad*, Frances Sheridan
1768	Death of Laurence Sterne
	A Sentimental Journey through France and Italy, Laurence Sterne
1774	Death of Goldsmith
1778	First Catholic Relief Act
1781	*The History of John Juniper, Esq.*, Charles Johnstone
	The Triumph of Prudence Over Passion, Anonymous ('An Irish lady')
1782	Grattan's Parliament; Dungannon Volunteer Convention
1786	*The Adventures of Anthony Varnish*, Anonymous [Charles Johnstone]
1791	United Irishmen founded by Theobald Wolfe Tone and others
1793	Relaxation of Penal Laws
1795	Battle of the Diamond, Armagh and founding of Orange Order
1797	Death of Edmund Burke
1798	United Irishmen lead insurrection resulting in 30,000 deaths

1800–1850

1800	Act of Union (takes effect 1801)
	Castle Rackrent, Maria Edgeworth
1803	Dublin uprising under Robert Emmet
1806	*The Wild Irish Girl*, Sydney Owenson (Lady Morgan)
1808	*The Wild Irish Boy*, Charles Robert Maturin
1812	*The Absentee*, Maria Edgeworth
	The Milesian Chief: A Romance, Charles Robert Maturin
1814	*O'Donnel: A National Tale*, Lady Morgan
1817	*Ormond*, Maria Edgeworth
1818	*Florence Macarthy: An Irish Tale*, Lady Morgan
1820	*Melmoth the Wanderer*, Charles Robert Maturin
1825–6	*Tales of the O'Hara Family*, John Banim
1826	*The Boyne Water*, John Banim
1828	*The Croppy*, Michael Banim
1829	Catholic Emancipation
	The Collegians, Gerald Griffin
1830–3	*Traits and Stories of the Irish Peasantry*, William Carleton
1833	*The Nowlans*, John Banim

1893	Eoin MacNeill and others form Gaelic League, with Douglas Hyde as president; second Home Rule Bill defeated
	The Celtic Twilight, William Butler Yeats
	The Heavenly Twins, Sarah Grand
1894	*Esther Waters*, George Moore
	The Real Charlotte, Somerville and Ross
	A New Note, Ella MacMahon
1897	*Dracula*, Bram Stoker
	Geoffrey Austin, Student, Patrick Augustine (Canon) Sheehan
	The Beth Book, Sarah Grand
1898	*The Triumph of Failure*, Canon Sheehan
1899	*Some Experiences of an Irish RM*, Somerville and Ross
	Autobiography of a Child [1898–9], Hannah Lynch

1900–1925

1900	Death of Oscar Wilde
	My New Curate, Canon Sheehan
1901	*The Triumph of Cuculain*, Standish James O'Grady
1902	*Cuchulain of Muirthemne*, Lady Augusta Gregory
1903	Wyndham Land Act
	The Untilled Field, George Moore
	The Riddle of the Sands, Erskine Childers
1904	Abbey Theatre opens in Dublin
	Gods and Fighting Men, Lady Augusta Gregory
	Séadna, Peadar Ua Laoghaire (Canon Peter O'Leary)
	John Chilcote, MP, Katherine Cecil Thurston
1905	Sinn Fein founded by Arthur Griffith
	The Lake, George Moore
	The Soggarth Aroon, Canon Joseph Guinan
1907	*The Northern Iron*, George A. Birmingham
1908	*The Moneylender*, Joseph Edelstein
	The Fly on the Wheel, Katherine Cecil Thurston
	When the Tide Turns, Filson Young
1909	Death of Synge
1910	*Deoraíocht*, Pádraic Ó Conaire
1911–14	*Hail and Farewell*, George Moore
1912	*Titanic*, built in Belfast, sinks on maiden voyage; third Home Rule Bill becomes law but in abeyance due to Great War and 1916 rebellion; Ulster Covenant (unionist) pledging resistance to home rule; Ulster Volunteer Force raised

Caisleáin Óir, Séamas Ó Grianna
The Loughsiders, Shan F. Bullock

1925–1950

1925   Dáil Éireann (Free State parliament) forbids bills seeking legal divorce
A Vision, William Butler Yeats
The Informer, Liam O'Flaherty
The Big House of Inver, Somerville and Ross [Martin d. 1915]

1926   Radio Éireann begins broadcasting
King Goshawk and the Birds, Eimar O'Duffy

1927   *Islanders*, Peadar O'Donnell

1928   Death of Standish James O'Grady

1929   Irish Censorship Board set up in Free State
An tOileánach, Tomás Ó Criomhthain
The Last September, Elizabeth Bowen

1930   *Sir John Magill's Last Journey*, Freeman Wills Crofts
A Flock of Birds, Kathleen Coyle

1931   *The Puritan*, Liam O'Flaherty
Women and God, Francis Stuart
Mad Puppetstown, M. J. Farrell (Molly Keane)

1932   Death of Lady Gregory
Pigeon Irish, Francis Stuart
Skerrett, Liam O'Flaherty
The Ladies' Road, Pamela Hinkson

1933   Death of George Moore
Fiche Blian ag Fás (Twenty Years A-Growing), Maurice O'Sullivan
Peter Abelard, Helen Waddell
Island Story, Olga Fielden

1934   *A Nest of Simple Folk*, Sean O'Faolain
The Islandman (An tOileánach), Tomás Ó Crohan
The Ante-Room, Kate O'Brien

1935   Death of George Russell (AE)

1936   IRA outlawed in Free State
Bird Alone, Sean O'Faolain
Mary Lavelle, Kate O'Brien

1937   New constitution for 'Eire', establishing presidency; forbids laws granting dissolution of marriages

	Famine, Liam O'Flaherty
	Peter Waring, Forrest Reid
1938	Douglas Hyde first President of Eire
	Murphy, Samuel Beckett
	The Green Fool, Patrick Kavanagh
	The Autobiography of William Butler Yeats
	Out of the Silent Planet, C. S. Lewis
1939	Death of Yeats
	At Swim-Two-Birds, Flann O'Brien (Brian O'Nolan)
	Finnegans Wake, James Joyce
	Call My Brother Back, Michael McLaverty
	My Cousin Justin, Margaret Barrington
1939–45	Second World War (Free State neutral, Northern Ireland a combatant)
1940	*Dutch Interior*, Frank O'Connor
	The Third Policeman (not published until 1967), Flann O'Brien
1941	Death of Joyce
	A House of Children, Joyce Cary
	An Béal Bocht, Flann O'Brien
	The Land of Spices, Kate O'Brien
1945	*The House in Clewe Street*, Mary Lavin
1946	*Odd Man Out*, F. L. Green
1948	Republic of Ireland Act establishes Free State as a republic
	Tarry Flynn, Patrick Kavanagh
1949	Death of Douglas Hyde; Eire declared Republic, leaves Commonwealth
	In a Harbour Green, Benedict Kiely
	Cré na Cille, Máirtín Ó Cadhain
	The Heat of the Day, Elizabeth Bowen

1950–1975

1950	Death of George Bernard Shaw; death of James Stephens
1951	*Molloy*, Samuel Beckett
1953	BBC begins television transmission to Northern Ireland
	Watt, Samuel Beckett
1955	*The Lonely Passion of Judith Hearne*, Brian Moore
1958	*Malone Dies* (*Malone Meurt*, 1951), Samuel Beckett
	Cadenza, Ralph Cusack
1960	*The Country Girls*, Edna O'Brien
	The Unnameable (*L'Innommable*, 1953), Samuel Beckett

1961	Broadcasts by Radio Telefís Éireann begin

1961   Broadcasts by Radio Telefís Éireann begin
1962   *The Lonely Girl*, Edna O'Brien
1963   *The Barracks*, John McGahern
        The Ferret Fancier, Anthony C. West
        Thy Tears Might Cease, Michael Farrell
1964   Death of Sean O'Casey
        The Maiden Dinosaur, Janet McNeill
        The Old Boys, William Trevor
1965   Talks between northern and southern premiers Terence
        O'Neill and Sean Lemass
        The Dark, John McGahern
        The Emperor of Ice-Cream, Brian Moore
1966   *Langrishe, Go Down*, Aidan Higgins
1967   Northern Ireland Civil Rights Association instituted
        An Eochair, Máirtín Ó Cadhain
1968   Riots and sectarian violence begin in Northern Ireland
        An Uain Bheo, Diarmaid Ó Súilleabháin
1969   Provisional IRA formed; Samuel Beckett awarded Nobel Prize
        for Literature
        Strumpet City, James Plunkett
        Poor Lazarus, Maurice Leitch
1970   *Godded and Codded*, Julia O'Faolain
        Troubles, J. G. Farrell
1971   Provisional IRA begins campaign of violence
        Black List, Section H, Francis Stuart
1972   'Bloody Sunday' riots in Londonderry; Stormont (NI)
        parliament prorogued
        Balcony of Europe, Aidan Higgins
        Catholics, Brian Moore
        Night, Edna O'Brien
        The Captains and the Kings, Jennifer Johnston
        The Poor Mouth (*An Béal Bocht*, 1941), Flann O'Brien
1973   Republic enters Common Market
        Birchwood, John Banville
1974   *How Many Miles to Babylon?*, Jennifer Johnston
        The Leavetaking, John McGahern

1975–2000

1976   *Dr Copernicus*, John Banville
        The Children of Dynmouth, William Trevor

1977   *A Hole in the Head*, Francis Stuart
        Proxopera, Benedict Kiely
1978   *Bogmail*, Patrick McGinley
1980   *Company*, Samuel Beckett
        No Country for Young Men, Julia O'Faolain
1981   Aosdána established to honour outstanding living Irish
        artists; hunger strikes by IRA detainees in Long Kesh prison
        Kepler, John Banville
1982   *The Obedient Wife*, Julia O'Faolain
1983   *Cal*, Bernard MacLaverty
        Cold Heaven, Brian Moore
        Fools of Fortune, William Trevor
        Bornholm Night-Ferry, Aidan Higgins
1984   *The Irish Signorina*, Julia O'Faolain
        The Summerhouse, Val Mulkerns
1985   Anglo-Irish Agreement protects majority wishes in Northern
        Ireland but provides for possible Irish unification
        Nothing Happens in Carmincross, Benedict Kiely
        The Trick of the Ga Bolga, Patrick McGinley
1986   *Ellen*, Ita Daly
        Mefisto, John Banville
1988   *The Silence in the Garden*, William Trevor
        Sionnach ar mo Dhuán, Breandán Ó hEithir
1989   Death of Beckett
        The Book of Evidence, John Banville
        There We Have Been, Leland Bardwell
        Ripley Bogle, Robert McLiam Wilson
1990   *Amongst Women*, John McGahern
        The Journey Home, Dermot Bolger
1992   Referendum in Republic approves Maastricht Treaty (EU)
        The Barrytown Trilogy, Roddy Doyle
        The Butcher Boy, Patrick McCabe
        Fat Lad, Glenn Patterson
1993   President of Republic (Mary Robinson) visits Queen Eliza-
        beth II in London
        Paddy Clarke Ha Ha Ha, Roddy Doyle
        The Heather Blazing, Colm Tóibín
1994   *Felicia's Journey*, William Trevor
        A Goat's Song, Dermot Healy
        Stir-Fry, Emma Donoghue

1995	Divorce referendum narrowly passes in Republic; Prince of Wales's visit
	The Wig My Father Wore, Anne Enright
	The Statement, Brian Moore
1996	*Reading in the Dark*, Seamus Deane
	The Woman Who Walked into Doors, Roddy Doyle
	Angela's Ashes, Frank McCourt
1997	*Grace Notes*, Bernard MacLaverty
	The Star Factory, Ciaran Carson
	The Untouchable, John Banville
1998	Belfast (or Good Friday) Agreement provides for devolved government in Northern Ireland
	Death and Nightingales, Eugene McCabe
1999	*Foley's Asia*, Ronan Sheehan
	The Blackwater Lightship, Colm Tóibín

2000–

2000	*What Are You Like?*, Anne Enright
2001	*At Swim, Two Boys*, Jamie O'Neill
2002	*That They May Face the Rising Sun*, John McGahern
	The Story of Lucy Gault, William Trevor
	Shroud, John Banville
2003	*Dancer*, Colum McCann
	The Parts, Keith Ridgway
2004	*The Master*, Colm Tóibín
2005	IRA announces cessation of armed struggle

JOHN WILSON FOSTER

Introduction

Beginnings

The Irish novel emerged in the tangle of social, cultural, commercial and literary interrelations of Great Britain and Ireland. It shares its genesis with the English novel, as do all English-language national traditions of the genre, though much older and distinctively native Irish narrative forms and energies influenced its course later. When we write of the eighteenth century (the century in which the novel written by Irish authors decisively appeared) and use the phrase 'the Irish novel', we are necessarily referring to novels written by authors who, irrespective of birthplace, inhabited both England and Ireland, but chiefly England, and who thought of themselves as English or possibly both English and Irish, with the first identity being the defining one. The once standard *History of the English Novel* (ten volumes, 1924–39) by Ernest A. Baker, and the once standard short histories of the English novel that took much from Baker – *The English Novel: A Short Critical History* (1954) by Walter Allen and *The English Novel: A Panorama* (1960) by Lionel Stevenson – like the once standard history of the genre's starting decades, *The Rise of the Novel* (1957) by Ian Watt, do not normally identify as Irish those early novelists who had in fact some claim to the title. If they did (Baker calls Thomas Amory 'half an Irishman'), the Irishness of the authors was regarded as of little consequence and this seemed to be a view derived from these almost exclusively Protestant or Anglo-Irish authors themselves, who failed to stake their claim to Irishness. True, thirty years ago and more, there was little sensitivity among British critics to matters of national pride or ethnic identity outside England and they would not have been scrupulous about Irish attribution. This may have been a vestige of an imperial attitude, certainly of a metropolitan attitude largely indifferent to regional identity, which was regarded as a mark of minor literature; but I recall it in my student days in Northern Ireland rather as a concern for literary texts instead of cultural contexts and national subtexts (Baker and Stevenson, after all, were North Americans). The English novel, like English literature, was as a literary matter largely sequestered from the anxieties of nationality; even James Joyce, though manifestly Irish, was seen as an ornament of both the English novel and English literature.

When Allen, Stevenson and Watt were writing, academic Irish Studies were in their infancy, though it had been assumed by many Irish readers ever since the first two decades of the twentieth century that Ireland had a literature that helped distinguish the country from Britain. William Butler Yeats (1865–1939) was to a degree interested in reclaiming Irish writers from the English canon and in recalling living expatriate Irish writers for duty in Ireland, but he was far more interested in building an entirely new canon by recovering the ancient or traditional native Irish sagas, folk tales and poems and encouraging young Irish writers to write a new national literature inspired by them. Yeats was aided in galvanising Irish writers into producing this national literature by Standish James O'Grady, Douglas Hyde, Lady Gregory and other 'culture-givers' of the early years of the twentieth century, and the abundant fruits of their success we call the Irish Literary Revival (c.1890–1930). When Irish Studies were gathering momentum thirty years ago, they were conducted in the long shadow of this revival, and thus the Irishness of writing by Irish writers outside the movement was not a given. The Irishness of the work of, say, Oscar Wilde and Bram Stoker was regarded as seriously qualified and indirect, since that work did not concern itself primarily with the new Ireland; these writers did not in an obvious way boast the Celtic eyes Yeats saw the novelist William Carleton (1794–1869) looking out from, and so their work was not a portion of the previously hidden or of the newly emerging Irish canon.

But recently, and encouraged by widespread contemporary academic interest in minority cultures, national beginnings, ethnic identities, minor literatures and anti- and post-colonialism (all components of Cultural Studies, into which literary studies have been largely absorbed), critics of Irish literature have made fascinating raids on the vast corpus of English literature and sought to unpick the English–Irish interrelations I have mentioned. *Castle Rackrent: An Hibernian Tale* (1800) had traditionally been read by English critics as a pioneering regional British novel but later Irish critics retrieved it as a pioneering national work, indeed the first truly Irish novel. Recent critics have tended to return it to the complex universe of colonial discourse while not detracting from its national importance. The author's biography would lend warrant to this: Maria Edgeworth belonged to an old English family long settled in Ireland; she was born in Oxfordshire and was fifteen before she arrived in Ireland; she did so in 1782, a year momentous for contemporary advocates of greater Irish autonomy; she lived her life in Ireland but spent productive periods in London. In the cases of Wilde (including *The Picture of Dorian Gray*, 1891) and Stoker (especially *Dracula*, 1897), it is largely courtesy of the new criticism and cultural studies, in which Irishness in texts is being detected in increasingly oblique and coded ways, that they are now staples of Irish literary studies, though of course, being Irish, they ought to have been so from the start. With some irony, the expanded Irish canon has almost achieved the amplitude it once enjoyed in such an anthology as Charles A. Read's *Cabinet of Irish Literature* (1879) and its 1902 revision by Katharine Tynan – an assembly too indiscriminately Irish to be of use to Yeats's Revival – but is now enveloped in an ideology that neither editor would have understood.

In any case, the search for early Irish novels uncovers further unfamiliar entanglements that are not obvious demonstrations of the ideology. For example, much work has been done on the genres and modes that fed into the early English novel, including the European picaresque novel, satire, travel narratives, biography, history, moral tracts and romances. The first and last of these are of particular interest, being narratives of comparable length to the novel proper.

Romances by English writers were inspired by Sir Philip Sidney's example and later by the vogue for French heroic romances in the middle of the seventeenth century. They are set in ancient Greece or Rome or equivalently exotic places and times; they are retellings of legends or classical stories, or narratives spun from characters and episodes from legend or history; they are peopled by royalty or nobles, with heroes and heroines tangled up in love and embarked on necessary quests (often at the insistence of oracles); they exhibit little realism of circumstance, motive or dialogue, but instead employ set pieces, indirect speech and civilised debates (often lengthy) on moral dilemmas. It is not surprising to find Irish contributors to the genre of romance. Roger Boyle (1621–79), 1st Earl of Orrery (son of the 1st Earl of Cork), studied at Trinity College Dublin; as both a royalist and a Commonwealth man, he periodically crossed from England, where he chiefly lived, to Ireland to help restore order there. For his loyalty, including military service during the Irish rebellion of 1641, he was rewarded with large grants of Irish land. *Parthenissa, That Most Fam'd Romance* (1651, 1654–65, 1676) is a long, unfinished prose fiction in six volumes (printed in Waterford) that opens with the arrival of Artabbanes from Parthia at the oracle of the Queen of Love in 'Siria'; the hero has been commanded by the gods to discover his destiny after disappointment in love and suffering melancholy, and his story, which he tells to a servant of the Queen, begins when he meets the 15-year-old Parthenissa and is smitten. This initially readable but cumbersome romance, with tales within tales, combines Roman history with fanciful invention, and martial combat with sexual longing. An important theme is the contest between kinds of love, an old and evergreen theme that the popular novel from the eighteenth century onwards inherited from the genre. The indelible power of love is also the subject of Boyle's incomplete *English Adventures* (1676), published anonymously under the name 'a Person of Honour'. Baker calls it a further deterioration of romance, a story which concerns the amours of the young Henry VIII, and related 'with the debauched cynicism of a romancer corrupted by a long life at the Restoration court'. The connected tales' employment of cold-blooded deceit, design and disguise, and the depiction of the amorous Izabella as the sexual prize (and 'prey') of numerous rivals turn heroic romance into erotic romance, yet the story cleverly sustains three extended metaphors for the machinations of love amongst intimates: stag-hunting, court intrigue and civil war (the barely historical action is set after the 'intestine' Wars of the Roses). The in-tale told by young Charles Brandon was the inspiration of Thomas Otway's tragedy, *The Orphan* (1680).

Roger's younger brother Robert was born in Lismore Castle, Co. Waterford, in 1627. Among his many accomplishments – physicist and chemist of European reputation (author of Boyle's Law), student of alchemy and theology – he was a writer, and in 1687 he published *Love and Religion Demonstrated in the Martyrdom of Theodora, and of Didymus*, a romance that recounts the fate of his heroine at the hands of the Roman authorities, for whom her Christian faith and celibacy are criminal rebellion against the civil government, and of his hero, her chaste lover who is also put to death. (Boyle's romance was the source of Handel's oratorio *Theodora*, 1750.) In a lengthy preface, Boyle claims he is rewriting the genre of heroic romance by making his heroine a pious Christian virgin and his hero a lover strictly bounded by his religion; he wishes 'to transform a piece of Martyrology into a Romance' even if it were regarded as 'a kind of Profaneness'. He is consciously combining the sermon or book of devotion (which provided models for his martyrs' speeches) and martyrologies with pagan romance to create something new. Boyle wished to show, in what we might call his Christian romance, that chivalry and heroic valour could be accompanied by 'eminent' piety. For the 'young Persons of Quality' who were his desired readers, he wanted unfashionably to substitute 'Patterns of Vertue' for mere 'Models of Skill or Eloquence', and serious themes for romance's customary lower aim 'to Delight the Delicate Readers'. Boyle defends the unfashionable intelligence of his heroine, who has to discourse learnedly on theology, and of women in general. The incongruity between hard matter and the pleasures of narrative, and the connection between romance and female readership, survived as both problem and opportunity when the novel proper retained some of the elements of the romance. Meanwhile, *Theodora and Didymus* is far more readable than *Parthenissa* and has some of the tempo and perspective of the genuine novel, incipiently visible behind the inherited static forms. Boyle was aware of the 'Liberties' he was taking by inventing speeches for his historical martyrs but felt at ease in borrowing this device from the heroic romances that he called 'disguised Histories'. Stevenson calls Boyle's romance a precursor of the historical novel, a claim all the more important given the popularity of the historical novel in Irish literary history, though the Christian story and its martyrs attracted only a handful of later Irish novelists, including George Moore and Helen Waddell.

A self-consciousness about romance as a genre became a component of it at the time the novel was emerging. It was perhaps when he was a student at Trinity College Dublin that William Congreve, born near Leeds in Yorkshire, published *Incognita, or Love and Duty Reconciled* (1692) under the pen name of 'Cleophil'. Critics have seen this work as transitional in form, gesturing in its mock-romance towards the future novel, realising Congreve's own prefatory distinction between the 'wonder' of romances and the 'familiar nature' of novels. This was his only fiction; Congreve moved to England where he achieved fame as a playwright. Congreve can hardly be claimed wholeheartedly as an Anglo-Irish writer, though before going up to Trinity he was educated at Kilkenny College, after his father moved to Ireland; but in returning to London he was treading a path already worn by Irish writers and artists who saw London as their cultural capital, and Congreve certainly represented a notable version of English–Irish interrelations.

The other major contributory to the novel, the picaresque narrative, can also claim an Irish exponent, though again it is not an unambiguous claim. The picaresque refers in reduced meaning to a novel in which the hero is plunged into all sorts of adventures and meets with all sorts of people during journeys that are too episodic to be called quests, in the romance sense. An English branch of the picaresque was the rogue biography, going as far back as the late sixteenth century. While insisting on its fidelity to truth and fact, rogue or 'cony-catching' literature mixed fiction, satire and what we might call reportage, all with relish, brio and the prurience of exposé. A late cony-catching novel was *The English Rogue Described in the Life of Meriton Latroon, a Witty Extravagant* (1665) by Richard Head; Stevenson claims it was banned for indecency and peddled underground for half a century.

In his Epistle to the Reader, Head hardly bothers to claim that he is writing the life of another and indeed confesses that he himself is a reformed rogue drawing profitably on personal experience. Yet the bookseller–writer who wrote a sequel to the highly popular *The English Rogue* insisted that Head declined to write a sequel because readers took it for autobiography instead of fiction. The bibliographic note to a 1928 edition accepts this to be true, though since the counterfeit and the spurious are the story's *raison d'être*, it pays the modern reader to be wary. Latroon's biographical circumstances read like Head's own. He is born in Carrickfergus, Co. Antrim, soon after his mother and father (an Anglican minister) arrive from England. When he is four, the 1641 rebellion breaks out and his brother is killed by roaming insurgents. His father and mother flee to Belfast with the remaining son but the Scots in Belfast rout his father, mistaking him in his Anglican garb for a Catholic priest, and the family escape to 'Linsegarvy' (Lisnagarvey) near Lisburn, Co. Antrim. There the father is soon murdered as a Protestant preacher. Mother and son take ship for England. In the book, the anti-hero becomes an English rogue and at one point, to escape creditors, hides out back in Ireland, in Dublin, 'Balle-more-Eustace' (Ballymore Eustace, a small town in east Kildare) and Baltinglass, where he has further adventures.

The English Rogue has been variously called fascinating, dreary, ill-written, disreputable, unsavoury and racy. George Saintsbury in *The English Novel* (1913) called it a quite openly picaresque novel and deplored it, yet devoted two pages to it. Head's perspective on Ireland certainly has interest. Dublin is itself a rogues' asylum (the descriptions of its appalling poverty are Swiftian before the fact), and Latroon's welcome is dysentery and crabs. He does not prosper in Ireland, where he finds that the Irish hate the English 'with a perfect antipathy'. Yet Latroon is not wholly English but rather occupies a strange hybrid place not yet classifiable as Anglo-Ireland. Recounting his childhood, he thinks it strange that the influence of Ireland on anyone born there overpowers 'the disposition of the parent': Ireland, he says, made him 'appear a bastard in disposition to my father'; whereas his father was naturally religious, he himself was roguish from the start. But his 'bastardy' is a memorable metaphor for the unrootedness of the British in Ireland, especially then but also thereafter, and it is an early figure in fiction for Anglo-Irish relations.

More important than *The English Rogue* itself are the ambient cultural factors of which it is the product and which are routinely adduced as necessary to the advent of the early novel written by Daniel Defoe and others: individualism, Protestantism, urbanism and capitalism, the latter in its shadowy guises here of theft, debt, swindling and get-rich-quick schemes.

The early novel of the eighteenth century shared Head's overall concern (however disingenuous) with vice and reformation. The book exhibits, too, the early novels' realism (a cynical realism here) and picaresque structure. *The English Rogue* is dedicated to promiscuity and the narrative is too episodic, unstable and disjointed to have the structure of the mature novel: there is a multitude of vices and sins (including blasphemy, incest, adultery), of scenes, of characters, of settings and of discourses. The book is likewise dedicated to duplicity (cheating, forgery, disguises and aliases), of which the cant words are its verbal equivalent. (There is a 'canting' glossary of rogues' argot by which they concealed their meanings and intentions from outsiders and 'conies', or marks.) But for all its crudity, the spirit of *The English Rogue* and rogue literature stayed alive in the English and Irish novel, and we can detect it in *Tristram Shandy* (1759–67) by Laurence Sterne (born and raised in Ireland) and James Joyce's *Ulysses* (1922).

Eighteenth- and nineteenth-century contexts

Congreve and Goldsmith, like Sterne, Farquhar, Sheridan and Steele, were late seventeenth- or early eighteenth-century writers, born or educated in Ireland, who settled in England; we must be content to describe them awkwardly as both English and Irish, but as chiefly English. Often, they disavowed their Irishness; even Irish geography could be disavowed. It has been said that in *The Vicar of Wakefield* (1766), Goldsmith – as he was to do in 'The Deserted Village' (1770) – transplanted to England an idealised portrait of Lissoy in Co. Westmeath where the author spent his childhood. (His novel has been called pastoral romance with picaresque elements.) 'Irish' in its unqualified use referred to the Catholic natives with whom these writers declined to identify. The more compact term, Anglo-Irish, was a nineteenth-century usage referring to those Anglican Protestants of English extraction who, from the early eighteenth century onwards, while still of dual nationality in the broadest sense, established a greater balance between their two identities and, as the eighteenth century progressed, began to shift some of their allegiance away from England towards Ireland: not the Ireland of the Catholic natives, but one made synonymous with themselves. We can watch this occur in the work of Jonathan Swift, whom Aileen Douglas discusses in chapter 1. The so-called Protestant Nation or Ascendancy, forming itself through colonial grievances against England, reached its constitutional apogee in Grattan's parliament of 1782–1800. At the same time, a colonial restiveness was growing among the Dissenters (or Non-conformist Protestants) of the North – mostly of Scots origin – whose liberal or radical philosophy troubled English–Irish relations and, coinciding with Catholic grievances for one tremendous moment, laid the intellectual foundation for the 1798 rebellion.

English–Irish relations came into sharper but not yet central focus in the novels written by those pre-1800 novelists, writing later than Swift, who are also of interest to Douglas. When those relations did move towards the centre of the novelists' field of view, they were revealed in all their instability and ambivalence. Genre vied with prescriptions and prejudices of a culturally political kind, as Miranda Burgess makes clear in her discussion of the varieties of tales that were popular in the late eighteenth and early nineteenth centuries, with those by Maria Edgeworth and Sydney Owenson (Lady Morgan) leaders in popularity and reputation. The eighteenth-century episodic novel was typically dominated by a hero's consciousness too worldly to subject itself sympathetically to others, especially to the 'Other', though romance elements survived. This was succeeded by the sympathy (one is tempted to say feminine sympathy) inherent in the tales; and in the tales, the strains between England and Ireland are embodied in their heroes and heroines.

The national tale, which Burgess discusses at some length in chapter 2, was a Romantic form that focussed its attention on Ireland as a setting and subject; it added to the English–Irish equation the third term of native Ireland and it fictionalised the cultural distinctiveness of Ireland. But recent critics have wondered how far the national tale tried to 'complete' the Union between Great Britain and Ireland of 1800, of which the genre has been seen as a product. Typically, an English visitor to Ireland or returned Anglicised Irish expatriate instigated the tale's proceedings; and the reader the novelist had chiefly in mind was English. On the other hand, how far does the genre express the grievances of a small country like Ireland? Or perhaps the genre belongs wholly to neither culture.[1] In any event, the influence of romance persisted and, through its satisfaction of wish-fulfilment, its unreality remained a feature of fictional treatments of English–Irish relations. Until recently, these relations never entirely vacated the Irish novel as a theme and, since those relations can run from the romance of Irish nationalism to practical economic and political reformism, the theme is a large and various one. The prescription in fiction of mere improvement (deriving from the Enlightenment) is one that ensured the neglect of novels that turn their back on nationalism; oddly, realism in the matter of deep Irish difference was, until recently, regarded as a denial of such difference.

The Gothic also contributed to the Irish national tale, which is hardly surprising, given that early Gothic novels have been called romances. Gothic is an adaptable form and its students have shown the role in it of science and the occult as well as radical (and conservative!) politics. Siobhán

Kilfeather demonstrates, in chapter 4, the versatility of the Gothic, especially after its heyday in the period 1760–1820, not just as subgenre but as a component and aspect of other kinds of novel. As well as paying heed to the romance and the national tale, the discussion of Irish Gothic as a tradition must root itself in the English Gothic and its international progeny and parallels. Horace Walpole's *The Castle of Otranto* appeared in 1764 and Irish Gothic is normally assumed to begin with Charles Maturin's *The Milesian Chief* (1812), though, pioneeringly, Kilfeather pushes the beginnings back to the 1770s and even 1760s. In any case, when setting and subject matter are Irish, though the tropes, themes, motifs or narrative formulas be English or international, the critic can make fair claim to Irishness. Just as English Gothic has been interpreted as a trope for English identity, so Irish Gothic has been interpreted as a trope for Anglican Ireland. Such are the intricacies of English–Irish relations that what seems like a late example of English Gothic or terror fiction, *Dracula*, has been read as a covert or subliminal text on English–Irish relations in general, and the degeneracy and delinquency of the Anglo–Irish Ascendancy landlords in particular. (Though it might equally be read as a covert text on the collision between the Enlightenment–inspired scientific and business culture of England and the Protestant North of Ireland – of which Stoker was a known admirer – and the Catholic, 'medieval', pre-industrial culture of native Ireland. In search of subtext and subthemes, English and American critics prefer the oddities of sexuality and anti-feminism in *Dracula*.)

Literary relations between England and Ireland reflect, and refract, the political and larger cultural relations, whereby Ireland is variously a province or region of Britain whose hub is the metropolis of London; a colony of Britain inhabited by those of a different race and religion; or a 'sister isle' or parallel kingdom, in theory equal though in fact unequal. These relationships have been differently inflected and expressed through the three hundred years of the novel and have involved, in different and changing ratios of power, the Anglo-Irish, the Catholic native Irish and the Northern Dissenters or Ulster Protestants. All three populations have maintained separate and evolving relations with England (and Britain) over time. The populations also represent points of view from which those relations have been interpreted, irrespective of the political facts of the matter at any one time; the English might see a province or region of Britain where the Irish see an incipient nation; the fact of colonisation might be refused by the colonised; the inhabitants of the 'sister isle' might repudiate sorority. Further, these relations have been internalised and imagined in a multitude of ways, coded, metaphorised and debated in novels and other literature.

Authors and texts inhabit this astonishing web as individuals, but both are also merchandise to be published, sold and consumed. Authors have developed changing cultural and economic relationships with each other and with society: authors have been wealthy self-subsidisers, patronised dependants, professional authors, Grub Street hacks, amateur loners, members of coteries or movements. Until the nineteenth century, the society in question was in the main (though not exclusively) British society, so that what Ian Watt and others have to say about publishing, bookselling and the reading public in England is of interest to students of the Irish novel. Loeber and Stouthamer-Loeber have calculated that there were 65 titles of original Irish novels and novelettes published in Dublin between 1750 and 1799, whereas there were 1,846 titles of original fiction published in London over the same period. The Dublin figure is a fraction of the English and French fiction titles republished in Dublin without authorisation. This 'piracy' of novels occurred because Dublin publishers did not recognise English copyright legislation, an attitude that expressed at once autonomy (and parallel development), economic opportunism and cultural dependency, and it is eloquent about the broad political and even constitutional situation. It has been inferred that Irish authors in the eighteenth century took their works to London to be published and that those who published their first novel in Dublin published their subsequent novels in London, a practice that continued in the nineteenth century. After the Union of 1800, the number of titles of original Irish fiction published in Dublin remained low: 50 between 1800 and 1829.[2]

Later, Irish publishing rejoined British publishing in legal partnership and mutual respect, and also sought to develop its own market and pool of authors. From the later nineteenth century onwards, there were Dublin (but also London and American) publishers who specialised in Irish writing, particularly fiction. By 1890 the regular school attendance rate in Ireland was more than 60 per cent and by 1911 only 12 per cent of the population could not read, so the reading public was there when the Revival got under way. The disparity in the size of the respective but contiguous markets in Ireland and Britain, however, has meant that there is still a great deal of traffic in contracts and writers between publishers in England and Ireland, especially nowadays in the publishing world of takeovers, mergers and subsidiaries. A telling footnote to this interdependence is that the London-based Man Booker Prize, the most famous, lucrative and commercially potent prize for novels in the world, is open to novelists from the United Kingdom, the Commonwealth – *and* the Republic of Ireland, though Ireland left the Commonwealth more than half a century ago. (The number of Irish novelists long-listed and short-listed has, over the years, been disproportionate to the island's tiny population of under five million.)

The changing literary context of the Irish novel in the main keeps pace with – sometimes in front, sometimes behind – the cultural and political situations. These have had their impact on the society out of which the novel springs. Since the mid-seventeenth century, the Irish constitutional positions have included limited parliamentary home rule in internal affairs enjoyed chiefly by Anglicans (1660–1782); parliamentary autonomy inside the British empire but with limited representation (1782–99); constitutional union with legislative differences (1800–1922); partition into dominion status outside the UK (the Irish Free State, 1922–37; Eire, 1937–49); limited self-government inside the UK (Northern Ireland, 1921–72); a republic (the twenty-six counties of Eire, 1949–); direct rule from Westminster with unsuccessful attempts at home rule in internal affairs through an elected assembly (Northern Ireland, 1972–). These constitutional experiments have been the product of political pressures, both constitutional and illegal, usually exerted on behalf of Irish freedom from English restraint of one kind or another. (Their violent counterpoints have been the famous modern rebellions – 1798, 1803, 1848, 1916, 1919–20, 1969–98 – to which the constitutional innovations have often been delayed reactions.) For example, the Catholic novelists of the early and mid-nineteenth century, with whom James H. Murphy is concerned in chapter 5, are difficult to think of without musing on the growth and consolidation of the Catholic Church in Ireland and, beyond that immense phenomenon, the increasing self-confidence and self-assertion of the native Catholic population, with its own middle class. These writers inherited or appropriated the forms to which Burgess addresses herself, including, as Murphy makes clear, the national tale. Much later, that Catholic self-confidence would reach the stages both of intellectual advocacy, for example Canon Sheehan, and of intellectual rebellion and apostasy, for example, George Moore, Gerald O'Donovan and James Joyce, all of whom permit Murphy to extend his story.

For its part, Anglo-Irish self-confidence could in the mid-nineteenth century take the form of rollicking storylines about the Irish in novels that appealed to, and were meant to appeal to, English readers, who apparently were entertained by quaint and humorous (and therefore unthreatening) Irish peasants and squires. Whereas writers of the national tale and its descendants attempted to educate their English readers about Ireland (however emotionally and sententiously in the main), the popular comic novelists of the nineteenth century settled for amusing their readers. But the amusement probably did not end there; surely it entrenched English images of the Irish, especially the peasantry, that affected English attitudes to Irish agitation for self-government, once it was realised that independence would be granted not to the old 'Protestant Nation' but to the mass of Catholic Irish, ignorantly thought to consist almost exclusively of childish, unreliable, humorous, duplicitous peasants? Most Irish writers have had an eye on the English reader (with whom he or she shares an anglophone literary culture and market) for obvious commercial reasons, but in this case the reader was courted even at the cost of distorting (or at least carefully selecting and editing) Irish truth and reality. Under these circumstances, plot and character were likely to be influenced, if not dictated, by the reader that the novelist had in mind. This largely, but not entirely, fictional countryside depicted in the pages of Charles Lever, Samuel Lover and Somerville and Ross was scornfully dubbed by Yeats 'the humourist's Arcadia' when he and others set about the task of reviving the literature of Ireland from the 1890s onwards. These authors were of course more complex than any epithet could capture – there is a good deal of reality in all of them – but the literary and historical past had to be in part misinterpreted to create a radically new present.

The Revival period

Since Yeats himself was not a populist, despite his early preoccupation with the customs, beliefs and lore of the Irish rural populace, it is not clear what readers he had in mind for the Irish Literary Revival; but they would surely have included the Irish themselves, while excluding prejudiced, middle-class English readers with whose preconceptions Yeats and the other revivalists wanted nothing to do, any more than they wanted anything to do with Irish Catholic middle-class preconceptions. The Irish Cultural Revival, in its breadth, and going far beyond Yeats's own ideas, was a vast educational project that indeed included the classroom but also extramural instruction, from agriculture through art, clothing, language, law and leisure to sports. A distinctive ancient Gaelic culture was to be revived and adapted to the modern world, and reform was to be so deep and widespread as to constitute cultural revolution. Political independence was certain to follow such a profound alteration and could therefore be mentally shelved, a shift in priorities that satisfied the Protestant leaders of the Revival, descendants of the Ascendancy. There were of course Catholic participants, but they dominated mostly in the sports and language revivals engineered by the recently founded Gaelic Athletic Association and Gaelic League. But even though Charles Stewart Parnell had been brought down in 1890 and the 1893 (Second) Home Rule Bill for Ireland failed, not all Catholics were giving up the idea of radical reform, or even actual revolution, as the Easter rebellion of 1916, which caught Yeats offguard, duly demonstrated.

The revival of the Irish (or Gaelic) language, which had been in retreat through most of the nineteenth century, despite sporadic efforts to silence the melancholy long withdrawing roar, was seen by some as the most important element of the proposed cultural revolution. Moore and Hyde experimented with writing fiction and drama in Irish (Moore needing the help of a translator) but with mixed success. Despite the centuries of achievement in narrative (sagas, genealogies and tales in Old and Middle Irish), the novel in Irish, as Alan Titley reminds us in chapter 9, was a late arrival on the literary scene (in the first decade of the twentieth century). Titley tracks the progress of the novel, one complicated by the fact that writing a literary work in Irish meant the onerous double duty of simultaneously defending and trying to advance the language front. As with the Irish novel in English, the novel in Irish had to compete with the romance, but was reinforced by the allied narrative forms of the folk tale and the autobiography. The enthusiastic Gaelic Revival, followed by decades of government support for Irish in the Free State and Irish Republic, together with that unbroken Irish gift for narrative, has despite setbacks resulted in the novel in Irish currently enjoying robust health, which is Titley's good news for this *Companion*. Moreover, many novels in English are available in Irish translation, which swells the Irish novel curriculum if not the canon.

For his part, because he was concerned with reviving and adapting ancient, pre-Enlightenment Irish kinds of writing and telling (which yet survived, particularly in the west of Ireland), Yeats paid little attention to the novel, or even the possibility of an Irish novel. This is perhaps why he dismissed most Irish novels of the nineteenth century. True, he admired Carleton, who had a promiscuous notion of his readers – Catholics, Protestants, English, Irish, unionists, nationalists. Carleton's picture of an Irish peasantry that he knew intimately was sympathetically dark and brutal as well as, by turns, comic and stereotyped, but Yeats was impressed less by his fiction *qua* fiction than by the evidence in that fiction of Carleton's knowledge of the peasantry and their ways. Yeats demonstrated his priorities when, in *Fairy and Folk Tales of the Irish Peasantry* (1888) and *Irish Fairy Tales* (1892), he asset-stripped nineteenth-century Irish novels and story collections (including those by Carleton), in order to liberate, as it were, the folk tales and folk beliefs inside them from the sophisticated distortions of the novelists. He himself attempted fiction that imitated traditional, anonymous folk tales and legends and largely eschewed modern fiction, with the exception of the unsatisfactory novella, *John Sherman* (1891) and the unfinished novel, *The Speckled Bird*. He pronounced Lady Gregory's literary translation of a Middle Irish manuscript saga, *Cuchulain of Muirthemne* (1902), the most important book to come out of Ireland in his lifetime and it has several features of the modern novel it was meant to supersede. Her literary translation of the feats of Finn and the Fenians, *Gods and Fighting Men* (1904), followed and it too has narrative qualities of a novel. During the Revival, numerous collections of folk tales appeared that read like short-story collections or novellas. The most creative adaptations of folk tales into a novel-length work were perhaps Padraic Colum's *The King of Ireland's Son* (1916) and *The King of Elfland's Daughter* (1924) by Lord Dunsany, the latter emulating non-Irish fairy tales.

The achievements of the Revival in the novel proper are there, and include works notably by James Stephens, but the novel of the Revival period belongs rather to what has been called the counter-Revival (a very various affair), and involves the names of Moore, Joyce, Brinsley MacNamara, Daniel Corkery (interested in a less Anglo-Irish and more truly native Revival), O'Donovan, Sheehan. There are also what we might call near-novels, including *The Interpreters* (1922) by AE (George Russell). We could call *The Interpreters* a philosophical fable and spiritual autobiography; Elizabeth Grubgeld, in chapter 12, claims that the life writing that traced the emergence of the self, while adapting some of the techniques of fiction, appeared during the Revival period. Several notable memoirs of the period that seem to hover between fact and fiction, between the novel and the autobiography, yet do not belong to that movement. They would include the entertaining sea-going picaresque, *Wide Seas and Many Lands* (1923) by Co. Down-born Arthur Mason, and Patrick MacGill's slum-novels (set in Donegal or Scotland) that are full of strange incident and character; all belong to a long tradition of itinerant, novelistic first-person adventures, including tramp and travel literature. MacGill published most of his prose works during or around the years of the First World War and his excellent Great War trilogy, written while he was in uniform, can be read either as reportage or imagination. Grubgeld mentions as a later example of the 'fictional' memoir *As I Was Going Down Sackville Street* (1937) by Oliver St John Gogarty, the model for Joyce's Buck Mulligan. Beside Gogarty's work we could put a comparable and neglected memoir of the same year that recruits as many techniques of the novel (and the cinema, one is tempted to say), swerves as far away from the autobiographical self and, like Gogarty's, puts fictional speech in the mouths of historical contemporaries: the lively political quasi-memoir of the Great War / Sinn Fein era by Gerald Griffin (not to be confused with the earlier novelist), *The Dead March Past: A Semi-Autobiographical Saga*.

But whereas the Revival itself constituted a hiatus in the Irish novel, the general resurgence of Irish literary energy – a kind of renaissance, irrespective of ideology and programme – inspirited the novel anyway, and it was during the Revival that Ireland's impressive contribution to Modernism was begun. Adrian Frazier, in chapter 6, reads Moore and Joyce as pioneers of Irish Modernism, the latter becoming one of the giants of international Modernism whose achievement in fiction could alone stand beside Yeats's achievement in poetry. Bruce Stewart, in chapter 7, draws our attention to both the internationalism of Joyce's experimental writings and the Irishness in which those experimental energies found their raw sources. And Frazier shows, too, the Modernist aspects of novels that otherwise participated in the folk flowering of the Irish Revival.

Outside the Revival, and taking little part in the general resurgence of literary energy I have referred to, the Irish novel as it developed in Victorian Ireland continued to appear throughout the 1890s and as late as the Great War. It had subsided into the popular novel which, in moments of benevolence, we can call the mainstream novel. Such mainstream novels are similar to their English counterparts, though many of them are somewhat less romantic and charged versions of the national tale (the English visitor to Ireland recurs as an instigator), but retain elements of the romance and, as in the national tale, English–Irish relations are a significant theme. The Irish authors can set whole novels in England (where many of them lived) as readily as in Ireland, or shift scenes between the two countries, and their plots and settings keep rough pace with broad social developments in Ireland. Chief among these is the continuing decline of the big house, reaching its lowest point with the various Land Acts of the late nineteenth and early twentieth centuries and the break-up of the huge demesnes. Vera Kreilkamp, in chapter 3, has analysed the power of the big house as a fictional venue and symbol, and shows its longevity by bringing the story down to our own day.

If we downsize the big house of the Ascendancy to the country house that was inhabited by the minor gentry, we have in combination a very populous and long-lived subgenre of the novel indeed. Many of the authors who wrote country house novels were women, and some of them hugely prolific: L. T. Meade (Elizabeth Thomasina Toulmin Smith) from Cork published at least 200 novels (many of them for schoolgirls); Katharine Tynan from Dublin published 105 novels; Mrs Hungerford (née Hamilton) from Co. Cork published 55 novels before dying at 42. Among other interesting, prolific or popular names are Hannah Lynch, M. E. Francis, Mrs J. H. Riddell, Katherine Cecil Thurston, B. M. Croker, Mrs Victor (Jesse Louise) Rickard, Lady Gilbert (Rosa Mulholland), Eleanor Alexander,

Jane Barlow, W. M. Letts, Ella MacMahon and Sarah Grand. Some were immensely successful in Ireland, Britain and beyond, and were the forerunners of today's bestselling novelists such as Maeve Binchy and Roddy Doyle. Thurston, from Cork, sold 200,000 copies of *John Chilcote, MP* (1904) in the United States alone (where it was entitled *The Masquerader*). These women novelists are as often Catholic as Protestant (and even upperclass Catholic) and often religious in spirit and observance as well as in name. Tynan (1861–1931) objected that Dublin booksellers tried to restrict Catholic readers to Catholic novels and Protestant readers to Protestant novels, and certainly there were Dublin (and American) publishers who catered to Catholic readers by publishing chiefly or exclusively Catholic novelists; if Tynan's objection had foundation, this is a fascinating sidebar to the Irish novel's literary sociology.

The novels of some of these women include elements of the New Woman novel, but the novels of Sarah Grand (born in Donaghadee, Co. Down) were entirely New Woman novels, not surprisingly, as she is credited with coining the term New Woman in 1894; her novel *The Heavenly Twins* (1893) was said to be more widely discussed and sold than any other novel of the day. Having a specific literary agenda to further her social aims, Grand was opposed to art for art's sake, but others among these writers, including Letts and MacMahon, displayed in their novels elements of the *fin-de-siècle* decadence that is associated with its most famous practitioner, Oscar Wilde; his novel *The Picture of Dorian Gray* is virtually a handbook to decadence, while Stoker's *Dracula* can be regarded as a qualified example that has an ambiguous relationship to the idea of the New Woman.

The novel since the Revival

After the founding of the Irish Free State and Northern Ireland in 1921–2, the two parts of the island went their separate political and cultural ways. Norman Vance, in chapter 8, shows how various and contested the literary scene was thereafter. Society in the Free State (later Republic) was itself divided along religious and ethnic fault-lines. Freedom of expression and behaviour were at the disposition of a state and a church that did not hesitate to outlaw, censor and ban. The Irish Censorship Board was set up in 1929, with statutory powers to ban books or periodicals that promoted contraception or abortion or were indecent. Many well-known novelists had their novels banned; there was double jeopardy, since many books also appeared on the Roman Catholic Index of proscribed publications. As early as the mid-1920s, Yeats protested fruitlessly as the Irish Catholic ethos was translated into legal proscriptions of one kind or another, but in fact the state became more theocratic in 1937 when the new Constitution replaced the more liberal 1922 Constitution. Such a society appeared to Sean O'Faolain and Frank O'Connor unconducive to artistic realism and therefore to the realist novel, indeed to the novel as a genre. In 1947, O'Faolain thought that only four realistic Irish novels had been written since 1922. In 1936, O'Faolain's novel *Bird Alone* and, in 1940, O'Connor's novel *Dutch Interior* were banned. Whether they were right or wrong in thinking that a healthy novel tradition required a certain kind of society, both writers turned almost exclusively to the short story (which they thought expressed best Ireland's fragmentation), in which they achieved international reputation.

In 1965, the critic Augustine Martin had a different explanation for the eccentric, uncooperative nature of the Irish novel when compared with the best contemporary English novels, which he thought saw English life steadily and saw it whole. Martin blamed the stance of dissent adopted by Irish writers – a stance inherited chiefly from George Moore and James Joyce and maintained by O'Connor and O'Faolain – which made it difficult for the Irish novelist to capture the tapestry and texture of the broader society and encouraged a retreat into lonely introspection that O'Faolain had claimed was the only alternative available to the alienated Irish writer.[3] Ironically, 1965 was the year *The Dark* by John McGahern was banned and the author sacked as a schoolteacher, but Martin was correct in seeing life and literature in mid-1960s Ireland as having reached a crossroads. Although Ireland had indeed been a broken and divided society that did not command assent, and although Martin seemed nostalgic for 'the social and religious pieties of Ireland' (this side of censorship, of course), he was right in detecting early the opening up of Irish society and how Irish fiction was lagging behind in registering it. (Censorship was relaxed somewhat in the late 1960s and has effectively petered out since.)

While it might be maintained that the novels that Samuel Beckett and Flann O'Brien wrote during the 1930s and 1940s obliquely reflect the instabilities and adversities of Free State society – veering as they do between solipsism and saga, structure and soliloquy – there is in those novels a momentum that is at once purely literary and universally philosophical and that carries them in compass beyond the facts of Irish life and most of Irish fiction. Terence Brown, in chapter 11, reads these two geniuses as important post-modernists whose novels compose what we might call a sophisticated intra-textuality as well as inter-textuality.

We might associate with Beckett and O'Brien the overlooked Ralph Cusack, whose *Cadenza: An Excursion* (1958) shares their grimly playful erudition, sustained interiority, gloom spiced with humour and sense of mind at the end of its tether. The narrator, apparent son of a big house, rides in a condemned train around Dublin and environs, all the while reviewing in disjointed sequence his life and adventures. This 'excursion' is a last flourish, the 'cadenza' of the title. Time (the Troubles to 1955) and place (Ireland, Scotland, Europe) are subjected to the vagaries of dreamlike memory, and structure is provided instead in musical fashion by motif and refrain. The whole has the purgatorial feel of Beckett's Trilogy and O'Brien's *The Third Policeman*.

Of course, Irish novels went on being written during the life of the Free State, as Vance makes clear. And if we were to consider 'category' or genre fiction, then the name of Freeman Wills Crofts would suggest itself. Crofts (1879–1957) was born in Dublin and spent his working life in Northern Ireland with the Belfast & Northern Counties Railway. His first detective novel was published in 1920, and thereafter he became one of the most famous practitioners of the subgenre anywhere. His novels belong to the tradition of the English whodunnit (though they are unusually dense and painstaking) and were set in England, though one, *Sir John Magill's Last Journey* (1930), is set knowledgeably in the young Northern Ireland and was published in Gaelic in 1935. Crofts joined M. McDonnell Bodkin (1849–1933) and Dorothea Conyers (1871–1949) as notable Irish detective novelists. An Irish novel that has never been out of print is *The Riddle of the Sands: A Record of Secret Service* (1903), a work that is at once a detective novel, a spy novel and an invasion story of the kind popular in Britain in the late nineteenth century. It is by Erskine Childers, born and educated in England, raised in Ireland, a British soldier and naval officer who became an Irish republican gunrunner and who was executed by the Free State forces! That other invasion story and detective novel (as well as horror story and late Gothic tale), *Dracula*, has likewise never been out of print.

Category fiction is popular by definition and includes the subgenre of science fiction. In *Out of the Silent Planet* (1938), C. S. Lewis, the popular children's author born and educated in Belfast, managed to combine the influences of H. G. Wells's scientific romances, the fantasies of Lewis's friend J. R. R. Tolkien, and *Gulliver's Travels*. It involved a voyage to Mars and thus followed *A Plunge into Space* (1890) by Robert Cromie, another popular Belfast author whose scientific romance pre-dated Wells's *The Time Machine* by five years. Like Wells and Cromie, Lewis used his scientific fantasy as a vehicle for social commentary and satire, as of course did Swift. Substituting religious faith for Swift's political and social preoccupations, Lewis, like the older writer, was drawn to the fable, as in *The Pilgrim's Regress* (1933).

The cultural malaise of the Free State appeared to affect male Catholic writers of mainstream fiction more than female writers, whether Catholic or Protestant. This may be in part because the women novelists of the 1930s–1960s – Pamela Hinkson, Kate O'Brien, Helen Waddell, Constance Malleson, Margaret Barrington and Elizabeth Bowen – all lived in England for lengthy periods. (O'Brien also lived in Spain and Hinkson in Germany; Kathleen Coyle, from the north of Ireland, lived in Paris before leaving for the United States.) These novelists – to whom we can add M. J. Farrell – continued the Victorian and Edwardian tradition of the Irish novel written by middle-class or upper-middle-class Catholic or Protestant women, which was highly dependent on the country house setting (or its latter-day townhouse equivalent), took love and marriage as a frequent theme, and had fitful recourse to other elements of romance and even of the national tale. The argument could be made in the teeth of the tacit Revival assumption of the un-Irishness of the novel and the explicit claim by O'Connor and O'Faolain of the contemporary inappropriateness of the novel genre, that there has been for several hundred years a strong continuous tradition in the Irish novel that is female more than it is male. Women writers of the 1930s–1960s are discussed in chapter 10 by Ann Owens Weekes. They were later joined by female novelists who started to write novels in the 1960s (such as Edna O'Brien), 1970s (Julia O'Faolain) and 1980s (Clare Boylan). M. J. Farrell is a fascinating bridge, for after silence as a novelist between 1952 and 1981, she resurfaced as Molly Keane and published several more novels.

Meanwhile in Northern Ireland, the Ulster regionalism on which Vance sheds light continued apace. But Northern Ireland, if protected from mono-lithic theocracy and state restrictions on freedom by the British connection and the relative liberalism of Protestantism, was nonetheless inhospitable to Catholics. It was a cramped and provincial sectarian society that declined to encourage artistic energy and was, on the strictly artistic level, even more inimical to creativity than the Free state, due in part to the darker side of Protestantism – its disapproving puritan philistinism. Irish Catholicism was likewise puritanical, but at least Free State writers lived where literature had been, and still was, valued by many and where the literary tradition was a saving grace, permitting a degree of underground activity and enlivening camaraderie in adversity. In the 1950s, Brian Moore took the measure of Northern Ireland in his early novels of Belfast, *The Lonely Passion of Judith Hearne* (1955) and *The Feast of Lupercal* (1957), and exploited the para-doxically rich material of its grimness, having by then shown the city and province a clean pair of heels.

A new and special grimness appeared in Northern Ireland from 1969, an eruption of violence soon called the Troubles, after the first Troubles of

1919–21. The frozen relations between the Irish state and the Northern Irish statelet had begun to thaw in the 1960s; it was in 1965 that the Taoiseach (prime minister) of the Republic and the prime minister of Northern Ireland met for the first time ever, and cordially. But this occurred only four years before the outbreak of renewed hostilities between Irish republicans and the British, preceded by Catholic agitation for full civil rights. IRA hostilities were immediately interpreted by Northern unionists or Protestants as an attack by Catholic nationalists on them and, after some delay and disarray, they responded accordingly. It became a sporadic thirty-year guerilla war that took more than 3,000 lives. During that time, Northern Ireland witnessed ironically a literary renaissance of real substance, at first in the genre of poetry but then in drama too and at last in the novel; Elmer Kennedy-Andrews, in chapter 13, examines both the serious and commercial novels of the last twenty-five years that have responded to the sordid and bloody Troubles and that have trafficked with the cinema, both Hollywood and the vigorous Irish film industry.

The state of affairs in the Irish novel today is a busy and multifarious one, as Eve Patten demonstrates in chapter 14. She has recourse to the concepts of post-nationalism and the metafictional to encompass a literary scene in which heretofore silent voices and subgenres are being heard and read: working-class novels of contemporary Dublin, women's novels more candid and feminist than before, gay fiction, and continuing first-rate work from the proven pens of John McGahern and John Banville. A crucial milestone in the cultural–political progress of Ireland was membership in the European Economic Community, which has since evolved into the European Union. Cultural movement towards pan-Europeanisation has been a feature of the member countries for thirty years, but there has been an acceleration in the last decade, fuelled by the movement of Europeans around the continent in the specific forms of tourism, migration and the flight of refugees. Multi-culturalism is a burgeoning ethnic reality. The resulting cultural phenomena and the social patterns that will emerge can only be guessed at. But it is certain that novels, highly adapted over the centuries for the job, will reflect these changes, while the best of them memorably express singular voices. After centuries of stagnation and decades of slow growth, Ireland is changing rapidly, and is now, astonishingly, an immigrant rather than emigrant society. The cultural, as well as spiritual, effects of the recent decline in the authority of the Catholic Church are at present incalculable. Things are changing faster in the Republic of Ireland than in Northern Ireland, but the end of the Troubles will almost certainly act like the release of a brake. The Irish novel will enter a new phase, no doubt extending an impressive and various canon in ways that are presently unforeseen.

NOTES

1. These questions are discussed by Ina Ferris in *The Romantic National Tale and the Question of Ireland* (2002).
2. See Rolf Loeber and Magda Stouthamer-Loeber, 'The Publication of Irish Novels and Novelettes: A Footnote on Irish Gothic Fiction', *Cardiff Corvey: Reading the Romantic Text* 10 (June 2003), 17–31. http://www.cardiff.ac.uk/encap/corvey/download/cc10_no2.pdf. See also James W. Phillips, *Printing and Bookselling in Dublin, 1670–1800* (Dublin: Irish Academic Press, 1998), pt I, ch. 4.
3. 'Inherited Dissent: The Dilemma of the Irish Writer', *Studies* (Spring 1965), 1–20. The question of genre in the post-Revival years is insightfully discussed by Terence Brown, 'After the Revival: The Problem of Adequacy and Genre', *Genre* 12 (1979), 565–89.

I

AILEEN DOUGLAS

The novel before 1800

Uses of romance

'When we speak of the People, we ought carefully to make a Distinction between *Irish* and *Irish*.' The voice is not that of a stage-Irishman committing a blunder, but a cosmopolitan Englishman in William Chaigneau's novel, *The History of Jack Connor* (1752). He continues: 'that is, we ought to regard the *Protestants* of *Ireland* as ourselves, because, in Fact, they are our *Brethren* and our *Children*; and so to manage the poor *Natives*, who are mostly *Papists*, that by *Clemency* and good *Usage* we may wean them from ill Habits, and make them *faithful* and *useful* Subjects'.[1] Use of the adjective 'Irish' clearly required distinctions. There may be a huge gap between Irish and Irish, but none between Irish and English: Irish Protestants are different from poor Irish natives, but essentially the same as the English speaker of Chaigneau's text. Acts of positioning, literary and geographical, of readers as well as characters, are crucial to eighteenth-century Irish fiction. Often, those acts are complicated by the fact that they are also, as in the present instance, silently redrawing earlier demarcations, correcting previous distinctions between 'ourselves' and 'them'.

Most eighteenth-century Irish fiction was produced by Irish Protestants, either the descendants of early Norman settlers (the Old English) or more recent arrivals. Yet the identity such writers shared determined neither their relationships with native culture – which ranged from the intimate to the remote – nor the strength of their attachment to the English mainland. Novelists such as Chaigneau and Thomas Amory self-consciously deployed Irish settings and subject matter; but there were also Irish novelists, among them Frances Sheridan and Oliver Goldsmith, who settled in England and whose fiction is apparently unmarked by their origins – the 'ourselves' to which such writers belonged being a general one of novelists writing in English. It is also important to consider that Irishness, however defined, can have effects beyond subject matter, influencing the construction, devices and projected readers of fiction.

That many Irish novels were published initially in London, and only subsequently in Dublin, suggests Irish writers wanted to reach a larger audience than Ireland alone could provide. Conversely, the fact that the British Copyright Act of 1709 had never applied to Ireland gave Irish publishers the opportunity to reprint for the Irish market popular English works in pirated editions. Yet in the latter part of the eighteenth century, a distinctive indigenous reading public was increasingly recognised, not only through original publication in Dublin of Irish fiction, but also in the way reprints directly addressed Irish audiences or made silent textual changes so as to appeal to their tastes.[2]

Two very early fictions, the anonymous *Vertue Rewarded, or the Irish Princess* (1693) and Sarah Butler's *Irish Tales, or Instructive Histories for the Conduct of Life* (1716), demonstrate the contrasting effects on fictional form of different understandings of Irishness. Both of these brief fictions are set in Ireland and have important romance elements: their plots unfold against the background of war and each tells in elevated language the story of a love affair. The texts nonetheless differ considerably in that *Vertue Rewarded* excludes the natives, the '*wild* Irish', from its rarified romance world, whereas *Irish Tales* equates romance civility with the riches of the ancient Gaelic past.

Vertue Rewarded is set in the midland town of Clonmel during the Williamite wars. The hero, a minor European prince fighting for William, falls in love with a local girl, Marinda. The class difference between the two causes the Prince to hope that he can seduce, rather than marry, the heroine, but eventually he recognises the heroine's virtue, and they marry. As befits characters in romance, Marinda and the prince share wit and breeding. They also share a commitment to Protestant values, as represented by King William. The native Irish are casually invoked to mark the limits of this world, as when a young man's appearance and civility are seen as so superior to other young men that 'they did look like our wild *Irish* to him'.[3] Or the natives actively threaten the protagonists, as when the heroine leaves the safety of Clonmel and is attacked by Irish-speaking rapparees. The '*wild* Irish', and Irish speakers, appear briefly only to emphasise their unsuitability for the romance world the protagonists share.

This exclusion is given added resonance by the use in *Vertue Rewarded* of the resources of Gaelic culture. Among the romance's interpolations is one 'from an ancient *Irish* Chronicle', of Cluaneesha, the only child of Machuain, King of Munster, whose chastity is wrongly suspected. Significantly, this interpolation is attached not to a character, but to a place: a fountain just outside Clonmel, instrumental – according to the chronicle – in the vindication of the princess. In re-telling this story, *Vertue Rewarded* draws on the Gaelic tradition of *dinnshenchas*, that is, the lore of places that turns landscape into narrative and perpetuates in the present the culture of the past. In *Vertue Rewarded*, however, the story is totally disconnected from a contemporary Gaelic culture which is seen as wild and lawless. Moreover, the structural position of the tale – specifically, its relation to other interpolations, one of which deals circumstantially with human sacrifice in Peru – reinforces the impression of dislocated exotica, rather than, as in the Gaelic tradition, a mark of the intimate way landscape enters culture.

Very little is known about Sarah Butler, the author of *Irish Tales*, but it is possible she was connected to the Ormonde Butlers, an Old English family with both Protestant and Roman Catholic branches. *Irish Tales* is set in the 'Ancient Kingdom of Ireland', at a time when the Milesian kings are fighting off Danish invaders. It tells of the unhappy love affair of Dooneflaith, daughter of the King of Meath, and Murchoe, son of Brian Boru, who was eventually to become High King and defeat the Danes at the battle of Clontarf (1014). The episodes listed on the title page – the Banish'd Prince, the Power of Beauty – prepare the reader for a romance, and, as the polemical preface makes clear, one with a political purpose. Butler preempts the charge that the language of her characters is 'too Passionate and Elegant for the Irish' and unsuitable for 'so Rude and Illiterate a People' by declaring that now the Irish are under a 'Yoke of Bondage', but that once the country was 'one of the Principal Nations in Europe for Piety and Learning; having formerly been so Holy, that it was term'd the Island of Saints'.[4]

The use of romance idiom to ennoble characters is not unique to Butler; Aphra Behn had employed a similar strategy in her depiction of the hero of *Oroonoko, or The Royal Slave* (1688). While for both Behn and Butler the use of romance is political, it is Butler who is the more radical of the two in this respect. Behn's use of romance is a kind of exceptionalism, applying only to Oroonoko, whereas Butler's is justified by a carefully supported argument about a whole culture. Her preface cites a range of sources in support of her view of ancient Gaelic society, the most significant of these being Geoffrey Keating's *Foras Feasa ar Éireann*, completed around 1634 but not published until 1723 – and which Butler must therefore have read in manuscript. Butler's use of romance is justified by the piety and culture of the Irish past, and that past is in turn used to suggest that the native Irish will, eventually, be able to reconstruct their ancient society. The invading Danes razed monastries and slew priests, throwing 'the sacred Host it self to the Dogs' (p. 52), but the Irish eventually succeeded in releasing themselves from their 'slavish Tyranny' (p. 76). In like manner, *Irish Tales* suggests, Irish Catholics oppressed in the aftermath of the Williamite wars will eventually succeed in asserting their 'native liberty' (p. 35).

Gulliver's Travels

Whereas *Vertue Rewarded* and *Irish Tales* orientate themselves differently in relation to Irishness, they share a literary mode – the romance – concerned with elite and circumscribed worlds. However, by the early eighteenth century, fiction had begun to accommodate the mundane, the imperfect and the low-born, and to deploy the realism of time and place characteristic of the early novel. As the eighteenth century progresses, Irish fiction too is significantly marked by an enlarged sense of the subjects suitable for fictional treatment and by an expansionist impulse. A historical moment in which even remote nations are increasingly bound together by commercial and imperial links is reflected in the constant movement of fictional characters now confronting cultures including, but also going beyond, those of the British Isles. At mid-century, emergent notions of national identity in Irish fiction are shaped not only by the old binary opposition between native and invader but also by the context of empire-building and global commerce. Beyond the reflection of quotidian social reality, eighteenth-century novelists also use the device of travel, and its potential for comparison, for reflection on the nature and extent of national character. Travel does not always lead to the recognition or development of identity; it can also have an abrading effect, softening distinctions and allowing new identities to emerge. The return to origins, the homecoming, does feature in eighteenth-century Irish fiction – as it does in eighteenth-century fiction generally – but origins are not always seen as decisively affecting identity.

The most profound and most extreme treatment of identity in eighteenth-century Irish fiction is *Gulliver's Travels* (1726) by Jonathan Swift (1667–1745). Swift's own complicated sense of identity was sharpened by acute feelings of displacement. He once claimed to have been born in Ireland by accident, and his novel is neither set in that country nor does it contain any explicitly Irish subject matter. Well into his forties, Swift still hoped to have an ecclesiastical career in England and regarded his appointment to the Deanship of St Patrick's cathedral in Dublin in 1714 as a kind of exile. Yet a decade later, Swift was to become known as the Patriot Dean for his passionate and inventive defence of Irish constitutional and commercial interests in *The Drapier's Letters*.[5] Significantly, although Swift wrote and published in Dublin on Irish matters and had close relationships with Dublin printers, his major literary undertaking was directed towards a metropolitan audience. He took considerable care that his best-known work, *Travels into Several Remote Nations of the World* (to give it Swift's own title) be published in London, making a rare trip to that city to deliver the manuscript himself.

Purporting to be an autobiographical account by a ship's surgeon, Lemuel Gulliver, *Travels into Several Remote Nations of the World* is, in its original title, elaborate detailing of time and place, and resolute empiricism, essentially indistinguishable from the works, such as William Dampier's *New Voyage around the World* (1697), it parodies to such unsettling effect. Like its non-fictional models, *Gulliver's Travels* satisfies the desire of sedentary readers to learn about exotic lands and beings of which Europeans were gradually becoming more aware. Gulliver has manifestly incredible experiences – visiting lands containing people six inches tall, giants and flying islands – yet, in appealing to verisimilitude as proof of their veracity, his *Travels* expose the constructed nature of truth-telling in the documentary narratives of his real-life predecessors.

Gulliver's Travels is not of course at all about the remote lands Gulliver visits, but about the unwarranted pride modern Europeans take in what they know and have: their modes of government, scientific achievements and civilisation. The antics of the Lilliputian court and Lilliput's war with neighbouring Blefuscu recognisably parallel political ambition in the Hanoverian court and English enmity towards France, yet when represented in miniature these things appear ridiculous. The Academy of Projectors, which Gulliver visits on his third voyage, satirises the pretensions of the Royal Society about scientific progress when, for example, mad projectors attempt to extract sunlight from cucumbers. Like Swift's earlier prose satires, *The Battle of the Books* (1704) and *A Tale of a Tub* (1704), *Gulliver's Travels* exceeds specific targets to satirise the self-involvement and self-congratulation which Swift took to characterise modernity generally. Unlike the early prose satires, however, *Gulliver's Travels* uses precisely those narratives features – a first-person narrator, reliance on circumstantial detail – central to the early eighteenth-century novel, a literary form which takes modern self-involvement with complete seriousness. The formal choices Swift made in writing *Gulliver's Travels* established a close and fundamental resemblance between his own work and Daniel Defoe's *The Life and Strange Surprizing Adventures of Robinson Crusoe* (1719), even though the latter's modern myth of self-sufficiency was entirely antithetical to Swift.[6]

Gulliver's Travels is a disturbing account of dislocation and habituation. The narrator's skill with languages and his ingratiating nature make him susceptible to the values and perspectives of the lands he visits. Even in

Lilliput, where he shows his superiority by disdaining to enslave the Blefuscudians, he manifests a petty, Lilliputian delight when he is awarded the honour of being made a Nardac. In Brobdingnag, Gulliver is a source of bewilderment to his captors and displayed as a freak. He faces further humiliation when his account of European society – which he innocently reveals as rapacious and violent – causes the King to denounce Gulliver's kind as 'the most pernicious Race of little odious Vermin that Nature ever suffered to crawl upon the Surface of the Earth'.[7] Gulliver manages to narrate this and keep his sense of self relatively intact, yet on his return to England he discovers that his perspective has been, at least temporarily, altered: everyone looks tiny; his attitude to his fellow Europeans has become Brobdingnagian.

The first three voyages chart Gulliver's oscillating sympathy with and resistance to the societies he encounters, as he sees himself or refuses to see himself through alien eyes. It is in his fourth and final voyage that he completely adopts the perspective of his hosts, and his sense of self is devastated. Unlike the other places he has visited, this society is clearly divided between a race of rational horses, the Houyhnhnms, and an enslaved race of Yahoos, 'animals' to which Gullliver instinctively feels a profound antipathy and which he subsequently discovers, with feelings of intense horror, to have a 'perfect human Figure' (p. 212). Despite Gulliver's own ability to speak and to reason, his Houyhnhnm masters see him as a Yahoo, an identification that Gulliver eventually accepts. Under his master's tutelage, Gulliver rejects humankind and is filled with self-loathing: 'When I happened to behold the Reflection of my own Form in a Lake or Fountain, I turned away my Face in Horror and detestation of my self' (p. 251).

Gulliver's Travels does not contain any explicitly Irish subject matter, although it does, in the account of Lindalino in Book Three, offer an allegory of Irish resistance to Wood's halfpence (a passage cut by the first London publisher). Yet it can be argued that Swift's searing account in Book Four of displacement and degradation owes a great deal to his own direct experience of colonialism. Speaking as the Dublin draper, Swift denounced 'our Neighbours' and their 'strong Contempt for most Nations, but especially for *Ireland*: They look upon us as a Sort of *Savage Irish*, whom our Ancestors conquered several Hundred Years ago'.[8] As an orthodox Christian, Swift believed that humankind was fallen, but he did not believe humankind to be immutable. The possibility that the degradation of the Yahoos is at least partly the result of their inhuman treatment by the Houyhnhnms is suggested not only by the destructive effects of Gulliver's sojourn in the land of the rational horses, but also by Swift's Irish writings. Gulliver is taught to despise himself by the Houyhnhnms; Swift was more than capable, on occasion, of despising the native Catholic population of Ireland, but he would not be taught to despise himself. The draper complained that the English know of Ireland 'little more than they do of *Mexico*; further than that it is a Country subject to the King of *England*, full of Boggs, inhabited by wild *Irish Papists*; who are kept in Awe by mercenary Troops sent from thence' (*Prose Works*, vol. x, p. 103). It does not belittle Swift to suggest that some of the force of his ferocious indignation on behalf of the 'savage Irish' came from the suspicion that he was, in certain eyes, numbered among them.

The History of Jack Connor

William Chaigneau (1709–81) shared with Swift an immediate experience of dislocation, being born in Ireland to a French Huguenot family. Jack Connor, the picaresque hero of Chaigneau's only novel, is like Gulliver a wanderer transformed by his experiences, but *The History of Jack Connor* (1752) is set in recognisable contemporary locations, and its mood is one of Enlightenment optimism. The novel contains several elaborate compliments to Henry Fielding, and while Chaigneau's imperfect, warm-blooded and good-natured hero clearly resembles Fielding's Tom Jones, an even closer model is provided by the hero of Tobias Smollett's *Roderick Random* (1748), an exile who confronts prejudice because of his Scottish birth. *The History of Jack Connor* is notable for its reflection upon prejudice as an increasingly salient feature of the way things are. We learn from the cruder characters in Chaigneau's novel that, by the mid-eighteenth century, the prejudicial view of the Irish as lazy, potato-eating bog-trotters was already established; but, in common with later writers such as Maria Edgeworth, Chaigneau believes fiction plays a part in dispelling the ignorance from which prejudice stems.

The illegitimate son of a Protestant landowner in Co. Limerick, who passes as the son of a Williamite soldier and who subsequently falls into the care of his mother's lover, a Catholic priest, Jack Connor embodies several strands of Irish social life. Abandoned as a child, he is taken in by the Truegoods, paternalistic English landowners, but is forced to leave the haven they provide when he seduces one of the maids. Jack's wanderings take him to Dublin, London, France and Spain and, after undergoing several different kinds of ignominious servitude, he eventually achieves considerable prosperity and returns to Ireland. In the course of his travels, Jack's Irishness is an uncertain quality, which fades and seems finally to be erased. On his setting out, his mentor changes his 'quite *Irish*' surname to Conyers and advises Jack, who has 'not much of the common *Irish* Manner of speaking', to lose the little he has (vol. I, p. 137). Jack follows this advice so successfully that soon his accent is unremarkable, and his Irishness only appears in a residual form. Possessing a fine voice, Jack has since his youth delighted audiences with his Irish songs; in London he ingratiates himself with his employer's family 'with Songs, and a thousand *Irish* Stories' (vol. I, p. 154). By the time Jack reaches Paris, even this controlled display of Irishness for the purposes of entertainment is abandoned and he passes as English. Giving an account of himself to the wealthy widow who will become his wife, Jack 'artfully avoided the Place of his Birth, or the least hint of Ireland, as it might occasion Scandal' (vol. II, p. 70).[9]

The condition of Ireland is given considerable treatment in the novel. On his arrival in the country, Truegood sees 'with real Uneasiness, the *wretched Condition* of the poor Inhabitants' (vol. I, p. 52) which he judges (in words very close to some of Swift's expressions on the subject) 'a *Scandal* to a Nation who piqued themselves as being *Polite* and *Humane*, and almost compell'd the *few Strangers* who visited the Country, to imagine they were rather with the Natives of the *Cape of Good Hope*, than in a *civilized Kingdom*' (vol. I, p. 53). This unhappy state of affairs is seen to arise from the laziness of the inhabitants, the malign influence of Catholic priests and the irresponsibility of landlords, and it can be redressed through educating the natives into habits of thrift and honesty. Chaigneau breaks the frame of the novel by having the schools Truegood establishes on his estate serve as models for those which were in fact established by the Incorporated Society for Protestant Schools in Ireland. This society, committed to proselytising the natives, is advertised at regular intervals in the novel's pages.

Jack Connor's metamorphosis is connected, then, to a vision of what Irish society might be if the natives can be weaned away from their old habits and transformed into good Protestants. Early in the novel, we are told that Truegood, to encourage this process, settles every year on his estate two or three poor Lancashire families to serve as good examples. Towards the novel's close, Truegood invites Jack, of whose identity he is unaware, to come to Ireland and enjoy the 'rational joy' of beholding 'a Colony of *human Creatures*, established by his *Care*, flourishing by his *Bounty*' (vol. II, p. 220). The abandoned barefoot boy has so successfully taken on the characteristics of a Protestant English gentleman that he can be invited to colonise his native land. In the novel, Jack is allowed to be a warm advocate for Ireland, but, as he passes in England as English, his advocacy is never understood as that of a native. It is only when the natives don't actually sound like natives anymore that they can be allowed to speak. Any consideration of Chaigneau's Protestant Enlightenment fantasy of transforming the natives should, however, be balanced by recognition of his sustained exploration of prejudice. If the ideal of the novel is a rational sameness, it offers at the same time a recognition of the injustice inflicted on difference. Nor is the novel's view of culture limited to the rational joy of a well-ordered estate. Its allusions to Jack's fine voice and love of stories testify, albeit hazily, to a more extensive view of culture and identity, as does the reaction of Jack on seeing his childhood hut: 'the idea of former times was so strong and every childish Circumstance recurr'd so clearly to his Memory, that it might have been fatal to him, had not his Eyes given Vent to the throbbings of his heart' (vol. II, p. 233). *The History of Jack Connor*, and its representation of identity, is more ample than its scheme of transformation suggests.

The Life of John Buncle Esq.

The narrator of *The Life of John Buncle Esq.* (1756–66) by Thomas Amory (?1691–1788), accounts for the difference of his life from 'that of the generality of men' by the fact that he 'was born in London, and carried an infant to Ireland' where he learned the Irish language and 'became intimately acquainted with its original inhabitants'.[10] This initial border crossing prefigures the extraordinary hybridity of the novel that follows: the character of the narrator combines aspects of the Enlightenment gentleman and the hero of ancient Irish sagas, its form simultaneously mimics oral storytelling and fully exploits the typographical possibilities of print, while its content veers between matter-of-fact observation and mesmeric fantasy. Purportedly based on a series of memoranda of 'men and matters, books and circumstances' that came the narrator's way, *The Life of John Buncle* incorporates a vast range of miscellaneous materials, including religious controversy, a reading list for a do-it-yourself medical education, an apologia for Gaelic historiography and information on how to strip a skeleton. In its bewildering variety and oddity, the novel does, nonetheless, offer three points of consistency: the narrator's staunch Unitarianism, his admiration of women and insistence that they have 'as strong reasoning heads as the men' (vol. I, p. 273) and his regular injunctions to the reader to 'be ready' (vol. I, p. 167) for the transition from this world to the next. It is these points, rather than the adventures – mostly in the north of England – of the eight-times married narrator that give the novel a semblance of coherence.

The son of an orthodox Anglican settled in the West of Ireland, John Buncle is educated at Trinity College Dublin where he reads Locke and is, apparently, acquainted with Swift. Learned in both modern and antiquarian topics, the narrator's interests include the potential of the microscope and the mathematical discoveries of Newton alongside the marginalia of medieval manuscripts and the transmission of the classics. Yet Amory's narrator is not simply a mouthpiece for extensive and eclectic Enlightenment learning. His relationships with women and his physical prowess – as a pole-vaulter he can penetrate mountains and leap his way into remote valleys – suggest a debt to ancient Gaelic story-telling, particularly to the feats of the legendary Fionn Mac Cumhaill. Written and oral cultures are further amalgamated in a narrative form deploying both an anecdotal style and a huge editorial apparatus.[11] The dynamic relationship between these aspects of the book is not only arresting in and of itself, but also illuminates – and contrasts with – subsequent conjunctions in Irish fiction of first-person narration and editorial commentary, most famously, Maria Edgeworth's *Castle Rackrent* (1800). The division of *Castle Rackrent* into the story told by the illiterate Thady Quirke and the controlling explication of that story by an anonymous editor, is reflected spatially and typographically in the book the reader holds. It is true, as Katie Trumpener observes, that at times the narrative in Amory's book is 'literally attenuated' because bulky footnotes take up much of the page, but both commentary and narration emanate from the same source.[12] The editor who provides extensive footnotes on ancient Irish manuscripts is also the voice who conversationally tells the reader of the excellent vegetables and extraordinary ale to be had in Jack Macklean's little public house in Ringsend (vol. I, p. 87). Like Butler before him, Amory pays tribute to ancient Gaelic culture, but his Ireland is not purely the product of antiquarian learning; it is also familiar and immediate, a place of inns and walks and the pleasures of daily life.

Amory's narrative projects a lively sense of an engaged reader who is to be exhorted, advised and simply talked to. Having decided after the death of his first love to place his hopes in the next world, the narrator breaks in: 'I wish I could persuade you, reader, to resolve in the same manner' (vol. I, p. 80). A learned disquisition is interrupted with the injunction: 'Get this book, if you can' (vol. II, p. 255). He praises an excellent inn so that the reader may know where to stop to advantage, 'if you should ever ride over the same ground I went that day' (vol. II, p. 260). Amory's eccentric erudition combined with his nuanced relationship with the reader irresistibly call to mind a more famous novelist who also combined dense textuality with the belief that 'writing properly managed is but another name for conversation'.[13] There is no evidence, unfortunately, that Laurence Sterne (1713–68) actually read Amory (we know very little of Sterne's reading in contemporary fiction). John Buncle claimed that the distinctive nature of his narrative was owing to his Irish childhood. It is tempting to speculate that

Sterne, who was born in Clonmel and lived in Ireland until he was ten, similarly derived some of the perceived oddity of his own narrative style from his early experiences. What is odd and delightful about Sterne and Amory is that they each show that writing in its most self-conscious and developed form can allow for a kind of intimacy: it can meet itself coming back as speech. Whether this ability was something they derived from a shared exposure to a native Irish tradition of anecdote and story-telling cannot in the case of Sterne be proven, but it is more than plausible.

Colonial exchanges

Amory represents the most capacious understanding of narrative form in eighteenth-century Irish fiction, but the novelist with the broadest literal sweep is Charles Johnstone (?1719–?1800). It seems appropriate that Johnstone, much of whose work has a global reach, was born in Limerick, lived in London and eventually settled in Calcutta. A satirist whose fiction insistently criticises the human appetite for power, fame and luxury, Johnstone still finds much to admire in British public life. Two late works attributed to him, *The History of John Juniper* (1781) and *The Adventures of Anthony Varnish* (1786), do contain scenes set in Ireland, but of all eighteenth-century Irish novelists, Johnstone most strenuously advocates the ideal of Britain. His most successful work, *Chrysal, or the Adventures of a Guinea* (1760–5) is narrated by the spirit of gold, embodied for much of the narrative in the form of a guinea. Set during the period just before and during the Seven Years War (1756–63) – a war which took place on fronts in North America and India as well as Europe and laid the foundation of the first British empire – the novel shows how an increasingly commercial society subordinates individuals to processes of commodification and exchange. The guinea never stays long in the possession of one individual, but is passed along, connecting all. The novel includes portraits of historical individuals, many of them politicians – the identification of whom was of much interest to contemporary readers – as well as fictional episodes, the whole driven by a logic of prostitution and peculation. While the narrative is leavened by some examples of private benevolence, it is significant that its most striking examples of virtue are public figures such as William Pitt and George II. Successive Johnstone narrators identify Britain with a 'great and happy nation' diffusing riches and blessings to the world.

For all his enthusiasm, Johnstone did recognise that the amalgamation Britain represented entailed difficulties. *Chrysal* satirises the plunder of Ireland by rapacious members of the English court. The same novel denounces 'national reflections' as proceeding from 'folly and malevolence'.[14] To counter prejudice, the Irish-born narrator of *Anthony Varnish* emphasises positive features of Irish life, such as hospitality, and makes a self-conscious attempt to explain Irish customs, such as the wake, not known to 'the generality of [his] readers'.[15] The short-sightedness of English economic policy towards Ireland – or America – is a possible target of one of the allegories in Johnstone's *The Reverie, or, a Flight to the Paradise of Fools* (1762), though even here the narrator insists that such victimisation is untenable, not because it is unjust but because the inhabitants of the secondary manor are 'connected by every tie of nature . . . having all removed from the principal one thither'.[16] It is perhaps not surprising, given the amenability of the genre of the tale to philosophical and general reflections, that Johnstone's most thoughtful treatment of empire and colonialism occurs in his Oriental tale, *The History of Arsaces, Prince of Betlis* (1774). An episodic novel set in the Middle East and North Africa, this sombre treatment of the cyclical rise and fall of empire views the process of colonisation as one of depletion and represents a mother country fatally weakened by its own appetite for luxury.

A feature of empire is that colonised countries may have relationships with each other, as well as with the imperial centre. Such is the perspective of *The History of Ned Evans* (1796), an anonymous work set in the late 1770s and early 1780s. The hero, apparently the son of a Welsh clergyman, leads an uneventful life in Snowdonia prior to the dramatic night he rescues the daughter of an Irish nobleman from highway robbers. This event leads to Ned's being granted an army commission by her grateful father and visiting Dublin before going off to fight for Britain in the American War of Independence. What is interesting about this pattern of movement is that it focuses on the fringes of the British Isles and on America. Dublin, rather than the more usual London, is the metropolitan centre here, with all the magnificence that this implies. Through Ned's rustic eyes we see Georgian Dublin in the process of being built. In several detailed chapters, he admires buildings such as the Duke of Leinster's residence – a 'dwelling fit for a sovereign' – and the library of Trinity College, while also noting defects, such as the ditch around St Stephen's Green and the fact that the building works are not in all cases complete.[17] Still, Dublin has its dangers and, in a neat counterpoise to earlier fictional scenes of the victimised Irish abroad, within hours of his arrival Ned is ridiculed for his Welsh accent and robbed.

In America, Ned's capture by Indians provides further cultural variety. While unhappy that his lot in life has cast him among savages, Ned resolves to enter 'into the full spirit of the Indian life' (vol. II, p. 122). This resolution has beneficial effects for all parties. Ned imparts to the Indians his superior agricultural and medical knowledge, while he himself undergoes a startling physical transformation. Hunting and roaming with his Indian fellows perfects his body so that by the time he eventually returns to Europe 'no statuary, even of antiquity, ever produced a more finished model of male beauty' (vol. II, p. 180). *The History of Ned Evans* is not sentimental about the processes of colonisation which bring different cultures together; it includes, for example, debate on the legitimacy of the American war and it deplores the suffering that war causes. At the same time, the novel's ability to see cultural contact as the opportunity for exchange, rather than simply the diffusion of European blessings, is a notable one.

Imagined geographies

Many of these expansive novels end with a homecoming in which the hero assumes the place that is rightfully his, but which, paradoxically, he has never known. Ned Evans may really be Lord Ravensdale, but the fact remains that identity – even in those novels deploying such romance conventions – has to be earned, not inherited. During the eighteenth century, a considerable number of Irish writers left Ireland to make a living in England. Unlike the fictional heroes discussed above, many of them never returned. The fact that it did not occur to such writers to represent Ireland in fiction, or that they chose not to do so, should not be taken to mean a lack of interest in Irish affairs or culture. The novels of Henry Brooke (1703–83), for example (including *The Fool of Quality*, 1765–70 and *Juliet Grenville*, 1774), contain no Irish content, yet this same writer – born in County Cavan – wrote a series of pamphlets on Irish political and economic matters and contemplated two ambitious works on Irish mythology and history.

In the novels of several Irish writers in England, as in the novels of English novelists generally, home was not understood as a geographical point of origin, but as a particular kind of non-localised space for the exploration of subjectivity and power. The mechanism most often chosen for this exploration was the courtship plot, with its endless variations on the submission of personal feeling and desire to parental scrutiny and ultimately to the sanctions of the law. Born in Dublin, Frances Sheridan (1724–66) moved to London in the late 1750s with her dramatist husband, Thomas. *Memoirs of Miss Sidney Bidulph* (1761–7), her epistolary novel, is dedicated to Samuel Richardson, several of whose major themes it rehearses. The explicit moral of Sheridan's work, as in Richardson's *Clarissa Harlowe* (1747–8), is that virtue is often unrewarded in life, but as Sidney's considerable sufferings are directly brought about by her accession to the will of her blinkered, intractable mother, the novel also undermines the desirability of unresisting obedience. It is a subtle and absorbing account of manipulation and constraint, an incisive anatomy of a heroine acting against her own desires with disastrous results.

In contrast, *Louisa Mildmay, or Memoirs of a Magdalen* (1767), an unusual epistolary novel by Hugh Kelly (1739–77), shows a heroine acting *from* her own desires – with, initially at least, disastrous results. Kelly's novel, like Sheridan's, pays explicit homage to Richardson. In this case, the heroine is 'undone' by her fiancé a few days before their wedding. Very few eighteenth-century heroines are permitted to slip into vice and then regain the virtuous shore; Louisa Mildmay is allowed to be prosperous, respected and happy. Kelly's novel both questions the absolute division between virtue and vice on which a good deal of eighteenth-century fiction depends and offers some cogent criticism of the ubiquitous sexual double standard. Several of the novel's scenes, particularly the morning after scene between hero and heroine, demonstrate Kelly's dramatic talent. In London (he was born in Killarney), he went on to have a successful career as a playwright.

In fact, in 1768, Kelly's *The False Delicacy* was competing for the attention of the London theatre public with *The Good Natured Man* by Oliver Goldsmith (1728–74). Goldsmith's *The Vicar of Wakefield* (1766) is, along with Jonathan Swift's *Gulliver's Travels*, distinguished from other eighteenth-century Irish fiction by being a canonical work of English literature. This shared status may well owe something to the fact that neither deals explicitly with Irish themes or shows any other signs of national particularity. In all other respects the two works are polar opposites: the first using the device of travel in remote regions to test European modernity and ideas of progress, the second, set in a timeless rural landscape, being an affectionately ironic portrait of paternal power.

Still, the line between domestic novels of feeling and their more outward looking counterparts should not be drawn too fast. Richardson's own novels have been legitimately read as having political valences, while the foremost Irish practitioner of the sentimental mode, Frances Sheridan, followed the success of *Sidney Bidulph* with another exploration of power, dependence and manipulation; *The History of Nourjahad* (1767) is a beautifully crafted Oriental tale given the public setting of a Persian court. Facile divisions between private and public are polemically disputed in *The Triumph of Prudence over Passion*, an anonymous epistolary novel published in Dublin in 1781, which deals with the courtships of four couples but also offers explicit commentary on political affairs. Set at the time of the Volunteer movement, then agitating for free trade – that is, the right of Ireland to trade directly with the colonies – the novel declares that there is 'no reason why women should not be patriots'.[18] Unlike Chaigneau's *Jack Connor*, whose paternalist attitudes towards the peasantry it shares, *The Triumph of Prudence over Passion* regularly distinguishes between Irish and English character, usually giving the preference to Ireland and thereby expressing a self-confident and distinct Irish Protestant identity. It was this identity which was to be severely eclipsed by the passing of the Act of Union in 1800.

Distinctions between public and private, home and abroad, are also challenged in Henry Brooke's singular novel, *The Fool of Quality*. The fool of the title is Harry Clifton, rationally educated by his uncle, free from conventional views and therefore foolish in prejudiced eyes. The novel has two main threads: one charts the fortunes of the Clifton family over a quarter of a century; the other consists of various interpolated tales – the life stories of the recipients of the extensive charity of Harry and his uncle. An evangelical novel of feeling, in which various characters are regularly born anew, the narrative dissolves boundaries between pleasure and grief, sexuality and sanctity, in ways that even some eighteenth-century readers, more flexible in this regard than their modern counterparts, found disturbing.[19] Yet more striking is the novel's unsettling treatment of origins and destinations, the local and the remote.

Ostensibly committed to a domestic ideal, the novel also insists that domestic space be ruptured for true social health: Harry's beneficial career is inaugurated by his abduction at his uncle's hands. This initial disregard for conventional notions of the domestic is subsequently offset by the particularly domestic version of the exotic at the novel's close, when the now adult Harry encounters a Moorish page. One of the first characters in Irish fiction to overcome racism, Harry is soon speaking of his former 'aversion' to blackness and denouncing prejudice. Then follow successive unpeelings of strangeness in which the page is revealed to be neither black, nor male, but Harry's half-Moorish female cousin once-removed.

Distinctions, including those between wild Irish and settler, between 'Irish and Irish', are common in eighteenth-century Irish fiction, but in its different forms – romance, picaresque, novel of ideas – it also discovers sameness in difference: Gulliver and the Yahoo; the Irish and the English; Harry Clifton and his Moorish cousin. The terrain on which this positioning occurs can be more or less real, more or less fantastic. When Chaigneau argued that Irish and English Protestants should be considered 'Brethren', he was articulating a relationship between familiar groups in a realistic setting; in contrast, Brooke's lines of consanguinity are extended and considerably more exotic. Seamus Deane has influentially characterised the Ireland projected by post-Union writers such as Edgeworth as a 'strange country'.[20] This phastasmagoric Ireland, this vision of remoteness, this site of absolute difference, has to some extent misted over literary history, obscuring both the familiar, intimate landscapes and the far-flung uncanniness of earlier fiction. Eighteenth-century Irish fiction mapped identity on to what is, for us, a still-to-be-recovered blend of real and imagined geography.

NOTES

1. William Chaigneau, *The History of Jack Connor*, 2 vols. (1752; London, 1753), vol. II, p. 113.

2. For example, Henry Brooke's *The Fool of Quality* was published originally in Dublin. In the anonymous *The History of Ned Evans* (Dublin, 1797), certain strictures on contemporary Dublin architecture are included 'agreeable to the London edition' (vol. I, p. 224), but the justice of the criticisms is disputed. In Irish reprints of Tobias Smollett's *Sir Launcelot Greaves*, a comment on the actor David Garrick is silently changed to one on the Irish favourite Spanger Barry. See Ian Campbell Ross, 'Prose in English 1690–1800', in Margaret Kelleher and Philip O'Leary (eds.), *The Cambridge History of Irish Literature* (Cambridge: Cambridge University Press, 2006), vol. I, p. 273.

3. *Vertue Rewarded; or, the Irish Princess*, ed. Hubert McDermott (1693; Gerrards Cross: Colin Smythe, 1992), p. 20.

4. Sarah Butler, *Irish Tales, or Instructive Histories for the Conduct of Life* (London, 1716), n.p.

5. These letters, supposedly written by a Dublin draper, urged resistance to Wood's halfpence. Without any consultation with the Irish parliament, Wood, an Englishman, had been given a patent to coin money for Ireland, leading to fears that the currency would be severely devalued.

6. The basic study of the early eighteenth-century novel is Ian Watt's *The Rise of the Novel: Studies in Defoe, Richardson and Fielding* (1957). Notable among more recent studies which consider Swift's relationship to the novel are Michael McKeon, *The Origins of the English Novel, 1600–1740* (1987), J. Paul Hunter, *Before Novels: The Cultural Contexts of Eighteenth-Century English Fiction* (1990) and 'Gulliver's Travels and the Later Writings', in Christopher Fox (ed.), *The Cambridge Companion to Jonathan Swift* (2003).

7. *Gulliver's Travels*, ed. Christopher Fox (1726; Boston: Bedford Books, 1995), p. 132.

8. *The Prose Works of Jonathan Swift*, ed. Herbert Davis, 16 vols. (Oxford: Blackwell, 1939–74), vol. X, p. 64.

9. Despite this feature of the novel, early reviewers noted not only the author's fondness for Ireland, but also his 'smart reprisals upon the *English*, for their national and vulgar prejudices against their brethren of *Ireland*' (*The Monthly Review* (June 1752), p. 447).

10. Thomas Amory, *The Life of John Buncle, Esq.*, 2 vols. (1756, 1766; New York: Garland Publishing, 1975), vol. I, p. vii.

11. See Ian Campbell Ross, 'Thomas Amory, *John Buncle*, and the Origins of Irish Fiction', *Éire-Ireland* 18 (1983), 71–85.

12. Katie Trumpener, *Bardic Nationalism: The Romantic Novel and the British Empire* (Princeton, NJ: Princeton University Press, 1997), p. 106.

13. Laurence Sterne, *The Life and Opinions of Tristram Shandy, Gentleman* (1760–7), ed. Ian Campbell Ross (Oxford: Oxford University Press, 1983), p. 87.

14. *Chrysal, or the Adventures of a Guinea*, 4 vols. (1756–63; London, 1767), vol. IV, p. 123.

15. *The Adventures of Anthony Varnish; or, a Peep at the Manners of Society* (London, 1786), p. 29.

16. *The Reverie, or, a Flight to the Paradise of Fools*, 2 vols. (1762; New York: Garland, 1974), vol. I, p. 130.

17. *The History of Ned Evans, interspersed with moral and critical remarks: anecdotes and characters of many persons well known in the polite world; and incidental strictures on the Present State of Ireland*, 2 vols. (1796; Dublin, 1797), vol. I, p. 191.

18. *The Triumph of Prudence over Passion: or, the History of Miss Mortimer and Miss Fitzgerald*, 2 vols. (Dublin, 1781), vol. I, p. 25. The 1783 London edition was entitled *The Reconciliation, or, History of Miss Mortimer and Miss Fitzgerald*.

19. Peter Garside, James Raven and Rainer Schöwlerling (eds.), *The English Novel 1770–1829: A Bibliographic Survey of Prose Fiction Published in the British Isles*, 2 vols. (Oxford: Oxford University Press, 2000), vol. I, pp. 135–6.

20. *Strange Country: Modernity and Nationhood in Irish Writing since 1790* (Oxford: Clarendon Press, 1997).

GUIDE TO FURTHER READING

Doody, Margaret. 'Frances Sheridan: Morality and Annihilated Time', in Cecilia Macheski and Mary Anne Schofield (eds.), *Fettered or Free? British Women Novelists, 1670–1815*. Athens, OH: Ohio University Press, 1986.

Douglas, Aileen. 'Britannia's Rule and the It-Narrator', *Eighteenth-Century Fiction* 6 (1993), 65–82.

Ferguson, Oliver. *Jonathan Swift and Ireland*. Urbana, IL: University of Illinois Press, 1962.

McMinn, Joseph (ed.). *Swift's Irish Pamphlets: An Introductory Selection*. Gerrards Cross: Colin Smythe, 1991.

Ross, Ian Campbell. 'Fiction to 1800', in *The Field Day Anthology of Irish Writing*. 3 vols. Gen. ed. Seamus Deane. Derry: Field Day Publications, 1991.

Ross, Ian Campbell. ' "One of the Principal Nations in Europe": The Representation of Ireland in Sarah Butler's *Irish Tales*', *Eighteenth-Century Fiction* 7 (1994), 1–16.

Ross, Ian Campbell. 'Rewriting Irish Literary History: The Case of the Irish Novel', *Etudes Anglaises* 39:4 (1986), 385–99.

Ross, Ian Campbell. 'An Irish Picaresque Novel: William Chaigneau's *The History of Jack Connor*', *Studies* 71 (1982), 270–9.

Ross, Ian Campbell. '*The Triumph of Prudence over Passion*: Nationalism and Feminism in an Eighteenth-Century Irish Novel', *Irish University Review* 10 (1980), 232–40.

2

MIRANDA BURGESS

The national tale and allied genres, 1770s–1840s

Tales and novels

To discuss the regional novels of nineteenth-century Ireland under the heading of 'the national tale' is to acknowledge the primacy of national tales among nineteenth-century regional fictions. I intend this acknowledgment in both historical and literary senses. National tales are the earliest Irish novels centrally concerned with definitions and descriptions of Ireland, but it is equally the case that examples of this genre are widely considered among the best and most significant of nineteenth-century Irish novels. Yet although it is a characteristically Irish form, the national tale is not limited to Ireland. Moreover, not every nineteenth-century Irish regional novel is best categorised under that rubric, though all in their different ways have at least some roots in the genre that it names. The label 'national tale', in short, is historically and aesthetically significant and at the same time slippery, still open to question or argument.

Despite this uncertainty of definition, the emergence of the genre is easily identified historically. The national tale is a distinctively Romantic genre. It belongs to the period bordered by the French Revolution in 1789 and the passage of a Reform Bill by the British parliament in 1832.[1] In specifically Irish terms, it thrives in the stretch of time between the 1801 Act of Union, which dissolved the Irish parliament that had legislated domestically since 1782 and folded all its legislative functions into the jurisdiction of Westminster, and Catholic Emancipation in 1829, which put a final end to political disabilities by allowing Catholics to sit in parliament.[2] Despite its distinctively Irish form, the genre shares motifs and concerns with other kinds of European Romantic fiction. In documenting the strengths and diagnosing the failings of the past, and in tracing the force of history on the present, it inspired and continued to influence the historical novel associated with Walter Scott. Its anatomies of the contemporary political economic scene resemble contemporary reformist fictions by such writers as William Godwin and Mary Wollstonecraft.

Above all, the national tale is dialogical, reproducing diverse accents, vocabularies and sometimes languages as it attempts to provide an overview of a national community – a national community that is continually in contact with representatives from other nations. It has a tendency toward generic agglomeration, enfolding snippets of letters, poems, travel writing and antiquarian and political economic treatises within its narratives. Taken together, these features associate the genre with the idealised field of political action and literary debate that contemporaries called a 'public sphere' or 'republic of letters' as it was being constituted in the Romantic period – or, in Ina Ferris's memorable phrase, with a 'dynamic notion of culture as encounter, often of an abrasive kind'.[3]

Although texts declaring themselves 'tales' of various kinds had been appearing frequently in Britain and Ireland since the early eighteenth century, until the 1770s these works were chiefly small and brief: anonymous chapbooks (printed on cheap paper and aimed at a labouring audience) and children's books, as well as narratives in verse. The chapbook 'tales' were transcriptions of oral stories or distillations of works so well known as to have taken on the status of folklore: the histories of popular heroes such as Robin Hood, European fairy stories and abridged renderings of Chaucer's broader *Canterbury Tales* and of Shakespeare's comedic plots. For children there were 'legendary tales' with subjects such as Alfred the Great and Richard I.

By the 1780s and 1790s, however, other, longer kinds of 'tales' were regularly being published. Two kinds are among the direct ancestors of the national tale. The first, the exotic or 'Oriental tale', purported to translate a legendary or a historical narrative from a foreign place. Its locations and plots often served as allegorical stand-ins for current social and political questions in Britain, especially imperial relations.[4] The geographical range of the exotic tale can be comprehended from a very partial list of titles, such as the anonymous *Rajah Kisna: An Indian Tale* (1786), George Cumberland's *The Captive of the Castle of Sennaar: An African Tale* (1798) and his American narrative, *Marraton and Yaratilda: An Indian Traditionary Tale* (1793).

The second, the 'historical tale', was either explicitly identified as such, as in Anne Fuller's *Alan Fitz-Osborne, an Historical Tale* (1787), or associated with distant histories in other more or less specific ways, as in Sophia Lee's *The Recess; or, A Tale of Other Times* (1785) and the anonymous *Count Roderic's Castle: or Gothic Times, a Tale* (1794). The historical tale differed from the historical novel as it emerged in the nineteenth century. The historical novel was a genre that investigated the effects of large changes in national or global history on the lives and actions of ordinary individuals.[5] Especially after the 1820s, it includes a good number of Irish works that, because of their preoccupation with the history of Ireland rather than British or European history, tend to be associated with the regional rather than the historical novel and overlooked by scholars of the latter.[6] For example, despite a title that references the national tale, the plot of Samuel Lover's *Rory O'More: A National Romance* (1837), in which an ordinary fellow is drawn into Theobald Wolfe Tone's revolutionary activities in 1798, closely resembles the outline of Scott's *Waverley*, the classic example of the genre. Anna Maria Hall's *The Whiteboy: A Story of Ireland* (1845) similarly imitates Scott, even to the English hero's arrival as a stranger in Ireland and his choice between the domesticated, religious and half-English Ellen, whom he eventually marries, and the 'Irish rebel' Lady Mary O'Brien, with whom he falls in love early in the novel. These women are Scott's Rose Bradwardine and his tragic Flora MacIvor, removed to an Irish setting.

By contrast, the historical tale, like the national tales that would eventually emerge from it, remained closely linked to antiquarianism. It paid more attention to fragmented material evidence and ancient texts than to the kinds of history that can be understood as seamless national narratives. A frequent marker of what are now called Gothic novels, the label 'tale' had come to connote exploration of historical fractures, conflicts and sufferings even as it continued to advertise its roots in oral narration and forgotten history. Lee's designation of her novel *A Hermit's Tale: Recorded by his own Hand, and Found in his Cell* (1793) is one example, and it is in this same sense that the Irish novelist Regina Maria Roche attached the 'tale' label to most of her novels. In particular, Roche's *The Children of the Abbey: A Tale* (1796) pieces together a series of oral narratives and found manuscripts with distinct voices and perspectives, heralding techniques that will characterise national tales by Maria Edgeworth, Sydney Owenson (later Lady Morgan) and Charles Robert Maturin after the turn of the nineteenth century.

Two more kinds of tale began appearing in the 1790s. In a subgroup of 'historical tales', such as John Palmer's *The Haunted Cavern: A Caledonian Tale* (1796) and Thomas Read's *The Enchanted Castle of Llewllyn [sic]; a Welch Tale* (1799), English writers arranged their plots against exotic backdrops that they located not in Europe, Asia or the New World, but in the far north and west of Britain itself. Still more typical of the 1790s were 'tales of the times'. Some of these were didactic novels that expressed alarm about what they represented as a recent decline in manners and virtue, as in Jane West's *A Tale of the Times* (1799). Others, however, dissected contemporary political corruption and disruption from a variety of political perspectives. The anonymous *The Rebel: A Tale of the Times* (1799) is an explicitly titled example, but works by so-called English Jacobin novelists, such as Godwin's *Things as they are; or, Caleb Williams* (1794) and *St Leon, A Tale of the Sixteenth Century* (1800), equally demonstrate the close connection of 'tales of the times' to 'historical tales' and thus to an interest in orality, antiquarian history and textual and generic pastiche.

Theories of the national tale

It is in 1806, amid a literary and political milieu shaped by these 'tales of the times' and 'historical tales' that the words 'national tale' make their first appearance together, in the title of *The Wild Irish Girl: A National Tale*, by the Dublin-educated novelist, essayist and poet, Sydney Owenson (?1776–1859). By adding these words to the title of her novel, Owenson names not only an individual text but also a species of texts, a set of objects to which her novel belongs. In classifying the book as 'a' national tale, Owenson identifies her novel as an exemplar of a recognisable literary form. But what are the parameters of the group to which this novel is nominated? How are they distinguished from the preoccupations of the 'tale' genre at large and of the historical tale in particular? Should membership of the group be identified by resemblances in theme or literary form or by matters of historical situation or rhetorical effect? These questions recur in any consideration of literary genres, not least eighteenth- and nineteenth-century novels, as the recent and thorough debates on the history and theory of genre as a category, and genre-formation as a process, suggest.[7] They are questions of especially urgent concern to scholars of the national tale, perhaps because the stakes are relatively high. The most pressing questions of definition concern the development and character of literary nationalism in Ireland and the relation of the Irish novel to the novels of Britain and Europe.

Existing theories of the national tale fall into two loosely identifiable groups. The first is associated with Gary Kelly and Nicola Watson, the first scholars to define the national tale as a genre. These scholars understand the national tale as a form of narrative proposing 'formal and thematic reso-lutions. . . for the alarming conflicts and social divisions revealed and exacerbated during the Revolutionary decade', in Britain and Europe as much as in Ireland.[8] The second group, with Katie Trumpener and Ina Ferris at its forefront, suggests that the national tale is concerned less with the achievement of a general kind of sociopolitical stability than it is with social and political dialogue and critical assessment, both within nations and between them.[9] National tales, for these readers, are texts concerned with examining the effects of writing on the formation and maintenance of national communities and at the same time with exploring the exchanges that take place among nations and their genres. To these two major accounts of the national tale as a genre should be added the many considerations of particular national tales in the context of literary histories of Ireland and histories of the Irish novel, by readers such as Mary Jean Corbett, Seamus Deane, Terry Eagleton, Declan Kiberd, Joep Leerssen, David Lloyd, W. J. McCormack and Julian Moynahan, among many others.[10] Although these readings do not consider the individual works discussed as members of a larger group of national tales, they nevertheless subdivide along related though not identical lines.

Kelly and Watson include examinations of the national tale within their general histories of the early nineteenth-century novel in English. To these readers, the genre is most closely related to the conservative 'tale of the times', with its pedagogical attempts at moral restoration. Both Watson and Kelly take novels by Maria Edgeworth (1767–1849) as primary examples of the genre. For Kelly, the thematic achievement of social harmony is paramount in Edgeworth's *Castle Rackrent: An Hibernian Tale taken from facts and from the manners of the Irish squires before the year 1782* (1800) and in the national tales that followed. He argues that the project of this novel in particular is the reform of the landed classes by such conventionally bourgeois means as domestic virtue, hard work and education, and the improvement and consequent quiescence of their tenants. The goal is furthered, in Kelly's view, by Edgeworth's double mode of narration. The 'author' of the avowedly factual tale is the steward Thady Quirk, whose exaggerated declarations of hereditary loyalty to the feckless and often exploitative Rackrent family make him a classically unreliable narrator. However, Edgeworth provides Thady with an 'editor' who adds an introduction, epilogue and footnotes that explain, contextualise, undermine and sometimes laugh at the servant's observations, for the benefit of an English audience 'ignorant' of Ireland's language, history and character.[11] Authority in Kelly's reading of *Castle Rackrent* rests with the educated, systematic presence of the 'editor', who demonstrates his own superiority to Thady's colloquial, popular style of narration at the same time as he censures Thady's 'pre-modern' attitude toward the Rackrents themselves.[12]

Similarly, Watson emphasises the unity Edgeworth imposes on the national tale. However, Watson views that unity as the inseparable formal counterpart of the orderly marriages with which the plots of these novels typically end. For Watson, the marriage ending is the key motif of what she calls 'national romance', an allegory of reconciliation between warring classes and cultures that unifies the nation. Contrasting the national tale as a genre to the epistolary forms of fiction that were popular in the last half of the eighteenth century, she argues that narrative cohesion mirrors and emphasises the displacement of national conflicts on to personal and emotional relations, where these conflicts can be resolved in virtuous domesticity. The novels, that is, arrive at a kind of narrative marriage between the multiple voices, narratives and perspectives they include. This formal cohesion is imposed on national tales by plots that limit the circulation of competing voices and assertions in letters, found documents and conversation and by narrators who evaluate and select among the various voices in the text, transforming first-person testimony into an authoritative third-person account. Watson's chief example is Edgeworth's *Ormond* (1817), which closes with a highly appropriate marriage between the hero Harry Ormond and his educated, docile neighbor Florence Annaly, sister to a major Anglo-Irish landowner. The marriage can be brought about only by a plot that abruptly cuts off Harry's earlier affection for Dora, heir to the Irish-speaking western 'kingdom' of the Black Islands, at the same time as it detaches Harry from the networks of French and Irish correspondence in which Dora is both a central object of discussion and an eager agent.[13] For Watson, the narrative technique of such novels is at least as significant as the themes of reconciliation, for it enacts rather than merely reflecting a new and centralised ideal of national unity. Its achievement of unity is born of an analogy between written texts and bodies.

Like most literary histories, Kelly's and Watson's accounts trace the progress of the genre they discuss. Certainly, their understanding of the narrator's role in Irish novels is suggested by a retrospective reading of the genre, from the regional novels of the mid-nineteenth century back through the national tales of the century's beginning, which assumes that the later works represent the maturity of the earlier. *Charles O'Malley, the Irish Dragoon* (1841) and *The O'Donoghue; A Tale of Ireland Fifty Years Ago* (1845), both by Charles Lever (1806–72), propose what Julian Moynahan calls a 'mystic notion of a feudal bond between landowners and their tenants, which had been mysteriously ruptured and which could be mended or restored whenever the proprietors got around to it', a reconciliation that is mirrored in the novels' blandly anglicised narrative voice.[14] In *Valentine M'Clutchy, the Irish Agent; or the Chronicles of Castle Cumber* (1847), William Carleton (1794–1869) – himself born into the native Irish labouring class – portrays the most unjust middleman in all of Irish fiction, pitting him against a peasantry whose thoroughly ironic conversation with him and uses of Irish language interjections as a secret level of communication convey the simmering danger of their opposition. But even against this turbulent linguistic and economic backdrop, the narrator retains a firm control of the characters' voices, primarily by appropriating the role of master ironist to himself.

Despite the apparent ties between Edgeworth's narrating 'editor' and the mainstream of nineteenth-century Irish regional fiction, three questions about gender and literary history might make it seem that the choice of Edgeworth's novels as objects of study obscures more than it illuminates the character of the national tale. First, although Watson and Kelly both draw their examples exclusively from the works of female writers – and until the Banim brothers published their novels in the 1820s, the Irish national tale remained a primarily female-authored genre – neither fully accounts for a gender association that they only implicitly recognise. Kelly elsewhere suggests that female writers are the principal purveyors of values, such as those he attributes to Edgeworth, that he links to a 'professional middle-class cultural revolution' taking place in Britain at the turn of the nineteenth century, but explains the connection by a conventional association of domesticity with women.[15] For Watson, the predominance of female-authored national tales mirrors the authorship of epistolary novels at the end of the eighteenth century. For this reason, she argues that the Irish national tale betrays the effects of the same social pressures that bear on contemporary epistolary narratives, especially fear of revolution and an associated redefinition of gender conventions, placing the national tale among the works of 'British' writers.[16] Neither Kelly nor Watson investigates the specific connections between gender and early nineteenth-century Irish nationhood that the history of the national tale makes available.

Second, although Edgeworth's first novel is named in most discussions of the national tale as the original exemplar of the genre, it has conventionally been considered as the first Irish novel though, as Siobhán Kilfeather has argued, it is more accurately described as the first Irish *regional* novel, taking up the land, people and problems of Ireland as primary matters of discussion.[17] The standing of Edgeworth's fictions is further complicated by such a reading as Norman Vance's which suggests that their amalgam of genres makes them something other than novels because it places them outside the tradition of the nineteenth-century novel in English, which Vance associates with Henry James and psychological depth.[18] These texts do not, then, immediately lend themselves to drawing the lines between national tales and the regional novels of which they are a subset, between regional novels and the generality of nineteenth-century Irish fiction or between the Irish novel and European fiction generally.

A third question about the emblematic status of Edgeworth's national tales arises from the continuing critical debate over the location of political, moral and narrative authority in *Castle Rackrent* and her other novels, which has left readers sharply divided. Responses to the narrative techniques of *Castle Rackrent* often range themselves on the side either of Thady or the 'editor', arguing that one perspective triumphs over the other. In this context, in emphasising the authoritative role of Edgeworth's narrators and their success in imposing order on narrative and political chaos, Watson and Kelly actually resemble more than they differ from Robert Tracy, who celebrates Thady's loyal rhetoric as a triumphant parody of colonial convention and argues that the servant's subversive rhetoric makes him a narrative surrogate for an anti-colonial nationalist Edgeworth.[19] In Watson's reading as in Kelly's, the national tale in so far as it is a genre of national cohesion deals with a nation defined in general terms, as a synonym for polity – even society – and in a context understood as homogeneously British.[20] For Tracy, it exists within the context of a Romantic nationalism that views Ireland as separate and unique. Both readings depend on an understanding of the national tale as an essentially insular genre, derived either from a Britain so uniform in its dedication to Union that writers from Ireland and Scotland cooperate in narrative opposition to disruptions they associate with French revolutionary influence, or from an Ireland already post-colonial in its narrative self-definitions.[21]

In contrast are readings by, for example, Corbett, Eagleton, Lloyd and Deane, who argue that the shifting of authority between narrators is more significant than any final accommodation that is reached. Eagleton and Corbett suggest that the textual encounter between the 'editor' and Thady constitutes an attempt to find a middle ground between the editor's narrative and political objectivity (which might border on callousness) and sympathy with Thady and the other Rackrent tenants (which risks being blinded by closeness to those whom it describes).[22] For Corbett, this 'middle way' is gendered, grounded in a critique of Anglo-Irish landowners and of their tenants as bad husbands and bad fathers, though Corbett points out that the novel neglects to acknowledge the dysfunctional contexts, the imperfect abolition of native landholding and kinship traditions and the incomplete adoption of British ones, in which both kinds of behavior flourish.[23] For Lloyd and Deane, on the other hand, a failure to impose narrative order is apparent in the competition between Thady and the narrator, and is evidence of what Lloyd calls a 'crisis of representation' caused by the unease of a genre whose key aim is to impose order on what it understands as chaos – as noise rather than conversation – while downplaying the historical factors that have created it.[24] For all these readers, the national tale exists on the uncertain terrain of negotiation between Ireland and Britain, both of which, in turn, are internally fractured according to politics, culture and class.

In short, the national tale divides its readers because novel and genre are alike divided by contending views and voices. Narrative divisions and divisions between readers are symptoms of transnational encounter.

Castle Rackrent

To read *Castle Rackrent* is to be introduced to an Ireland that is unique, but the uniqueness of which depends on an opposition to Britain and perhaps equally on the intimate and contested relations between settler and indigene, tradition and progress, that are a lasting outcome of this transnational relation. Edgeworth traces the fate of a landed Irish property in the hands of the Rackrents – constantly in debt, in default of heirs-male and given to dying young from hunting mishaps, drink and duels. Because the estate is inherited by brothers and cousins more often than by sons, it changes hands five times in the single lifetime of Thady Quirk before being bought by his son Jason, an attorney who makes himself the Rackrents' principal creditor. The property is a staging ground for the economic consequences of domestic misconduct, but the novel's subtitle – 'taken from facts and from the manners of the Irish squires before the year 1782' – also emphasises the larger metaphorical status of the estate. Edgeworth's 'year 1782' saw the establishment of a Dublin parliament, for which all landed Protestants (and, after 1793, freeholding Catholics) could vote. Despite this retrospective dating, however, the gentry in Edgeworth's subsequent novels – the dissolute Lord Glenthorn in *Ennui* (1809), the rackrenting, free-spending Lord and Lady Clonbrony of *The Absentee* (1812) and the paired, flawed guardians in *Ormond*, the 'old Irish' King Corny of the Black Islands and the Dublin politician Sir Ulick O'Shane – often differ little from members of the Rackrent family. To read the novels in sequence is to observe an ironic denial of social improvement in the years since 1782. This irony raises questions about the utility of legislative autonomy – a solution proposed by mid-eighteenth-century Irish Patriots and by the Volunteers who armed against a feared French invasion of Ireland during the American Revolutionary War – as a cure for Ireland's ills.[25] It also implies that ills are an intrinsic condition of Ireland.

Yet the plot of *Castle Rackrent* also has broader historical and geographical implications. That the Rackrent family was formerly called O'Shaughlin suggests that its members embody not only the failings of the Protestant Ascendancy (established, as W. J. McCormack has shown, as the novel was being written) but also those of the assimilated or *déclassé* native gentry the Ascendancy has finally displaced.[26] In documenting the struggles for power and the rhetoric of affection that characterise relations between native and settler, this novel removes the historical boundaries dividing one from the other. Moreover, even as the novel traces the distressing continuities of the Irish past and present, the rapid transfer of the Rackrent estate from each owner to the next mirrors the pace of regime change in the revolutionary Europe of the 1790s. Both domestically and internationally, the novel explores the metaphor of 'an entailed estate' (caught between heirs who encourage incremental improvements and those who advocate demolition and reconstruction) to which Edmund Burke had compared the nation states of Europe in *Reflections on the Revolution in France* (1790).[27]

The complexly metaphorical character of Edgeworth's plot, then, is at once national and transnational, locating its Irish themes firmly within the context of pan-European historical conflict. Lacking an indisputable centre of ethical and narrative gravity, it appears critical by turns of native Irish claims on a share of landed and political power, Ascendancy demands for order and Enlightenment projects for gradual social and economic improvement. But it is in Edgeworth's pioneering narrative mode that the ambiguities of *Castle Rackrent* chiefly reside. Moynahan draws attention to the relations of verbal 'impersonation and mimicry' that link Thady Quirk to Edgeworth.[28] Edgeworth comically assumes the language of an Irish peasant, Moynahan suggests, just as such a peasant would likely have mocked the speech and behavior of a landlord. The relation between writer and narrator is contradictory, at once sharply critical and approaching the familial. It is unlike, for example, the relationships Homi Bhabha uses to illustrate his post-colonial theory of mimicry, in which colonised subjects aspire to emulate the colonisers and in which a critical impulse is latent in the mimetic failures of the colonised, exposing the cruelty (or silliness) of the conventions they imitate.[29] Imitation in *Castle Rackrent* passes back and forth between the propertied and the poor, the settler and the native, refusing any stable account of the emotional or political relations between them.

Against this backdrop of mimicry and geographic and historical complexity, the stubborn problem of Edgeworth's relation to the fictional 'editor' is less surprising, less anomalous. It helps to explain the contradictions between the claims of the editor and arguments Edgeworth makes elsewhere. The editor, for example, praises Arthur Young's *Tour in Ireland, with General Observations on the Present State of That Kingdom* (1780) as a depiction of Irish 'shrewdness, and blunder' as faithful as the contemporary Irish portraits on the London or Dublin stage (p. 121). Yet this evaluation differs markedly from the denial of association between Irish speech and verbal error in the *Essay on Irish Bulls* (1802) that Edgeworth coauthored with her father. Considered alongside the *Essay*'s assertion that 'the bulls and blunders, of which [Irish speakers of English] are accused, are often attributable to their neighbours', the imitation of an anglicised, apparently judicious voice reads like a parodic reproduction of dynamics typical of the transnational exchanges within which readers, writers and speakers consolidate their national identities.[30] This mimicry is not, exactly, an instance of 'minor literature' as Gilles Deleuze and Félix Guattari define it: the act of writing in a major language by minority users of the language, which dislodges metropolitan assumptions about the national ownership of languages while helping to consolidate a minority group identity.[31] But *Castle Rackrent* is a good fit with two important modifications of the theory in an Irish context. Ferris emphasises that minor literatures voice the claims of small nations against large ones in language borrowed from the latter; for Lloyd, even more relevant to this novel, the crucial point is that 'minor' works refuse to succumb to a unified narrative or a stable national identity.[32]

The national tale and metropolitan genres

The unceasing movement of *Castle Rackrent* from perspective to perspective among competing narrators, voices and documents is inherited from the historical tale of the 1790s – itself, it should be noted, a genre that remains minor within the history of the novel as well as within the nineteenth-century literary canon, despite its contemporary popularity.[33] As such, it is closer to a mix of characteristics from the liberal 'tales of the times' and 'exotic tales' than it is to conservative didactic fiction. It is precisely such a repudiation of a stable centre of narrative judgment and national definition that recurs in subsequent national tales, making Edgeworth's novel at once prophetic and typical. Among the best examples is Owenson's *Florence Macarthy: An Irish Tale* (1818), the first volume of which is entirely taken up by the lengthy conversations of two new arrivals in Ireland. One, a 'brave Guerilla chief, whose life and fortune have been devoted to South American independence', is by birth the lost heir to the Norman Irish Marquis of Dunore.[34] The other is apparently English, a romantic and reader of picturesque tours, but in reality is son and heir to the Anglo-Irish usurper of the Dunore estate. Travelling incognito, the pair debate about women, taste, the best way to live, the character of America and, especially, the political economy of Ireland, without interruption or resolution.

A similar series of conversations, presented in epistolary form without an authoritative editor, takes place in *The Wild Irish Boy* (1808) by Charles Robert Maturin (1782–1824). Maturin's text is not, as has sometimes been suggested, a parody of *The Wild Irish Girl*. It is closer to, but precedes, Edgeworth's *Ennui* in recounting the history of an Anglo-Irish heir who has bored himself with too much pleasure, though Maturin's Ormsby Bethel, unlike Edgeworth's Earl of Glenthorn, is aware from the start of the harm he is causing himself and his estate. The novel's events, unlike Owenson's, take place almost entirely in urban social settings, in London as well as in Dublin and rural Ireland. Nevertheless, it imitates Owenson's frameless epistolary form. Further examples include two important novels by the middle-class Catholic Irish novelist John Banim (1798–1842): *The Boyne Water* (1826), whose paired heroes present heartfelt opposing perspectives on the Williamite wars of 1689–90, and *The Anglo-Irish of the Nineteenth Century* (1828), with an opening volume devoted to a clash of religious, political and moral opinions on post-Union Ireland, arriving at neither reconciliation or consensus. In each of these novels, the visible sharing of narrative authority underscores a similar theme: the lack of a single uniform ethical and political standpoint, the impossibility of consensus, characterises the 'nation' whose tale is being told.

I have suggested that the national tale's descent from the 'historical tales' and 'tales of the times' of the 1790s is one reason for its inclusion of diverse voices, texts and genres. The most detailed and complex accounts of the national tale as a distinctive genre, by Trumpener and Ferris, go a long way to explain why these predecessor forms of fiction should have attracted the writers of national tales. Trumpener begins her account with a history of literary representations of Ireland by metropolitan writers. She demonstrates that Ireland and the Scottish Highlands were perceived in Romantic-period England as at once exotic and familiar, part of the national family of Britain and yet insufficiently well known to be fully and safely assimilated. It was in writing that Englishmen sought to domesticate the differences: in tours and surveys such as Young's *Tour in Ireland* and Samuel Johnson's *Journey to the Western Islands of Scotland* (1775), which presented the land, people and languages of the Highlands and Ireland as a romantic spectacle and, at the same time, as a wasteland to be reclaimed and modernised.[35] As Susan Stewart might put it, they 'distress' the peripheries – not only in the sense of Highland clearances and prejudicial Irish trade laws, but also in the sense of antiquing them, treating Ireland and the Highlands as surviving pockets of a pre-modern past that England has long since left behind.[36] In short, these texts acted as a cultural counterpart to Union. For this reason, Trumpener argues, the earliest national tales were created in reaction against them.

Irish and Scottish writers drew on 'historical tales' to respond with a pastiche of conventions and quotations imitated from metropolitan genres such as landscape description and antiquarian research. At the same time, they reinserted the stories of historical change that had left their traces on peripheral landscapes, literatures and histories.[37] As with the 'tales of the times', the very form of their novels promoted the idea of a public sphere. Here, periphery and metropole would debate their relations on literary terms, at least, of equality.[38] Irish national tales in particular insisted on the complex, ancient and continuing history of Ireland and its inhabitants, while documenting the fractures caused by transnational conflict and metropolitan control. In this way, Trumpener argues, Irish novelists made their own descriptions of Irish speech and landscape into vehicles for the self-definition of the inhabitants of Ireland as a distinct people within Britain and thus, in some cases, for the self-assertion of the smaller nation against the larger. Ironically, however, the national tale did not remain a genre of anti-colonial protest or small-national self-assertion. In Ireland, as it faded into the gentler regional novels of a Lever or a Griffin, the representation of sublime landscapes and peasant speech was taken up by metropolitan sojourners like Anthony Trollope (1815–82), whose Irish regional novels – especially *The Kellys and the O'Kellys; or, Landlords and Tenants* (1848), which transmutes the national tale's theme of a dispossessed native Irish aristocracy into a purely comic register – were popular in England. Moreover, because of its origins in such acts of transnational self-definition, the national tale is uniquely fitted, once exported to the colonies of the nineteenth century, to provide a model for new self-definitions as the colonies began to define themselves, and eventually came to be recognised, as nations.[39] Though the differences between them are real, they are not intrinsic: there is no absolute distinction between the native and the settler, the original and the imitation. Rather, the divergence is a product of specific transnational histories.

Edgeworth's *Ennui*, John Banim's *The Anglo-Irish of the Nineteenth Century* and Owenson's *Wild Irish Girl* are especially fine examples of the simultaneous imitation and criticism with which the national tale responded to metropolitan genres. In *Ennui*, the aristocratic English tourist Craiglethorpe comes to Ireland to collect materials for 'a Tour through Ireland, or a View of Ireland, or something of that Nature', a book to resemble Arthur Young's. He is fed 'absurd anecdotes, incredible *facts*, stale jests, and blunders, such as were never made by true-born Irishmen' by the witty Lady Geraldine, who plans to 'show him what a farrago of nonsense he has collected as materials for his quarto; and convince him at once how utterly unfit he is to write a book . . . on Irish affairs'.[40] The implication is that Young might have benefited from similar lessons and a similar circumspection. But Edgeworth's novel refuses to validate either the metropolitan or the nationalist claim of Irish exceptionalism, for, as well as being an Englishman, Craiglethorpe is the cousin of the patriotic Lady Geraldine.

His cousin's name simultaneously associates her with the United Irishman Lord Edward Fitzgerald and with the Fitzgerald family, or Geraldines, descendants of the original Norman invaders of Ireland, including the Earl of Kildare who helped defeat the 1641 rebellion of his Norman Irish peers and their native allies, which had transformed the two groups into a unified Irish interest. No generalised Enlightenment notion of a family of man and a common humanity results from the cousinship. Rather, the relationship is the sign of a complex sense of modern Irish history as the product of a very long series of encounters with England and with Europe.

Banim's parody of the metropolitan genres of Irish reform is at once more extended and more pointed. Seeking to thicken the exoticism of their descriptions of Ireland, English tour writers had often transcribed quotations from Irish peasant speech. The most bitingly funny moment in *The Anglo-Irish of the Nineteenth Century* comes as Banim turns the tables on the metropolitan observers. He records a series of undigested quotations from the political economy of Thomas Malthus, the Irish surveys of Young, tracts against the Catholic Association and its Emancipation petitions and didactic Irish tours that mingle in the conversation of social, judicial and political leaders at an Ascendancy evening party:

> 'Convert them,' said Lord Harmer.
>
> 'Keep them down,' recommended Sir John Lumley.
>
> 'And begin with the demagogues,' added the Judge's son, 'and the counsellors,' with a sneer.
>
> 'Make them tidy,' exhorted Miss Flint. . . 'teach them to go neat, and to turn small loans, and to whitewash.'. . .
>
> 'Set them to drain all the bogs,' said Lord Offally. . .
>
> 'Thin them,' advised a young Fellow of Dublin College. . .
>
> 'Yes, ship them off, in fleets, to our colonies,' recommended Mr Blake.
>
> 'And afterwards,—indeed, immediately,—make marriage amongst those who stay at home, except under prescribed circumstances, and at a certain age, penal,' said the young clergyman. . . a deep student in Malthus.[41]

In other scenes, too, the traffic between periphery and metropole moves more than one way. One of Banim's parodies of the Irish survey tour is situated in London rather than rural Ireland. Here, even 'in the very core of English cleanliness, order, and comfort, was a picture of. . . Irish nastiness and misery, as vivid as if. . . on Irish ground' (vol. I, p. 46). The Irish, it seems, have as much impact on London as Londoners do on Ireland, but their effect does not stem from any intrinsic national character. Rather, the patriotic clergyman Mr Knightly underlines the historical relations and cultural assumptions that have created such scenes, in England as in Ireland.

He asks why the street cleaners of London are encouraged to stop outside the Irish quarter of the city (vol. III, p. 106).

It is in Owenson's *Wild Irish Girl* that the classic response to the metropolitan writing of Ireland may be found. This national tale is itself a metropolitan tour, composed of the letters of Horatio M. to his father, who has banished him to Ireland for a series of romantic indiscretions, and to his friend J. D. Esquire, MP, who acts as the confidant of his Irish impressions. As Horatio's journey begins, he is ignorant of Ireland, though he takes on faith the little he has read in exploration narratives – even the wildest Elizabethan stuff. In consequence, he says, it has long been the case that 'whenever the Irish were mentioned in my presence, an *Esquimaux* group circling round the fire which was to dress a dinner, or broil an enemy, was the image which presented itself to my mind', and he declares what he calls 'a *confirmed prejudice*' against Ireland and its people. In Horatio's responses to his reading and to Ireland itself, his prejudices are those of the metropolitan survey. To his mind, Ireland is a colony whose differences from England can only be understood as a 'barbarity' of land and people, in need of improvement in so far as improvement is possible and control where it is not.[42] When at length he encounters the heroine, Glorvina, and her father, the dispossessed Prince of Inismore, he turns from survey to romantic exoticism: Ireland becomes for him a 'region of wonders' (p. 60).

Where Ireland does correspond with Horatio's expectations, it is in ways equally conditioned by travel narratives and surveys. He expects to discover the aesthetic pleasure of the sublime and indeed finds it almost immediately. When he praises Ireland's 'cloud-capt mountains, the impervious gloom of its deep embosomed glens, the savage desolation of its uncultivated heaths, and boundless bogs', he does so in terms that perfectly accord with the conventions of the metropolitan tour, which transform the uncultivated evidence of Ireland's damaged economic history into picturesque effects (p. 18). Among the peasantry, he is not surprised to find a 'living Chronicle', who recounts the romantic events of ancient oral history as though it were continuing in the present (p. 39). And on meeting Glorvina and her father, he portrays them for J. D. in a picturesque tableau, helpfully ending with the exclamation, 'What a picture!' (p. 50).

Glorvina and her father, however, resist their picturesque entrapment. Instead they testify, repeatedly and forcefully, to the continuing significance of Irish history, in which they educate Horatio. The Prince seems to Horatio to have a 'memory. . . rich in oral tradition' (p. 63). What the text attributes to him, however, is a memory well stored with Owenson's own apparatus of Irish intertextuality. Whereas in *Castle Rackrent* a learned narrator undermines the claims of a native Irishman, in *The Wild Irish Girl* a similar 'editor' supports the claims of the Prince and Glorvina against the prejudices of Horatio. Everything they say is backed up by footnoted quotations from Irish informants: Joseph Cooper Walker's *Historical Memoirs of the Irish Bards* (1786), Charlotte Brooke's *Reliques of Irish Poetry* (1789), Edward Ledwich's *Study of Irish Antiquities* (1781) and numerous other antiquarian texts. The effect is to convey the complexity of Irish culture and the continuing vibrancy of its history in a way that contests and reframes the printed accumulation of metropolitan assumptions. What Horatio thinks of as 'my *Hiberniana*,' is, it becomes increasingly clear, actually Glorvina's – and Owenson's – Irish textbook (p. 161).

Marriage and multiplicity

For Ferris, the textual contest that takes place when an educated Englishman enters Ireland is the key plot dynamic of the national tale. Removed from his native context and immersed in a new one, the metropolitan observer finds that his reading and his cherished assumptions are not universal orthodoxy, nor are they wholly confirmed by his material experience. This plot dynamic is paired with a reading dynamic in which the presentation of Ireland as a 'problem' to be comprehended and addressed by a metropolitan audience is displaced by the demands of Ireland to be heard speaking for itself. 'What matters', says Ferris, 'is the dynamic of contestation rather than the content of rival representations.'[43] In this space of linguistic encounter, Ireland enters the public sphere.

That its entry is not in itself a subject for celebration in the national tale is a suspicion raised by two further aspects of *The Wild Irish Girl* and perhaps of other national tales as well. In most of these novels – *Florence Macarthy* and *The Boyne Water* also stand out – the decentralisation of narrative authority and the inclusion of multiple histories of places and events uneasily coexist with the kind of orderly marriage ending identified by Watson. Thus at the conclusion of *The Wild Irish Girl*, Horatio's father presides over his marriage to Glorvina, declaring his hope that 'this family alliance' may be 'prophetically typical of a national unity of interests and affections between those . . . who are naturally allied' (p. 250). Feminist readers have pointed out the inequality of an alliance in which the female and Irish Glorvina gains protection in return for her complacent submission to the Englishman Horatio, often arguing that such a depiction of union hides political as well as gender inequities beneath a veil of sentimental romance.[44] In writing of Edgeworth's similar endings, however, Claire Connolly has importantly argued that in the national tale 'politics can, at times, be a mere foil in matters of sexual manners rather than the other way round'; at the very least, 'politics and sexuality exist in dynamic relation'.[45]

If the inequities of marriage law raise critical alarm, as indeed they often do in the 'tales of the times' that precede the national tale, then there is insufficient reason to conclude, with Deane, that such marriages are inevitably an 'analgesic version . . . of Anglo-Irish relations'.[46] In some tales, such as *The Boyne Water*, the marriages that make the heroes and heroines happy seem entirely irrelevant to political reconciliation, which remains beyond the reach of an essentially tragic historical narrative. In others, these marriages come under critical scrutiny. Indeed, the discomfort raised by the metaphoric substitution of bodies for nations is represented within *The Wild Irish Girl* itself – in the scene, for example, where Horatio remarks that 'the sentiment the daughter of the Prince inspired, only made *a part* in that general feeling of curiosity, which everything in this new region of wonders continued to nourish into existence', even as he fears the emotional pull of Glorvina's 'dangerous presence' (p. 60). Glorvina's physical presence is inadequate to an allegory of the nation, of which she is able to represent only 'a part'. But her presence also exceeds the requirements of her allegorical role, creating desires in Horatio that have nothing to do with their transnational relation and that threaten to dwarf it in significance and power.

The analogy between narrative cohesion and physical marriage that persists in the national tale means that Horatio's thematic discomfort is mirrored in the novel's treatment of text. Although Horatio uses books such as Rousseau's *Julie; or the New Héloïse* (1761) and Goethe's *The Sorrows of Young Werther* (1774) to educate Glorvina in the language of sexual feeling, he quickly comes to view their teaching as at once imperfect and excessive. When he sees Glorvina reading letters from another friend or suitor, he fears that he has awakened imaginings and desires that stretch dangerously beyond himself. He responds by condemning the inadequacy of the written word and longing for smiles, blushes and tears, the only 'testimonies' he can trust (pp. 209, 216). This simultaneous presentation of the practical failures of marriage allegory and textual dialogue, however idealistically advanced, makes *The Wild Irish Girl* a profoundly sceptical narrative. A similar scepticism is mirrored in the Irish Gothic narrative tradition founded by Maturin's *The Milesian Chief* (1812), in which letters and love are equally and tragically unreliable media of exchange between Irish and English – and perhaps in the national tale in general.

Above all, it is this swing between utopian and sceptical views of transnational dialogue as a medium of protest and a remedy for Ireland's ills that defines the national tale from its beginnings, after the Act of Union, through its flourishing in the 1810s and 1820s. The regional novels that followed after Catholic Emancipation retain much of its morphology, including the marriage ending and the borrowing of genres from metropolitan discourse on Ireland: landscape description, surveys and comical representations of peasant speech. In this context it makes sense to argue, with Liz Bellamy, that the national tale was the original regional novel.[47] But the regional novel in general does not share in the generic self-scrutiny of the national tale. The assimilation of all these novels into an Irish literary tradition culminating in the radical experimentation of a Beckett or a Joyce has tended to obscure these important differences by aligning nineteenth-century Irish fiction with a quiet, traditionalist cultural nationalism that makes very limited political claims.[48] The recent scholarship on the national tale's specificity has not only expanded the ways in which it is possible to read early nineteenth-century Irish fiction but also enriched the existing picture of the nineteenth-century Irish novel – and, indeed, of Irish literature as a whole.

NOTES

1. Katie Trumpener, *Bardic Nationalism: The Romantic Novel and the British Empire* (Princeton, NJ: Princeton University Press, 1997), pp. 12–13.
2. Ina Ferris, *The Romantic National Tale and the Question of Ireland* (Cambridge: Cambridge University Press, 2002), pp. 5–7.
3. Ferris, *The Romantic National Tale*, p. 9. See also Jon Klancher, *The Making of English Reading Audiences, 1790–1830* (1987); Kevin Gilmartin, *Print Politics* (1996); Paul Keen, *The Crisis of Literature in the 1790s* (1999).
4. Felicity Nussbaum, *Torrid Zones: Maternity, Sexuality, and Empire in Eighteenth-Century English Narratives* (Baltimore, MD: Johns Hopkins University Press, 1995), pp. 127–34; Srinivas Aravamudan, *Tropicopolitans: Colonialism and Agency, 1688–1804* (Durham, NC: Duke University Press, 1999), pp. 202–3.
5. Georg Lukács, *The Historical Novel*, trans. Hannah Mitchell and Stanley Mitchell (Lincoln, NE: University of Nebraska Press, 1962), ch. 1.
6. Joep Leerssen, *Remembrance and Imagination: Patterns in the Historical and Literary Imagination of Ireland in the Nineteenth Century* (Cork: Cork University Press, 1997), p. 51.
7. Especially relevant works for the Romantic-period European novel are Fredric Jameson, *The Political Unconscious* (1981), Michael McKeon, *The Origins of the English Novel, 1600–1740* (1987), Franco Moretti, *Signs Taken for Wonders: Essays in the Sociology of Literary Forms*, rev. edn, trans. S. Fischer, D. Forgacs and David Miller (1988) and Clifford Siskin, *The Historicity of Romantic Discourse* (1988) and *The Work of Writing: Literature and Social Change in Britain, 1700–1830* (1998).
8. Gary Kelly, *English Fiction of the Romantic Period 1789–1830* (London: Longman, 1989), p. 71. See also Nicola J. Watson, *Revolution and the Form*

of the British Novel, 1790–1825: Intercepted Letters, Interrupted Seductions (Oxford: Clarendon Press, 1994).

9. Trumpener, *Bardic Nationalism*; Ferris, *The Romantic National Tale.*

10. Mary Jean Corbett, *Allegories of Union in Irish and English Writing, 1790–1870* (Cambridge: Cambridge University Press, 2000); Seamus Deane, *Strange Country: Modernity and Nationhood in Irish Writing since 1790* (Cambridge: Cambridge University Press, 1997); Terry Eagleton, *Heathcliff and the Great Hunger: Studies in Irish Culture* (London: Verso, 1995); Declan Kiberd, *Irish Classics* (London: Granta, 2000); Joep Leerssen, *Remembrance and Imagination* (1997); David Lloyd, *Anomalous States: Irish Writing and the Postcolonial Moment* (Dublin: Lilliput Press, 1993); W. J. McCormack, *From Burke to Beckett: Ascendancy, Tradition and Betrayal in Literary History* (Cork: Cork University Press, 1994); Julian Moynahan, *Anglo-Irish: The Literary Imagination in a Hyphenated Culture* (Princeton, NJ: Princeton University Press, 1995).

11. Maria Edgeworth, *Castle Rackrent*, in *Castle Rackrent and Ennui*, ed. Marilyn Butler (London: Penguin, 1992), p. 63; subsequently cited in the text.

12. Kelly, *English Fiction of the Romantic Period*, pp. 74–8.

13. Watson, *Revolution and the Form of the British Novel*, pp. 109–11, 118–27.

14. Moynahan, *Anglo-Irish*, p. 99.

15. Gary Kelly, *Women, Writing, and Revolution, 1790–1827* (New York: Oxford University Press, 1993), passim.

16. Watson, *Revolution and the Form of the British Novel*, pp. 73–8; for reaction to the French Revolution as a 'crisis of gender', see Claudia L. Johnson, *Equivocal Beings: Politics, Gender, and Sentimentality in the 1790s* (Chicago: University of Chicago Press, 1995), pp. 3–12.

17. Thomas Flanagan, *Irish Novelists, 1800–1850* (New York: Columbia University Press, 1959), p. 100, named *Castle Rackrent* the first Irish novel; Claire Connolly suggests, in '"I accuse Miss Owenson": *The Wild Irish Girl* as Media Event', *Colby Quarterly* 36 (2000), 98, that this identification remains conventional. See also Siobhán Kilfeather, '"Strangers at home": Political Fictions by Women in Eighteenth-Century Ireland', diss., Princeton University, 1989, p. 390.

18. Norman Vance, *Irish Literature since 1800* (London: Longman, 2002), p. 50. For counter-arguments to this association of psychological depth with the Romantic novel, see especially Andrea K. Henderson, *Romantic Identities: Varieties of Subjectivity, 1774–1830* (Cambridge: Cambridge University Press, 1996), chs. 2, 5.

19. Robert Tracy, *The Unappeasable Host: Studies in Irish Identities* (Dublin: University College Dublin Press, 1998), p. 21.

20. See Marilyn Butler, *Maria Edgeworth: A Literary Biography* (Oxford: Clarendon Press, 1972), pp. 345–51, 358.

21. This view of Britain conforms with that of Linda Colley's influential *Britons: Forging the Nation, 1707–1837* (1992).

22. Eagleton, *Heathcliff and the Great Hunger*, pp. 172–3.

23. Corbett, *Allegories*, pp. 45–6.

24. Lloyd, *Anomalous States*, pp. 132–6; see also Deane, *Strange Country*, pp. 30, 47.

25. R. B. McDowell, *Ireland in the Age of Imperialism and Revolution, 1760–1801* (Oxford: Clarendon Press, 1979), pp. 271–2.
26. W. J. McCormack, *From Burke to Beckett*, pp. 63–89.
27. W. J. McCormack, *Ascendancy and Tradition in Anglo-Irish Literary History from 1789 to 1939* (Oxford: Clarendon Press, 1985), pp. 108–22.
28. Moynahan, *Anglo-Irish*, p. 21; Kiberd, *Irish Classics*, p. 245, makes a similar point.
29. Homi Bhabha, 'Of Mimicry and Man', in *The Location of Culture* (London: Routledge, 1994), pp. 85–92.
30. Maria Edgeworth and Richard Lovell Edgeworth, *Essay on Irish Bulls* (London: Johnson, 1802), p. 308.
31. Gilles Deleuze and Félix Guattari, *Kafka: Toward a Minor Literature*, trans. Dana Polan (Minneapolis: University of Minnesota Press, 1986), pp. 16–17.
32. Ferris, *The Romantic National Tale*, p. 50; David Lloyd, *Nationalism and Minor Literature: James Clarence Mangan and the Emergence of Irish Cultural Nationalism* (Berkeley: University of California Press, 1987), p. 22.
33. The association of the historical tale with the fragmented material culture of antiquarianism, rather than with progressive national historiography, might explain its minor status; see Yoon Sun Lee, 'A Divided Inheritance: Scott's Antiquarian Novel and the British Nation', *ELH* 64 (1997), 537–67.
34. Sydney Owenson (Lady Morgan), *Florence Macarthy: An Irish Tale*, 4 vols. (London: Colburn, 1818), vol. III, p. 48.
35. Trumpener, *Bardic Nationalism*, chs. 1–2.
36. Susan Stewart, *Crimes of Writing: Problems in the Containment of Representation* (Durham, NC: Duke University Press, 1994), ch. 3.
37. In this sense, the re-historicised landscape descriptions that are Owenson's *Patriotic Sketches of Ireland, written in Connaught* (London: Phillips, 1807) might also count as a national tale.
38. Trumpener, *Bardic Nationalism*, ch. 3. This argument offers a different account of Joep Leerssen's influential and more sceptical characterisation of the national tale in *Remembrance and Imagination*, pp. 37, 50, as a genre of 'auto-exoticism' that transforms Irish history into 'an undifferentiated pool of diverse mementos and memories wholly separate from the present'.
39. Trumpener, *Bardic Nationalism*, chs. 5–6.
40. Edgeworth, *Ennui*, in *Castle Rackrent and Ennui*, pp. 211–12.
41. John Banim, *The Anglo-Irish of the Nineteenth Century*, 3 vols. (London: Colburn, 1828), vol. II, pp. 270–1; subsequently cited in the text.
42. Sydney Owenson, *The Wild Irish Girl*, ed. Kathryn Kirkpatrick (Oxford: Oxford University Press, 1999), p. 13; subsequently cited in the text.
43. Ferris, *The Romantic National Tale*, pp. 50, 52.
44. See especially Corbett, *Allegories of Union*, pp. 53–4.
45. Connolly, introduction to Edgeworth, *Ormond*, ed. Connolly (London: Penguin, 2000), p. xxii.
46. Deane, *Strange Country*, p. 30.
47. Liz Bellamy, 'Regionalism and Nationalism: Maria Edgeworth, Walter Scott and the Definition of Britishness', in J. D. M. Snell (ed.), *The Regional Novel in Britain and Ireland* (Cambridge: Cambridge University Press, 1998), pp. 54–77.

48. Vance, *Irish Literature: A Social History: Tradition, Identity and Difference* (Oxford: Blackwell, 1990), pp. 1–15; Deane, *Strange Country*, p. 18. See also Miranda Burgess, 'Violent Translations: Allegory, Gender, and Cultural Nationalism in Ireland, 1796–1806', *MLQ: A Journal of Literary History* 59 (1998), 33–70.

GUIDE TO FURTHER READING

Anderson, Benedict. *Imagined Communities: Reflections on the Origin and Spread of Nationalism.* Rev. edn. London: Verso, 1991.

Ferris, Ina. *The Achievement of Literary Authority: Gender, History, and the Waverley Novels.* Ithaca, NY: Cornell University Press, 1991.

Habermas, Jürgen. *The Structural Transformation of the Public Sphere.* Trans. Thomas Burger. Cambridge, MA: Massachusetts Institute of Technology Press, 1989.

Leerssen, Joep. *Mere Irish and Fíor-Ghael: Studies in the Idea of Irish Nationality, its Development and Literary Expression prior to the Nineteenth Century.* 2nd edn. Cork: Cork University Press, 1997.

Rafroidi, Patrick. *Irish Literature in English: The Romantic Period.* 2 vols. Gerrards Cross: Colin Smythe, 1980.

Sloan, Barry. *Pioneers of Anglo-Irish Fiction, 1800–1850.* Gerrards Cross: Colin Smythe, 1986.

Vaughan, W. E. (ed.). *Ireland Under the Union, I (1801–1870).* Vol. v of *A New History of Ireland.* Oxford: Clarendon Press, 1989.

3

VERA KREILKAMP

The novel of the big house

The term 'big house' – an ambivalently derisive expression in Ireland[1] – refers to a country mansion, not always so very big, but typically owned by a Protestant Anglo-Irish family presiding over a substantial agricultural acreage leased out to Catholic tenants who worked the land. As rural centres of political power and wealth in Ireland, most big houses occupied property confiscated from native Catholic families in the sixteenth and seventeenth centuries. Their presence in the landscape, unlike that of England's 'great houses', long asserted the political and economic ascendancy of a remote colonial power structure.[2] Whereas by the nineteenth century the English country mansion could be incorporated into a triumphal concept of national heritage, for most of Ireland's population, Ascendancy houses signalled division, not community.[3] In a colonial country, such division reflected not just the typical disparities of class and wealth between landlords and tenants, but also difference of political allegiance, ethnicity, religion and language. Thus in a speech advocating the 1800 Act of Union, Lord Clare notoriously described Irish landlords as 'hemmed in on every side by the old inhabitants of the island, brooding over their discontents in sullen indignation'.[4]

Ireland's architectural flowering during the eighteenth century suggests the eagerness of a newly secure Anglo-Irish Protestant oligarchy to display its wealth and power – and indeed its permanence – through a classically inflected building programme. This rapid spread of Ascendancy architecture in the classical mode indicates that parts of Ireland were being visually transformed into replicas of an England that was increasingly imagining itself as the modern version of the imperial Roman state.[5] But even in its grandest and most rationalised eighteenth-century form – the wide-spreading Palladian edifice with a centre block joined to subordinate wings – rural big houses adapted themselves to local needs. In Ireland, the wings of a Palladian mansion were as likely to be occupied by offices and farm buildings as reception rooms. Other houses, reflecting centuries of accretion by improving landlords, grew more organically as medieval fortresses were expanded and embellished with Gothic or classical additions. A severely vertical rather than horizontal Georgian house was a more characteristic form of classical eighteenth-century estate architecture. Three stories tall, with five to seven bays, such smaller homes were built as Elizabeth Bowen notes, to house 'a family, its dependents, a modest number of guests'.[6] Significant late nineteenth- and twentieth-century fiction by Somerville and Ross, George Moore and Elizabeth Bowen emerged from these austere country seats.

Novels about the big house survived as a stubbornly persistent genre in Irish fiction, even as nineteenth-century landed estates faced growing social and financial marginality. Emerging as a national literary form in 1800, with Maria Edgeworth's slyly subversive depiction of gentry decline in *Castle Rackrent*, they continued to appear long after political independence in 1922. Women writing from within Ascendancy society and a range of largely middle-class male authors were to transform the subject matter of domestic gentry life into an insistently (if often covertly) political fiction. These novels flourished in the late nineteenth and early twentieth centuries, a period of precipitous Ascendancy collapse under the assault of new land laws and emerging nationalism. Thus for some critics, writing alike from nationalist and unionist perspectives,[7] the genre necessarily constitutes a nostalgic or reactionary form, rooted in elegiac longings for a threatened hierarchical reciprocity characterising British country house literature from Ben Jonson's 'To Penshurst' (1616) to Evelyn Waugh's *Brideshead Revisited* (1945). Although a conservative rural ideology surfaces in many of the works examined here, most Anglo-Irish big house novels are far from elegiac, typically directing considerable irony toward an improvident class of social and economic losers. Attempts to place this fiction into the nostalgic anglophone tradition of a wider country house literature or into the context of W. B. Yeats's revivalist yearning for an eighteenth-century Anglo-Irish hegemony mistakenly sentimentalise what is, for the most part, a fiercely self-lacerating genre.

Maria Edgeworth

The major conventions of the big house genre were established by Maria Edgeworth (1767–1849) in her subversive first novel about Ireland. Both its preface and its full title – *Castle Rackrent, An Hibernian Tale Taken from Facts, and from the Manners of the Irish Squires, before the Year 1782* – maintain that this chronicle of ruling class inadequacy describes a 'long past era'.[8] Many readers, however, would interpret *Castle Rackrent* against the authorial grain as a precursor of future Ascendancy crisis, not simply as an account of past disorder. Despite Edgeworth's insistence that the unruly Rackrent landlords belonged to a corrupt and well-lost system of land governance (one that the author self-protectively identified with a native rather than Anglo-Irish genealogy), the novel establishes the conventions of an enduring literary genre: the neglected house as symbol of family and class degeneration, the improvident landlord alienated from his duties, the native Irish usurper of the Ascendancy estate.

Edgeworth's fast-paced account is narrated through the voice of a seemingly devoted Irish house servant, Thady Quirk, presented as a colonial exotic to the British readers addressed in *Castle Rackrent's* preface, notes, glossary and epilogue. Although early critics generally viewed Thady as a transparently naive and unreliable narrator, he is increasingly read as a servile, colonised consciousness, masking his own self-interest in a professed loyalty to his reckless and doomed masters.[9] At the conclusion of *Castle Rackrent*, Thady's ambitious son Jason, a lawyer portrayed as an unscrupulous land-grabber, dispossesses his father's employer of house and land. Jason Quirk's final triumph anticipates decades of Anglo-Irish authorial anxiety before an emerging Catholic middle class that was to undermine the big house, symbol of British control of the countryside.

The house that is finally lost to its former owners in *Castle Rackrent*, as in so many subsequent novels of the genre, is less grandiloquent than its name might imply – typically characterised by fading dilapidation rather than opulence or authority. It is indeed castle-like in comparison to surrounding cabins in the Irish landscape, but signs and smells of the farmyard intrude on the pretensions of its owners. Repeatedly in the big house genre, an account of physical decay merges with the saga of social crisis and political decline. Moreover, recurring depictions of crumbling walls, leaky roofs, shabby furnishings, overgrown drives and neglected demesne gardens suggest how domestic disorder in the gentry house replicates reports of those notoriously slipshod rural hovels that English tourists transformed into a trope of Ireland's savage and baffling 'otherness'. This conflation of two versions of Ireland's ramshackle dwelling places endures well into the twentieth century. Almost two centuries after the publication of *Castle Rackrent*, Molly Keane's *Loving and Giving* (1988) describes how the last Anglo-Irish occupant of a big house contentedly retreats to a second-hand caravan parked near the rotting mansion.

With her Irish novels written after *Castle Rackrent* – *Ennui* (1809), *The Absentee* (1812) and *Ormond* (1817) – Edgeworth abandons a subversively ironic native narrator, instead adopting key elements of the national tale plot that Sydney Owenson (Lady Morgan) had recently popularised.

In *The Absentee*, as in Owenson's *The Wild Irish Girl* (1806), a young landlord, long resident in England, finds his authentic identity in Ireland. Appalled by the deracinated and debt-ridden London life of his absentee parents, scorned hangers-on in a snobbish metropolitan society, Edgeworth's Lord Colambre journeys through Ireland's post-Union social and political landscape and initiates a didactic narrative of cultural encounter. He observes a range of houses on his travels: a vulgarly 'improved' Bray villa that a grocer's wife has named after a fashionable Roman resort and decorated with vying classical and Gothic motifs; the pretentious estate house of Killpatrick, overlooking 'ornamented, picturesque cottages', built by a fashionable but injudicious Anglo-Irish landlord to improve his visual prospect; and, more promisingly, the tasteful seat of the resident Oranmore family, of a 'becoming magnificence, free from ostentation'.[10] Each of these retreats conveys *The Absentee's* insistent moral agenda: Ireland can be brought to order and civility only by well-educated resident landlords who will eschew over-building or decorating in a crass imitation of styles that are both inappropriate and dangerously costly to the estate's economic survival. The showy orientalised spoils of the British empire that the hero's mother flaunts in her London drawing room are anathema to the modest classical or Gothic country house aesthetic of Edgeworth's ideal Irish home.

As a virtual trope of social deracination, the absentee landlord appears frequently in nineteenth-century big house novels, not only by Edgeworth, but also by Sydney Owenson, John Banim, Charles Maturin, William Carleton and Charles Lever. Edgeworth's *The Absentee* takes as its moral subject those landlords who regard their Irish properties and tenants as mere sources of income to be squandered abroad. Unlike the idealised lord of the manor in the English country house tradition, the figure of the Irish absentee signals distance rather than a nurturing propinquity. The recurrent appearance of such rootless characters in the nineteenth-century novel certainly over-represents the actual absenteeism of economically strapped post-Union landlords, suggesting that the literary deployment of the absentee exists less as an exact rendition of social reality than as a formative intervention into it.

Edgeworth's insistent motif of the bad agent whose greed and chicanery exploit the landlord's absenteeism for his own benefit reflects Arthur Young's widely disseminated critique of the Irish landlord and his oppressive middleman.[11] A key scene in *The Absentee* depicts the return of the long non-resident heir to his patrimony, the rescue of the small leaseholders and the expulsion of the thieving agent who condemns the tenants to lives of misery and want. Such ideologically charged celebrations of a quasi-feudal benevolence demonstrate how well big house motifs could serve

Ascendancy ideology. The trope of the absentee becomes, in part, a means of critiquing a colonial land policy that has dispossessed an indigenous population with an improvident class of wastrels living abroad. But by demonising the native bailiff or agent who thwarts the owner's more benevolent intentions, absenteeism is as commonly deployed by Catholic as by Protestant writers to avoid a more radical critique of existing arrangements. Thus in many big house novels, a seeming complaint about contemporary conditions both registers an abuse and wards off more radical criticism of colonial land settlements. But despite the restoration of order following the dramatic expulsion of the agent in *The Absentee*, his land-hunger and greed raise the spectre of Anglo-Irish defeat before a rising Catholic class. Jason Quirk's appetite for the Rackrent property, a nightmare of class displacement haunting the first major big house novel, would be anxiously negotiated throughout the nineteenth century.

Charles Lever

In an often cited 1834 letter to a brother serving as an imperial British administrator in colonial India, Maria Edgeworth implied the failure of her Enlightenment ideal of benevolent resident landlords rationally reforming a dysfunctional land system. Responding to the new political order ushered in by Daniel O'Connell's challenge to Ascendancy domination, she wrote that Irish social order now constitutes 'a distorted nature': 'realities are too strong, party passions too violent to bear to see, or care to look at their faces in the looking-glass'.[12] But for Charles Lever (1806–72), Edgeworth's successor as a realistic chronicler of the big house, such 'party passions' – the turbulent social reality that Edgeworth rejected as a fit subject for a mimetic genre – shaped what was to become one of nineteenth-century Ireland's most popular bodies of fiction. Lever's now neglected *œuvre* records the growing challenges to patterns of social and political deference that had long sustained the landlord.

The Martins of Cro' Martin (1854), published more than three decades after Edgeworth's last Irish novel, depicts the fall of a Connemara estate in the period between Catholic Emancipation (1829) and the Great Famine (1845–9), when the historical Martin property on which the novel is loosely based fell into the hands of the Encumbered Estate Courts. Lever's engagement with an acute period of social and political transformation for Irish proprietors emerges from an ideologically split consciousness. Even as he asserts that the fall of the landed gentry brings disastrous upheaval to a traditional society, Lever insists on the inevitability of such collapse. His pessimistic assessment of the belatedness and inevitable failure of estate reform serves not only as a retrospective judgment of Edgeworth's didactic agenda in her post-*Rackrent* fiction, but as a dark prophecy of the future of the big house.

Having little in common with the ramshackle Castle Rackrent, Lever's Cro' Martin Castle first appears as the centre of a private kingdom in the west of Ireland. Its layers of stone accretions attest to its successive architectural incarnations – from fourteenth-century Norman watchtower to opulent nineteenth-century home. In his initial descriptions of this ancient and organically developing edifice, Lever draws heavily on the classical European trope of the great house, a marker of civilising culture. Cro' Martin's 'vast drawing rooms' and dining room with its 'noble fireplace of gigantic dimensions' imply centuries of hospitality.[13] Its library, 'calm, quiet and secluded' but 'fitted up in the most luxurious taste', suggests the enlightened connoisseurship and scholarship of that aristocratic Ascendancy society W. B. Yeats was to invoke a half-century later.[14] But despite such an initial appraisal of a quasi-feudal big house, viewed from the awed perspective of the visitor, Lever depicts Cro' Martin not as a Yeatsian fantasy of high culture but as a mere shell of such civilised life – as an object-laden monument to acquisition, destined for the auction block.

Lever's narrative distaste before rancorous middle-class voices advocating democratic change embodies the class anxiety of much nineteenth- and early twentieth-century Anglo-Irish fiction, from Edgeworth to Somerville and Ross. Writing in 1817, Maria Edgeworth could still envision a rescue operation for the big house, as the hero of her last Irish novel, *Ormond*, retires to a semi-feudal island estate, presumably to bring just and rational governance to a disorderly traditional society. But in *The Martins of Cro' Martin*, Lever's reforming Anglo-Irish heroine Mary Martin is doomed to defeat and early death, unable to stem the costs of her absentee family's arrogant isolation from their tenants and neglect of their responsibilities as landlords. The novel's idealised native Irish political figure, Joe Nelligan, is a local shopkeeper's son, whose high honours from Trinity College and chaste devotion to Mary Martin and Cro' Martin Castle isolate him from vulgar O'Connellites. The creation of Nelligan marks Lever's wish fulfilment, a retreat from the political realism with which he so unsparingly depicts the fate of the big house.

William Carleton

The reputation of William Carleton (1794–1869) as Ireland's first great modern recorder in the English language of a Gaelic-speaking peasantry seemingly excludes him from the conventions of the largely Anglo-Irish tradition of big house fiction. Historian Oliver MacDonagh emphasises the striking differences between those novelists like Edgeworth, who write about the big house from within the demesne walls, and those observing it from without. Thus for MacDonagh, Carleton depicts landlordism with 'Marxist indignation not Tschekovian melancholy'.[15] Certainly, such indignation shaped much of Carleton's work. But after a youthful immersion in traditional Irish society and an adult career working for unionist periodicals as a Protestant convert, Carleton also appropriates conventions being established by middle-class or gentry novelists of the big house. In his incendiary attack on the Irish land system in *Valentine M'Clutchy*, as in his short story 'The Poor Scholar', the return of the good landlord – mirroring the classic redemptive scene Edgeworth staged in *The Absentee* – reverses the agent's cruelty and injustice. In 'The Poor Scholar', a returned absentee landlord contemplates his abandoned and mouldering big house, an image charged with a similar symbolic association of mismanagement and loss for Edgeworth and Lever.

Carleton's big house novel *The Squanders of Castle Squander* (1852) depicts a familiar gentry estate, shamefully neglected and convivially debauched – virtually a mid-nineteenth-century Castle Rackrent. Despite the growing indignation its narrator Randy O'Rollicke directs toward the riotous profligacy of the landlord, this novel again suggests the shaping role of a range of existing literary conventions. Randy elicits considerable sympathy for the improvident and reckless landlord class he serves and judges. A household tutor and a son of the estate bailiff, he offers, as does Edgeworth's Thady Quirk, a servant's view of the big house. However, Carleton's narrator is an upstanding intimate of the improvident Squanders, attempting to rescue and reform his employers rather than sycophantically defer to them.

The novel's most pressing ideological agenda – its condemnation of ruling-class neglect during the Famine – cannot be contained by a single, dramatically conceived narrative voice. Instead, *The Squanders of Castle Squander* becomes clogged with stretches of interpolated and unassimilated authorial commentary and propaganda: detailed statistics of Famine evictions, parliamentary reports and condemnations of secret societies. Vying with this flood of unassimilated data, Randy's pity for his improvident landlord emerges: Squander is not a man of 'bad heart', and 'impossible not to like'.[16] Even as Randy describes the arrogant Mrs Squander, forced to sleep on a borrowed bed as creditors strip the over-mortgaged house of its furniture, he finds parallels between the dispossession of the gentry and the tenantry. The peasant narrator compares the 'woeful decline and desolation' of Castle Squander to the 'decline and desolation of the country', a landscape plunged in the worst horrors of the Famine – hunger, disease, evictions, mass deaths.[17] By insisting on such mutual suffering rather than merely dwelling on the obvious differences between the experiences of the ruined gentry and the brutally evicted tenants, Randy invokes a shared national disaster. Thus Carleton's radical critique of the landlord's sons as brutal evictors, sexual marauders of peasant girls, or extravagant wastrels is moderated by literary conventions developing among upper- or middle-class Protestant writers. Moreover, the generic instability of *The Squanders of Castle Squander*, alternately polemic and dramatic novel, underscores the shaping role of ideology on the genre.

Big house Gothic

Throughout the nineteenth century, allegorical Gothic motifs invoking the anxiety of a beleaguered Ascendancy interact with and intrude upon the developing conventions of a more transparently realistic big house fiction. As one reader has put it, nineteenth-century Ireland can be seen as a 'living gothic' for a post-Union ruling class slowly acknowledging its failure to maintain hegemony over a newly emboldened tenantry.[18] Proprietors of rural estates were surrounded by the material and psychic conditions encouraging a turn to the Gothic: crumbling mansions, anxiously anticipated violence and casts of eccentrics, marooned in their walled demesnes and condemned by their isolation from the surrounding community.[19] Certainly, the political insecurity conveyed by Gothic conventions expresses, often in distorted or sublimated forms, the reality of Anglo-Irish conditions during the long century of local violence accompanying the development of the big house novel.[20] Maria Edgeworth's neglected estate and declining social class in *Castle Rackrent*, as well as her plots of disinherited heirs and missing wills in *Ennui* and *The Absentee*, already suggest a convergence between Gothic conventions and Ascendancy preoccupations. Charles Maturin (1782–1824) and Sheridan Le Fanu (1814–73), and later in the century, Bram Stoker and Somerville and Ross, develop full-blown Protestant Gothic novels deploying a range of characteristic motifs: deranged and demonised landlords, settings in decaying houses, a growing class obsession with racial pollution and cultural decline, as well as sadistic threats against helpless young women.[21]

Although *Melmoth the Wanderer* (1820) reads as a phantasmagoria of sectarian and sadomasochistic violence in the hidden dungeons of Spain, India and the South Seas, Charles Maturin frames his Gothic tour de force with scenes set in a decaying house on the Irish coast – a familiar motif in the realistic big house tradition. The Melmoth estate, confiscated land bestowed on a seventeenth-century Cromwellian, is in ruins: the lodge is collapsing, the avenue reduced to mud, the garden desolate. A dying land-lord protests his impoverishment at the hands of his brutalised, vampire-like retainers, and the ancestral absentee Melmoth assumes the role of a lurid satanic protagonist. Such a framing strategy underscores how even a strik-ingly un-provincial Gothic Irish novel retains a specifically local and class-bound anxiety. Although big house proprietors managed to hold on to much of the island's property until the late nineteenth-century land acts, already in the century's early decades a fictional landlord dies burdened by the corrupt sources of his power and by premonitions of future loss. Illustrating the continuing relationship between Gothic conventions and those of the big house novel, Irish writers after Maturin, for example, Sheridan Le Fanu, Somerville and Ross, and Bram Stoker, continued to create doomed satanic landlords residing in their encumbered, decaying or strikingly archaic mansions.

Sheridan Le Fanu was reportedly haunted by a recurring dream of a crumbling old mansion that threatened to fall upon him, crushing him to death.[22] This nightmare of personal extinction – of dispossession of life itself – invokes the terror threatening the big house protagonist of his masterpiece of Gothic sensation, *Uncle Silas* (1864). Although set in Derby-shire country houses at the behest of its publisher,[23] the novel's Irish antece-dents have remained insistently present.[24] Depicting an innocent young woman's victimisation at the hands both of a proudly reclusive father and a murderous uncle, each living on an isolated estate, *Uncle Silas* returns to a plot Le Fanu had created in an 1838 short story that was set in Galway.[25] Obsessed with family pride, a dying father bequeaths his daugh-ter as ward to a viciously depraved brother. In the later novelistic version, the ordeal suffered by the young narrator – terrifying isolation at her father's estate and murderous assaults at her uncle's decaying big house at Bartram-Haugh – collapses any Yeatsian fantasy of a benevolent or eight-eenth-century Ascendancy culture. W. J. McCormack points out how the repetitious reciprocity between father and uncle in *Uncle Silas* establishes a collaborative sense of evil between the past and the present.[26] Remote and neglected country houses entrap the young heiress – an innocent pawn in a social landscape of brooding greed and violence.

In Maturin's *Melmoth The Wanderer* and Le Fanu's *Uncle Silas*, villains in the big house novel are no longer outsiders – ambitious Catholic upstarts such as Jason Quirk in *Castle Rackrent* or Lever's ambitious Irish agent Scanlan, soliciting a gentry bride in *The Martins of Cro' Martin*. They appear, rather, as criminal family presences, beleaguered and tormented souls who on occasion turn upon their own young. The motifs of a threatened inheritance in *Uncle Silas* and *Melmoth the Wanderer* and of detailed legal documentation in Stoker's *Dracula*, like Edgeworth's or Lever's preoccupations with the disorderly passing on of property, suggest the anxiety of a gentry society confronting the illegitimate sources of its patrimony and its growing fears of dispossession.

George Moore and Somerville and Ross

Although occasionally drawing on Gothic conventions in *A Drama in Muslin* (1886), George Moore (1852–1933) reduces a vitiated Ascendancy to its basest materiality through the techniques of French naturalism he had recently mastered in Paris. As the economic and political foundations of the Ascendancy increasingly fall under attack, a decadent big house society auctions its convent-raised daughters to the highest bidders at the levees, drawing rooms and balls of Dublin Castle's annual debutante season. The novel's action occurs in the decades surrounding the 1879–82 Land War and subsequent Plan of Campaign, a period characterised by ruthless evictions of tenants and organised violence directed against landlords. That Moore was both heir to one of Mayo's great liberal Catholic estates threatened by the Land League and a productive member of avant-garde circles in London and Paris undoubtedly influenced his rejection of any straightforward nationalist or democratic political agenda against a heritage he defied. Although *A Drama in Muslin* conveys Moore's unrelenting contempt for an Ascendancy society obsessed with its waning virility, it envisions the threatening underclass – brutalised peasants or squalid Dublin slum dwellers – with a comparable naturalist repugnance.

In focussing on the ordeal of young Ascendancy women in a vitiated social order, Moore anticipates central thematic concerns of subsequent big house novelists. Earlier fiction by Edgeworth or Lever had, on rare occasion, depicted women who resisted patriarchal entrapment – for example, the Rackrent wives who manage to retain their wealth or an array of Lever's characters who choose radical alliances. But in a liberating choice that foreshadows Stephen Dedalus's triumphant flight from provincial Dublin to nurture his artistic destiny, Moore's Alice Barton transgresses class lines by marrying an Irish doctor and abandoning Ireland to become a middle-class writer in London. Alice's entrapment in the paralysing social forms of a big house society suggests the ordeal of Anglo-Irish women in later novels by Somerville and Ross, Elizabeth Bowen, Molly Keane and Jennifer Johnston. However, her escape from such social constriction in *A Drama in Muslin*, through a radical plot turn choreographed by a self-exiled male artist openly defying his Ascendancy roots, remained largely unavailable to a range of female characters in subsequent big house fiction by women.

When *An Irish Cousin* inaugurated a literary partnership between two young gentry women in 1889, only three years after the appearance of *A Drama in Muslim*, Anglo-Irish landowners continued to reel from the crises of economic under-capitalisation and accelerating political insecurity. Publishing collaboratively as Somerville and Ross, the two cousins Edith Somerville (1858–1949) and Violet Martin (1862–1915) belonged to an extended clan of big house families. Like most members of their class, they scorned the parliamentary process of land reform, viewing the land laws as London's craven abandonment of Irish proprietors. (A growing animosity towards the sister country, appearing already in Edgeworth and Lever's parodies of tourists to Ireland, expresses itself in a range of Somerville and Ross's hostile portrayals of English visitors to big house territory.) The 1903 Wyndham Land Act, cutting the gentry house and its demesne adrift from its rental properties, decisively undermined surviving fantasies of quasi-feudal bonds between the lord of the manor and his tenants. Although nostalgic memories of harmonious landlord–tenant relationships appear frequently in Violet Martin and Edith Somerville's essays,[27] their novels are startlingly clear-headed about the historical dubiousness of such idylls.

An Irish Cousin recycles a range of, by now familiar, Gothic tropes: an isolated transgressor driven by class pride and personal greed, a decaying big house and the mysterious death of the big house's legitimate heir. Within this cauldron of Ascendancy guilt, Somerville and Ross develop a recurring theme in late nineteenth-century big house fiction: a narrative distaste before misalliance – specifically viewed as racial miscegenation between Catholic and Protestant Ireland. Just as the degeneracy of Le Fanu's Silas Ruthyn became manifest in his marriage to an Irish barmaid and his fathering of a debased son, so in *An Irish Cousin* the landlord's youthful affair with an Irish servant engenders criminality and madness. Such dark readings of the native Irish woman's contribution to Ascendancy decay reflect a growing obsession with pure blood lines (in horses and dogs as well as in the inhabitants of the big house) when power and privilege are receding. Lever and Le Fanu had earlier replaced the national tale's allegorised versions of marital union between aristocratic Gaelic and English cultures with a horror before the boorish (i.e. native Irish) suitor of the big house woman. As the native vulgarian gazes longingly at the gentry estate, the defensive response of its occupants invokes ethnic and sectarian overtones; thus colonial and post-colonial Irish fiction adds a specifically racial dimension to the familiar class narrative of the English novel.

Somerville and Ross's *The Real Charlotte* (1894) exists for critics as that rare Irish novel aspiring to be a totalising work of social realism, on occasion compared to George Eliot's *Middlemarch*.[28] It dissects the insatiable class ambition constituting the thematic focus of much nineteenth-century European and English fiction, but always with an acute sense of the political shifts occurring within provincial Anglo-Irish society. In one of its many plot strands, *The Real Charlotte* casts a devastatingly comic eye on a rural big house fading into ineffectual torpor. Although the novel's middle-class protagonist Charlotte Mullen attains status by rapaciously acquiring property from those descending the social ladder, Charlotte's ambitions to marry her young cousin into local big house society are decisively thwarted. In *The Real Charlotte*, Somerville and Ross anatomise not criminal culpability or Gothic excesses in the big house as they do in *An Irish Cousin*, but rather effeteness and depletion of will that increasingly characterise Ascendancy progeny in twentieth-century fiction. Thus Charlotte's cousin, a vital but impoverished young Dublin ingénue whose unschooled energy might have revitalised an aristocratic house and its descendants, is doomed instead to disastrous romantic choices and catastrophic death. Francie Fitzgerald's fate is engendered not just by her own tawdry romantic fantasies, but by her suitor Christopher Dysart's effete decency and self-conscious intellectual circumspection: in short, by a pervasive failure of sexual energy and purpose characterising the diffident big house male.

Still writing as Somerville and Ross after her collaborator's death, Edith Somerville published *Mount Music* (1920) and *The Big House of Inver* (1925), novels that expose the resolutely philistine life of the landed gentry, even as W. B. Yeats was elegising the beleaguered big house as a squandered source of national vitality and high culture. Celebrating and simultaneously undermining the achievements of Ascendancy culture, *The Big House of Inver* conflates that culture's defeat with a violence and moral shoddiness already inherent in its eighteenth-century aesthetic flowering. The history of the Prendeville family – whose motto 'Je Prends' flaunts an acquisitive colonial presence in Ireland – warrants reading *The Big House of Inver* as a *Castle Rackrent* interpreted against the authorial grain. The landlord's greed, rackrenting, womanising and drunken roistering – the very behaviour that Edgeworth's preface to *Castle Rackrent* relegated to the 'bad old times' before the Union – now anticipates the continuing disorder of Somerville's improvident nineteenth-century Prendevilles. Moreover, *The Big House of Inver* suggests the malevolence of such history through recognisably Gothic flourishes; the ghostly animation of ancient family portraits in a ruined house signals how ancestral arrogance dooms the living. The civilisation that the eighteenth-century Prendevilles bring to the west of Ireland is characterised not only by extraordinary physical beauty – of houses, paintings, horses and young men – but also by insolent pride, hedonism and shiftless improvidence.

Bowen, Keane, Johnston

Edith Somerville published *The Big House of Inver* during a revolutionary decade that witnessed the burning of more than two hundred big homes as alien presences in the Irish landscape. Like several other post-independence novels, it concludes with the fiery destruction of an eighteenth-century Georgian mansion. Although Somerville's narrative voice in *The Big House of Inver* conveys little empathy for the native Irish, who are perceived as the disorderly abettors of Ascendancy arrogance and appetite, neither does it sentimentalise a flawed ruling caste's supreme imaginative achievement. Thus even as the big house is described as a triumphant work of art, it is, finally, ripe for burning. Published shortly after *The Big House of Inver*, *The Last September* (1929) by Elizabeth Bowen (1899–1973) concludes with the conflagration of yet another eighteenth-century building. Bowen's fictional Danielstown is destroyed by the IRA, not, as in the case of Somerville's Inver House, by a former owner's senile carelessness. Alternatively anticipated, denied, longed for and dreaded, the burning of Danielstown evokes a complex response. But once again, amid the shock elicited by the wasteful destruction of a beautiful cultural artefact, emerges a subversive sense of necessary completion.

Although in plot and setting *The Last September* is a representative big house novel, Elizabeth Bowen's modernist sensibility continues the shift toward a psychological reading of character and action initiated in George Moore's *A Drama in Muslin*. Like Moore, Bowen reveals how the costs of the Anglo-Irish experience express themselves most fully in the private consciousness of its young victims. Moreover, she grasps how those who occupy the big house, isolating themselves from their island community, are, like the diffident Ascendancy heir in Somerville and Ross's *The Real Charlotte*, isolated from their own emotional cravings. The ordered surface of gentry life in *The Last September* deludes with promises of continuity, while menacing trench-coated figures, filled with a passionate purpose so absent in Anglo-Irish society, stride through the demesne grounds. Bowen's young protagonist Lois Farquar, helpless before her own aimlessness and inability to love, is haunted by her ties to a house whose inhabitants evade facing their own drifting purposeless. Drawn to the vitality of the trespassing gunmen, but socially isolated from them, Lois cannot respond to her conventional English admirer. Instead she turns to deracinated visitors – both male and female – for an unavailable love. Her passionate bonding with Marda in *The Last September*, like the more explicitly lesbian desires characterising one of Moore's young muslin martyrs, anticipates Molly Keane's, Jennifer Johnston's and William Trevor's explorations of the celibate or homoerotic life choices of characters who respond to the failures of heterosexual love, marriage and parenthood in the big house.

Bowen's examination of women's struggles for selfhood are inseparable from her recurring descriptions of domestic spaces – not only the Anglo-Irish houses of *The Last September*, *The Heat of the Day* (1949) or *A World of Love* (1955), but also the suburban villas, townhouses and seaside retreats in other novels. Her identification with her ancestral home, an austere eighteenth-century mansion in west Cork, became the subject of her major work of non-fiction, *Bowen's Court* (1942), providing both a biographical and historical context for the sense of homelessness of her fictional protagonists. Like Somerville and Ross and George Moore writing big house fiction before her, and M. J. Farrell (Molly Keane, 1904–96), Jennifer Johnston (b. 1930) and William Trevor (b. 1928) after, Bowen perceives how a seemingly permanent domestic space, appearing fortress-like in its physical solidity, first deludes and then fails to sustain Anglo-Irish children.

Twentieth-century novels about the big house continued to expose the cost of such a failure, expressed in an increasingly rigid adherence to elaborate social lies and rituals disguising unpalatable truths about country and home.[29] Both Somerville and Ross in *The Big House of Inver* and Molly Keane in *Two Days in Aragon* (1941) create illegitimate daughters of Anglo-Irish landlords and Irish servant women who sacrifice themselves to Ascendancy illusions, fiercely defending a society which condemns them to domestic service in their fathers' houses. As a former imperial order of local magistrates and estate proprietors confronts its political impotence, novels about the big houses depict landlords who withdraw into hunting and drinking – or into sexual relationships that their society deems aberrant. Molly Keane's womanising patriarch in *Good Behaviour* (1981) ends his days as a paralysed and drooling old man, in thrall to the illicit masturbatory pleasure doled out to him by the Irish servant he had once pursued. In Johnston's *How Many Miles to Babylon* (1974) and *The Captains and the Kings* (1972), the harsh social condemnation of suspected homosexual longings assures a culture of loneliness and deprivation.

Bowen's *The Last September*, and later novels by Keane and Johnston, describe gentry chatelaines who move into family roles abdicated by their increasingly ineffective husbands. But without an adequate arena for their domestic and social ambitions, monstrous wives and mothers prey on the young, creating a fiction of lonely, terrorised or guilt-ridden children who turn from generative sexuality and love. The daughter of the big house in Keane's *Two Days in Aragon* realises that sexual alliance with a local Irish man will appear to his mother 'as wrong . . . as the love of black and white people seemed to her'.[30] Keane's dark depictions of maternal cruelty in *The Rising Tide* (1937), *Good Behaviour*, *Time After Time* (1983) and *Loving and Giving* (1988), like Johnston's portrayal of a lonely big house child in *How Many Miles to Babylon*, strip the domestic novel of its foundation in sentiment. Such fiction, exposing savage parental exercises of power over children as the dark side of a waning imperial sway, undermines the triumphal marriage plot of English fiction. Responding to an Anglo-Irish culture unable to transcend its history of violence, William Trevor constructs in *Fools of Fortune* (1983), *The Silence in the Garden* (1988) and *The Story of Lucy Gault* (2002) historicised allegories of primal guilt and atonement in which children, both within and outside the demesne walls, fall victim to Ireland's colonial past.

Higgins, Farrell, Banville

The survival of big house fiction throughout the twentieth century suggests its generative power rather than, as Seamus Deane would have it, the 'comparative poverty of the Irish novelistic tradition'.[31] Joyce Cary's *Castle Corner* (1938) chronicles the relentless decline of a Donegal estate under the late nineteenth-century land laws, a trajectory that is undeterred by family forays into African imperialism. Cary strives to reassert the claims, now refracted through a liberal rather than conservative ideology, of the expansive social and political realism that Charles Lever had deployed in the nineteenth century. Later twentieth-century novelists, however, subvert and arguably reinvent a realistic form. Thus *Langrishe, Go Down* (1966) by Aidan Higgins (b. 1927) re-casts the big house genre as post-Joycean fiction, approaching a familiar setting and subject through the conventions of literary modernism: a stream of consciousness narration, a thematic preoccupation with anomie and despair, and a transformation of a supramimetic Irish landscape into a dense pattern of symbolism. Moreover, by boldly transforming the big house's native antagonist into a 1930s Weimar intellectual with ambiguous political leanings, and by introducing newspaper headlines reporting a progressive Fascist expansion in Europe, Higgins thrusts the narrative of gentry decline into a far wider political and cultural debacle.

Troubles (1970) by J. G. Farrell (1935–79), appearing as the first in a trilogy marking key moments in the dissolution of the British empire,[32] alternatively writes the big house novel directly into a wider post-modern and post-colonial discourse. The protagonist of *Troubles*, a shell-shocked English veteran of the First World War, pursues the daughter of a big house who is dying, significantly, of a fatal blood ailment. Farrell's bizarrely intertextual novel – interpolating early twentieth-century newspaper clippings about the collapse of empire and describing a decaying rural mansion invaded by stray cats and tropical vegetation before its final conflagration – parodies the very conventions that it deploys.

Realistic novels of Anglo-Irish decline are again both reinvented and subverted in the post-modern metafiction of *Birchwood* (1973) and *The Newton Letter* (1982) by John Banville (b. 1945). Banville exploits the conventions of a traditional form to expose the process by which historical illusions are themselves created and sustained. Playing with the familiar tropes of a Gothic big house form in *Birchwood* – the decaying house, the disputed inheritance, the improvident landlord and threatening intruders – Banville tosses in stock characters from other traditions ('the quest, the lost child, the doppelganger') as though to emphasise the random inclusiveness of his metaliterary enterprise.[33] Banville's insistence on how memory fails to recreate reality, but instead reinvents subjective versions of the past, suggests that his innovations return to the central demythologising drive of an enduring Anglo-Irish big house tradition. 'We imagine that we remember things as they were, while in fact all we carry into the future are fragments which reconstruct a wholly illusionary past.'[34]

NOTES

1. The use of the term elsewhere to denote a threatening institution such as a prison or mental institution suggests negative connotations transcending any national setting. Elizabeth Bowen, for example, notes the slight inflection of a possible 'hostility' or 'irony' that accompanies the expression. See 'The Big House' in *The Mulberry Tree: Writings of Elizabeth Bowen*, selected and introduced by Hermione Lee (New York: Harcourt Brace Jovanovich, 1986), p. 26.
2. Arthur Young calculated in 1776 that Catholics owned but 5 per cent of the land of Ireland, even though they constituted 75 per cent of the total population: see R. F. Foster, *Modern Ireland, 1600–1972* (London: Penguin, 1989), p. 210. Still, Kevin Whelan suggests that there were as many as 350 Catholic landed families in the early eighteenth century, 'An Underground Gentry? Catholic Middlemen in Eighteenth-Century Ireland', in J. S. Donnelly Jr and Kerby A. Miller, (eds.), *Irish Popular Culture, 1650–1850* (Dublin: Irish Academic Press, 1998), pp. 120–1. In the nineteenth century, many Catholics purchased estates from the Encumbered Estates Court (later the Landed Estates Court), but

it is difficult to arrive at a figure for Catholic ownership of big houses in that century or the one before, and the ascendancy of Protestant land owners and big house occupants is incontrovertible.

3. See Terence Dooley, *The Decline of the Big House in Ireland* (Dublin: Wolfhound Press, 2001), p. 252.

4. Quoted in W. E. H. Lecky, *A History of Ireland in the Eighteenth Century*, 5 vols. (London: Longmans Green, 1892), vol. v, p. 372.

5. For an illustrated architectural history of the Irish big house, see Mark Bence-Jones's *Burke's Guide to Country Houses: Ireland* (London: Burke's Peerage Ltd, 1978).

6. Bowen, 'The Big House', p. 26.

7. For a nationalist perspective, see Seamus Deane, 'The Literary Myths of the Revival', in Deane, *Celtic Revivals: Essays in Modern Irish Literature* (London: Faber & Faber, 1985), pp. 31–2. For a unionist perspective, see Malcolm Kelsall, *Literary Representations of the Irish Country House: Civilisation and Savagery under the Union* (London: Palgrave Macmillan, 2003), pp. 27–8.

8. Maria Edgeworth, *Castle Rackrent*, ed. George Watson (Oxford: Oxford University Press, 1995), p. 4.

9. See Michael Neill, 'Mantles, Quirks, and Irish Bulls: Ironic Guise and Colonial Subjectivity in Maria Edgeworth's *Castle Rackrent*', *Review of English Studies* 52 (2001), 76–90.

10. Maria Edgeworth, *The Absentee* (Oxford: Oxford University Press, 1998), pp. 87–9, 108, 128.

11. Arthur Young, *Arthur Young's Tour in Ireland (1776–1779)*, 2 vols., ed. Arthur Wollaston Hutton (London: George Bell & Sons, 1892), vol. II, pp. 25–8.

12. Maria Edgeworth to Michael Pakenham Edgeworth, 19 February 1834, in Augustus J. C. Hare (ed.), *The Life and Letters of Maria Edgeworth*, 2 vols. (1894; Boston: Houghton Mifflin, 1895), vol. II, p. 550.

13. Charles Lever, *The Martins of Cro' Martin*, 2 vols. (Boston: Little Brown and Co., 1895), vol. I, p. 148.

14. Lever, *The Martins of Cro' Martin*, pp. 148, 141.

15. Oliver MacDonagh, *The Nineteenth-Century and Irish Social History: Some Aspects* (Dublin: National University of Ireland, 1970), p. 7.

16. William Carleton, *The Squanders of Castle Squander*, 2 vols. (London: Office of the Illustrated London Library, 1852), vol. I, p. 219.

17. Carleton, *The Squanders of Castle Squander*, vol. II, p. 249.

18. Julian Moynahan, *Anglo-Irish: The Literary Imagination in a Hyphenated Culture* (Princeton: Princeton University Press, 1995), p. 111.

19. On the failure of big house proprietors to achieve hegemony, see Terry Eagleton: 'But the real test of hegemony is whether a ruling class is able to impose its spiritual authority on its underlings, lend them moral and political leadership and persuade them of its own vision of the world. And on all these counts, when the record is taken as a whole, the Anglo-Irish must be reckoned an egregious failure' ('Ascendancy and Hegemony', in *Heathcliff and the Great Hunger* (London: Verso, 1995), p. 31).

20. Nineteenth- and twentieth-century big house novels reflect Anglo-Ireland's response to a range of violent threats: memories of the United Irishmen Rising of 1798, the early nineteenth-century Tithe Wars and rural faction fighting, as

well as the later rise of Fenianism and the hostility directed at landlords in the Land War and the War of Independence.

21. For discussions of the 'Protestant Gothic', see W. J. McCormack, 'Irish Gothic and After', in *The Field Day Anthology of Irish Writing*, gen. ed. Seamus Deane (Derry: Field Day, 1991), vol. II, pp. 832–54; R. F. Foster, 'Protestant Magic: W. B. Yeats and the Spell of Irish History', in *Paddy & Mr Punch* (London: Allen Lane, 1993), pp. 212–32; Terry Eagleton, 'Form and Ideology in the Anglo-Irish Novel', in *Heathcliff and the Great Hunger*, pp. 187–99.

22. Devendra P. Varma, general introduction to *The Collected Works of Joseph Sheridan Le Fanu* (New York: Arno Press, 1977), p. ii.

23. W. J. McCormack, introduction to *Uncle Silas* by Sheridan Le Fanu (Oxford: Oxford University Press, 1981), pp. xvi–xvii.

24. See Bowen, 'Uncle Silas', in *The Mulberry Tree*, p. 101. Bowen identifies as typically Anglo-Irish the 'hermetic solitude and the autocracy of the great country house, the demonic power of the family myth, fatalism, feudalism and the "ascendancy" outlook'.

25. 'Passages in the Secret History of an Irish Countess', in *The Purcell Papers* (New York: Garland, 1979), pp. 1–102.

26. See McCormack, introduction to *Uncle Silas*, pp. vii–xx.

27. E. Œ. Somerville and Martin Ross, *Irish Memories* (1918) and *Wheel-Tracks* (1924).

28. See Eagleton, *Heathcliff and the Great Hunger*, p. 215.

29. See Margo Backus, *The Gothic Family Romance: Heterosexuality, Child Sacrifice, and the Anglo-Irish Colonial Order* (Durham, NC: Duke University Press, 1999).

30. Molly Keane (M. J. Farrell, pseud.), *Two Days in Aragon* (London, Penguin/ Virago Press, 1985), p. 15.

31. Deane, 'The Literary Myths of the Revival', p. 32.

32. *The Siege of Krishnapur* (1973) and *The Singapore Grip* (1978).

33. John Banville, 'My Readers, that Small Band, Deserve a Rest', an interview with Rudiger Imhof, *Irish University Review* 11 (1981), 11.

34. John Banville, *Birchwood* (London: Granada, 1984), p. 12.

GUIDE TO FURTHER READING

Flanagan, Thomas. *The Irish Novelists 1800–1850*. New York: Columbia University Press, 1959.

Frehner, Ruth. *The Colonizers' Daughters: Gender in the Anglo-Irish Big House Novel*. Tübingen: Francke, 1999.

Genet, Jacqueline (ed.). *The Big House in Ireland: Reality and Representation*. Dingle, Ireland: Brandon, 1991.

Kreilkamp, Vera. *The Anglo-Irish Novel and the Big House*. Syracuse, NY: Syracuse University Press, 1998.

McCormack, W. J. *Ascendancy and Tradition in Anglo-Irish Literary History from 1789 to 1939*. Oxford: Clarendon Press, 1985.

Rauchbauer, Otto (ed.). *Ancestral Voices: The Big House in Anglo-Irish Literature*. Hildesheim: Georg Olms Verlag; Dublin: Lilliput Press, 1992.

4

SIOBHÁN KILFEATHER

The Gothic novel

Origins of the Gothic novel

[W]hatever is fitted in any sort to excite the ideas of pain and danger, that is to say, whatever is in any sort terrible, or conversant with terrible objects, or operates in a manner analogous to terror, is a source of the sublime.[1]

It is something for a man to be able to walk from his own door to his place of worship without being shot at from behind his father's tombstone.[2]

After 1757, a large number of novels in English adopted, explored, adapted and perverted the aesthetic theories set out in Edmund Burke's *A Philosophical Enquiry into the Origin of our Ideas of the Sublime and Beautiful*. They did this through new attention to landscape, through the deployment of historical settings and themes, and through an interest in the sensational and the supernatural. The most obvious influence of Burke's treatise is found in the subgenre of terror fiction that quickly identified itself as Gothic.

The sublime is produced by great and terrible objects, including natural phenomena like oceans, mountains and waterfalls, as well as great buildings whose size overwhelms the spectator. Burke emphasises that a certain amount of obscurity is necessary for the creation of terrible effects. To enter a ruined abbey on a moonlit night would be to invite the experience of the sublime. Small and pleasing objects are beautiful, and, in terms of landscape, the beautiful is associated with domesticity and cultivation. Burke leads his readers to associate the sublime with masculinity and the beautiful with femininity.

The term Gothic first appeared in the seventeenth century, and its original meaning – pertaining to the Goths (or Germans) and their language – was derogatory. It implied crudity and barbarism. It was primarily used as a descriptive term for medieval architecture. By the mid-eighteenth century, a Gothic revival was under way in British architecture and Gothic effects had become fashionable in landscape gardening and in painting. The English novelist Horace Walpole, whose *The Castle of Otranto* (1764) was described on the title page of its second edition as 'a Gothic tale', identified two possible origins for his story, which continue to engage the interest of readers and critics:

> I waked from a dream . . . of which all I could recover was, that I had thought myself in an ancient castle (a very natural dream for a head filled like mine with Gothic story) and that on the uppermost bannister of a great staircase I saw a gigantic hand in armour. In the evening I sat down and began to write . . . – add that I was glad to think of anything rather than politics . . . [3]

The turn away from politics and the emergence of subconscious anxieties and desires in dreams suggest an intimate relationship between a psycho–sexual dynamic and the macro-political world. The mixture of sex and power, dreams and history, costume drama and terror, fired the imagination of writers and readers and the popularity of Gothic fiction became one of the most striking publishing phenomena of the late eighteenth century. In London the Minerva Press, a publishing house established by William Lane, was closely identified with the publication of Gothic novels from 1790 to 1820. Irish writers who published with Lane include Sydney Owenson (Lady Morgan, ?1776–1859) and Regina Maria Roche (née Dalton, 1764–1845). There was no Irish equivalent of Lane in the eighteenth century, although Harriet Colbert of Dublin, who ran a circulating library, published several Irish novels. The extension of the 1709 British copyright laws to Ireland after the Act of Union meant that Irish publishing was in significant decline in the first thirty years of the nineteenth century. In the 1830s, the main outlet for the Irish Gothic was in the pages of the *Dublin University Magazine,* the *Dublin Penny Journal* and *Blackwood's Magazine* (published in Edinburgh); from the 1840s through the rest of the nineteenth century, James Duffy in Dublin was a major publisher of Irish fiction.

In 1760, the Scottish writer James Macpherson published his *Fragments of Ancient Poetry,* which were supposedly translations of the poems of Ossian, a third-century Highland bard, but are now regarded more as reworkings of Scots-Gaelic ballads and stories collected by Macpherson on his tours of the Highlands. *Fingal* (1762) and *Temora* (1763), two collections of epic poems by 'Ossian', followed swiftly and, in spite of accusations of forgery, Macpherson's work was highly valued and influential in Britain and Europe, where it chimed with and influenced the development of bardic nationalism. It was also part of eighteenth-century popular antiquarianism, which encompassed such collections as Evan Evans's *Some Specimens of Ancient Welsh Poetry* (1764), Thomas Percy's *Reliques of Ancient English*

Poetry (1765), Francis Grose's *A Classical Dictionary of the Vulgar Tongue* (1785) and *Antiquities of England and Wales* (1773–87), Joseph Walker's *Historical Memoirs of the Irish Bards* (1785) and Charlotte Brooke's *Reliques of Irish Poetry* (1789). Ossian is a particularly useful reference point for the ways in which Gothic novels regularly make a theme – perhaps even a moral – of translation. In the first edition of *The Castle of Otranto*, Walpole assumes the guise of a translator, and Gothic fiction in general often seems to suggest that the relationship between cause and effect is the matter lost in translation.

The fusion of interest in Ossianism, antiquarianism and the sublime is found in some of the earliest British Gothic novels. If one popular version of the eighteenth-century Gothic novel inherited from Jacobean tragedy a strong flavour of anti-Catholicism, a pre-occupation with the Machievel and the Inquisition and a preference for Mediterranean locations, then there was also from the start a Celtic Gothic which appropriated the newly realised sublimity of the wild landscapes of Wales, Scotland, Ireland and Cornwall and traded on a blend of popular superstitions and native insurgency to produce its terrors. Sophia Lee (1750–1824), who was born in London but spent much of her early life in Dublin, and lived in Bath and Clifton (near Bristol) in the company of Irish patriots, based her influential Gothic novel, *The Recess* (1783–5), on the life of Mary Queen of Scots and her (fictional) daughters, taking the story with the Earl of Essex to Ireland, where Lee describes the devastation of the defeated Irish. Ann Radcliffe was a pupil at Lee's boarding school in Bath, and Radcliffe's first Gothic novel, *The Castles of Athlin and Dunbayne: A Highland Story* (London, 1789; Dublin, 1794), exhibits the popular taste for Celticism and antiquarianism.

The first phase of the Gothic novel was between the 1750s and the 1820s and involved the self-identified Gothic fictions that flooded the Atlantic market-place, during which time the major Irish Gothic writers were Regina Maria Roche, Sydney Owenson and Charles Robert Maturin. Irish Gothic novels which appeared in this heyday of the genre include Thomas Leland's *Longsword, Earl of Salisbury* (1762); Elizabeth Griffith's *The History of Lady Barton* (1771) and *Conjugal Fidelity: Or Female Fortitude. A Genuine Story* (1779); Anne Fuller's *Alan Fitz-Osborne* (1787); James White's *Earl of Strongbow* (1789); Stephen Cullen's *The Haunted Priory* (1794); Anne Burke's *The Sorrows of Edith* (1796); Elizabeth Ryves's *The Hermit of Snowden* (1797); [Mrs] F. C. Patrick's *More Ghosts!* (1798); Anna Millikin's *Plantagenet; or, Secrets of the House of Anjou* (1802); Catharine Selden's *Villa Nova* (1804); Marianne Kenley's *The Cottage of the Appenines or the Castle of Novina* (1804); Luke Aylmer Conolly's *The Friar's*

Tale; or, Memoirs of the Chevalier Orsino (1805); W. H. Maxwell's *O'Hara* (1825); George Croly's *Salethiel, or The Wandering Jew* (1828). Many of these novels are only partly Gothic (or mock-Gothic) but that is typical of the genre. A substantial number of anonymous novels and novelettes have been rediscovered recently through the researches of Rolf Loeber and Magda Stouthamer-Loeber.[4] Among anonymous works are *The Adventures of Miss Sophia Berkley*, by 'a young lady' (1760) and *The Cavern in the Wicklow Mountains, or, The Fate of the O'Brien Family* (1821).

Before 1798, the Irish Gothic was close to the English Gothic in terms of its dual interests in early British and Irish history (see Leland, Fuller and White) and in ghosts and sensational terrors (Griffith, Cullen, Roche and Patrick). But it also resembled North American Gothic in that it seemed to press the reader in the direction of rather generalised allegorical readings which emphasised the resemblance between the oppressed virtue of the characters and the fate of the nation. After 1798, the terrors of the Gothic became much more explicitly related to those of contemporary life in Ireland, and the realism became much more horrific and dangerous than previous fantasy literature had suggested.

Conventions and Irish Gothic

Take – An old castle, half of it ruinous.

> A long gallery, with a great many doors, some secret ones.
> Three murdered bodies, quite fresh.
> As many skeletons, in chests and presses.
> An old woman hanging by the neck, with her throat cut.
> Assassins and desperadoes, 'quant. suff.'
> Noise, whispers, and groans, threescore at least.

Mix them together in the form of three volumes, to be taken at any of the watering places before going to bed.[5]

Amongst the many tropes which pervade Gothic texts are portraits, doubles, veils, the confessional, hunger, bleeding corpses, treasure chests, live burial, madhouses, deformity, inquisition, dismemberment, miscegenation, restlessness, surveillance, footsteps, inarticulate howls, nightmares, insomnia, fire, shipwreck and mob violence. *Melmoth the Wanderer* (1820) by Charles Robert Maturin (1782–1824) has almost all these features, but most novelists are content to pick and mix just a few ingredients.

Since the elements of the Gothic are so predictable, what pleasure do they offer? One pleasure must surely be that predictability itself. In an imaginative world where the characters are, for at least part of the time, powerless, the reader has the pleasurable sensation of foreseeing disasters and predicting outcomes. The repetition of Gothic plots can be the source of another pleasure, and many of the narrative strategies of the Gothic closely resemble the narrative strategies of pornography, and involve the terrorisation, sometimes leading to the rape and murder, of young women. The strongest similarity between the Gothic and pornography – and many Gothic novels, including M. G. Lewis's *The Monk* (1796) and Bram Stoker's *Dracula* (1897), might fairly be described as pornographic – is not so much what happens to women in these texts as the way in which the central characters learn nothing from experience. The heroine who is terrorised by the sinister monk in the dark cellar one night will embark the next night to explore the ruined abbey, just as unprepared for the horrors that await her. There is another – more political – dimension to the repetition of Gothic plots. It represents a formal enactment of one of the major Gothic themes of particular significance in Ireland, namely that history is repeating itself and that its victims cannot stop themselves banging on about the same old story.

Gothic writing is sensational in the most primitive ways in so far as it emphasises how people decode the information presented to them via their senses (the flickering candle in the empty house, the footsteps in the room overhead, the smell of flowers in the deserted cavern) and interpret that information in the light of their prejudices. 'This cannot be happening to me' is the first assumption of the narrative voice in a significantly large number of Gothic texts. The rational mind rejects the apparent evidence of the supernatural. In its attitude to the supernatural and its conflation of Roman Catholicism with expressions of belief in the supernatural, Gothic texts often appear as much indebted to David Hume's essay on miracles (1748) as to Burke on the sublime. In other words, Gothic novels depend on the presumption that the implied reader is sceptical, a person for whom the likelihood of an occurrence of the supernatural or the miraculous is so small that it would be nearly miraculous to find a person whose belief was founded solely on witness. Such an implied reader might, of course, be very different from 'real' readers, and one recurrent convention of the Gothic novel is to present characters who are primed by their reading habits to be more credulous.

If one aspect of the pleasure of reading Gothic novels is to appreciate the ways in which they resemble one another, as so well parodied in Jane Austen's *Northanger Abbey* (1818), then there is another – perhaps more literary – kind of satisfaction to be derived from the way in which an individual novelist takes the Gothic template and does something original, perhaps unusually poetic, perhaps unpredictably amusing, with it. The best

Gothic novels work with the comic, and particularly with the camp possibilities of the genre. They also embrace generic impurities, enacting their own forms of literary miscegenation. Although the Gothic is so clearly recognisable, it has a habit of putting itself about, suddenly emerging in texts that appear to be playing by the rules of some quite different genre, such as the realist novel, the oriental tale, lyric poetry, autobiography and even history writing.

If by the Gothic one understands a series of conventions concerning the representation of landscape, character, history, plot and the supernatural, and which give a distinctive stamp or character to certain types of fiction, then it is possible to identify elements of the Gothic in Irish writing from the 1590s to the present. Indeed, the Gothic appears more often than not as a response to modernisation, a mode of registering loss and of suggesting that new forms of subjectivity are necessary to deal with the new forms of knowledge and power that are conquering past systems and beliefs. But if an interest in memory and loss were to be seen as the defining features of the Gothic, there would be a risk that the genre would be asked to encompass almost all of modern Irish writing. However, what distinguishes Gothic writing from sentimental, melodramatic, sensational or realist texts is a set of tactics and an overriding interest in the sublime, not simply as something one encounters in the world but as a particular kind of reading experience. In Gothic novels, the reader is at least temporarily unsettled in terms of his or her belief in the power of reason and the presence of the supernatural, but also confounded by the status of certain information offered by the text and overwhelmed by sensations of shock and apprehension. One of the most common conventions of Gothic novels is to present the author as an editor and the text as 'found' – an edited manuscript, a confession to the editor, a series of embedded tales, a collection of fragments. The emphasis on the materiality of the text sits in paradoxical contrast to the insubstantial nature of the stories of sights possibly seen and sounds allegedly heard by witnesses who are frequently frightened, criminal, insane or otherwise unreliable. *Dracula* famously ends with the comment that 'in all the mass of material of which the record is composed, there is hardly one authentic document; nothing but a mass of typewriting . . . '.[6] This reverses a prevailing trope in the romantic Gothic, where – in an age of mechanical reproduction – the Gothic emphasises the mystique of manuscript and oral transmission. The Gothic novel presents itself as an alternative form of history writing, one which questions official sources, excavates guilty secrets and pulls skeletons from the closet.

The Irish Gothic has a special dynamic around matters of translation, given that in pre-Famine Ireland the Gothic was usually a printed text in

English which apparently sought to represent or mediate manuscript and/or oral traditions composed, and generally received and interpreted, in Irish. Maria Edgeworth's *Castle Rackrent* (1800), Sydney Owenson's *The Wild Irish Girl* (1806) and Michael Banim's *Crohoore of the Bill-hook* (1825) all wrestle with the idea that translation from Irish to English, and from English to Irish, operates 'in a manner analogous to terror'.[7] This is because translation is rarely a matter of choice. Critics writing about the Gothic often emphasise that the vocabulary for describing Gothicism was originally developed in criticism of the visual arts and especially architecture. The narrowest definition of the Gothic is that it is a way of describing windows with pointed arches. Gothic novels tend to merit the description 'Gothic' by virtue of their descriptive passages. The foreign settings and historical displacements characteristic of Gothic fiction raise questions about the location of cognitive processes – can people living in different places, at different times, with different religious beliefs and other ideological constraints, be translated in ways that do justice to their differences as well as similarities to their readership?

Northanger Abbey, Jane Austen's brilliant parody of the Radcliffian Gothic, suggests that the middle-class English reader uses the Gothic almost completely as an allegorical device for decoding patriarchal power and domestic victimisation. In order to accomplish such a decoding, the Gothic novel must appear uninterested in specificities of character. The reader cannot enjoy Radcliffe's *The Italian* (1796) if he or she is wondering how Vivaldi and Ellena developed so much Protestant scepticism against the grain of the Catholic *mentalité* in which they were educated. The Irish Gothic, on the other hand, characteristically confronts its readers with a cast list divided in its experience of time and history. *The Wild Irish Girl* and *Melmoth the Wanderer* both posit the theory that the sublime can be produced through the clash in world views that occurs when people who are experiencing historical progress and modernisation in different ways – say the powerful and the powerless, or the rich and the poor – attempt to establish either a conservative ethos of marketplace exchanges or a liberal ethos of translation and comprehensibility.

In *Melmoth the Wanderer*, a powerful figure (the wanderer) is repeatedly thwarted in his attempts to negotiate a new contract with vulnerable individuals because the excessive misery of their situations has driven them beyond the scope of argument into forms of abjection and insanity. *The Wild Irish Girl* idealises the possibility of translation and mutual comprehension between different languages, religions and cultures, but can only find a fairy-tale narrative to encompass such possibilities. As if to emphasise its fantastic dimensions, it uses one of the favourite Gothic tropes, the interrupted wedding, as its penultimate scene. Parodies of the Gothic novel often mock its impoverished characterisation – all those interchangeable heroines and villains – as compared with the rich, complex sense of interiority created for characters in the realist novel. In fact, the Gothic novel shifts the ground for thinking about interiority from an exploration of fictional character to the production of a reader whose sense of his or her own inner life is created through reading about terror and desire, and experiencing desire and terror while reading.

Varieties of Irish Gothic

A variety of definitions might justify the inclusion of particular texts in the canon of the Irish Gothic. There are Gothic stories written by Irish writers and set wholly or partially in Ireland, of which Regina Maria Roche's *The Children of the Abbey* (1796), Michael Banim's *Crohoore of the Bill-hook* and Mrs J. H. (Charlotte) Riddell's *The Nun's Curse* (1888) are examples. Gothic novels by Irish writers not chiefly set in Ireland, but with striking and interesting references to Ireland in their pages, include Charles Robert Maturin's *Fatal Revenge* (1807) and *Melmoth the Wanderer* (1820). Amongst novels by English writers set wholly or partly in Ireland are Caroline Lamb's *Glenarvon* (1816) and Mary Shelley's *Frankenstein* (1818). There are novels by British authors with Irish Gothic characters, or significant allusions to the Irish, for example M. G. Lewis's 'The Anaconda' (1808) and John Buchan's *The Three Hostages* (1924). Stories by second- and third-generation emigrants which evoke aspects of the Irish Gothic suggest that those writers are still consciously and unconsciously working through aspects of their Irish heritage; such claims can be made for Emily Brontë's *Wuthering Heights* (1847) and several stories by Arthur Conan Doyle. There are also stories by Irish writers not set in Ireland but about which it is regularly argued that a significant Irish aspect is discernible: Sheridan Le Fanu's *Uncle Silas* (1864), Oscar Wilde's *The Picture of Dorian Gray* (1891) and Bram Stoker's *Dracula*.

Finally, there are translations into English and Irish of Gothic texts, which might be said to pick up Irish resonances in those acts of translation: *Eachtra Uilliam*, a seventeenth- or eighteenth-century translation of the medieval werewolf tale, *William of Palerne*; John Anster's translation of Goethe's *Faust* (1820–35); James Clarence Mangan's many translations from the German for the *Dublin University Magazine*; *Sidonia the Sorceress* (1849), translated from the German of J. W. Meinhold by Jane Elgee (later Lady Wilde); Dion Boucicault's version of Pushkin's *The Queen of Spades* (1851); Mary Hely-Hutchinson's translation of Merimée's *Colomba* (1840) into English (1905) and Cormac O Cadhlaigh's Irish translation (1929); C. S. Ó Fallamhain's *An Dr Jekyll agus Mr Hyde* (1929); W. H. Maxwell's *Sealgaireacht an Iarthair (Wild Sports of the West)*, translated by Sean O Ruadhain (1933); Seán Ó Cuirrín's *Dracula* (1933); Nicolas Toibin's *Cu na mBaskerville (The Hound of the Baskervilles)* (1934). To take one example, Elgee's translation of *Sidonia the Sorceress* brings out the vulnerability of the peasantry under interrogation and the ruthless indifference of institutional power; these were themes to resonate in Ireland in the 1840s.

Gothic after 1798

Gothic novels provide writers with an opportunity either to probe or to hide (perhaps even hide from) certain kinds of knowledge about the self and the world. This paradox is one of the most distinctive features of the Gothic. It can be a vehicle for both radical and conservative ideas, although there are currents of literary criticism which represent the Gothic as a coherent corpus working to a specific ideological agenda. The essential subversiveness of the Gothic is the starting point for many feminist arguments, in particular. The Gothic can explore the innermost recesses of the human heart and/or trot out a series of stereotypes. It predicts as well as presents lived experience as always involving the uncanny. At the heart of every Gothic novel is a mystery, but it is an eminently predictable mystery. Only a reader so naive as not to realise that Portia can only be won through choosing the lead casket could really doubt that Melmoth has made a pact with the devil, that Uncle Silas is plotting to kill Maud, that Donnel M'Gowan (in William Carleton's 1847 novel, *The Black Prophet*) is a murderer, or that Lucy Westenra is preyed upon by a vampire. The narrative structure of the Gothic novel (as well, perhaps, as its moral) is usually close to that of the folk story or fairy tale, and its characterisation is generally as formulaic.

For most of the nineteenth century, Irish Gothic cannot be defined so much in terms of a subgenre as much as in terms of an extra dimension apparent in many works of Irish fiction. One can in fact trace this generic mixture back to the work of Roche, Owenson and Maturin. Each of these writers produced novels which crossed the Gothic with the sentimental novel, the novel of manners or – most commonly – the national tale. *Melmoth the Wanderer* is exceptional for the degree to which it sits very squarely in the Gothic tradition. The presence of the supernatural, or, as commonly of superstition – in other words, a belief in the supernatural – is a feature of much of the later nineteenth-century Irish fiction of Thomas Moore, the Banim brothers, Gerald Griffin, Samuel Lover, Sheridan Le

Fanu, Frances Browne and Emily Lawless; and 'gothic traces'[8] continue to surface in the twentieth-century novel.

It is not difficult to imagine why the events of 1798 might have reinvigorated a belief, or at least a hope, that death is not final, and that those people whose lives had been so suddenly erased might somehow live on as presences for their surviving friends. John Banim's *The Fetches* (1825) is one of many European romantic novellas to draw on superstition and folklore for a reservoir of strategies by which to imagine possible relations between the living and the dead. In Irish romanticism, 'the memory of the dead' has a very specific reference to the dead of 1798. But memory is not the only way in which the living and the dead jostle up against one another in the 1820s. At either end of the decade, Charles Robert Maturin and Jonah Barrington (1760–1834) create extended prose works which demand that their readers look at the faces of the dead in a very direct and specific way. From young John Melmoth's initial confrontation with his ancestor's portrait, looking into the face of the wanderer is a demand repeatedly made of characters in the novel. Such a gaze brings death or madness because it forces the character in his or her notional present to recognise the undeadness of the dead, and to feel their pain. The past will not go away and leave people in peace. Since Melmoth's mission is to exchange places with a new victim of his curse, he necessarily poses as a doppelgänger in each of his encounters with putative victims. Jonah Barrington's comic autobiography, *Personal Sketches of his Own Time* (1858), is inflected with the macabre, not least because of Barrington's account of his own experiences in 1798. As he (under)states it: 'General Lake . . . had ordered the heads of Mr Grogan, Captain Keogh, Mr Bagenal Harvey, and Mr Colclough, to be placed on very low spikes, over the courthouse door of Wexford . . . The mutilated countenances of friends and relatives, in such a situation, would, it may be imagined, give any man most horrifying sensations.'[9]

A survey of the periodical literature of the 1830s and 1840s suggests that tales of the fantastic and supernatural dominated Irish taste. In periodicals, Gothic texts are fragmented by serialisation and illustration, and there is contamination with contiguous political discourses. This is particularly evident in the first decade of the *Dublin University Magazine*, where the language of haunting, terror, dismemberment and monstrosity, along with explicit references to Frankenstein, is repeatedly deployed in essays on politics. The fact that the contributions are largely anonymous heightens this sense of 'contagion'. In the same decade, in the *Dublin Penny Journal*, the dominance of architectural and scenic illustrations with an accent on Gothic perspectives suggests that Ireland itself is a Gothicised space.

Although relatively few of these Gothic stories were serialised or grew into novels, they are an important part of the fragmentary poetics of the Irish Gothic and it is in the periodicals that some important examples of the Irish Gothic first appeared: *Confessions of a Reformed Ribbonman* (1830) by William Carleton (1794–1869), *Chapters from a College Romance* (1834–5) by Isaac Butt (1813–79) and the major novels and stories of Sheridan Le Fanu (1814–73). James Wills is one of the writers who did not progress from the periodicals to greater fame, but his tales in the *Dublin University Magazine*, sometimes published under the pseudonym 'George Faithful Mendax', deserve to be better known, and in that journal there are many striking Gothic tales which remain unattributed. William Maginn (1793–1842) contributed several mock-Gothic and macabre short stories to English and Scottish periodicals, but also some genuinely unusual and frightening tales, including 'The Man in the Bell' (*Blackwood's*, 1821) and 'A Night of Terror' (*Bentley's 'Miscellany'*, 1836).

One of the distinguishing features of the nineteenth-century Irish Gothic is its interest in dismemberment. The discovery of a skull in a grave, as happens at the opening of Le Fanu's *The House in the Churchyard* (1861–3), is a favourite trope. The Irish Gothic engages with the generic dominance of realist fiction through a poetics of fragmentation. In the context of such atrocities as the 1798 rebellion and the Famine, the 'morselisation' of bodies is both ultra-realist as well as ultra-fantastic. In Carleton's *Confessions of a Reformed Ribbonman* (*Wildgoose Lodge*) and in *Crohoore of the Bill-hook* by Michael Banim (1796–1874), there is an interesting Irish take on the 'explained supernatural' as practised by Ann Radcliffe and some of her contemporaries, and owing something to her writing about Italian *banditti*. The explanation in Banim and Carleton for mysterious activities at night is that secret societies use the cover of the supernatural to disguise the organisation of political violence. This would be interesting enough, but both Carleton and Banim pursue a more apparently formalist concern with the ways in which the invocation of the supernatural produces a transformation in the people who employ it. The meeting in the chapel before the attack on Wildgoose Lodge is a clever and rational strategy, but during the meeting a blasphemous and diabolical presence takes possession of the conspirators. Banim's interest in deformity challenges corporeal theories of identity and incorporates a sophisticated linguistic strategy for misrepresenting the Irish language in deformed morsels.

Another trope in the Irish Gothic for representing the demonisation or repression of Gaelic culture is the howl. Amanda Fitzalan hears it at a wake; Melmoth's demonic laughter is a version of the howl; and there is a remarkable story devoted to it in Isaac Butt's *Chapters from a College*

Romance: chapter 4, 'The Murdered Fellow'. The almost obsessive interest in decapitation in the Irish Gothic – and there is of course a remarkable example in *Crohoore of the Bill-hook* when the mother runs off with her son's head – reminds the reader of the background of the history of state violence which forms a backdrop to personal crimes. The twin trope of the corpse which identifies its murderer – central to Carleton's *The Black Prophet* – and of the corpse desecrated by the mob are common to fiction, memoirs, travel writing and popular histories. There isn't space here to investigate those genres, but it is worth pausing on the remarkable *Autobiography* of James Clarence Mangan (1803–49). When Mangan writes that '[i]n my boyhood I was haunted by an indescribable feeling of something terrible', he cuts to the heart of the Gothic and demonstrates how it is possible to distil its meanings. The reader knows to what the indescribable in Mangan refers, and that its indescribability is part of how we know it. It is both an illumination and a critique of those Gothic novels which are too simply allegorised into ideological statements.

Gendered Gothic

Amanda pressed her hand in silence and trembling departed from the chapel. She stopped at the outside to listen, for by her ear alone could she now receive any intimation of danger, as the night was too dark to permit any object to be discerned; but the breeze sighing among the trees of the valley, and the melancholy murmur of the water falls were the only sounds she heard. She groped along the wall of the chapel to keep in the path, which wound from it to the entrance of the Abbey, and doing so, passed her hand over the cold face of a human being; terrified, an involuntary scream burst from her, and she faintly articulated, 'Defend me, Heaven!'[10]

There are two archetypal Gothic plots, one generally associated with the female Gothic, the other with the male Gothic. In the female Gothic, an innocent young woman is terrorised by an older man who is trying to seduce her or to kill her. There are usually incestuous overtones to his interest in her. *The Children of the Abbey* and *Uncle Silas* are variations on this plot. The beleaguered heroines are incarcerated in rambling big houses, on isolated estates. Their oppressors are fathers, guardians, husbands, clerics and/or teachers. These conventions represent all too obviously women's sense of entrapment in domestic ideology, under patriarchy. The Gothic is particularly effective in suggesting that women have little or no practical access to law or to communal support when they come into conflict with their families. Lyn Pykett notes that ghost stories are 'in many cases, stories about power, in which the seduced, betrayed, persecuted, wronged, or dispossessed return to right or avenge their wrongs or repossess what has been taken away'.[11] The link between ideas of dispossession and of sexual betrayal are part of the way in which Irish Catholics are regularly feminised within the Irish Gothic. In the nineteenth century, to the extent that Irish Gothic novels deal with dispossession and guilt, the dynamics are usually intra-denominational rather than inter-denominational. Nevertheless, figures like Griffin's 'colleen bawn' (*The Collegians*, 1829) and Emily Lawless's Grania (*Grania*, 1892) are associated with essential identity, with qualities put at risk by the embourgeoisement of the emerging Catholic middle classes.

In the masculine Gothic, a central character makes a Faustian pact, offering his soul in exchange for material advantage or some form of knowledge. *Melmoth the Wanderer* and *The Picture of Dorian Gray* are the best known examples of the Irish Faustian plot. Maturin sent his novel to the publisher piecemeal, claiming that he hardly knew himself if it was a collection of tales or a novel. The style veers between the intense, rhapsodic descriptions of terror and an accomplished naturalism which does justice to the miseries of materialism. *Melmoth the Wanderer* develops many of the tropes which go on to dominate the Irish Gothic: the watcher, the traveller, the voices, the portrait, the window, hunger, dismemberment, the unspeakable, death from fright. For all its baroque architecture and the melodrama of the plot, *Melmoth* is at its most brilliant on the terrors of intimacy and the horror of family life. Central to the development of the male Gothic is the fear/desire of uncovering the monster within the self. 'Then followed – I saw myself; and this horrid tracing of yourself in a dream, – this haunting of yourself by your own spectre, while you still live, is perhaps a curse almost equal to your crimes visiting you in the punishments of eternity'.[12]

For this reason, the nineteenth-century male Gothic became a particularly valuable route for the exploration of taboo sexual feelings. In the work of Wilde and Stoker, such taboos involve fears of miscegenation, violence, misogyny and disease, as well as a mode of negotiating the outlawed terrain of the homoerotic. Basil Hallward describes his first meeting with Dorian Gray: 'When our eyes met, I felt that I was growing pale. A curious sensation of terror came over me. I knew that I had come face to face with someone whose mere personality was so fascinating that, if I allowed it to do so, it would absorb my whole nature, my whole soul, my very art itself . . . '[13] For Wilde, the Gothic is the appropriate aesthetic in which to explore those desires 'monstrous laws have made monstrous and unlawful'.[14] In *Melmoth the Wanderer*, and particularly in the chapters of 'The Lovers' Tale', the feeling of terror that accompanies the significant look is generated by the consciousness of sexual taboo. John Sandal goes insane when he realises that he has sacrificed his first love to a false understanding of its illegitimacy. Sandal is the victim of the powerful competing ideological inheritances of aristocratic feudalism and puritanism. Wilde adapts these motifs to a contemporary world in which the competing ideals of platonic pederastic love and promiscuous sexual practices are destructively polarised by being forced underground.

The gender division in the genre is not a matter of the gender of the author – there are women writers including Mary Shelley who use the Faustian plot – and many Gothic novels incorporate both plotlines. The female Gothic is obviously an allegory of the terrors of the family romance and the dangers of domesticity, and it is also concerned with the limits of sensibility. The Faustian plot is more likely to dramatise an encounter with the sublime. A reader who discovers either of these plots knows that there are guilty secrets to be excavated in the novel. W. J. McCormack has argued that one of the most common plot devices in the Irish Gothic is disputed inheritance, and that this reflects the unease of the Protestant landed gentry in particular as to the legitimacy of their tenure.[15]

Whether one reads the Gothic as a coherent corpus or a heterogeneous collection of texts, there is some consensus that it is a mode of excavating certain cultural anxieties, particularly anxieties about racial, religious and sexual identities. If one looks at the continuities between English Jacobean drama and the English Gothic novel, one notices that extreme violence, sexual anxiety, racial hatred and anti-Catholicism are significant ingredients in the brews of both genres. These are also ingredients in Elizabethan and Jacobean descriptions of Ireland. One way of tracing the emergence of the Gothic in the eighteenth century would be to suggest that a generation after the apparent collapse of political Jacobitism, the Jacobite wars were re-fought in the cultural realm, with the Irish playing a central role as both an enemy without – the last site of unresolved conflict in the metropolitan colonies – and the enemy within – a population whose difference was not always clearly inscribed on the body, but had as much to do with hearts and minds. The teasing question would remain as to whether those demonised by the Gothic, for example the Gaelic Irish, women, Jews, Catholics, gypsies, homosexuals and Jesuits, were able to fight back within the conventions of the genre. Is the Gothic always the nightmare of the oppressor, or can it be a vehicle for dissent from below?

Gothic novels and the Irish language

Irish language writing is very rarely brought into discussions of the Irish Gothic, partly because the nineteenth-century novel is its most recognised form, but Gothic poetry and Gothic drama were both popular forms of writing, particularly in the romantic period. Anglophone writers adopted themes and literary conventions from what they knew of Gaelic literature. The influence of Ossian on the European tradition has been well documented. It is less clear that there was a reciprocal influence on Irish poetry from either English or from continental European poets, but in a poem such as the anonymous 'Cill Chais' (c.1802) one finds a familiar Gothic/romantic scene, which may be attributable to the reading of English poets such as James Thomson, and the influence of 'graveyard poetry', which certainly coloured the development of Gothic sensibilities in English.

Seán Ó Coileáin's 'Machtnamh an Duine Dhoilíosaigh' (1813), a meditation on the ruins of Timoleague Abbey, deploys a number of Gothic conventions to which translators Thomas Furlong, Samuel Ferguson and James Clarence Mangan were clearly attracted.

> The memory of the men who slept
> Under those desolate walls – the solitude – the hour –
> Mine own lorn mood of mind – all joined to o'erpower
> My spirit – and I wept![16]

The closest attempt to a nineteenth-century Gothic novel in Irish is the collection of tales by Aomhlaith Ó Súileabháin, linked through the figure of Calmar. Ó Súileabháin several times uses the term *gothamla* to describe the architectural features of the ruins in which these tales characteristically begin, and there are marked stylistic as well as thematic similarities between these tales and the short stories that were being published in Irish periodicals such as the *Dublin Penny Journal* and the *Dublin University Magazine* in the 1830s.

Peadar Ua Laoghaire's *Séadna* (1904), often identified as the first novel to be published in the Irish language, is a Faustian tale whose narrative strategies are pegged to oral tradition rather than to the varieties of writing characteristic of a Gothic fiction. It raises in a particularly pointed way the question of how and why the Gothic needs to be distinguished from surviving and evolving native folk stories in Irish and in English.

Pádraic Ó Conaire is doing something rather different in *Deoraíocht* (1910), which resembles the work of Stoker, Wilde and Pushkin, in exploring the fusion of Gothic monster and *flâneur* as a figure for modern alienation. Ó Conaire anticipates one of the favourite cinematic devices for representing the Gothic by replacing the traditional framing narratives and the fragments of anecdote and manuscript with the use of flashbacks. Like Frankenstein's creature, Micil is an outcast because of his monstrous body, but part of the raw modernity of Micil's condition is that his amputations are the result of accident, rather than design. Ó Conaire prefigures the interest in freak shows and in amputation that is so characteristic of later American Gothic, particularly the work of Flannery O'Connor, Carson MacCullers, Eudora Welty and Tod Browning. Micil's story is set in contemporary London and Galway. The Gothic tropes include Micil's obsession with his bag of gold and his seduction by drinking companions, both of which link the novel to themes common in German and Russian romantic tales: the snowy landscape in which he meets a sailor; his impersonation of a lunatic and later his role as a circus freak; the phantasmagoric crowd scenes; the incestuous dimension to sexual desire as it erupts between the various characters; and the recurrence of hunger.

The dead souls who speak from their graves in Máirtin Ó Cadhain's *Cré na Cille* (1949) are not, on the whole, telling Gothic tales, but there are links to the ways in which the Gothic flourished elsewhere, following both the First and Second World Wars. In the somnambulant murderer in Robert Wiene's *The Cabinet of Doctor Caligari* (Germany 1919), critics have seen the shell-shocked victims of the First World War, whilst *Nosferatu*, directed by F. W. Murnau (Germany, 1921) and almost destroyed after a copyright dispute with Stoker's family, gave a new and specific resonance to the vampire story in the eerie echoes in the desolation on the vampire ship of the huge losses suffered by both Germany and the allies in U-boat attacks, and in the representation of a man journeying with his box of earth, as it were from the trenches. The ghosts of war, and the fear of the dead repossessing the living, haunted many marriage nights. Akira Kurosawa claimed that his first inspiration for *Rashoman* (Japan, 1951) came to him when he was walking round Nagasaki with his father after the nuclear holocaust. It would be reductive merely to say that the central conceit of *Rashoman* and *Cré na Cille* is that truth resides in a site of conflicting testimonies, but that is certainly one concern of both narratives. The particular resonance in post-war Ireland may have had something to do with the 'telling' images of the Jewish dead in the liberated concentration camps. During the 'Emergency' (as the Second World War was known in the Irish Free State), news of the holocaust had been largely censored in Ireland. The French airman in *Cré na Cille* is a reminder that Ireland had made itself marginal to the fight against continental European fascism. At the same time, the location of Gaelic voices in graves is a sharp warning that the culture of the Gaeltacht (the Irish-speaking part of Ireland) is at risk of annihilation.

Twentieth-century anglophone Gothic

In the twentieth century, and particularly after the Irish civil war, the Gothic became increasingly entwined with the genre of big house novels (see chapter 3). Although Molly Keane ('M. J. Farrell', 1904–96) is less interested in the supernatural than some other big house novelists, what she captures from the Gothic is the impact of space on sensibility and the jokey, camp qualities of domestic enmities. Elizabeth Bowen (1899–1973) carries on from Sheridan Le Fanu and Mrs J. H. (Charlotte) Riddell (1832–1906) the excellent tradition of Irish ghost stories, which became particularly resonant during the Second World War. The chief inheritor and exploiter of the modernist impulses in the Gothic is Samuel Beckett.

In the 1970s and 1980s, Ian Cochrane (1941–2004) and E. L. Kennedy (1927–85) produced a form of 'Free Presbyterian' Gothic, building on the lonely landscapes and puritan repressiveness of Michael McLaverty's *In This Thy Day* (1945), Anne Crone's *Bridie Steen* (1948) and Sam Hanna Bell's *December Bride* (1951), Ulster novels which combine regionalism with a Gothic accent on the persecution of passion and the dominance of patriarchy. Cochrane and Kennedy fracture the tormented lyricism of those earlier novels with the voices of *idiot savant* children, brutalised by religion, poverty and ignorance, but still capable of experiencing Wordsworthian spots of time. Cochrane's *A Streak of Madness* (1973) and Kennedy's *Twelve in Arcady* (1986) are Gothic in the mode of Flannery O'Connor and Carson McCullers, existing in a self-enclosed world where deformity is the dominant metaphor and terror frames everyday rather than exceptional experience. They are the precursors of the more popular Patrick McGinley and Dermot Healy, and Patrick McCabe, whose novel *The Butcher Boy* (1993) was filmed by Neil Jordan (1997). McCabe (b. 1955) has coined the term 'bog Gothic' to characterise his own reformulation of the genre. 'Bog Gothic' might be pitched in opposition to the 'big house' Gothic which has continued to surface in the past fifty years in the works of John Banville, Aidan Higgins and William Trevor. Banville's *Mefisto* (1986), though it can hardly be described as wearing its debts to Goethe, Kleist and Beckett *lightly*, is the most brilliant recent incarnation of the fantastic tale in Irish writing. The American poet and undertaker Thomas Lynch, who has for many years lived part of the time in Ireland, made an original and distinctive contribution to Gothic autobiography with his memoir *The Undertaking: Life Stories from the Dismal Trade* (1997), which begins and ends with photographs of Moyarta Cemetery, Carrigaholt, Co. Clare. Several contemporary women writers – including Caroline Blackwood, Anne Devlin, Emma Donoghue, Anne Enright, Deirdre Madden, Gerardine Meaney and Moy McCrory – have self-consciously built on feminist criticism, and particularly on Sandra Gilbert and Susan Gubar's *The Madwoman in the Attic*, to adapt the Gothic as a vehicle for female anger. Peter Mullan's film, *The Magdalene Sisters* (UK 2002), suggests that Ireland may yet have a number of Gothic institutions which remain unexplored.

NOTES

1. Edmund Burke, *A Philosophical Enquiry into the Origins of our Ideas of the Sublime and the Beautiful*, ed. J. T. Boulton (1757; London: Routledge, 1958), p. 39.
2. Samuel Ferguson, 'A Dialogue Between the Head and Heart of an Irish Protestant', *Dublin University Magazine* (November 1833); reprinted in *The Field Day Anthology of Irish Writing*, gen. ed. Seamus Deane (Derry: Field Day Publications, 1991), vol. II, p. 586.
3. *The Yale Edition of Horace Walpole's Correspondence*, ed. W. S. Lewis et al. (New Haven: Yale University Press, 1937–83), vol. I, p. 88; quoted in E. J. Clery's introduction to Horace Walpole, *The Castle of Otranto: A Gothic Story* (Oxford: Oxford University Press, 1996), p. vii.
4. R. Loeber and M. Stouthamer-Loeber, 'The Publication of Irish Novels and Novelettes: A Footnote on Irish Gothic Fiction', *Cardiff Corvey: Reading the Romantic Text* 10 (June 2003), 17–31. See http://www/cardiff.ac.uk/encap/corvey/download/cc10_no2.pdf.
5. Burke, *A Philosophical Enquiry*, p. 39.
6. 'Terrorist Novel Writing', in *The Spirit of the Public Journals* for 1797 (London, 1798), pp. 223–5; quoted in Clery's introduction to Walpole, *The Castle of Otranto*, pp. xvi-xvii.
7. Bram Stoker, *Dracula*, ed. John Paul Riquelme (Boston: Bedford/ St Martin's, 2002), p. 368.
8. Fred Botting, *Gothic* (London: Routledge, 1996), p. 113.
9. Jonah Barrington, *Personal Sketches of his Own Time* (New York: Redfield, 1858), p. 173.
10. Regina Maria Roche, *The Children of the Abbey* (Philadelphia, PA: Lippincott, 1873), p. 459.
11. Lyn Pykett, 'Sensation and the Fantastic in the Victorian Novel', in Deirdre David (ed.), *The Cambridge Companion to the Victorian Novel* (Cambridge: Cambridge University Press, 2001), pp. 192–211.
12. Charles Robert Maturin, *Melmoth the Wanderer*, ed., with introduction and notes, Victor Sage (London: Penguin Books, 2000), pp. 262–3.
13. Oscar Wilde, *The Picture of Dorian Gray* (London: Penguin Books, 1985), p. 28.
14. Wilde, *The Picture of Dorian Gray*, p. 42.
15. W. J. McCormack, 'Introduction to Irish Gothic and after 1820–1945', in *The Field Day Anthology of Irish Writing*, vol. II, pp. 831–53.
16. Mangan, 'Lament over the Ruins of the Abbey of Teach Molaga', *The Nation*, 1846.

GUIDE TO FURTHER READING

Carson, James P. 'Enlightenment, Popular Culture, and Gothic Fiction', in John Richetti (ed.), *The Cambridge Companion to the Eighteenth-Century Novel*. Cambridge: Cambridge University Press, 1996.

Fitzgerald, Mary E. F. 'The Unveiling of Power: Nineteenth Century Gothic Fiction in Ireland, England, and America', in Wolfgang Zach and Heinz Kosok (eds.), *Literary Interrelations: Ireland, England, and the World*. Vol. ii, *Comparison and Impact*. Tübingen: Gunter Narr Verlag, 1987.

Gibbons, Luke. *Gaelic Gothic: Race, Colonialism and Irish Culture*. Galway: Centre for Irish Studies, 2004.

Glover, David. *Vampires, Mummies, and Liberals: Bram Stoker and the Politics of Popular Fiction*. Durham, NC: Duke University Press, 1996.

Hogle, Jerrold E. (ed.). *The Cambridge Companion to Gothic Fiction*. Cambridge: Cambridge University Press, 2002.

Kilfeather, Siobhán. 'Origins of the Irish Female Gothic', *Bullán* 1:2 (Autumn 1994), 35–46.

Killeen, Jarlath. *Gothic Ireland: Horror and the Anglican Imagination in The Long Eighteenth Century*. Dublin: Four Courts Press, 2005.

McCormack, W. J. *Sheridan Le Fanu and Victorian Ireland*. Oxford: Clarendon Press, 1980.

McCormack, W. J. 'Introduction to Irish Gothic and after 1820–1945', in *The Field Day anthology of Irish Writing*. Gen. ed. Seamus Deane. Derry: Field Day Publications, 1991. Vol. ii, pp. 831–53.

Malchow, H. L. *Gothic Images of Race in Nineteenth-Century Britain*. Stanford: Stanford University Press, 1996.

Stewart, Bruce (ed.). *That Other World: The Supernatural and the Fantastic in Irish Literature and Its Contexts*. London: Colin Smythe, 1998.

Valente, Joseph. *Dracula's Crypt: Bram Stoker, Irishness, and the Question of Blood*. Urbana: University of Illinois Press, 2001.

Watt, James. 'Gothic', in Thomas Keymer and Jon Mee (eds.), *The Cambridge Companion to English Literature 1740–1830*. Cambridge: Cambridge University Press, 2004.

Wynne, Catherine. *The Colonial Conan Doyle: British Imperialism, Irish Nationalism, and the Gothic*. Westport, CT: Greenwood Press, 2002.

5

JAMES H. MURPHY

Catholics and fiction during the Union, 1801–1922

Catholicism and the novel

During the funeral of Mrs Daly in *The Collegians* (1829), Gerald Griffin's narrator notes that 'two or three clergymen made their appearance and were, with difficulty, accommodated with places'.[1] Griffin was a Catholic and was later to join a religious order, yet there is little direct reference to Catholic life in *The Collegians*. The novel's reticence about religious practice belies its theme of Ascendancy decadence and rising Catholic leadership in rural Irish society, but is typical of the treatment of religion by mainstream Catholic writers.

The nineteenth century witnessed a 'devotional revolution', an extraordinary growth in the institutional cohesion of the Catholic Church in Ireland and in the conformity of ordinary Irish Catholics to orthodox religious practice.[2] However, this was not matched by an assertive advocacy of Catholicism in fiction, except by a number of literary priests who had international experience of the struggle between Catholicism and modernity. Ireland also experienced modernisation, largely as a result of changes to the land system, but it was of a special form which favoured the farming family rather than the urban individual. Its emphasis on collective – or at least family – identity rather than on individual identity created a favourable environment for the Church. The Irish Catholic cultural environment thus diverged from the European mainstream in which urban experience and the triumph of individual experience were prized, especially in fiction.

The situation did not favour a literary culture. Irish Catholics were not to experience the crisis of faith in Britain brought on by biblical criticism and Darwinism. There, Protestantism had embraced Enlightenment concepts of knowledge and was disconcerted no longer to be able to live up to them. For many British Victorians, the novel became at least a partial substitute for religion. Not so in Ireland, where such a powerful religious narrative was available throughout society and where supernatural reality remained almost palpable. Thus in Gerald O'Donovan's *Father Ralph* (1913), the young Ralph O'Brien asks his nurse why Catholics did not write novels as good as *David Copperfield* and *Treasure Island*. O'Donovan, for satiric effect, has her reply starkly that novels were lies and that 'Catholics write true stories about Lourdes and St Aloysius and the like.'[3]

There were other reasons, too. The Irish Catholic community generally had utilitarian ambitions when it came to intellectualism, higher education, the professions and the middle classes. Novel writing was an English or an Anglo-Irish business, not only in terms of authors but also largely in terms of publishers and markets. The culture of the United Kingdom remained inimical to Catholics throughout the many decades of the union of Great Britain and Ireland (1801–1922), on account, initially, of its pronounced Protestantism and, latterly, of its increasing secularism. Irish Catholics preferred to remain reticent about their religion or simply to insist on its respectability. This understandable defensiveness was not, however, a promising basis for fiction. But the hostility that elicited it partly explains the ready audience for the work of oppositional Irish Catholic writers after 1891, the year of the death of the disgraced nationalist leader Charles Stewart Parnell. Blame for that event, vividly recalled in the argument during Christmas dinner in *A Portrait of the Artist as a Young Man* (1916) by James Joyce (1882–1941), was laid by many at the door of the Church. Members of the small but vocal Catholic intelligentsia came to see the latter as a dominating and coercive social and moral force in society. These journalists, teachers and others used fiction in the period between 1891 and Irish independence in 1922 to argue both against personal limitation and in favour of a more liberal society.

The Ireland which intelligentsia writers claimed had come about after 1891 was something like the one which Ascendancy writers feared would eventuate from the granting of Catholic Emancipation in 1829. Allowing Catholics to sit as members of parliament, though itself a limited measure, removed the last of the penal laws and seemed to presage the final accession of the Catholic majority into public life. Early nineteenth-century Whig politicians and novelists such as Sydney Owenson (Lady Morgan, ?1776–1859) had urged it on grounds of prudence but, to their consternation, saw it achieved by the populist agitation of Daniel O'Connell in the 1820s. During that decade, the Catholic novelists Gerald Griffin (1803–40) and the brothers Michael (1796–1874) and John (1798–1842) Banim acceded to the national tale, the genre of Owenson and Maria Edgeworth (1767–1849), and transformed it into an instrument of cultural combat in favour of Catholic Emancipation.[4]

The 1820s

John Banim's *The Boyne Water* (1826) combines the national tale with the historical novel. Introductory remarks made by the narrator indicate a desire to transcend the partisan myths surrounding the conflict between King James and King William in the 1690s, so that Irish people of all political and religious persuasions might recognise 'each other as belonging to a common country and exchanging the password, "This is my native land."'[5] In the novel, Robert Evelyn wishes to marry Eva McDonnell and his sister Esther to marry her brother Edmund. The Protestant Evelyns, from an Old English family long-settled in Ireland, are identified as English, the Catholic McDonnells – of contested Irish or Scots ancestry – as Irish. The novel tests whether these personal relationships can survive the political and sectarian polarisation of the times and perhaps even serve as national marriages for a prophetic future time, such as the one within which Banim was writing, if not for the 1690s: 'Other times will naturally create another spirit' (p. 552).

Historical events are witnessed at first hand through Evelyn's tolerant eyes. He reproves those who hold 'a right to scoff at the devotions of others' (p. 86) and wishes for religion to be kept out of politics: 'shall the world ever grow old enough to limit priests to the inculcation of a peacemaking creed and let honest men, nay, even knaves, mind their own business and fight their own quarrels?' (p. 156).

As Ireland begins to divide militarily, suspicions within the two couples grow and their joint marriage ceremony ends in disarray and division, exacerbated by the intransigent clergy present. Amity is restored only when isolating extremes of topography and climate allow the principal characters to set historical circumstances aside. The two couples initially meet at a precipice during a storm and Edmund and Evelyn are later reconciled while escaping waves by scrambling up a cliff at night: 'A renewal of friendship, then, solider foes though we are' (p. 249). Relationships across the sectarian divide need, it seems, to be nurtured in an entirely private sphere. 'National' marriages are fraught with difficulty and, indeed, Esther actually dies. The corollary to the retreat of the couples to the private sphere is their increasing invisibility in the historical realm. They move across the lines of the siege of Derry (1688–9) with little difficulty, and Evelyn manages to have conversations with both King William and King James during the Battle of the Boyne. Even gender seems to lose its specificity when, for a time, Eva appears to have been transformed into a young man.

The Boyne Water exemplifies the difficulties of writing an historical novel in Ireland, where characters are unable to steer a moderate course between extremes as they do in the fiction of Sir Walter Scott. Michael Banim thought his brother's novel too polemical. His own historical novel of Irish sectarian and politican divisons, *The Croppy* (1828), about the 1798 rebellion, tries to strike a more moderate note and was well received in England.

If *The Boyne Water* looks backwards to the romantic writing of Morgan, John Banim's *The Nowlans* (1826) appears to look forwards to a realistic engagement in fiction with the life of the Catholic community itself. As the puritanism of the 'devotional revolution' took hold over the following decades, however, little came of this new trend. Indeed, it is possible to see *The Nowlans* as helping to close off the very opportunity it was also opening up.

At the centre of the novel is a morality tale about Fr John Nowlan, once his comfortable farming family's 'hope and pride; afterwards their shame and afflication'.[6] What proves his undoing is the friendship between him and his sister Peggy and Letty Adams and her brother Frank, members of the Ascendancy. John finds himself 'on fire'(p. 79) for Letty and engrossed by the library of her uncle Charles Long, though when Frank urges him to marry Letty he somewhat imprecisely retorts, 'I have vowed my vow, sir' (p. 91). Both couples soon marry, however, though these are not politically healing national marriages but examples of an almost Gothic moral miscegenation. Villainous Frank seduces Peggy and marries her only at the point of John's pistols. John and the virtuous Letty elope, but even she knows that their religiously and tribally transgressive union will be punished by social ostracism and his own sense of guilt: 'I knew you would immolate yourself, John, to your wretched Letty' (p. 145).

The novel's candour in dealing with such issues as abortion, prostitution, marital abuse and clerical sexuality strikes a surprisingly modern note. Yet this candour is chiefly a warning of the dangers of a lack of a strict moral education and of Catholics associating with the Ascendancy. In many ways, therefore, *The Nowlans* advocates the greater puritanism and reticence which did come about in the later nineteenth century and which would make its own very candour largely impossible in subsequent fiction.

Griffin's *The Collegians* begins and ends with a national marriage. The first is the secret marriage of volatile, romantic Hardress Cregan, of marginal Ascendancy background, to the Catholic peasant, Eily O'Connor, which ends in her murder by Cregan's servant so that his master can pursue a more remunerative match. The second is the marriage of ultra-respectable Kyrle Daly, son of a Catholic middleman, to the Ascendancy-born Anne Chute. Though liked by readers – to Griffin's dismay – Cregan was designed to represent the anachronistic, personalised power of the Ascendancy.

When arrested by impartial enforcers of the law, neither the aristocratic hauteur of his mother nor the feeble resistance of his drunken duellist friends can save him. Yet there is something unintentionally chilling about Daly, whose face is 'pale and bright with the serenity of triumphant virtue' (p. 279).

As with *The Nowlans*, ecclesiastics are not the disciplined group they would be seen to be later in the century. Cregan and O'Connor are married by a shady priest 'that was disgraced by his Bishop' (p. 93). Even Eily's uncle, Fr Edward O'Connor, a positive clerical presence, is endowed with less than self-sacrificing zeal. He resents the loss of the '[q]uiet lodgings, a civil landlady, regular hours of discipline and the society of my oldest friends' of his city curacy and exile to a country parish 'in so dreary a peopled wilderness' (p. 159).

William Carleton

The period between Catholic Emancipation (1829) and the Famine (1845–9) was a time of Whig reform in Ireland and thus a period of particular anthropological interest in the habits of the Irish peasantry. This was the context for the work of the peasant novelist William Carleton (1794–1869), from Co. Tyrone. Converting to Protestantism in early adulthood, he began to move in evangelical circles and wrote short stories in the late 1820s and early 1830s which were hostile to Catholicism and yet deeply insightful into peasant Catholic life. His tone had begun to moderate when he turned to writing novels in the late 1830s, not least because he was being published by Catholic as well as Protestant publishers.[7]

Fardorougha the Miser (1839) is a morality story, with little specifically religious context. Like Silas Marner, Fardorougha's problem is an avarice which even he comes to recognise as a disability: 'I can cry, but I'm still as hard as a stone.'[8] The death sentence, later changed to transportation, which his affectionate and loyal son Connor incurs for arson, is the result of the machinations of a rival in love. But it is attributed to God's punishment for Fardorougha's refusal initially to welcome his son as a blessing. This may be a superstition, according to Carleton, but it is one he approves of and it provides the story with a moral teleology, as Fardorougha's conversion to feeling coincides with his son's vindication. Carleton complements the focus on individual morality with a critique of Irish social morality which approved of the culture of revenge, 'the sacred code of perverted honour by which Irishmen are guided' (p. 159).

In his preface to *Valentine M'Clutchy, The Irish Agent* (1845), Carleton signals that this novel is to be something new.[9] Though he has not abandoned his conservatism, the work will be an attack on the Orange Order and its links with the Established Church, and on landlords. The novel is said to be set in 1804, but it is clear from its descriptions of the attempts by evangelicals to convert Catholics that Carleton has the period from the 1820s onwards very much in mind. The long and rambling plot centres around the machinations of Val 'the Vulture' M'Clutchy and his son Phil, who are corrupt land agents for Lord Cumber and pillars of the Orange Order. Things are put right when Cumber's brother, who has already inserted himself as an anonymous observer into the situation, inherits the title and estate. He reflects that 'until property in this unfortunate country is placed upon an equal footing between landlord and tenant . . . so long will there be bloodshed and crime' (vol. ii, p. 345). The narrative emphasises the point to its landlord readers: 'Think of this, gentlemen, and pay attention to your duties' (vol. ii, p. 358).

The novel satirises representatives of various religious denominations: the violently zealous Catholic curate, Patrick McCabe; Solomon McSlime, dissenter, evangelical zealot, corrupt attorney and sexually abusive employer; and the Rev. Phineas Luce, ambitious Established Church parson, who in Dublin worshipped 'the Lord Lieutenant – and in London, the King, whilst his curate was only worshipping God in the country' (vol. ii, p. 213). There are two good clerics: Mr Clement, Lucre's aforementioned curate, who believes in Catholic Emancipation and is opposed to the evangelicals, and the Catholic parish priest, Fr Francis Roche. Carleton tries to endear Roche to those of his readers who were not Catholics. Though reviled by M'Clutchy, the priest manages to frustrate two plots against the agent's life, thus acting as a restraint on social disturbance. And, as a religious figure, he is portrayed as in fact being mildly Protestant. He recites prayers for a dying man 'replete with the fervour of Christian faith, to raise the soul to hopes of immortality' (vol. ii, p. 186). His primary authority comes not from his office, but from his personal integrity: 'Will you obey the old man who loves you?' (vol. ii, p. 316), he thus pleads with one group contemplating violence. Another character on his deathbed rebuffs both Luce and McCabe in favour of Roche: 'Here is a Christian gentleman and under his ministry I will die' (vol. ii, p. 323). Though Catholic writers later in the century were keen to present priests as exercising a social constraint, it was within a context of accentuated rather than elided denominational differences.

Like its two predecessors, *The Black Prophet: A Tale of Irish Famine* (1847) has a monstrous patriarch as its core. Donnel Dhu, the black prophet, claims to be the seventh son of a seventh son. He is a 'prophecy man', making his living in predicting good or bad fortune, and exploiting current millenarian expectations among the peasantry. Written during the Great Famine in part as a plea for relief, the novel is yet set in 1820 and draws on Carleton's experience of earlier famines, particularly in 1817, to paint harrowing pictures of the effects of starvation and disease, especially social disintegration. The novel is a murder mystery, a love story and, in the case of the prophet's daughter Sarah, a story of moral regeneration.

Carleton occasionally sermonises about religious toleration: 'it is not for those who differ with them in creed . . . to quarrel with the form of prayer when the heart is moved as theirs were, by earnestness and humble piety'.[10] And the prophet's final unredeemed condition is testified by the fact that he 'refused all religious consolation' (vol. III, p. 935) before his execution after his various crimes catch up with him. However, religion is really of less interest in the novel than folk belief and practice. It is only after one of the characters dies, for example, that someone remembers to mention that he had received the last rites of the Church.

The Emigrants of Ahadarra (1848) combines criticism of the land system with praise for the more prosperous Catholic farmers as an indispensable class for the prosperity of the country. Unrenewed leases, illicit stills, controversial elections, treacherous friends and conflicted lovers are spiced by the exotic presence of Hycy Burke, a self-styled 'chartered libertine' who tells his mother that a neighbouring family 'is but an upstart one at best; it wants antiquity, ma'am'.[11] Sober Bryan McMahon, to Hycy a 'clodhopping boor' of the mountain farm of Ahadarra (vol. II, p. 539), is beset by many trials and narrowly avoids having to emigrate. He is a representative of the 'independent class of farmers and yeomen' which for Ireland is 'the very class of persons that constitute its remaining strength' (vol. II, p. 572). At the end of the novel the landlord tells his father, 'the country cannot spare such men as you and your admirable son' (vol. II, p. 639).

McMahon is denounced from the altar by the local curate and subsequently dragged from the chapel and beaten for the way he has voted at the election. However, the narrative denounces such priests as 'low and bigoted firebrands' and reassures the reader that 'Such scenes are repulsive to the educated priest' (vol. II, p. 600). Indeed, the cleric in question is reprimanded and the parish priest assures everyone that 'a single word of politics I shall never suffer to be preached from the altar while I live' (vol. II, p. 637). Of more significance, perhaps, is the way in which Kathleen Cavanagh, whose impending marriage to McMahon is delayed by disputes over his voting behaviour, is criticised. Dora McMahon wishes 'she'd be more of a woman and less of a saint' (vol. II, p. 602) and caustically hopes she will marry the pope 'for I don't know any other husband that's fit for her' (vol. II, p. 622). In these respects the novel anticipates the satiric tone of some intelligentsia novelists of half a century later.

Victorian Catholic fiction

In the interim, fiction writing by Catholics tended to become the preserve of those who were keen to vindicate the Victorian respectability of Ireland, and especially of the Irish peasantry as the most politically visible class as far as English audiences were concerned. Many of these were upper-middle-class women writers, clustered around *The Irish Monthly*, a review founded in 1873 by the Jesuit litterateur Matthew Russell (1834–1912). They included M. E. Francis, Attie O'Brien and Katharine Tynan, though May Laffan derided Catholic pretensions to respectability. By the 1880s, some of these novelists were projecting a conclusion to the land war conducive to their class interests. *Marcella Grace* (1886) by Rosa Mulholland, one of the most important of these Catholic gentry novels, imagines the advantages of a new class of Catholic landlords.[12] Its heroine, a poor Dublin Catholic girl, inherits a large estate and manages it well in the face of opposition from almost all shades of political opinion.

Novels were little read in the wider community, apart from *Knocknagow* (1873) by Charles Kickham (1828–82), which achieved an unlikely totemic status, given its author's controversial status as a Fenian at odds with the Church. Russell's 1887 preface to the novel, with its recollections of Kickham's religious faith, helped create a more acceptably pious version of the author.[13] The novel is a saga of Irish rural life, of venal land agents and long-suffering lease holders, of evictions, poverty and emigration. The key to its success was its capacity to present an oppressed community that was riven with conflict, and yet simultaneously united and harmonious. This duality mirrored that of the self-image of the Ireland that emerged triumphant from the land war and whose values would soon be so execrated by the Catholic intelligentsia. It was an Ireland of shopkeepers and farmers who saw themselves as the heirs to a noble history of suffering but who, in the peasant ownership of farms, the fruit of the land war, had reached a settlement which must not be disturbed.

Unlike Griffin in *The Collegians*, Kickham is demonstrative in the central role he gives to Catholic religious practice in the life of the locality. The chief communal events in the opening chapters of the book are the Christmas morning mass in Kilthubber chapel and a station mass held in the home of the principal family in the novel, the middle-class Kearneys. These latter masses were biannual events in particular parts of a parish, to enable people to go to confession and communion. The mass at the Kearneys is conduced with decorum and piety, the confessions are heard with propriety and the priests involved are noted for their frugality and lack of avarice. Before the 'devotional revolution' these were three issues about which concern was very often raised. *Knocknagow* thus subtly acknowledges the reforms, as well as the greater religious uniformity, of the previous quarter century.

As Catholicism became normalised within Irish life (outside Ulster), there was little reason to use fiction to defend or protect it. Those who did tended to be priests who had worked outside Ireland for a time and who had a sense of the fragility of Catholicism in the modern world. Among them were R. B. O'Brien (1809–85), an advocate of the ultramontanism of Pope Pius IX, and Joseph Guinan (1863–1932), who valorised the emotional bond between priests and people in Irish Catholic culture as a defence against attack. Canon [P. A.] Sheehan (1852–1913), the best known of such novelists, also valued that bond but suspected its capacity to withstand the assault of modernity.[14] The heroes of his fiction, many of them priests, thus find themselves torn between the bond and a middle-class intellectualism, though the strategy of embracing intellectualism in order to defend the faith often turns into an alluring obstacle to it.

In *Geoffrey Austin, Student* (1895), the eponymous hero moves away from his faith, while his friend Charlie Travers comes to see the need for 'zealous Catholic laymen in Ireland' because the country is not living up to its 'great vocation as the Catholic nation of the West'.[15] Charlie is also a nationalist, though of a particular religious kind, identifying British values as a threat to Ireland and advocating a cultural quarantining of Ireland from Britain which, outside fiction, was to become typical in Ireland for the first half of the twentieth century. *The Triumph of Failure* (1899) is a sequel. Here, Geoffrey immerses himself in philosophy and gets a reputation for being a free thinker before his conversion back to Catholicism, while Charlie burns all his non-religious books and becomes a lay missionary, inveighing against the paganism of modern civilisation, before his own premature death. Central to his mission is an attempt to distinguish between a true and false intellectualism: 'What shall it be when the intelligence of Ireland, emancipated from the shackles of a false education, shall go forth to stir the world with the watchword: Christ and Rome?'[16] In spite of such enthusiasm for a militant Catholicism, however, the novel ends on a pessimistic note about whether Ireland can live up to such a vision.

What made Sheehan's subsequent and largely unwarranted popular reputation for bland affability was his semi-humorous *My New Curate* (1900), in which the contentment and wisdom of the priest narrator is contrasted with the zeal and inexperience of his reforming curate. Most of the latter's initiatives end in disaster, including a fishing vessel designed to boost the local economy but which sinks. The curate ultimately learns the lesson from a paralysed local woman that true sanctity is to be found in a certain type of passivity and that, as with Charlie Travers, defeat and even death are not inimical to a true Christian victory.

Sheehan returned to intellectualism and its perils in *Luke Delmege* (1901). Its priest-hero begins his career with the assertive certainties of his seminary education. He is sent to work in England, where he is overawed by the social refinement of the friends he makes there, and comes to believe that faith and intellect can easily be reconciled. However, his social pretensions and intellectual pride lead to disaster when one of his friends goes to found a new religion called Eclectic Catholicism, under what he claims is Luke's influence. In order to be saved he has to purge himself of his Anglicisation, abandon intellectualism and return to the simplicities of life and faith in Catholic Ireland. There, he looks forward to 'the creation of a new civilisation, founded on Spartan simplicity of life, and Christian elevation of morals, and the uplifting to the higher life, to which all the aspirations of his race tended'.[17] *The Blindness of Dr Gray* (1909) also acknowledges that intellectualism may be more of an instrument of modernity than a weapon against it. In Sheehan's last novel, *The Graves of Kilmorna* (1915), Ireland is seen to be a place more of selfishness than idealism. Sheehan's fiction thus ends on a pessimistic note, disappointed by the inability both of intellectualism and of Irish Catholic culture to resist the corrupting effects of modernity.

Catholicism and the new Ireland

Though still somewhat in the tradition of the Catholic gentry novel, *When We Were Boys* (1890) by William O'Brien (1852–1928) is the first major example of the sort of novel the social, political and religious attitudes of which would become typical of the style of Catholic intelligentsia novels during the next thirty years.[18] In these novels, what was derided as Ireland's new puritanical and philistine establishment of lower-middle-class shopkeepers, farmers and priests becomes the problem, succeeding the now largely defunct landlord class.[19] This pessimistic analysis was balanced by the sense that the new establishment was far from secure and that these years (roughly 1890–1920) were a time of change and potential. This was the age of Gaelic League, of the cooperative movement, of the Anglo-Irish literary revival and even of hope for a more liberal spirit within the Church itself, to which many intelligentsia novelists were committed. Catholic intelligentsia writers, a largely male group, believed that a new form of society was about to emerge and that their novels could make a contribution towards it. By defining what true Ireland was, a new Ireland might be born.

During this time, the novel came to be seen as a vehicle for semi-fictional autobiographies of the struggle with Catholic Ireland for a new Ireland. These struggles, however, often ended in various forms of failure, as Catholic Ireland proved to be more intractable than had been imagined. This autobiographical dimension was the reason for the great success of *Father Ralph* (1913), by the former priest Gerald O'Donovan (1871–1942). The novel follows the education of Ralph O'Brien, a member of a relatively wealthy family who becomes a priest of the fictional diocese of Bunnahone and then leaves the priesthood in disillusionment. The clergy, with a few notable exceptions, are boorish, unintelligent and venal, and aligned with the interests of the stronger farmers and shopkeepers. Ralph is sustained by his friendship with a number of pastorally minded and intellectual priests and far-sighted laymen. One of the priests wants to build 'a Church that feels and voices the aspirations of every man of good-will in the world'. Meanwhile, the editor of a radical newspaper hopes to 'make religion intelligible in the light of progress'.[20]

Ralph's own efforts at reform, however, and especially the club for working men which he founds, are crushed and the progressive theology which has sustained him is condemned as modernism by the Pope. His suspension over the theology issue and subsequent departure from the priesthood are greeted with incomprehension by his clerical colleagues: 'If it was drink now, or women, there'd be some meaning in it! But theology!' (p. 367). The novel ends with Ralph on the boat for Holyhead, declaring 'I have found myself at last' (p. 376). The departure of the defeated reformer, but free individual, into exile would become a standard plot resolution in such books. O'Donovan himself had been a nationally known progressive priest; his own departure from the priesthood had none of the climactic quality of Ralph's theological dispute. After some successful years as an author, much of the rest of his life was to be spent in a disappointing lassitude.[21]

In *Waiting* (1914), O'Donovan moves over the same territory as his previous novel, though this time from the point of view of a layman. Maurice Blake, in conflict with a tyrannical and ambitious parish priest, Fr James Mahon, is suspicious of almost everything from the Irish language movement to agricultural improvement. Blake loses his job as a teacher when he marries a Protestant without the requisite ecclesiastical approval under the recent papal decree, *Ne Temere* (1907). O'Donovan brings the novel to an almost histrionic climax when Blake loses an election to parliament and Fr Mahon refuses the last rites to an old friend who had supported Blake.

Towards the end, the novel moves in the direction of satire, especially in the description of the priests who are brought in to preach against Blake's candidacy. Earlier on, though, O'Donovan shows an interest in delineating Blake's complex reaction to expressions of religious faith which appear naïve to a person of his educational level. Thus, when he is given a religious medal he tries to throw it away but then keeps it: 'He felt angry and sought round in his mind for a cause. Not with the superstition. That was even interesting. There might be a good deal of folk lore in that' (p. 211). The satiric trend in O'Donovan's writing, itself a sign of a waning interest in battling the issues involved, reaches it apogee in *Vocations* (1921), a hilarious account of convent life somewhat in the style of the young Evelyn Waugh.

In their differing ways Aodh de Blacam, Patrick MacGill, Edward MacLysaght, Brinsley MacNamara, Eimar O'Duffy and Seumas O'Kelly made contributions to Catholic intelligentsia fiction in the decade before Irish independence. They were preceded by W. P. Ryan (1867–1942), a radical journalist who was the kind of religious and social reformer whom O'Donovan imagines in his novels; one of Ryan's newspapers was closed under pressure from the Archbishop of Armagh. *The Plough and the Cross: A Story of New Ireland* (1910) is his own, albeit less well-known, equivalent to *Father Ralph*. Ryan's hero is the editor Fergus O'Hagan, a thinly disguised self-portrait, who mixes with theosophists, altruistic industrialists and reforming priests interested in social Christianity and 'immanentism', a central tenet of theological modernism.[22] An important concern of the novel is the need for a real intellectual engagement with religion. As one reformer laments: 'A man with a fair intellect must really turn away in despair or weariness from the majority of Irish sermons and the generality of stuff that is called "Catholic literature".'[23]

This is confirmed by the sinister bishop who warns O'Hagan off after the publication of an 'unsound and unIrish' article (p. 254). The bishop privately admits that the article is 'bold and cruelly true' (p. 311): 'our religion in Ireland has been emotional and in a measure sentimental' (p. 304). But education will disturb the social order, and O'Hagan stands 'in the way of episcopal and British and Vatican policy in Ireland' (p. 312). He ends with almost risible menace: '[w]e can generally do it in a quiet way; it is seldom necessary to hit an editor very hard' (p. 311). Though ultimately defeated, O'Hagan remains in Ireland in a sort of internal exile, rendered possible by his immanentist views: 'the great Ireland is in ourselves, and it is full of beauty, divine activity and boundless hope. The outer Ireland, agitated or stagnant, is something incidental to keep our souls in training' (p. 373).

Moore and Joyce

Versions of other historical characters appear in Ryan's novel, including George Moore (1852–1933) in the guise of Geoffrey Mortimer, who is well summed up by O'Hagan as having been 'pathetically full of Ireland' (p. 20) when he had arrived some years before to participate in the Anglo-Irish literary revival, but is now leaving the island. Moore's *The Lake* (1905, rev. 1921) fits the pattern of Catholic intelligentsia fiction, though, as his relatively exalted social position protected him from the ill effects of rebellion, it lacks the intensity of O'Donovan's and Ryan's work and shows none of their initial concern with reforming Catholic Ireland. Its central character is Fr Oliver Gogarty, who is in part based on O'Donovan. Gogarty engages in a correspondence from which he learns much with a young woman who appears as Rose Leicester in the 1905 version of the book and as Nora Glynn in the 1921 version. He had forced her to leave his parish where she worked as a teacher because she was pregnant and unmarried, an action he now regrets. His involvement with her moves from concern for her faith – especially as she works for a literary figure who is an atheist – to an acknowledgment of the human emptiness of his own existence. He has nothing to look forward to but 'the Mass and the rosary at the end of his tongue, and nothing in his heart'.[24] Losing his faith and acknowledging his love for her, he comes to believe that 'there is no moral law except one's own conscience' (p. 173). The novel ends with his dramatic bid for freedom, staging his own apparent drowning in a lake so that he can escape to become a journalist in New York.

Moore had initially intended the story to cap his collection of short fictions, *The Untilled Field* (1903), in which both peasants and members of the intelligentsia struggle against the common strictures of Catholic Ireland. In *The Lake*, the former teacher's employer researches a book on the origins of Christianity, though it may 'disturb people in their belief in the traditions and symbols that have held sway for centuries' (p. 87). Moore thought it incumbent upon himself to perform a similar task and produced *The Brook Kerith* (1916). In it, he deploys 'the swoon theory', a scenario which had never enjoyed much credit among scholars, to explain Jesus's resurrection. Here, Jesus regains consciousness after his crucifixion and goes off to make a new life for himself, while his followers wrongly suppose that he has risen from the dead and found a religion in his memory. The novel reaches unintentionally comic heights towards the end, when St Paul has to explain Christianity to a bemused Jesus, who himself tends to prefer Gogarty's doctrine that conscience is what really matters.

It should by now be apparent how well James Joyce's seminal *Bildungsroman*, *A Portrait of the Artist as a Young Man* (1916) fits into the pattern of the Catholic intelligentsia novel, though it is by no means confined to it. Most critics have tended to see Joyce as *sui generis*, standing aloof from the Irish Revival and forging his own artistic path. However, even the trope of the solitary path, of 'silence, exile and cunning', of forging 'in the smithy of my soul the uncreated conscience of my race', is a familiar device, as has already been noted.[25] Indeed, Joyce's Stephen Dedalus makes a joke about Holyhead, whither Ralph O'Brien is travelling at the end of O'Donovan's earlier novel.[26] And, rather like O'Brien, Stephen moves through a variety of attitudes to religion through childhood, adolescence and young adulthood.

A Portrait makes a number of original contributions to the genre of the Catholic intelligentsia novel. One is representation of the relationship between sense experience and religious memory and imagination: 'There was a cold night smell in the chapel. But it was a holy smell', reflects Stephen early on (p. 15). Another is Joyce's delineation of the relationship between sexuality, guilt and religion in adolescence. 'The preacher's knife had probed deeply into his diseased conscience and he felt now that his soul was festering in sin' (p. 123). In the end though, Stephen's parting from religion occurs quietly and almost coldly: we are told that 'he felt the silent lapse of his soul' (p. 175). Stephen's rebellion is a general rather than exclusive one, and he embraces Fr Arnall's summation of Lucifer's sin, *'non serviam: I will not serve'* (p. 126), as his own manifesto: 'I will not serve that in which I no longer believe whether it call itself my home, my fatherland or my church' (p. 268). However, this rebellion is not part of the more general reforming mission often seen in other Catholic intelligentsia novels, where the achievement of individual freedom is often counted as a marker towards a more general change. Stephen's freedom leads him towards the vocation of an artist, which he envisions significantly in terms borrowed from the religious tradition he has left behind – he will be 'a priest of the eternal imagination' (p. 240), thus subtly harnessing religion to the service of art. Stephen's final prayer is to the mythic and pagan Daedalus for aid for what is to come: 'Old father, old artificer, stand me now and ever in good stead' (p. 276). This is a form of looking to the future not generally achieved at the end of Catholic intelligentsia novels, with their focus on what had turned out to be the less promising world of social reality. After Irish independence in 1922, that world seemed even less conducive and the tradition of such novels came to an end.

NOTES

1. Gerald Griffin, *The Collegians* (1829; Belfast: Appletree Press, 1992), p. 212.
2. Emmet Larkin, 'The Devotional Revolution in Ireland', *American Historical Review* 80 (1975), 625–52.

3. Gerald O'Donovan, *Father Ralph* (1913; Dingle: Brandon, 1993), p. 28.
4. See James M. Cahalan, *Great Hatred, Little Room: The Irish Historical Novel* (Dublin: Gill and Macmillan, 1983), pp. 43–66; Ina Ferris, *The Romantic National Tale and the Question of Ireland* (Cambridge: Cambridge University Press, 2002), pp. 128–52; Thomas Flanagan, *The Irish Novelists, 1800–1850* (1959; Westport, CT: Greenwood Press, 1976), pp. 167–251; James H. Murphy, *Ireland: A Social, Cultural and Literary History, 1791–1891* (Dublin: Four Courts Press, 2003), pp. 49–64; Barry Sloan, *The Pioneers of Anglo-Irish Fiction, 1800–1850* (Gerrards Cross: Colin Smythe, 1986), pp. 76–130.
5. John Banim, *The Boyne Water* (1825; New York: Sadlier, 1881), p. 13.
6. John Banim, *The Nowlans* (1826; Belfast: Appletree Press, 1992), p. 10.
7. Murphy, *Ireland*, pp. 82–3; Robert Lee Wolff, *William Carleton: Irish Peasant Novelist. A Preface to his Fiction* (New York: Garland, 1980), p. 52.
8. William Carleton, *Fardorougha the Miser* (1839; Belfast: Appletree Press, 1993), p. 77.
9. William Carleton, preface to *Valentine M'Clutchy, The Irish Agent* (1845), in *The Works of William Carleton* (New York: Collier, 1881), vol. II.
10. William Carleton, *The Black Prophet: A Tale of Irish Famine* (1847), in *The Works of William Carleton* (New York: Collier, 1881), vol. III, p. 827.
11. William Carleton, *The Emigrants of Ahadarra*, in *The Works of William Carleton* (New York: Collier, 1881), vol. II, pp. 617, 507.
12. James H. Murphy, *Catholic Fiction and Social Reality in Ireland, 1873–1922* (Westport, CT: Greenwood Press, 1997), pp. 1–75.
13. Murphy, *Catholic Fiction*, pp. 79–88.
14. Murphy, *Catholic Fiction*, pp. 115–26.
15. Canon Sheehan, *Geoffrey Austin, Student* (1895; Dublin: M. H. Gill, 1914), p. 153.
16. Canon Sheehan, *The Triumph of Failure* (Dublin: Phoenix, 1899), p. 231.
17. Canon Sheehan, *Luke Delmege* (London: Longmans, Green, 1901), p. 459.
18. Murphy, *Catholic Fiction*, pp. 65–75.
19. Murphy, *Catholic Fiction*, pp. 89–113, 127–52.
20. O'Donovan, *Father Ralph*, pp. 252, 211.
21. Peter Costello, 'Gerald O'Donovan', in Robert Hogan (ed.), *Dictionary of Irish Literature* (Westport, CT: Greenwood Press, 1996), vol. II, pp. 947–9.
22. Immanentism looks inward to the human spirit for sustaining energy, meaning and even the divine. This general philosophical trend was associated in the nineteenth century with Henry Bergson and others. In the late nineteenth century, a movement known as modernism grew up within the Catholic Church, later condemned by Church authorities, which looked more towards human experience than doctrine for religious authority.
23. W. P. Ryan, *The Plough and the Cross: A Story of New Ireland* (Dublin: Irish Nation Office, 1910), p. 177.
24. George Moore, *The Lake* (1921; Gerrards Cross: Colin Smythe, 1980), p. 124.
25. James Joyce, *A Portrait of the Artist as a Young Man* (1916; London: Penguin, 1992), pp. 269, 276.
26. Stephen tells his Catholic friend Davin that the shortest way to Tara, associated with St Patrick and thus with Catholicism, is by way of Holyhead, associated

with Irish exile and emigration (p. 273). He is thereby presumably associating humorously – since he is not a Christian believer – his artistic exile with a form of Christian apotheosis.

GUIDE TO FURTHER READING

Boué, André. *William Carleton: Romancier Irlandais (1794–1869)*. Série Sorbonne 6. Paris: Publications de la Sorbonne, 1978.

Brown, Stephen J. *Ireland in Fiction: A Guide to Irish Novels, Tales, Romances and Folklore.* 1915. Dublin: Maunsel, 1919.

Corbett, Mary Jean. *Allegories of Union: Irish and English Writing, 1790–1870: Politics, History and the Family from Edgeworth to Arnold.* Cambridge: Cambridge University Press, 2000.

Cronin, John. *The Anglo-Irish Novel. Vol. 1: The Nineteenth Century.* Belfast: Appletree Press, 1980.

Cronin, John. *Gerald Griffin 1803–40: A Critical Biography.* Cambridge: Cambridge University Press, 1978.

Escarbelt, Bernard. *Les Frères Banim: témoins et peintres de l'Irlande.* Paris: Université de Paris III, 1985.

Foster, John Wilson. *Fictions of the Irish Literary Revival: A Changeling Art.* Dublin: Gill & Macmillan, 1987.

Hawthorne, Mark D. *John and Michael Banim (the 'O'Hara brothers'): A Study in the Early Development of the Anglo-Irish Novel.* Salzburg: Institut für Englische Sprache und Literatur, 1975.

Kirkpatrick, Kathryn, (ed.). *Border Crossings: Irish Women Writers and National Identity.* Tuscaloosa: University of Alabama Press, 2000.

Krause, David. *William Carleton, the Novelist, his Carnival and Pastoral World of Tragicomedy.* Lanham, MD: University Press of America, 2000.

Mercier, Vivian. *Modern Irish Literature: Sources and Founders.* Oxford: Clarendon, 1994.

Murray, P. J. *The Life of John Banim.* 1857. New York: Garland, 1978.

Tracy, Robert. *The Unappeasable Host: Studies in Irish Identities.* Dublin: University College Dublin Press, 1998.

Vance, Norman. *Irish Literature: A Social History.* 1990. Dublin: Four Courts, 1999.

6

ADRIAN FRAZIER

Irish modernisms, 1880–1930

The un-Englishness of Modernism

'Modernism' does not just refer to the literature of a certain period of time, say 1890 or 1910–1940. The '-ism' suggests it was a distinctive doctrine, or at least a distinctive practice. Yet it is best not to attempt a strict definition of the typical modernist work. No two writers wrote to one formula (though Ezra Pound, an impresario of the modern, tried to get many to do just that). Modernist works deploy devices or manifest traits that include the following: (a) perspectivalism: knowledge limited to the point of view of specific persons (the most radical form being 'stream of consciousness'); (b) juxtapositions without copulas: the omission of transitional matter that would indicate grammatical, chronological or logical relationships; (c) presentation of images or events without commentary or explanation; (d) style of presentation so radically in service of subject matter that, paradoxically, style becomes the subject of attention; (e) parody of popular literary styles and, by implication, mockery of the general readership that made such styles popular; (f) learned allusions to literary classics; (g) mythic parallels to contemporary life and demythologising treatment of Christianity; (h) a governing principle of 'art for art's sake': self-conscious neglect of a utilitarian purpose for the work, such as to teach a moral or move the public to action; and (i) the manifestation of literary art in every sentence or line, as Joseph Conrad demanded of prose writers equally with poets.[1]

The phenomenon of works with such attributes has been assigned a history of causes and effects by literary historians. The beginnings are said to be a revolt against Victorian values and forms in the 1890s and a reaction to the accelerating modernisation of society during the Edwardian period (1901–10). The catastrophe of the First World War (1914–18), it is claimed, made writers across Europe and North America struggle to find forms to represent disillusion with, and distaste for, the present. Across the West, new times required new forms. So while Victorianism is a British phenomenon, Modernism is an international one.

Most English literary modernists were not English. Among the poets, Eliot and Pound were American and Yeats was Irish. Of the great novelists of the period, Henry James was American, Joseph Conrad was Polish, Ford Madox Ford was both German and English, George Moore and James Joyce both Irish, while Woolf and Lawrence are the only major modernist novelists who were English. Furthermore, the modernists were not writing solely out of the tradition of English literature. They sought models in other languages: Irish, Chinese, Italian, Russian and especially French – Gustave Flaubert, Emile Zola and Maupassant were particularly influential pacesetters. They also attended to the literary implications of the Paris art movement called 'Modern Painting' or 'Impressionism'. Subsequent twentieth-century art movements like Cubism inspired further literary equivalents, as painting led and literature followed. Schopenhauer and Nietzsche, both pessimistic German philosophers with brilliant prose styles, enchanted Moore, Conrad, W. B. Yeats, Eliot and, to a lesser degree, Joyce.[2] For the most part, the Englishness of the English-born writers seems to have restrained them from following the example of German thinkers or French artists, whatever their disgust with Victorian conventions in manners, morals and art. As a result, the great writers of early twentieth-century literature are not Edwardian or Georgian, as Browning and Tennyson are Victorian. The great works of twentieth-century fiction in English are often not by English people or about English life as lived under English monarchs.

Moore and Modernism

If one removes from English literature for the period 1890 to 1950 the works of Irish writers – Oscar Wilde, George Moore, W. B. Yeats, James Joyce, George Bernard Shaw and Samuel Beckett – half the major achievements disappear. Is there a subcategory of international Modernism (vague category though that already is) that is identifiably Irish? This question would normally require a book-length answer, but as this chapter concerns fiction alone, there are only two main cases to consider, George Moore and James Joyce, and Joyce is dealt with separately in this volume. Irish Modernism in fiction for our purposes comes down to George Moore. The fictions of Yeats, Wilde, Bram Stoker, Somerville and Ross and James Stephens exhibit one or two aspects of modernist style; Moore's novels have the full complement.

Moore (1852–1933) was the oldest son of a Catholic member of parliament from Moore Hall, County Mayo. He spent his childhood partly at

Moore Hall and partly at a Brighton boarding school, with spells at a Kensington townhouse. Upon the sudden death of his father, Moore became at eighteen the landlord of a vast estate with thousands of tenants in the impoverished west of Ireland, just then beginning its swift decline in land values, rents and social stability. Moore, however, did not then return to Ireland; at twenty-one, he moved from London to Paris to become a painter. There he began the journey of a quintessential modernist author.

Upper-class and downwardly mobile, with a gift for ingratiation, between 1873 and 1879 Moore became closely acquainted with modern French writers and painters. He knew Mallarmé, Zola, Degas, Manet, Pissarro and Monet. At cafés, he participated in their arguments about the theory of modern art and how to represent the new urban, bourgeois, commodified, transformed world of Paris after the Commune (1870–1). Moore became a hero-worshipper of Baudelaire and Flaubert, the predecessors of modern French art. By the time the Irish Land War cut off his income and forced his return from Paris in 1879, Moore was more thoroughly versed in contemporary European aestheticism than any other English-speaking person. In 1881, he decided to become a novelist and introduce modern art to (as he saw it) a stuffy and conventional English public.

His first novel, *A Modern Lover* (1883), bears in its title this intention: a story so entitled will not be the old thing once again, and it will be risqué, as Victorian literature was not permitted to be. The story concerns a painter in London who entices one woman after another to be his lover and advance his career. 'Happily ever after' is not how his marriage turns out. The background to the story is a struggle between the 'Moderns' – a group of painters sometimes like French Impressionists, at other times like English pre-Raphaelites – and the Traditionalists. The narrator is clearly on the side of the Moderns.

With his next novel, *A Mummer's Wife* (1885), Moore furnished a textbook illustration of Zolaesque naturalism in telling the story of Kate Ede, the wife of a disabled linen-draper from a town in northern England who runs off with an actor. Like Flaubert's *Madame Bovary* (1845), the book includes a running parody of popular romances, so that healthy truth is opposed to the morally sickening illusions of most fiction. Like Zola's *Thérèse Raquin*, Kate Ede undergoes a change of character when her environment changes, and dies a dipsomaniac. This second novel, like Moore's first, was banned by the companies that monopolised book distribution, establishing typically adversarial relations between modernising art and providers of traditional popular entertainment.

Moore's first two novels have nothing Irish about their idioms, subject matter or narrative traditions, but there is something of the Irish landlord about the attitude they take up toward English life. That attitude is coldly intelligent, estranged, condescending and contemptuous of moral hypocrisy (which Moore assumes is a way of life in Victorian England). The habitual point of view of the Protestant English coloniser had been to look down – in ridicule laced with fear – upon the colonised Catholics of Ireland. Many Irish writers had been compelled when publishing their books in London to resort to disarming self-ridicule, gentle humour or harmless fancifulness in order to make their appeal. Even Wilde and Shaw sugared the pill of their own contemptuous writings on English life with witticisms. As a socially confident landowner, however, with his cultural ancestry in Paris, Moore made no such concessions. His early fiction is a deadly and humourless realism. It became one of the characteristics of modernist fiction as a whole that it left out the humour of earlier English fiction (for example, Dickens and Thackeray) and projected the novel as a serious art form.

A Drama in Muslin (1886) is the first of Moore's three novels about Ireland. (He wrote fifteen novels in all.) It depicts Irish society on the eve of Home Rule, from the point of view of 'the passionless observer, who, unbiased by any political creed, comments impartially on the matter submitted to him for analysis'.[3] The immediate 'matter for analysis' is the choice of a future for Alice Barton, one of three daughters in a family of minor Catholic gentry who go to a debutante ball in Dublin Castle in the hope of arranging matches, as if dynastic marriages among the gentry and British officers would make one's future safe in the revolutionary Ireland that is vividly etched in the novel's background. Because of its accuracy of observation, variety of Flaubertian set pieces (a play in a convent school, a dress fitting, a Castle ball, an eviction, etc.) and intellectual courage, A Drama in Muslin has won a place in the canon of Irish literature. Declan Kiberd, for instance, gives it a chapter in Irish Classics (2001). However, A Drama in Muslin bears little resemblance to other nineteenth-century Irish fiction. Not until Joyce's Ulysses (1922) would such an artistically ambitious novel about the Irish totality be undertaken. Modernism of form aside, A Drama in Muslin was too modern by far in morals and politics to be welcome either in England or Ireland. Its point of view is against God, Catholicism, landlordism and Dublin Castle, and in favour of free love, vocations for women, metropolitan life and science (as in so many naturalist works, the liberated woman marries a medical doctor and goes off to the city). There was something in it to offend everyone.

While A Drama in Muslin had no traceable impact on contemporaries, Moore's autobiographical Confessions of a Young Man (1888) was a major influence on the younger generation of modern authors. Two of those who learned from the book are Arthur Symons (the quintessential nineties man of letters) and James Joyce, whose *A Portrait of the Artist as a Young Man* (1916) echoes much more than the title of his forerunner's book. Masquerading as an autobiography of Moore's first thirty years, *Confessions of a Young Man* is a guidebook to becoming a bohemian author decorated with all the latest fads: 'Naturalism I wore round my neck, Romanticism was pinned over the heart, Symbolism I carried like a toy revolver in my waistcoat pocket.'[4] *Confessions* taught young men the lifestyle of the aesthetic avant-garde: how to dress, how to decorate a bachelor flat, how to be effeminately male, what to read, what to buy, how to deal with publishers and how to write in many styles. The various chapters on Moore's experiences in Ireland, Paris and London are an anthology of contemporary literary styles in Europe, with the implied lesson that form should suit function.

The narrator of *Confessions* presents his round-up of contemporary fiction in English in chapter 10 and concludes with praise for Walter Pater's *Marius the Epicurean* (1885) as the first work of English prose he had ever read that gave him genuine pleasure by its language, 'the combination of words for golden or silver chime, and unconventional cadence' (p. 166). It was for him a sacred book in a special modernist sense; that is, a profane work in which completeness of artifice gives to the words an aura, a sanctity and presence above and beyond their signification. What Moore had to offer was a bible to young male hell-raisers, so the *Confessions* both imitates and parodies the concept of a sacred book.

'The School of Pater'

Moore may have been the first of the major modern Irish writers to admire Pater, but, remarkably, nearly all of them came to do so, including Wilde, Yeats, J. M. Synge and Joyce. They all paid heed to his elegant and passionate appeal in the famous conclusion to *The Renaissance* (1878) for the young to become individuals on whom nothing is lost, not one pulsation of experience, and, as the wisest course, to spend their short lives in the making of art, which for Pater was the beautiful stylisation of one's own sharpest impressions.[5] The young Irish writers would also have agreed with Pater that the word *renaissance* should not refer to the revival of antiquity in Italy, England or Ireland; it was the name

> of a many-sided but yet united movement, in which the love of the things of the intellect and the imagination for their own sake, the desire for a more liberal and comely way of conceiving life, make themselves felt, urging those who experience this desire not only to the discovery of old and forgotten sources of enjoyment, but to the divination of fresh sources thereof – new experiences, new subjects of poetry, new forms of art. (p. 1)

The search for art as the best life, and a personal search for what was new, led all the Irish followers of Pater in the direction of Modernism. Their commitments were to something other than morality, nationality or religion: more than anything else, they wanted to be great writers. That is one of the chief distinctions between the forgotten foot soldiers of the Irish Renaissance and its Nobel prize winners and saints of modernism.

Their strict aestheticism was brilliantly set forth by Oscar Wilde (1854–1900) in the epigrammatic preface to his 'poisonous book', *The Picture of Dorian Gray* (1891):[6]

> No artist desires to prove anything.
> No artist has ethical sympathies. An ethical sympathy in an artist is an unpardonable mannerism of style.
> All art is at once surface and symbol.
> All art is quite useless.
> Diversity of opinion about a work of art shows that the work is new, complex, and vital.

Critical opinion about *Dorian Gray* was certainly diverse. The novel tells the story of Dorian and two men, the painter Basil Hallward and the cynical aesthete Lord Henry Wotton. Hallward paints a portrait expressing his admiration for the young man's beauty; Wotton, who equally admires Dorian's charms, teaches him to gratify every impulse, for nothing is forbidden. Dorian breaks hearts, kills, feasts, drinks and smokes, all through the years of dissipation keeping his bloom of youth. Meanwhile, in the attic his portrait turns old and ugly with sin. When Basil Hallward sees the ruin of Dorian's life in the ravaged portrait, Dorian murders the painter. Finally, stabbing the canvas with a knife, Dorian kills himself.

Many reviewers thought *The Picture of Dorian Gray* a fetid celebration of drugs, decadence and homosexuality; some young Oxonians (for example, part-Irish Lionel Johnson, utterly English Lord Alfred Douglas) took it as a *delightful* celebration of these things. What was most modernist about the tale – paradoxically, it is an obvious morality tale – was its extension of the model of Pater's *Marius the Epicurean*, an account of the growth of the hero's soul. Wilde's narrative style was even more ornately ritualistic than Pater's.[7] While the story involves suicide, murder and corruption, in the foreground one finds only long passages of unrealistically epigrammatic dialogue and longer passages of airless description, apparently for the sake of the rarefied nouns and adjectives in the description. Here is the second sentence of the novel:

> From the corner of the divan of Persian saddlebags on which he was lying, smoking, as was his custom, innumerable cigarettes, Lord Henry Wotton

could just catch the gleam of the honey-sweet and honey-coloured blossoms of a laburnum, whose tremulous branches seemed hardly able to bear the burden of a beauty so flame-like as theirs, and now and then the fantastic shadows of birds in flight flitted across the long tussore-silk curtains that were stretched in front of the huge window, producing a kind of momentary Japanese effect, and making him think of those pallid jade-faced painters of Tokio who, through the medium of an art that is necessarily immobile, seek to convey the sense of swiftness and motion.

The far-fetched similitude between nature (shadows of birds on drapes) and art (Japanese painting), with all its attendant and irrelevant detail – 'jade-faced'? – is typical of a book that is more professedly art-fiction than any English novel before it.

The early art-fiction of W. B. Yeats (1865–1939) grew out of his edited collections of Irish stories and lore about Irish faeries. With *The Secret Rose* (1897) and *Rosa Alchemica, The Tables of the Law* and *The Adoration of the Magi* (published in one volume in 1897), his prose proceeded to emulate that of Pater. 'The Crucifixion of the Outcast', an aesthetic version of a medieval Irish fable, resembles *Imaginary Portraits* (1887), although Yeats's prose is not so opaque or syntactically devious as Pater's. Still, the long lists and parallel repetitions so frequent in the Irish tale are both aggressively anti-realist rhetorical figures. They create the effect of a dreamlike beauty of mood. For instance, here is a speech by Cumhal, son of Cormac, a medieval minstrel who is about to be crucified by Irish friars outside an abbey. The minstrel, surrounded by the friars and curious outcasts, is trying to decide to whom to give the food in his wallet:

> I am myself the poorest, for I have traveled the bare road, and by the edges of the sea; and the tattered doublet of parti-coloured cloth upon my back and the torn pointed shoes upon my feet have ever irked me, because of the towered city full of noble raiment that was in my heart. And I have been the more alone upon the roads and by the sea because I heard in my heart the rustling of the rose-bordered dress of her who is more subtle than Aengus the Subtle-hearted, and more full of the beauty of laughter than Conan the Bald, and more full of the wisdom of tears than White-breasted Deirdre, and more lovely than a bursting dawn to them that are lost in the darkness. Therefore, I award the tithe to myself; but yet, because I am done with all these things, I give it to you.[8]

With which weirdly complacent oration, he flings some strips of bacon to the beggars, then undergoes the nailing to the cross.

The significance of Yeats's medieval parable is characteristically modernist: in modern times, the artist is a martyr to the beauty he invents. The poet-figure is truth-telling, woman-loving, impoverished yet aristocratic, hated by the religious (who fear his rhymes), yet also rejected by the crowds of poor, by the birds and by the other creatures of the earth, who at the end eat his crucified body.

Social origins of Irish Modernism

The aesthetic fiction produced by Irish writers in the late nineteenth century (call them 'the School of Pater')[9] had certain elements of modernist form: style as subject, mythic parallels to contemporary life, the philosophy of 'art for art's sake', realist parody of popular literary styles and literary art sustained throughout the prose. It did not, however, feel an obligation to treat modern Irish life directly. The writers who did that best in the 1890s were Edith Somerville (1858–1949) and 'Martin Ross' (pseud. Violet Martin, 1862–1915), second cousins who wrote books collaboratively.

In 1894, Somerville and Ross produced *The Real Charlotte*, the finest depiction of Irish gentry society during this decade of its swift decline. Charlotte Mullen is astonishingly detestable for a title character. She is a shabby and Hibernicised middle-class Protestant of forty years, very ugly in face and worse in nature. Her principal business is secretly lending out money at interest to the very poor or to friends in a fix, but she also schemes and steals and betrays in order to climb up higher in the social scale of a West Cork village. Her shambling 'Tally Ho Lodge', overrun with cats, is as far from being a big house as it is from being a thatched cottage. The driving interest in the plot is Charlotte's relationship to her lively young Dublin cousin and ward, Francie Fitzpatrick, whom everyone loves at first sight and whom Charlotte therefore hates. Charlotte cheats Francie out of her inheritance and then pushes her to marry the feeble but sensitive heir of Bruff Castle. Francie prefers a young captain in the British army, garrisoned near the village. In his absence, she flirts with the local canon; any man, in fact, attracted to Francie attracts her in return. The captain – a cad – deserts Francie, who is then successfully pursued in wedlock by the local land-agent, upon whom Charlotte had set her own sights. So Charlotte schemes to bring about the destruction of Francie, her own cousin and a most innocent soul.

The novel was obviously written in a spirit of hatred for the specific person on whom Charlotte was modelled,[10] but if the feeling is personal, the observation of social types, manners and speech in Dublin suburbs and the Irish countryside is clear-sighted and entertaining. The subject matter is contemporary ('modern' would not be the word for Cork in the 1890s) and the social types represented belong to one moment, and not to a period before or after that moment. The narrative form, however, is not modernist. The book is written as Jane Austen would have written it had she lived in Castletownsend, Co. Cork, at the end the nineteenth century, rather than Steventon, Hampshire, at the start of the nineteenth century. In fact, *The Real Charlotte* alludes several times to Austen's famous ironic epigram, 'that a single man in possession of a good fortune must be in want of a wife'. Most of the single men in the Irish tale, as in *Pride and Prejudice* (1813), are in no hurry to get to the altar. In fact, there is a remarkable infertility in all the houses represented in *The Real Charlotte* (the interior life of the cabins is not represented). This infertility is not thematised by the authors, but it implicitly depicts the Protestant population of Ireland as having lost its capacity to provide the next generation. The Ascendancy is on its last legs, decrepit, like its houses. In such fashion, *The Real Charlotte* silently registered the effect of the Land Acts of 1881, 1885 and 1891.

The rapid revolution in Irish property ownership, set in train by these acts, is the main social cause of the Irish Revival and a factor in the modernism of major Irish authors. The Irish Revival does not (*pace* Yeats) begin with the 1891 fall of Parnell, the leader of the Parliamentary Home Rule Party. The radical leader of the Land League, Michael Davitt, is its first mover. Nor does it prophetically culminate in Patrick Pearse and the Irish Rebellion of 1916, as Yeats's subsequent, more nationalist literary history proposed. In a speech celebrating the Irish Literary Theatre in May 1899, George Moore spun a theory to this effect. It was, he said, no surprise that the agrarian revolt of peasants had been followed by a movement inspired by the desire of art for art's sake. 'Having gained property, formerly landless people ask, "What is property for?"'[11] And those who had lost property, he might have added, asked what the spiritual legacy of that property had been. Indeed, if there is something Irish about Irish modernists, one of the most distinctively national traits is that they were living through a period when the material basis for their own social class was melting away.[12] They could descry that, sooner or later, Ireland would break from Britain, and the Catholics would be in a majority in the new and smaller electorate thus created. The old dominant class would then have not just less property, but less power too. Non-Irish historians of international Modernism are accustomed to naming as principal causes of the new stylistic features of twentieth-century writing the impact of the decline in faith and moral values during the Victorian period, and, more traumatically, the impact of the First World War. But those are less important to non-English writers, and most of the modernists, as indicated above, were not English. For the Irish modernists, the key social transformation was what Michael Davitt called 'the fall of feudalism' in Ireland. Wilde, Moore, Yeats, Shaw, Bram Stoker and others turned to literature to forge in new circumstances identities that were no longer secured in material and social realities.

Many turn-of-the-century Irish writers staged their works in the England of their residence rather than the Ireland of their birth, for example, all of Wilde's plays and most of Shaw's, the novels of Wilde, Shaw and Bram Stoker, and all but one of Moore's pre-1900 fictions. Recent Irish critics have often read such works as somehow about the Ireland they do not mention. *Dracula* (1897) by Bram Stoker (1847–1912) has particularly been targeted for re-nationalisation by means of allegorical readings. The tale requires no summary; everyone has seen at least one of the 250 films it inspired; and once imagined, the figure of the bloodthirsty vampire stays in the memory. Original reviews, while condescending to its literary mechanisms, acknowledged the qualities that made *Dracula* an immediate bestseller: that the horrid details and thrilling plot of maidens-at-risk made it a successfully spine-tingling fleshcreeper, like the best of Wilkie Collins or Sheridan Le Fanu.[13] In the last ten years, scholars have seen not just Irish matters in it, but much more – nearly everything, indeed. It is said to be about the threat to England of immigrant Germans, Jews, gypsies and syphilitics; about colonisation, reverse colonisation and empire at risk; about questionable genders and sexualities; about urbanisation, professionalisation, bureaucratisation and technologies of communication. Among the Irish interpretations, Dracula is said to be Parnell, Wilde or starving tenants; an upstart Catholic miscegenist or Ascendancy bloodsucker.

A more likely candidate for re-nationalisation courtesy of allegory might be *Esther Waters* (1894), George Moore's most successful book. The novel follows the fortunes of a servant in a large Sussex, horse-racing household. She becomes pregnant by the footman, loses her job, and goes to London to have her baby and then to support her son by her wages as a wet-nurse. The Sussex house in which the novel begins and ends is partly based on Moore Hall in Mayo; some of the house servants are modelled on specific Moore Hall servants. Moore's empathy with the underclass and recognition of the moral dignity of each individual's struggle for survival is exemplary of an Irish landlord who declined to shore up landlordism. The whole point of his novel is that the masses were really individuals who had as much right to live as any other. But for all that, *Esther Waters*, like *Dracula*, was not meant to be a comment on the Irish situation or an expression of the Irishness of its author, nor was it taken to be by anyone at the time of publication.

Irish modernist projects

The interrelationships between Victorian literature, literature by Irish people or literature about Ireland, and international modernist literature during the period between 1880 and 1920 can be illuminated by a look at the specific publishers of this literature. A key London publisher of Irish-interest books was Edmund Downey, a Waterford writer who began his editorial career with William Tinsley of Tinsley Brothers, which issued the novels of Mrs Braddon and the travels of Sir Richard Burton.[14] It had been Tinsley who in 1883 brought out George Moore's *A Modern Lover*. In 1885 Downey and a partner set up their own firm, Ward and Downey. The firm made a special place for Irish writers and its list included fanciful, verbose and humorously Irish works like those by J. Fitzgerald Molloy, John Augustus O'Shea and Downey himself; Irish antiquarian work by Lady Wilde and Standish O'Grady, modernising books such as Moore's *Mike Fletcher* (1889) and Arthur Lynch's *Modern Authors* (1891), and the first fruits of the 'Irish Revival', such as Yeats's poems (*A New Poet*, 1892) and W. P. Ryan's breathtakingly premature history of the movement, *The Irish Literary Revival* (1894). One can detect in the boil of publication by Irish people in London an inchoate Irish Modernism coming to the surface.

In the 1890s, two other young publishers established themselves and would become channels of new Irish writing to the wider English-reading public. The first, William Heinemann, had a particular sympathy for European literature and literature that aimed to achieve classic status. Heinemann published English translations of Hauptmann, Balzac, Ibsen, Freud and Turgenev, and new fiction by Henry James, H. G. Wells, Israel Zangwill and Bram Stoker. After the very positive critical reception given *The Real Charlotte*, Somerville and Ross changed from Edmund Downey's house to Heinemann, who brought out *The Big House of Inver* in 1925, which indicates the authors' transition in the market from Irish-interest books to novels of quality. However, between those two novels, Somerville and Ross worked for Longmans, Green & Co., publishers, writing stories in the series that began with *Some Experiences of an Irish RM* (1899). These proved so successful (*Some Experiences* sold particularly well in India from Longmans' Bombay printing house) that Somerville and Ross remained for thirty years within the category of 'Irish humour'.

In the 1890s, Heinemann set out to add George Moore to his list, a natural fit with its European and high-art features. Before he succeeded in this aim, he had to await the termination of Moore's relationship with T. Fisher Unwin. This publisher issued a number of series that included Irish authors – the Pseudonym Library, the Children's Library and the Cameo Series all had titles by Yeats, for instance, and the New Irish Library published five books by Charles Gavan Duffy, including *The Revival of Irish Literature* (1894). The principal modern authors in Unwin's list were Joseph Conrad, Pearl Craigie (pen name John Oliver Hobbes) and Moore.

While Unwin was a very commercial person, with no self-sacrificing attachment to Ireland or great literature, he was happy to do business distributing books by Irish people, if the business was good.[15] He profitably issued Yeats's *Poems* (1895) and entered into a distribution deal with Sealy, Bryers and Walker, a Dublin publisher, for *Samhain,* an occasional magazine relating to the new Irish theatre. These co-publication arrangements became significant when the Revival shifted its base from London to Dublin at the turn of the century.

Inspired by his friends Yeats and Edward Martyn, Moore moved to Dublin in 1901 to lend his talent and force of personality to the cultural revival. One of his first projects was to write short stories and to have them translated into the Irish language, so that they might serve as models of modern prose literature for young Irish-speaking authors. Thus, *The Untilled Field* (1903) was deliberately conceived as a schoolbook for short-story writers. Moore had already published a considerable number of stories in British magazines since the early 1880s, and some of those stories he rewrote with Irish settings; stylistically, they are excellent examples of the naturalist method of Guy de Maupassant, as modified for English tastes and subjects, and later modified once more for Irish tastes and subjects.[16] New stories were drafted, based on what Moore saw and heard upon his return to Ireland after years away, and these he self-consciously conceived in the manner of Turgenev: a gentlemanly, poignant, philosophical view of provincial life. The collection as a whole was united by the question, is it possible to regenerate a degenerate Ireland? (One title Moore considered was *Ruin and Weed.*) Six of these stories were translated by Pádraig Ó Súilleabáin and published in 1902 as *An t-Úr-Gort* by Sealy, Bryers and Walker in Dublin. There is no sign that any Irish-speaking young author began to write stories in any of the narrative styles displayed in the volume, but 21-year-old James Joyce began in the same year a remarkably similar project of thematically linked short stories, *Dubliners,* not published until 1914.

Neither Moore nor Joyce was primarily concerned with writing books for Irish-speakers, or for Irish people of any language; they had wider ambitions. In April 1903, *The Untilled Field* was co-published by Unwin in London and by Bell's Indian and Colonial Library, throughout the British empire. An American edition came out from Lippincott in the same year; a European edition was distributed in bookstores across the continent by Tauchnitz also in 1903. *The Untilled Field* and *Dubliners* are representative cases of the intersection between the Irish Revival and Modernism. Both are closely concerned with the Irish scene and matters of interest to Irish people at the time (anti-clericalism is a dominant note in each), but they are written in cutting-edge, realist prose styles, and ultimately published for readers of masterly writing throughout the world.

Moore planned a climax of anti-clericalism for *The Untilled Field* – a final story about a priest who, by thinking long and hard about why he had denounced an attractive, pregnant single woman in his parish, decides to give up the priesthood and secretly disappear from Ireland. Self-declericalisation, in other words, was the wished-for remedy for an Ireland weighed down by a wealthy and oppressive church, as it had once been weighed down by an Ascendancy. The appropriate narrative method for such a tale seemed to Moore to be a version of *le monologue intérieur* invented by his French *bon ami*, Edouard Dujardin, in *Les Lauriers Sont Coupés* (1887). Moore sank himself lyrically into the mental associations that arose in the mind of Father Gogarty, in walks along the banks of Lough Carra. The priest gradually comes to realise that he is being dishonest with himself, and impious as well, for one must love life not curse it. The capstone short story grew into a novel, published in 1905 by William Heinemann as *The Lake*. It was an entirely new form of fiction in English, 'the stream of consciousness', a technique that Joyce would carry much farther in *Ulysses* (1922).

As soon as Moore finished *The Lake*, he abandoned that technique and invented still another for his three-volume autobiography on the Literary Revival, *Hail and Farewell* (1911–1914). There are several daring innovations in this book. The most shocking was Moore's decision to treat living people under their own names as if they were characters in a novel, who would be described, have their conversations reported and their motives investigated, as if by a superhumanly perspicacious (and funny) authorial presence. A second innovation was to structure the whole parodically on the story of St Patrick's arrival in Ireland to Catholicise the pagans; Moore's equally grand aim was the very opposite: to paganise the Catholics. Thirdly, Moore introduced to English fiction Wagnerian leitmotifs, so that characters are announced as they re-enter the narrative by certain reiterated attributes, almost like horn calls in a symphony.[17] This enterprise had many imitators – Oliver St John Gogarty, for instance, in *As I was Going Down Sackville Street* (1937). Few of the subsequent comic novelistic Irish autobiographies, however, attempted either the candour, mythic structure or Wagnerianism of Moore's *Hail and Farewell*, apart from James Joyce's *Ulysses*, which is not a novelistic autobiography and is only partly an autobiographical novel.

O'Donovan and Stephens

In the first decade of the twentieth century, Moore and AE (George Russell) held open house in Dublin on specific nights of each week. Writers, artists and other intellectuals would gather for talk and readings from manuscripts-in-progress. Yeats would sometimes attend, and at the Abbey Theatre he was at the centre of comparable events, part seminar, part seance, part banquet. Each of the three authors was a master of the art of conversation; each was an advanced thinker about art and culture. Certainly, the impact of this free university on the young in Dublin during those years was great, greater perhaps than the impact of an Oxford, Cambridge or Trinity College under Dowden upon the cultural productivity of its fee-paying, test-taking students. Yeats was, George Moore somewhat sarcastically remarked, 'a very fine schoolmaster'.

> I owe something to him myself . . . He seems to me to have devised a method of teaching, or to speak more plainly, he has devised literary formulae not unlike the pictorial formulae that Walter Sickert invented and that have enabled countless ladies to paint gable ends barely distinguished from the 'master's' . . . But there is one great difference between Walter Sickert and Yeats. Yeats began by being a great poet; he has written almost as much good poetry as Coleridge and has thereby earned his right to teach ladies how to shape their sentences.[18]

Sarcasm apart, Moore wanted to find students too, but in Dublin he located only a few young people who could take advantage of his lessons on how to shape their narratives. A priest from Loughrea, Father Gerald O'Donovan (1871–1942) influenced Moore (his departure from the priesthood for journalism gave Moore an ending for *The Lake*), and Moore influenced O'Donovan, more notably in O'Donovan's later fiction *Vocations* (1921) than in his first, best, and self-declericalising novel, *Father Ralph* (1913) – the only novel in which an author depicts fellow priests in the privacy of their own company. Another strange soul attracted to Moore's work was the socialist and Irish-language enthusiast, W. P. Ryan, but he managed only two novels, *The Plough and the* Cross (1910) and *The Pope's Green Island* (1912). Moore did not make the acquaintance of Joyce until 1929. By the end of his sojourn in Dublin, his efforts to modernise Irish prose narrative seemed to have made little headway.

However, in December 1913, with Moore settled once again in London, John Eglinton sent him a book by a follower of AE, James Stephens (?1880–1950).[19] The novel was *Here are Ladies* (1913), Stephens's third and not his best. In Moore's opinion, the book showed little ability to tell a tale, but Stephens, he judged, 'writes better than anyone now living'.[20] By the following August of 1914, Moore had read more by Stephens, 'the only writer that interests me'.[21] Stephens's first three books are all radically different in kind. *A Charwoman's Daughter* (1912) is precise in its descriptions of Dublin tenements, laced with authorial indignation at the injustices of capitalism, and wish-fulfilling in its guidance of the plot, which sees its lovely heroine, Mary Makebelieve, escape the attentions of a big Dublin policeman and discover true love at the book's end. *Here are Ladies* is a unique book: nineteen stories telegraphically setting forth different domestic situations, in which men are equally bedevilled and entranced by the mysteries of women's incomprehensible personalities. *The Crock of Gold* (1912), Stephens's masterpiece, is also original in form: it mixes up Yeatsian tales of leprechauns and Celtic gods with pictures of rural life and Blakean philosophy. The story concerns the Philosopher, who is married to the cranky Thin Woman of Inis Magrath, and his quest to rescue the lovely peasant girl Caitilin from the god Pan, with the aid of the Irish god of love, Angus Og. As in other books by Stephens, humorously block-headed policemen have a part to play.

The novel is the beginning of an Irish tradition of twentieth-century fiction that includes the anti-capitalist Cuanduine trilogy of Eimar O'Duffy (1926–33), and Flann O'Brien's *At Swim-Two-Birds* (1939) and *The Third Policeman* (written 1940, published 1967). Along with the policemen, the characters out of Irish myth, the leprechauns and the philosophising, Flann O'Brien's books share with *The Crock of Gold* the technique of dialogue running absurdly on two different rails, one of them orotund, self-serious and full of maxims, the other colloquially bathetic. Here is part of a conversation between Stephens's Philosopher and Meehawl MacMurrachu, a small farmer seeking assistance in the recovery of his wife's missing washboard:

> 'Well, anyhow, the washboard is gone, and my wife says it was either taken by the fairies or by Bessie Hannigan – you know Bessie Hannigan? She has whiskers like a goat and a lame leg!'
>
> 'I do not,' said the Philosopher.
>
> 'No matter,' said Meehawl MacMurrachu. 'She didn't take it, because my wife got her out yesterday and kept her talking for two hours while I went through everything in her bit of a house – the washboard wasn't there.'
>
> 'It wouldn't be,' said the Philosopher.
>
> 'Maybe your honour would tell a body where it is then?'
>
> 'Maybe I could,' said the Philosopher; 'are you listening?'
>
> 'I am,' said Meehawl MacMurrachu.
>
> The philosopher drew his chair closer to the visitor until their knees were jammed together. He laid both his hands on Meehawl MacMurrachu's knees –
>
> 'Washing is an extraordinary custom,' said he. 'We are washed both on coming into the world and on going out of it, and we take no pleasure from the first washing nor any profit from the last.'

'True for you, sir,' said Meehawl MacMurrachu.

'Many people consider that scourings supplementary to these are only due to habit. Now habit is continuity of an action, it is a most detestable thing and is very difficult to get away from. A proverb will run where a writ will not, and the follies of our forefathers are of greater importance to us than is the well-being of our posterity.'

'I wouldn't say a word against that, sir,' said Meehawl MacMurrachu.

'Cats are a philosophical and thoughtful race, but they do not admit of the efficacy of either water or soap, and yet it is usually conceded that they are cleanly folk . . .'[22]

Meehawl has to listen to a good deal more before the Philosopher (correctly) locates the cause of the disappearance of the washboard and its current whereabouts. Stephens's mastery of multiple idioms and originality of invention made him a favourite of other writers. Not only was he openly admired by Moore and secretly imitated by Flann O'Brien, James Joyce proposed that if he died before completing *Finnegans Wake*, Stephens should finish it for him.[23]

In the summer of 1916, Moore met Stephens in Dublin and made a proposition over lunch: that, for a fee, the younger writer assist Moore in the composition of stories in an Irish idiom, stories that would be 'poetical but highly sexed'.[24] The stories appear in a fictional autobiography entitled *A Story-Teller's Holiday* (1918). It concerns Moore's visit to Dublin after the 1916 Easter Rising and his travels out to Moore Hall, where he meets Alec Trusselby, a *seanchaí*. The traditional and modern narrators have a story-telling contest. Alec's tales are about medieval monks and nuns who excite themselves sexually by voluntarily undergoing temptations, supposedly in order to test the mettle of their chastity. The tales by Moore the character are re-tellings of famous works by Milton, Balzac, Dostoevsky and Moore himself ('Albert Nobbs'). Stephens's job was to touch up the idiom of Trusselby's tales, and this he did deftly.

After this successful experiment, Stephens went on to write more books under his own name – retellings of Irish myths, biographies, short stories, etc. – but he diverted much of his energy into verse, on the misconception that his true talent lay there. Overblown with fancifulness, neither his poetry nor later fiction equalled the condensation of social perceptiveness, anger and brio of his first two novels.

A Story-Teller's Holiday, however, proved to be a productive intervention in Irish fiction. It led to a further collaboration between the two authors on Moore's medieval love story, *Ulick and Soracha* (1926), a book in full flight from the modern world into a heavily wooded Ireland of horses, poets and beautiful women, a country without political parties, motor cars or suburban developments. Poet Austin Clarke added to the subgenre with *The Bright Temptation* (1932, dedicated to Moore), *The Singing Men of Cashel* (1936) and *The Sun Dances at Easter* (1952). The Irish subgenre of poetical fantasies set in medieval Ireland, written in beautiful sentences, with an overall mood of wonder amid the splendours of pre-modern nature and innocent sexuality, did not, of course, belong to the future of modernist fiction. It was an Irish solution to an Irish problem. In the impoverished, morally repressive new Catholic Irish Free State, many writers were disillusioned. Some left the country in the 1920s and early 1930s. But others felt both loyal to church and state, and yet oppressed by them; censored not celebrated. They became 'inner émigrés', to adapt Seamus Heaney, dwelling on fantasies of a pre-Reformation, Irish-speaking Ireland. Even if their books are sometimes motivated by sexual wish-fulfilment, the fictions of Stephens, O'Duffy, Clarke and Padraic Colum have a fey quality that is not very adult. Their books came to belong in the market of children's literature.

Conclusions

The Irish gift to Modernism in the 1920s and 1930s – and it was the greatest gift of all – occurred elsewhere than in Dublin. On 2 February 1922, Shakespeare and Co. in Paris issued James Joyce's *Ulysses*. Its impact on world literature was rapid and immense; its impact on literature written in the Irish Free State, established just a month earlier on 7 January 1922, was a longer time in coming. The new Ireland deliberately turned away from international modern literature as something frequently sinful and always un-Irish. A hyperactive censorship of film and literature was set up by the new state; work in the Irish language was promoted above work in English, and Catholic values were the only values to be entertained. Of those surviving Protestant authors who had contributed heavily to the Irish Revival all but Yeats left the country, and so did quite a few Catholic authors – Moore, Colum, Gogarty, Gerald O'Donovan. The contribution of Ireland to modern literature had been so immense that it can hardly be expected that it would continue at the same rate. Masterpieces are rare events. Everything that came before, and everything that came after, is small compared to the weight of one great novel, 'Stately, plump' *Ulysses*, the sacred book of modern fiction. But *Ulysses* is not the unique expression of literary Modernism in Ireland at the turn of the century. Several of its elements – perspectivalism, style as subject, presentation of images without commentary, parody of popular literary styles, mythic parallels to contemporary life, and constant manifestation of literary art – had found a place in the novels of Wilde, Yeats and especially George Moore.

The question of the Irishness of Irish Modernism remains open. The spotlight in this chapter fell on George Moore, who personally knew – and either sparked or caught fire from – fellow Irish writers, even when he was uninterested in, or positively disenchanted by, the national dimension of the Irish Revival. He was a boyhood playmate, and later rival man of letters, of Oscar Wilde; a collaborator with Yeats; a business associate of Bram Stoker; a patron of James Stephens; an acknowledged forerunner of Joyce; and a mentor of Austin Clarke. But these writers did not just have relationships to Moore; many knew one another. Wilde welcomed the young Irish poet Yeats to London and gave him Christmas dinner; Yeats sent young Joyce off to London and Paris with a loan and a letter of introduction. When they happened to be living in Dublin at the same time, these writers were part of a very small literary set who published in the same small weeklies and monthlies, attended the same plays at the Abbey Theatre and frequented one another's houses for periodic *conversazione*. When they were in London, 'Micks on the make', in Roy Foster's phrase, gave one another a helping hand, opened doors for one another.[25] This fraternity of modern Irish writers also allowed the transmission of lessons in the art of fiction to move quickly among them. Modernism skips quickly from Moore to Wilde to Yeats and ultimately to Joyce who drew together their stylistic innovations and those of many others. After Wilde's London stardom, young Irishmen seeking to make a name for themselves as new, brilliant, irreverent wordsmiths inhabited for a period of years a role that always had to be fulfilled by one or another, and this very drive to become the next new thing itself was a force for Modernism in fiction. Before Ezra Pound invented the slogan, the turn-of-the-century Irish were 'making it new'.

NOTES

1. Joseph Conrad, preface, *The Nigger of the 'Narcissus' and Typhoon* (1897; London and Toronto: J. M. Dent & Sons, 1923), p. i.
2. For a severe commentary on the influence of Nietzsche on modernist novelists, see John Carey, *The Intellectuals and the Masses: Pride and Prejudice among the Literary Intelligentsia, 1800–1939* (London: Faber & Faber, 1992).
3. GM to Dear Sir [unidentified editor], Tuesday [January 1885], Tillyra Castle; quoted in Adrian Frazier, *George Moore 1852–1933* (London and New Haven: Yale University Press, 2000), p. 118.
4. George Moore, *Confessions of a Young Man*, ed. Susan Dick (Montreal and London: McGill-Queen's University Press, 1972), p. 149.
5. Walter Pater, *The Renaissance: Studies in Art and Poetry* (Oxford: Oxford University Press, 1986), pp. 150–3.
6. A *Daily Chronicle* (London) review of Wilde's novel called it a 'poisonous book', quoted in *The Picture of Dorian Gray*, ed. Isobel Murray (Oxford:

Oxford University Press, 1998), p. vii. The maxims quoted from the preface are selected and rearranged.

7. See remarks on Pater by Isobel Murray (ed.), *The Picture of Dorian Gray*, pp. viii–x.

8. William Butler Yeats, *Mythologies* (New York: Collier Books; Macmillan, 1969), pp. 155–6.

9. For an intelligent account of Pater's work and some notes on his influence, see Denis Donoghue, *Walter Pater: Lover of Strange Souls* (New York: Random House, 1998), pp. 55–90.

10. One Emily Herbert, who did the Somervilles out of an inheritance: see *Selected Letters of Somerville and Ross*, ed. Gifford Lewis (London and Boston: Faber & Faber, 1989), p. 235.

11. 'Irish Literary Theatre, Interesting Speeches', *Daily Express* (Dublin), 12 May 1899; Frazier, *George Moore*, pp. 274–5.

12. See also Vivian Mercier, 'Victorian Evangelicalism and the Anglo-Irish Literary Revival', in Peter Connolly (ed.), *Literature and the Changing Ireland* (Gerrards Cross: Colin Smythe, 1982), pp. 59–101.

13. Carol A. Senf (ed.), *The Critical Response to Bram Stoker* (Westport, CT, and London: Greenwood Press, 1993), pp. 59–61. Bruce Stewart reviews some Irish interpretations of the novel in 'Bram Stoker's *Dracula*: Possessed by the Spirit of the Nation?', *Irish University Review* 29 (Autumn/Winter 1999), 238–55. A recent book is Joseph Valente's *Dracula's Crypt: Bram Stoker, Irishness, and the Question of Blood* (2001).

14. Edmund Downey, *Twenty Years Ago* (1905).

15. See Warwick Gould, '"Playing at Treason with Miss Maud Gonne": Yeats and His Publishers in 1900', in Ian Willison, Warwick Gould and Warren Chermaik (eds.), *Modernist Writers and the Marketplace* (London: Macmillan, 1996), pp. 56–63.

16. For a scrupulous account of the changes to these stories, see Edwin Gilcher, *A Bibliography of George Moore* (Dekalb: Northern Illinois University Press, 1970), pp. 62–7.

17. For more on this subject, see William F. Blissett, 'George Moore and Literary Wagnerianism', in Douglas Hughes (ed.), *The Man of Wax: Critical Essays on George Moore* (New York: New York University Press, 1971), pp. 185–216.

18. George Moore to Ernest Boyd, 17 August 1914, Healy Collection, Stanford University.

19. George Moore to W. K. Magee ['John Eglinton'], 11 December 1913, Harry Ransom Humanities Research Center, Austin, Texas.

20. George Moore to Hilda Hawthorne, 19 December 1913, Berg Collection, New York Public Library.

21. George Moore to James Stephens, 26 August [1914], Berg Collection, New York Public Library.

22. James Stephens, *The Crock of Gold* (1912; New York: Macmillan, 1926), pp. 18–19.

23. Richard Ellmann, *James Joyce* (Oxford: Oxford University Press, 1983), pp. 592–3. Joyce appears to have been led to the conclusion that Stephens could carry on with *Finnegans Wake* because he and Joyce had the same first name and same birthday. See James Stephens, *James, Seumas, and Jacques* (New York: Macmillan, 1964), pp. 147–55.

24. James Stephens, 'A Conversation with George Moore', *The Listener*, 16 January 1947, n.p.; George Moore to Viola Rodgers [18 May 1917], Bancroft Library, Berkeley.

25. R. F. Foster, 'Marginal Men and Micks on the Make: The Uses of Irish Exile, c. 1840–1922', in *Paddy and Mr Punch: Connections in Irish and English History* (London: Allen Lane, Penguin, 1993), pp. 281–305.

GUIDE TO FURTHER READING

Bradbury, Malcolm and James MacFarlane (eds.). *Modernism, 1890–1930*. Harmondsworth: Penguin, 1976.

Dibattista, Maria and Lucy McDiarmid (eds.). *High and Low Moderns: Literature and Culture, 1889–1939*. Oxford: Oxford University Press, 1997.

Foster, John Wilson. 'Irish Modernism', in *Colonial Consequences: Essays in Irish Literature and Culture*. Dublin: Lilliput Press, 1991.

Kenner, Hugh. *A Colder Eye: The Modern Irish Writers*. London: Allen Lane, 1983.

Levenson, Michael (ed.). *The Cambridge Companion to Modernism*. Cambridge: Cambridge University Press, 2002.

7

BRUCE STEWART

James Joyce

Joyce the modernist

James Joyce (1882–1941) was the international modernist *par excellence* of his day, yet the question of where his modernism sprang from is difficult to answer. While the conditions of national life during his formative years in Ireland are often regarded as pre-modern, the point is worth observing that the capital in which he was born had one of the most advanced communication systems in Europe when he left it in 1904 – a fact which made its imprint on his novel *Ulysses*, in the shape of trams and telephones. At that time, Ireland was gripped by a mood of romantic nationalism which did not readily embrace modernist ideas in politics and religion, other than those which confirmed the importance of the 'imagined community' (in Benedict Anderson's famous epithet for the *nation*); and just as romanticism seemed preferable to realism for nationalists of the day, archaism rather than innovation was the dominant mode for literary revivalists (though that inevitably involved some degree of literary experiment). Joyce turned away from nationalists and revivalists alike, and identified strenuously with a 'movement already proceeding out in Europe' which he identified as 'the modern spirit',[1] before quitting Ireland in 1904 to become part of it.

It was not, of course, until after he had left Ireland that he made any personal contact with anglophone modernists, and then it was the modernists who contacted him in the person of the leading exponent, the poet and critic Ezra Pound. In December 1913, Pound wrote to Joyce in Trieste seeking permission to include in his collection *Des Imagistes* (1914) a poem shown to him by W. B. Yeats (1914). Thus began a literary association that resulted in the serial publication of *A Portrait of the Artist as a Young Man* (1916) and *Ulysses* (1922) in the literary journals where Joyce's international reputation became established. In promoting the Irish writer, Pound insistently compared him to French standard-bearers of modern literature, writing in one place that Joyce 'produces the nearest thing we have to Flaubertian prose in English today' while, in another, expressing dismay at his national origins ('It is surprising that Mr Joyce is Irish'), before putting matters on a properly international basis: 'Joyce has fled to Trieste and into the modern world . . . He writes as a European, not as a pro-vincial.'[2] After 1919, having passed the First World War in Switzerland where he wrote much of *Ulysses*, Joyce moved to Paris at Pound's sugges-tion, there to remain until the Second World War drove back him to Zurich, where he died in 1941.

For Valéry Larbaud and others in the Paris of the 1920s, it was the 'interior monologue' which gave Joyce his salient position in the *avant garde*. In 1923, T. S. Eliot confirmed his importance for Anglo-American modernists when he wrote that the 'mythic order' of *Ulysses* had 'the importance of a scientific discovery . . . making the modern world possible for art'.[3] 'Work in Progress' (later published as *Finnegans Wake* in 1939) was, however, a discovery too far for Pound, who wrote to Joyce in 1926: 'Nothing short of divine vision or a new cure for the clapp can possibly be worth all that circumambient peripherisation.'[4] At about this time Eugene Jolas, the editor of *transition*, identified Joyce's latest experiment with 'the revolution of the word' and took on the publication of 'Work in Progress' from April 1927. For the wider readership throughout all this, Joyce's art was implicitly identified with the psychoanalytical movement associated with Sigmund Freud and Carl Jung. This was an often hostile as-sociation as when, for instance, a *Sunday Express* reviewer pronounced that *Ulysses* had been 'adopted by the Freudians as the supreme glory of their dirty and degraded cult'.[5] Yet Joyce's attitude to psychoanalysis was essentially ambivalent, and there is little question of direct influence. For while he prided himself on the modernity of his ideas, he was often scornful of his imputed affinity with those whom he called 'the Swiss Tweedledum [and] the Viennese Tweedledee',[6] asking why they were always talking about the *unconscious* and what they knew about the *conscious* mind. There is no doubt, however, that, like Freud, he placed the sexual instinct at the centre of human life and that mental processes greatly interested him.

It did not always suit Joyce to be thought a modernist as the term was understood by contemporaries and, once this aspect of his work was widely recognised, he began to speak of his conservatism along with it. Talking to an Irish friend in Paris in the 1920s, for example, he insisted that he was a medieval writer, just as the Irish were a medieval people.[7] There is some truth in this: in his youth, Joyce had laboured to convert a 'garner of slender sentences' gleaned from Aristotle and St Thomas Aquinas into an aesthetic philosophy.[8] In later life, he identified the Book of Kells as a precursor of his own sense of literary design. (A lengthy passage in *Finnegans Wake* takes the form of a parody of Sir Edward Sullivan's introduction to the *Studio* facsimile of the Book of Kells, a copy of which Joyce sent to his patron Harriet Shaw Weaver at Christmas 1922.)[9] Much of this was camouflage on the part of a writer who disliked the suggestion that his 'discoveries' had been anticipated by contemporaries, and equally a check on too easy an identification with the Anglo-American, and essentially Protestant, version of modernity identified with the liberal and implicitly imperialist themes of *civilisation* and *progress*. At the same time, it can be taken as alluding to a paradox that underlies his art at every point: Joyce was Irish and therefore implicitly pre-modern; yet he was also European in his own estimation, regarding Ireland as 'an afterthought of Europe' (*SH*, p. 52) and the Irish as the 'most belated race in Europe'.[10] Just as he aimed to make Ireland European, effecting a juncture between medievalism and modernity might be regarded as the chief intellectual task that he set himself in early manhood.

Joyce was unique among his student peers in his openness to modern ideas; yet, while most of those who stayed at home when he went into exile remained in the combined grip of Catholic and nationalist orthodoxies, they were hardly members of the 'shivering society' that he castigates in *Stephen Hero* (p. 38). Con Curran, a college friend, gave the lie to that unflattering estimate in an impressive memoir.[11] The most telling difference between Joyce and his contemporaries at University College lay perhaps in his peculiar biographical circumstances. The sharp decline in his family's social status, brought about by his father's gregarious alcoholism, combined with an unshakable sense of his own worth seem to have set up a reaction in Joyce's mind that produced the air of intellectual superiority reflected in his autobiographical writings. As a young man, he knew himself to be excluded from the courtship rites of his school and college fellows and was correspondingly dismissive about the 'colleen' dress of 'marriageable daughters' in the households he frequented through their friendship (*SH*, p. 45). At the same time, he espoused the politics of sexual liberation, perhaps to justify a habit of frequenting brothels which in itself marked his sense of remoteness from the prospects of a 'good match' in middle-class Dublin. The decision to leave Ireland in 1904 with Nora Barnacle, a sexually aware young woman who was working as a chambermaid when they met, was therefore the outcome of a social alienation produced by the familial consequences of his father's economic downfall.

If Joyce was radicalised by his father's failure, his critical intelligence found an apt focus in the moral poverty to which he was exposed in the localities where the family was forced to live. On arriving in the inner city, he found that the 'dull phenomenon of Dublin' (*Portrait*, p. 68) offered 'a new and complex sensation' to which he responded by reading 'subversive writers whose jibes and violence of speech set up a ferment in his brain before they passed out of it into his crude writings' (*Portrait*, p. 80). Besides these writers (nationalists and anarchists), Joyce's self-directed reading led him towards such modern authors as Gustave Flaubert and Henrik Ibsen, excluded from the timid syllabus of the Royal University. From both he learned about the place of sexuality in the human mind. From Flaubert he also learnt the novelistic technique known as *style moyen indirect*, which excerpts phrases from the consciousness of the characters in order to convey reality as they experience it. Joyce knew Flaubert's letters, too, and a famous sentence which Stephen lavishes almost verbatim on Cranly in *A Portrait*, asserting that the artist must remain 'within or behind or beyond or above his handiwork, invisible, refined out of existence, indifferent, paring his fingernails' (p. 219), is taken from the *Correspondence*.[12]

Greater by far than the influence of Flaubert, however, was that of the Norwegian playwright Ibsen, whose name was synonymous with the overturning of bourgeois convention at that time. In Joyce's account of it, the mind of 'the Old Norse poet' and that of 'the young Celt' met 'in a moment of radiant simultaneity' (*SH*, p. 41) in 1899. In 1900, Joyce wrote a review of Ibsen's latest play, *When We Dead Awaken*, and this was published in the April issue of *Fortnightly Review*. On learning that Ibsen approved, he studied Norwegian sufficiently to write a letter in that language which characteristically ends with a suggestion that he himself will succeed the object of his homage. In the summer of 1901, he translated two plays by Gerhart Hauptmann for the Irish Literary Theatre, but these were refused. Other European authors who attracted him at this time included Turgenev and Maupassant, Herman Sudermann and Gabriel D'Annunzio. Of Irish contemporaries, he read Yeats most closely; of English contemporaries, Meredith and Hardy – though without abandoning the conviction that he had 'little or nothing to learn from English novelists', as he told Stanislaus in a letter of November 1906 (*SL*, p. 124). At the same time, Joyce made a close study of Dante Alighieri while still in Dublin and, in an important departure, the sixteenth-century philosopher Giordano Bruno. For if his literary instincts led him to the moderns, the actual building blocks of his mind were very different.

Pre-modern Joyce

Joyce remained in important ways the product of a Jesuit education, versed in the terminology of scholasticism rather than any more modern brand of philosophical thinking. If Joyce's intuitions were modern, his vocabulary was medieval. The best example of this tendency is his application of the term 'epiphany': a word employed in Christian liturgy to mean the 'shewing-forth of Jesus in the temple', but redefined by Joyce to mean 'a sudden spiritual manifestation' in which the significance of some ordinary person or object is revealed with great clarity in spite of being 'the most delicate and evanescent of moments' (*SH*, p. 188). It is pertinent, moreover, that the location of the first epiphany in *Stephen Hero* is Eccles Street, afterwards the 'home' of Leopold Bloom in *Ulysses*, and at any time a common abbreviation for *ecclesia* (church) – though actually named after the land owner Sir John Eccles. Joyce's strategy was thus to found his own church, in rivalry with the one which he regarded as 'the tyrant of the islanders' (*SH*, p. 52). (Joyce was fascinated by Yeats's monkish aesthetes Michael Robartes and Owen Aherne, who likewise attempted to 'inhabit a church apart . . . having chosen to fulfil the law of their own being', as he puts it in *Stephen Hero*, p. 178.)

The role that Joyce had in mind for himself was partly that of a 'priest of the eternal imagination' (*Portrait*, p. 225) and partly that of a literary messiah who would 'forge in the smithy of [his] soul the uncreated conscience of [his] race' (*Portrait*, p. 257). Yet in spite of the juvenile egoism of this conception, the underlying idea was essentially realistic and, more precisely, intellectually grounded in the Realism of Aristotle. In 1903, Joyce sat in the Bibliothèque de Sainte-Geneviève in Paris reading Aristotle's *De Anima* (or *Psychology*) in French, and from this he derived the terms 'form of forms' and 'entelechy' – both of which Stephen bandies in episodes of *Ulysses* – which allowed him to define the 'soul' of the individual and its process of development. When it came to applying these in practice, Joyce made the stylistic discovery that governs the literary structure of *A Portrait*. Here, each successive episode is written in a style that corresponds to a definite embryological stage in the development (or *telos*) of the central character. From childhood through adolescence to early manhood, along a line that reveals his growing awareness of his mission as an artist, the narrative prose imitates the mentality of its living subject.

To many of its early readers, *A Portrait* was especially shocking for the scene in which Stephen visits a prostitute, but hardly less so for the 'hellfire' sermon which occupies eighteen pages in the standard edition (about one fifteenth of the whole). This serves as an extended specimen of Catholic authoritarianism, religion being one of the 'nets' which Stephen is determined to elude – the others being 'nationality' and 'language' (p. 207). The last refers to the way in which conventional ideas imprison the growing mind but also, more specifically, to the Irish-language movement, increasingly gaining ground among young Dublin intellectuals of the day. Contemporary Irish reviewers objected to *A Portrait* on the grounds that, 'instead of pointing to the stars overhead', Joyce had 'degraded' it into 'a muck-rake'.[13] This was at once true and false: in *Dubliners* and *A Portrait*, Joyce had indeed begun to forge the bond between literary art and the psycho-sexual realism which was to be the hallmark of his work in decades after, and ultimately the reason for his lasting reputation. It is in *Ulysses* that this new ethos was to be most comprehensively displayed.

Ulysses

The most important strands of Modernism to be met with in *Ulysses* concern its psychological realism and its literary experimentalism, these being closely combined in the 'stream of consciousness' technique which brings the sexual instinct to the surface of the text, along with all the bric-a-brac that makes up the ordinary human mind. The profusion of such materials calls for some organising principle other than the elements of plot and motivation common to all naturalistic novels. *Ulysses* possesses these in modified degrees – the main 'events' happen offstage, for instance – but is artistically structured by means of an extended parallel between the events of a single day in Dublin and the episodes of Homer's *Odyssey* as retold in Charles Lamb's *The Adventures of Ulysses* (1803), which Joyce knew from school. Hence, if Bloom is Odysseus, Michael Cusack ('the citizen') is Polyphemus or the Cyclops in the episode of that name. By the same token, Stephen is Telemachus, the son of Odysseus, but also Hamlet, the betrayed prince walking through the cathedral of himself (in Baudelaire's phrase). Eliot calls this the 'mythic method' but *intertextual* is a better term, since little about Joyce's way of handling the Homeric parallel reflects Eliot's concern with 'controlling . . . the immense panorama of futility and anarchy which is contemporary history'[14] – an anxiety that the American poet shared with W. B. Yeats, as 'The Second Coming' shows.

Nor was Joyce interested in symbolism in the same sense of the others. In sharp contrast to the poetry and prose of Yeats, for instance, the greater part of *Ulysses* is given over to stylistic parodies, whether the subject is the mentality of a given character, such as Fr Conmee,[15] or the thirty-two samples from George Saintsbury's *History of English Prose Rhythm* (1912) which Joyce parodied at chapter-length in the 'Oxen of the Sun' episode, which itself resembles an embryological chart of the development of the language. (T. S. Eliot saw this characteristically, if erroneously, as a revelation of the 'futility of all styles'.)[16] 'Sirens', at the halfway point, marks the beginning of the more remorselessly experimental chapters of *Ulysses*.

Everything before this episode, excepting 'Oxen' and 'Aeolus', is a clear development of the *style moyen indirect*. Henceforth, parody and pastiche are the governing laws of *Ulysses*.

Probably, Joyce would not have taken things to such lengths had he not been committed to serial publication in 'little magazines', with their compulsively *avant garde* dynamic. Yet even in this context, he saw his styles as essentially mimetic – that is to say, each was representationally appropriate to its subject. In a letter to Harriet Shaw Weaver, he spoke of the challenge of writing the chapters of *Ulysses* from 'eighteen different points of view and in as many styles' (*SL*, p. 284). From this we may infer that *style* is primarily connected to the idea of psychological perspective. In conveying the state of mind of a young man traumatised by his mother's death alongside the disquiet of a middle-aged man whose wife is engaged in a sexual affair with the aptly named Blazes Boylan, Joyce plumbed the depths of psycho-sexual life in an entirely new way. In intention and effect, the thrust of *Ulysses* is at one with the principle Joyce enunciated in a letter to his brother in speaking of a host of Dubliners and others better known in the world of letters: 'I am nauseated by their lying drivel about pure men and pure women and spiritual love and love for ever: blatant lying in the face of truth.' He then turns the focus on himself: 'If I put down a bucket into my own soul's well, sexual department, I draw up [their] dirty water along with [my] own', adding immediately after, 'I am going to do that in my novel' (*SL*, p. 129).

Although the novel that he meant was *Stephen Hero*, it is *Ulysses* that most relentlessly explores human sexuality in both its normal and abnormal aspects – constructing in the 'Circe' chapter, for example, a series of hallucinatory scenes involving sadomasochistic and trans-sexual episodes where Bloom's and Stephen's underlying anxieties are acted out in a kind of psycho-analytical nightmare, like the *Walpurgisnacht* in Goethe's *Dr Faust*. In 'Penelope', Joyce gives us immediate access to Molly Bloom's consciousness through a stream of unpunctuated sentences which embrace her sexual history (real and imagined), and which still retains the capacity to shock through its intense psychological realism, culminating in the life-affirming 'yes' with which she ends the novel.

Finnegans Wake

The exceptional materiality that Bloom, Stephen, Molly and all the others in *Ulysses* possess as literary characters derives in large measure from a host of encyclopaedic details which Joyce methodically transposed from such sources as Hely Thom's *Dublin Directory* for 1904. These permitted him to make the claim that if Dublin were destroyed, it could be rebuilt from the pages of his novel. Joyce told Arthur Power that if he could get to the heart of Dublin, he could get to the heart of all the cities of the world, in the belief that we can only reach the universal through the particular.[17] In his next book, however, he abandoned the naturalistic method that anchors *Ulysses* firmly in temporal and physical reality, in order to construct a kind of literary cosmology that embraces all times and places through the sheer multiplicity of its cultural allusions. In 1926, Joyce offered Miss Weaver this explanation of the experimental language of *Finnegans Wake* (1939): 'One great part of every human existence is passed in a state which cannot be rendered sensible by the use of wideawake language, cutandry grammar and goahead plot' (*SL*, p. 318). Whether or not the subject of the book is a dream, it certainly exhibits a dreamlike texture. This is produced by a fabric of multilingual puns, portmanteau words and Freudian 'slips of the tongue', all born out of Joyce's knowledge of European languages and supplemented by samples from others such as Burmese, thanks to a word list supplied by his ex-colonial friend Frank Budgen. The result sounds very much as if humanity itself were speaking through the text in all its 'diverse tonguesed'.[18]

In so far as the *Wake* calls for a uniform plot, Joyce supplies it in the notion that everything that happens passes through the sleeping mind of an Irish giant, stretched out in the Dublin landscape 'like a god on pension' (*FW*, p. 24). This explains the structure of the book only in a very provisional way, however, and must be measured against the implications of the title – a well-kept secret up to the day of publication – which derives from an Irish-American ballad about a bricklayer called Tim Finnegan, who falls to his death but is suddenly revived by a splash of whiskey during the ructions at his wake. The theological implications of this are made quite clear at the outset: 'Phall if you but will, rise you must: and none so soon either shall the pharce for the nunce come to a setdown secular phoenish' (*FW*, p. 4). In this view, reproduction and resurrection are ultimately the same – a view with which Artistotle concurs (as Joyce carefully recorded in an early notebook).[19] At the same time, the topographical setting, bounded by the River Liffey and Howth Head, provide a backdrop for a vast census of *Wake* 'characters', though each in turn appears to correspond to one or other member of the primordial *Wake* family: Humphrey Chimpden Earwicker (HCE), Anna Livia Plurabelle (ALP), Shem, Shaun and Issy (of Tristram and Isolde fame). Relations between these are variously amorous and bellicose, fratricidal and parricidal, incestuous and oedipal.

At an even deeper level, however, the 'characters' themselves are little more than *sigla* (Latin 'letters') in a schematic counterpart of a map of

Dublin scratched graffiti-wise in the jakes of the pub in Chapelizod (now a suburb of Dublin), like the 'outwashed engravure that we used to be blurring on the blotchwall of his innkempt house' (*FW*, p. 13). As such it is inevitably scatological, being labelled the 'whome of your eternal geomater' (*FW*, p. 291) in a sex lesson taught by one of the siblings to the others in the 'Night Lessons' episode of the *Wake*. This is the stuff that dreams are made of, at least in a Freudian universe, and the whole movement of the work can consequently be described as 'a sot of a swigswag, systomy dystomy, which everabody you ever anywhere at all doze' (*FW*, p. 597).

Joyce the Irishman

In 1923, the Irish critic Ernest Boyd took issue with Valéry Larbaud's assertion that Ireland 'makes a sensational re-entry into European literature' with the publication of Joyce's *Ulysses*, objecting that Larbaud had overlooked the real context of the work: 'The fact is, no Irish writer is more Irish than Joyce; none shows more unmistakably the imprint of his race and traditions.'[20] Much of recent Irish commentary on Joyce has been concerned with demonstrating this. In regard to theme and treatment, each of his works can arguably be seen to participate in a Celtic heritage of comic writing that stretches back into remote antiquity – albeit without his being fully aware of it, as Vivian Mercier controversially suggested in *The Irish Comic Tradition* (1962).[21] More recent commentaries see as ingenious Joyce's response to a national history that confronted contemporary Irish writers with an apparent choice between assimilation to the dominant English culture and a romantic return to the 'native' language, in a programme that Douglas Hyde called 'the de-Anglicising of Ireland' in 1892.[22] Joyce emphatically did not participate in that programme, and indeed regarded it as reactionary and anti-modern, but he did remark on an inherent dissonance in modern Irish culture connected with linguistic colonialism in Ireland in a well-known passage of *A Portrait*, in which Stephen Dedalus and the Dean of Studies speak to one another: 'His language, so familiar and so foreign, will always be for me an acquired speech. I have not made or accepted its words. My voice holds them at bay. My soul frets in the shadow of his language' (*Portrait*, p. 215).

Stephen's sensitivity on the point might be seen as anticipating Joyce's radical assault on standard English in *Ulysses* and *Finnegans Wake*. Sir Shane Leslie, an Anglo-Irish man of letters, wrote of the former that it was like a 'Clerkenwell explosion in the well-guarded, well-built classical prison of English literature',[23] while Joyce's friend Arthur Power made a comparable observation about the man himself: 'I realized that there was

much of the Fenian about him . . . a literary conspirator, who was determined to destroy the oppressive and respectable cultural structures under
which we had been reared.'[24] Others less friendly (and therefore less
amused), such as H. G. Wells, speaking up for the liberal-progressive tradition in English letters, regarded Joyce as an anarchic force motivated by
Catholic malice against Protestant civilisation.[25]

It was not Joyce's political ideas so much as his attitude to language that
threatened the English literary tradition. By means of a ludic approach to
the primary stuff of literature itself, Joyce reveals the language of narration
as a 'discourse of power' (in Michel Foucault's phrase) pertaining to the
cultural outlook of the dominant social group. It is this power-relation that
Joyce eroded by constructing books from various 'styles' without intrud-
ing an authorial voice of his own. The effect, when carried to its logical
conclusion, is to set the language of the text free to bear often contradictory meanings. This, for instance, is how *Finnegans Wake* is described in its
own pages: 'this Eyrawyggla saga [though] readable to int from and, is
from tubb to buttom all falsetissues, antilibellous and nonactionable and
this applies to its whole wholume' (*FW*, p. 48), while, in another part we
are told that '[t]he unfacts, did we possess them, are too imprecisely few to
warrant our certitude' (*FW*, p. 57). If those irrational negations ('unfacts'
and 'imprecisely') render the sentence unamenable to commonsense interpretation, they also reveal a fundamental distrust of language as the bearer
of forensic truth – at least in Ireland. This distrust is tragically consistent
with a colonial experience that made it impossible for any nineteenth-
century Irish novelist to construct a univocal narrative which spoke equably
for the society as a whole. Indeed, there was no *society as a whole*. (Ironically perhaps, the most forthright account of this predicament comes from
the English novelist W. M. Thackeray, who asked in his *Irish Sketchbook*
(1842): 'Where is the truth to be found in Ireland? There are two truths' –
each corresponding to the Catholic and Protestant viewpoints on history
and society in Ireland.)[26]

The complexity of Joyce's relationship with the English language is usefully conveyed by a further passage in *Finnegans Wake*: 'Behove this sound
of Irish sense. Really? Here English might be seen. Royally? One sovereign
punned to petery pence. Regally? The silence speaks the scene. Fake!' (*FW*,
pp. 12–13). This addresses the question whether the book is written in 'the
King's English' or an Irish version of the same and, if the latter, whether it
is not in fact a downright counterfeit of the other. An apparent reference to
St Peter's pence further suggests that Joyce regards his revolution of the
word as a kind of counter-Reformation, undermining the cultural hegemony
of the Anglican Communion which once ruled Ireland by means of the

Penal Laws, as well as the general climate of Protestant rationalism that gave rise to the English novel. A Swiftian undertone may possibly be detected in the covert allusion to Wood's halfpence, the subject of his *Drapiers Letters* (1724). Comparably, Joyce's new literary coinage is, in effect, a challenge to the sovereignty of English. There is a pervasive wealth of allusion to Irish texts (both printed and oral) in the novels themselves, as well as linguistic practices which are distinctly Irish. These latter variously exemplify ways of using English for the purposes of gossip, song and story-telling, political oratory and patriotic dock speeches.

Joyce's youthful antipathy to the Irish Revival would supply him with numerous examples of brilliant excess for purposes of literary parody. At the same time, it fortified his authority as a classicist among romantics in literary Dublin. In a college oration of 1902, Joyce theorised the difference between classical and romantic in terms of a cognate distinction between realist and idealist, writing that the 'romantic school' finds expression for its ideals under 'insensible figures' which later degenerate into 'feeble shadows' (*CW*, p. 74) – a fate that presumably awaits W. B. Yeats and AE (George Russell) no less than their English antecedents. In contrast to this, the 'classical temper' which he himself espouses is represented as a patient, elaborative art that 'bends up . . . present things and so . . . fashions them that the quick intelligence may go beyond them to their meaning, which is still unuttered' (*CW*, p. 74). This distinction would later serve to fuel Stephen Dedalus's scornful criticism of the Platonist tendency among the literary revivalists in the 'Library' episode of *Ulysses*: 'creepycrawl after Blake's buttocks into eternity of which this vegetable world is but a shadow' (p. 238). A year before that oration of 1902, he had issued a pamphlet entitled 'The Day of the Rabblement', scourging the Irish Literary Theatre for its failure to act as the 'champion of progress' (*CW*, p. 70). In it, Joyce insisted that the business of the theatre was to produce the plays of the modern continental playwrights, since even those of 'the second rank' could 'write very much better plays' than the Literary Theatre had yet has staged (*CW*, p. 70). This was in keeping with his conviction that 'a country which never advanced as far as the miracle play affords no literary model to the artist, and he must look abroad' (*CW*, p. 70), a conviction that shortly afterwards led him into literary exile when he departed from Ireland with Nora Barnacle in 1904, after several preliminary trips to Paris in 1902 and 1903.

Joyce and Moore

In 1905–6, while settled in Pola as a language teacher, Joyce defined his position as an Irish author in a series of letters to Grant Richards, the

London-based publisher of *Dubliners* (1916). Asserting at first the originality of his subject matter, he wrote: 'I do not think any writer has yet presented Dublin to the world. It has been a capital of Europe for a thousand years [and] is supposed to be the second city of the British Empire . . .' He then concluded blithely: 'I think people might be willing to pay for the special odour of corruption which, I hope, floats over my stories.'[27] By May 1905, having met with objections to the realism of the stories, Joyce was still more forthright: 'My intention was to write a chapter in the moral history of my country and I chose Dublin for the scene because that city seemed to me the centre of paralysis . . . I cannot alter what I have written' (*SL*, p. 83). In June, he warned the publisher that he (Richards) would 'retard the course of civilisation in Ireland by preventing the Irish people from having one good look at themselves in my nicely polished looking-glass', before returning once again to the aroma of the collection in a revealing repetition of the earlier phrase: 'It is not my fault that the odour of ashpits and old weeds and offal hangs about my stories' (*SL*, pp. 89–90).

The appeal to authenticity in this last is an obvious hallmark of the kind of realist writer that Joyce aimed to be, but the assertion that Dublin had never been the subject of literary fiction was highly questionable, since Irish novelists had been setting their scenes there since Maria Edgeworth's *The Absentee* (1812). More recently, Somerville and Ross had opened *The Real Charlotte* (1894) with a snapshot of Mountjoy Square that shares an awareness of the brown-brick houses 'brow-beating' each other across the intervening space with an opening sentence in Joyce's 'Araby' set in nearby North Richmond Street. Joyce was inclined to dismiss contemporary Irish writing as 'ill-written, morally obtuse, formless caricature',[28] but there was one work which certainly did not correspond to this description. In 1903, George Moore had published *The Untilled Field* (1903), a book that brought the method of French realism to the matter of Ireland for the first time. Yet Moore's collection was about rural Ireland in the main, and Joyce was therefore right to place his emphasis on the place name in the title. Dublin, as he told Richards, had been chosen because it was 'the centre of paralysis', and a portrait of Dublin was therefore a portrait of Ireland. It is significant, however, that while he was writing *Dubliners*, Joyce already formed the idea for another collection to be called *Provincials* (*SL*, p. 63), presumably dealing with the rest of Ireland and based on the trips he had made to Cork and Mullingar with his father. Though purely notional, this reveals his thinking about the relation between the capital and the country as a whole: all the rest apart from Dublin could comfortably be left to Moore.

The Untilled Field is sometimes seen as a precursor of Joyce's collection, yet Joyce's letters indicate that he had not, in fact, read Moore's stories until after he commenced his own – indeed, until after he had reached Pola in 1904, when he met with them in a continental edition which only appeared that year.[29] On reading it, Joyce wrote to his brother of 'that wretched book of Moore's . . . which the Americans found so remarkable for its "craftsmanship"', adding: 'O, dear me! It is very dull and flat, indeed: and ill written.'[30] Previously, he had dismissed the older novelist in writing that 'it is plain from *Celibates* [1895] and the later novels that [he] is beginning to draw upon his literary account' and that 'his new impulse has no kind of relation to the future of the art' (*CW*, pp. 70–1). Ironically however, some of the stories in *Celibates* are more like stories in *Dubliners* than any in *The Untilled Field*. In all of these transactions, we witness Joyce defending his position against Moore as the first Irish modernist in a way that he did not have to do in dealing with contemporaries such as Seumas O'Kelly, whose tales of 'beautiful, pure faithful, Connacht girls and lithe, broad-shouldered open-faced young Connacht men' he ridiculed in another letter (*SL*, pp. 133–4). Yet if Joyce was modern and continental, he was also deeply Irish; and, in retrospect, his engagement with the Irish world he left behind explains the magnitude of his achievement better than his departure from it. Joyce the modernist and Joyce the Irishman are not ultimately in conflict.

Joyce and a national literature

W. B. Yeats liked to quote Oscar Wilde's saying that the Irish were the greatest talkers since the Greeks, and the dramatis personae of *Ulysses* arguably prove the case. Yet their actual conversation forms a compara-tively small part of the total text of that novel, the rest being made up of passages that draw their 'styles' from the literary environment. In this respect, his works can be seen as a census of the books that Irish men and women were reading or had read as well as a catalogue of the cultural influences which, in a very definite and linguistically identifiable sense, constituted them as the men and women that they are. In the case of Little Chandler, shackled to a 'sober inartistic life',[31] it is the poetry of the Irish Literary Revival which drives his ambitions, causing him to imagine the reviews that his yet-unwritten volume will receive: '*Mr Chandler has the gift of easy and graceful verse. . . A wistful sadness pervades these poems. . . The Celtic note*'. Joyce gives further twist to his literary scalpel in writing next: 'It was a pity his name was not more Irish-looking', a fault which Little Chandler sets out to amend (*Dubliners*, p. 80). A comparable fantasist is Gerty McDowell, the young woman in the 'Nausicaa' episode of *Ulysses* who throws herself into an imaginary relationship with the 'dark stranger' (Leopold Bloom), allowing him to glimpse her underwear on Dollymount Strand. Joyce called the manner adopted in this chapter a 'namby-pamby marmalady drawsery (*alto là!*) style' (*SL*, p. 246) and the language that reflects her counter-factual habits of thought and feeling is gleaned from the columns of the *Princess Novelette* and the *Lady's Pictorial*, women's journals replete with tips from the 'leaders of fashion' (*Ulysses*, pp. 453, 455).

The most extended exercise in stylistic parody with a specifically Irish bent in *Ulysses* is unquestionably the 'Cyclops' chapter, broadly narrated by an anonymous 'Thersitic' figure, whose acid comments are conveyed in the local demotic ('and be damned but a bloody sweep came along and he near drove his gear into my eye', p. 377). This is in sharp distinction to the 'gigantism' of other passages, for which Victorian translations of Irish hero-tales are the chief model: 'The figure seated on a large boulder at the foot of a round tower was that of a broadshouldered deepchested stronglimbed frankeyed redhaired freely freckled shaggybearded wide-mouthed largenosed longheaded deepvoiced barekneed brawnyhanded hairylegged ruddyfaced sinewyarmed hero' (p. 382). To this concoction is added an inflection that owes less to the Irish manuscript tradition than to the special ineptitude of stylistically footless writers ('Lovely maidens sit in close proximity to the roots of the lovely trees singing the most lovely songs', p. 379), while yet another manner is devised to convey the atmosphere of 'heroticisms', an epithet coined in *Finnegans Wake* (p. 614) which well suits the humour of a largely feminine crowd in attendance at a patriotic martyrdom in Joyce's remorselessly irreverent burlesque of national sacrifice on the gallows. All in all, the chapter captures a politico-cultural landscape of such emotional rancidity that the plain truth of Leopold Bloom's naïve appeal for love as the moving principle of all social life ('I mean the opposite of hatred', p. 432) provides the only moral light in the chapter.

Joyce's antipathy to the national revival did not prevent him admiring individual writers and none more than W. B. Yeats, whose story 'The Tables of the Law' he knew by heart – so very different in surface and symbol from his own fiction. Stephen Dedalus carries the poem 'Who Goes with Fergus?', from *The Countess Cathleen*, in his heart since the refrain 'no more turn aside and brood / Upon love's bitter mystery' answers so well to his tormented memory of his own dead mother (*Ulysses*, p. 681). It was, however, the Irish *poète maudit* James Clarence Mangan (1803–49) whom Joyce saw as most representative of the predicament of the Irish artist whose country's history encloses him 'so straitly that even in his hours of extreme individual passion he can barely reduce its walls to ruins', as Joyce told a university audience in Trieste in 1907 (*CW*, p. 185). The implication that he should transcend his country's historical legacy in order to fulfil his individuality was a key doctrine with the young Joyce. Mangan is thus, in almost every way, the epitome of an Irish racial destiny that Joyce himself intended to elude: 'Love of grief, despair, high-sounding threats - these are the great traditions of the race of James Clarence Mangan, and in that impoverished figure, thin and weakened, an hysterical nationalism receives its final justification' (*CW*, p. 86).

By a large measure, however, it is the 'national poet' Thomas Moore (1779–1852) who occupies most space of all Irish writers in the works of James Joyce. Moore, a Catholic educated at Trinity College Dublin, the friend of Robert Emmet and of Lord Byron, was the author of saccharine drawing-room songs accompanying Irish airs arranged for the piano by Sir John Stevenson. Moore promulgated the poetical idea of a lovable Irishman bearing secret sorrows for lost national glories, but manfully resisting the extremes of nostalgia or revolution in pursuit of the unattainable in a modern British world. The scale on which Joyce's books reverberate with lines from Moore's *Irish Melodies* (issued from 1808 and collected in 1820) can be judged from the fact that he carefully incorporated the initial phrase of each melody in *Finnegans Wake* with a nearby reference to the associated air on each occasion. This act of total recall is barely more than a just acknowledgment of the immense familiarity of Moore's lyrics in Irish society of the time, from 'Erin, The Tear and the Smile in Thy Eyes' and 'The Harp that Once Through Tara's Halls', to 'She Is Far from the Land' and 'The Last Rose of Summer'. All too often abjectly sentimental, the melodies represent an ambiguous legacy that Joyce pilloried in his glancing sketch in *A Portrait* of the 'servile head [and] shuffling feet' of Moore's statue in College Street, 'humbly conscious of its indignity' (*Portrait*, p. 183). Moore's complicity in the project of what might be called Irish auto-exoticism is perfectly captured in the *Dubliners* story that takes its title from the song which includes these wistful lines:

> I'll sing thee songs of Araby
> And tales of far Cashmere,
> Wild tales to cheat thee of a sigh,
> Or charm thee with a tear.
>
> And dreams delight shall on thee break,
> And rainbow visions rise,
> And all my soul shall strive to wake
> Sweet wonder in thy eyes.

In Joyce's 'Araby', a harsh verdict on the form of delusion crystallised here is issued in the final sentence: 'Gazing into the darkness I saw myself as a creature driven and derided by vanity; and my eyes burned with anguish and anger' (*Dubliners*, p. 36).

For Joyce, Moore embodied perfectly a tendency among Irish writers which he identified as the 'court jester' syndrome. Thus, when Stephen reflects how Buck Mulligan – the 'gay betrayer' (*Ulysses*, p. 15) – expects him to drip-feed the Celtophilic English visitor Haines with specimens of Irish wit in the opening chapter of *Ulysses*, he feels the lethal old infection hovering near:

> For Haines's chapbook. No-one here to hear. Tonight deftly amid wild drink and talk, to pierce the polished mail of his mind. What then? A jester at the court of his master, indulged and disesteemed, winning a clement master's praise. Why had they chosen all that part? Not wholly for the smooth caress. For them too history was a tale like any other too often heard, their land a pawnshop. (*Ulysses*, p. 29)

Anglo-Irish writers in the Protestant tradition who served up Irish peasants for affectionate ridicule include Samuel Lover (1797–1868) and Charles Lever (1806–72). Many of the former's comic-romantic songs such as 'The Low-Backed Car' and 'O, Thady Brady You Are My Darlin'' feature frequently in *Ulysses*, as does a virtual anthology of Irish ballad and story, rann and song (in Yeats's phrase), from throughout the Victorian period. Among Catholic songsters, Charles Joseph Kickham (1828–82) is best represented with songs such as 'Patrick Sheehan' and 'Rory of the Hill', both of which adorn the 'Cyclops' episode of *Ulysses*, where his nationalist credentials are implicitly honoured. At the same time, a somewhat different Ireland, tinged with atavistic violence, became the stock-in-trade of the Victorian authors who created the Irish Gothic novel (see chapter 4 above), and Joyce was sufficiently attentive to this tradition to take Sheridan Le Fanu's *The House by the Churchyard* (1863), a novel concerning a murder in the Phoenix Park and set in Chapelizod, as an important source for the setting and the narrative of *Finnegans Wake*.

In November 1906, Joyce asked Aunt Josephine in Dublin to send him 'any old editions' of Kickham, Gerald Griffin, William Carleton and the Banims (John and Michael),[32] together with 'Xmas present made up of tram-tickets, advts, handbills, posters, papers, programmes, &c.' (*SL*, p. 124). There is scant indication that he engaged with these writers in any extended way and, though each represents a phase in the rather unhappy attempt to produce a prose literature for Catholic Ireland, all belong more or less indiscriminately to the subliterary sounding-chamber of *Ulysses*, along with the operas which provide a distinct element in the sing-a-long culture of contemporary Dublin. Prominent among these are *The Bohemian*

Girl (1843) and *The Rose of Castile* (1857) by the Irish composer-dramatist Michael Balfe. The former plays a prominent part in 'Eveline' of *Dubliners*, while his aria 'I Dreamt that I Dwelt' from it and 'Killarney' from another opera (*Innisfallen*) supply important hinges of meaning in 'Clay' and 'A Mother'. However, it is the 'The Lass of Aughrim', an anonymous ballad which Nora sang to Joyce, that provides the climactic musical moment in the last story and the collection as a whole (*Dubliners*, pp. 240ff). As a young man Joyce consumed the melodramatic fare of the Queen's Theatre, Dublin, and the most commonly referenced Irish dramatist in his work is Dion Boucicault, master of the genre. *Arrah-na-Pogue* (1841) and *The Shaughraun* (1874) are much in evidence in *Finnegans Wake*, and there is suspicion that Joyce identified Nora Barnacle with Arrah; Shaun the Post, who marries her in the play, is an alias of one brother in the *Wake*, while the other is identified as Shem the Penman – based on *Jim the Penman*, a nineteenth-century forger who became the central character of a play by Sir Charles Young. Forgery is much to the point, since, in the chapter of *Finnegans Wake* devoted to Shem and dealing with the phenomenon of artistic personality and artistic representation, *Ulysses* is described as an 'epical forged cheque' drawn at the public's expense (p. 182).

The owner of a good tenor voice, Joyce nearly won the *Feis Ceol* in 1904 with a rendering of Yeats's 'The Sally Gardens', losing to the future Count John McCormack only because he refused to sing from score. More than three hundred songs and fifty nursery rhymes are quoted in *Ulysses* alone, and to this can be added an equal number of references to European operas – most of them part of the currency of turn-of-the-century Irish cultural life and hence the reason for their inclusion. In fact, the idea that the Irish are *not* a separate race or nation – that a Jew like Leopold Bloom can be an Irishman in both a pragmatic and affective sense; that Irish minds are permeated by European culture – is the fundamental trope of *Ulysses* and the explanation of its 'mythic method' and intertextual procedures. By the same token, the greatest strength and weakness of Joyce's final book consists in the compulsion to build up a holistic image of humanity by synthesising the totality of its cultural manifestations in all times and places: that is to say, by 'totalising' Everyman 'in lashons of language' so as to reconstruct a post-Edenic image of the original Adam who – according to the Christian mythos – is 'ultimendly respunchable for the hubbub caused in Edenborough' (p. 129). In this way, *Finnegans Wake* is first and foremost a testament to the very idea of a global culture, or even a 'global village', as Marshall McLuhan has called it. James Joyce was an Irish writer who set his sights on the universal, and the course of his career from *Dubliners* to *Finnegans Wake* is the implacable consequences of that design. In this sense,

Joyce the European and Joyce the Irishman are no more contradictory than Joyce the modern and Joyce the medievalist. What unites all of these is his uniquely perspicacious grasp on the true complexity of the modern world and a corresponding ability to translate it into radically innovative literary fiction.

NOTES

1. James Joyce, *Stephen Hero: Part of the First Draft of* A Portrait of the Artist as a Young Man, ed. Theodore Spencer, rev. edn (1944; London: Triad Grafton, 1986), pp. 36, 167. Hereinafter *SH*.
2. Forrest Read (ed.), *Pound/Joyce* (New York: New Directions, 1970), pp. 28, 89, 32.
3. *The Dial* (November 1923); quoted in Richard Ellmann, *James Joyce* (1959; Oxford: Clarendon Press, 1965), p. 541.
4. Letter of 15 November 1926; repr. in Read, *Pound/Joyce*, p. 228.
5. Quoted in Stan Gébler Davies, *James Joyce: A Portrait of the Artist* (Davis-Poynter, 1975), p. 247.
6. *Selected Letters of James Joyce*, ed. Richard Ellmann (London: Faber & Faber, 1975), p. 282. Hereinafter *SL*.
7. Arthur Power, *Conversations with James Joyce* (London: John Millington, 1974), p. 91.
8. James Joyce, *A Portrait of the Artist as a Young Man*, definitive text corrected by Chester Anderson, ed. Richard Ellmann (1916; London: Jonathan Cape, 1968), p. 180.
9. James Joyce, *Finnegans Wake* (London: Faber & Faber; New York: Viking Press, 1939), pp. 119–23. Hereinafter *FW*.
10. *The Critical Writings of James Joyce*, eds. Ellsworth Mason and Richard Ellmann (New York: Viking Press, 1964), p. 70. Hereinafter *CW*.
11. See C. P. Curran, *James Joyce Remembered* (Oxford: Oxford University Press, 1964), p. 61.
12. In a letter to Mme de Chantepie, 18 March 1857, Flaubert wrote: 'L'artiste doit être dans son œuvre comme Dieu dans la Création, invisible et tout-puissant, qu'on le sente partout, mais qu'on ne le voie pas.' ('An artist must be in his work like god in creation, invisible, and all-powerful: he should be everywhere felt, but nowhere seen.') In Francis Steegmüller (trans.), *Selected Letters of Gustave Flaubert* (London: Farrar, Straus & Young, 1954), p. 186.
13. *Freeman's Journal* (7 April 1917), repr. in Robert Deming (ed.), *James Joyce: The Critical Heritage* (London: Routledge & Kegan Paul, 1970), pp. 98–9.
14. Quoted in Ellmann, *James Joyce*, p. 541.
15. James Joyce, *Ulysses* (1922; London: Bodley Head, 1960), p. 248. Pagination in this edition is shared by *Ulysses: Annotated Students' Edition*, introduction and notes by Declan Kiberd (London: Penguin Books, 1992).
16. Quoted in Ellmann, *James Joyce*, p. 490.
17. Ellmann, *James Joyce*, p. 650.
18. Joyce, *Finnegans Wake*, p. 381.
19. Ellmann, *James Joyce*, p. 212.

20. Ernest Boyd, *Ireland's Literary Renaissance* (1923 rev. edn; Dublin: Allen Figgis 1968), p. 302.
21. Vivian Mercier, *The Irish Comic Tradition* (Oxford: Oxford University Press, 1962), p. 239.
22. Douglas Hyde delivered his influential lecture, 'The Necessity for De-Anglicising Ireland', to the National Literary Society in November, 1892.
23. *Quarterly Review* (October 1922); repr. in Deming (ed.), *James Joyce: The Critical Heritage*, p. 210.
24. Power, *Conversations with James Joyce*, p. 69.
25. Letter to James Joyce of 23 November 1928. In Stuart Gilbert (ed.), *Letters of James Joyce*, vol. I (New York: Viking Press 1966), pp. 274–5.
26. W. M. Thackeray, *The Irish Sketchbook* (1842; Belfast: Blackstaff 1985), p. 364.
27. Stuart Gilbert and Richard Ellmann (eds.), *The Letters of James Joyce* (New York: Viking Press 1966), vol. II, pp. 122–3.
28. Gilbert and Ellmann, *The Letters of James Joyce*, vol. II, p. 99.
29. Gilbert and Ellmann, *The Letters of James Joyce*, vol. II, p. 71.
30. Gilbert and Ellmann, *The Letters of James Joyce*, vol. II, p. 112.
31. James Joyce, *Dubliners* [1914], corrected text, with an explanatory note by Robert Scholes (London: Jonathan Cape, 1967), p. 80.
32. Gerald Griffin (1803–40); William Carleton (1794–1869); John Banim (1798–1842) and Michael Banim (1796–1874).

GUIDE TO FURTHER READING

Attridge, Derek (ed.). *The Cambridge Companion to James Joyce*. Cambridge: Cambridge University Press, 1990.

Aubert, Jacques. *The Aesthetics of James Joyce*. Baltimore: Johns Hopkins University Press, 1992.

Beja, Morris. *James Joyce: A Literary Life*. Basingstoke: Macmillan, 1992.

Brown, Richard. *James Joyce and Sexuality*. Cambridge: Cambridge University Press, 1985.

Cheng, Vincent J. *Joyce, Race, and Empire*. Cambridge: Cambridge University Press, 1995.

Ellmann, Richard. *The Consciousness of Joyce*. London: Faber & Faber, 1977.

Fairhall, James. *James Joyce and the Question of History*. Cambridge: Cambridge University Press, 1993.

Gifford, Don. *Joyce Annotated: Notes for* Dubliners *and* A Portrait of the Artist as A Young Man. Rev. edn. Berkeley: University of California Press, 1988.

Gifford, Don. *Ulysses Annotated: Notes for James Joyce's* Ulysses. Berkeley: University of California Press, 1988.

Gilbert, Stuart. *James Joyce's Ulysses: A Study*. London: Faber & Faber, 1930.

Herr, Cheryl. *Joyce's Anatomy of Culture*. Urbana: Illinois University Press, 1986.

Howes, Marjorie and Derek Attridge (eds.). *Semicolonial Joyce*. Cambridge: Cambridge University Press, 2000.

Kenner, Hugh. *Dublin's Joyce*. Bloomington: Indiana University Press, 1955.

MacCabe, Colin. *James Joyce and the Revolution of the Word*. London: Macmillan, 1979.

McHugh, Roland. *Annotations to* Finnegans Wake. London: Routledge & Kegan Paul, 1980.

Norris, Margot. *A Companion to James Joyce's* Ulysses. New York: Bedford Books, 1998.

Peake, C. H. *James Joyce: The Citizen and The Artist.* London: Arnold, 1977.

Potts, Willard (ed.). *Portraits of the Artist in Exile: Recollections of James Joyce by Europeans.* Seattle: University of Washington Press, 1979.

Scott, Bonnie Kime. *Joyce and Feminism.* Bloomington: University of Indiana Press; London: Harvester Press, 1984.

Tindall, William York. *A Reader's Guide to James Joyce.* New York: Noonday, 1959.

8

NORMAN VANCE

Region, realism and reaction, 1922–1972

Irish regionalism

'Regionalism' is a topical theme, kept before us by the regional policies of the European Union, of which Ireland is a member, and by recent discussions of regionalism in connection with the contemporary phenomenon of economic globalisation. But the concept of 'region' or 'regionalism' in Irish fiction is not straightforward, either before or after the establishment of Northern Ireland and the Irish Free State in 1920–2. Within the tradition of regional fiction in English, Maria Edgeworth made a pioneering contribution with her Irish novel *Castle Rackrent* (1800), and this was generously acknowledged by Sir Walter Scott, who helped to pass on the lessons to subsequent regional writers. But Edgeworth's example did not of itself produce strongly localised Irish fiction. The main market for Irish fiction has always been outside Ireland, and from the outset this rather discouraged a regional or sub-regional specificity which would not be appreciated at a distance. In consequence, the whole of Ireland, or at least rural Ireland, tended to be identified as a single non-metropolitan 'region', the literary province of nineteenth- and indeed twentieth-century Irish writers in English, just as a largely undifferentiated Scotland tended to be seen as a single region, the province of Scottish writers.[1]

Broadly speaking, this external perception of Ireland has not been seriously challenged from within, at least within what is now the Irish Republic (the old Free State). If one discounts the Dublin metropolitan area and the remaining Irish-speaking areas as special cases, then county, provincial and regional identities and rivalries throughout the rest of Ireland survive, if at all, mainly through sporting fixtures and other competitions. Since independence, the strongly centralised tradition of government has generally encouraged the sense of the whole country as a single region administered from Dublin. In 1975, after the Republic of Ireland became a member of the European Community, it was, at its own request, classified as a single region for the purposes of the Community Regional Policy, and Dublin retained full central control over regional funds allocated to Ireland.

This strategic appearance of homogeneity is reflected in twentieth-century Irish fiction, which often continues to present a largely undifferentiated rural Ireland. In her pioneering study *The English Regional Novel* (1941), the Yorkshire novelist Phyllis Bentley felt able to compile a table of 'English Regional Novelists (Arranged by County)'. It would be very difficult to do the same for every county in Ireland, even if exceptions could be made for Cork or Kerry. Many of the more rural Irish counties have historically had such small populations and have received so little specific literary attention that nil returns would be inevitable. In recent years, numerous literary summer schools have sprung up across rural Ireland, including the John Hewitt Summer Schools in Antrim and Armagh and the Brian Merriman Summer School in Clare, following the older-established Yeats Summer School in Sligo. Though these schools have done something to increase awareness of the local base of particular writers, they have addressed general and national as much as regional issues, and in any case Hewitt, Merriman and Yeats, and many of the other writers thus honoured, were poets rather than novelists. The concept of an Irish regional (or subregional) novel has still not really established itself. The first three of the four provinces of Ireland – Munster, Leinster, Connaught and Ulster, each perhaps too large and varied to have much geographical distinctiveness – have long ceased to have much administrative or political significance either, so arrangement by province rather than county would be little better: the term 'Leinster novelist' has no more currency than 'Leitrim novelist' or 'Louth novelist'.

On the other hand, 'Ulster novelist' does convey something, even if 'Ulster', historically the nine most northerly counties, is used inaccurately as a synonym for the six counties of present-day Northern Ireland. In a recent comparative study of partition and literature, Joe Cleary has observed that the political partition of the island of Ireland, strenuously resented in extreme nationalist circles both north and south, has led to a kind of cultural partitioning as well: 'the state division has cut quite deeply into the imaginative contours of contemporary Irish literature'.[2] Cleary does not directly acknowledge that perceived cultural difference was one of the factors leading to partition in the first place. In so far as 'Ulster' constitutes a distinct region or imagined community in Irish fiction, this is attributable to an incoherent mixture of regional history and geography, distinctive local dialects and aggressively insecure rival traditions in religion and politics which have become more concentrated and embittered since partition. But 'Ulster', variously prosperous and impoverished, urban, suburban and rural, Protestant, Catholic and mixed, is not itself homogeneous, and different Ulster novels reflect that variousness.

Quite early in the nineteenth century, when the Irish novel was still a new form, James McHenry (1785–1845) wrote a series of novels presenting the distinctiveness of the topography, the Scots-influenced speech and the hardy, largely Presbyterian people of the north-eastern corner of Ulster. Though born in the north of Ireland, in Larne, Co. Antrim, and educated for the ministry of the Presbyterian Church in Belfast and Glasgow, McHenry had emigrated to Philadelphia where he worked as a doctor and journalist. He was proudly conscious that earlier Presbyterian settlers from Ulster had made a distinctive contribution to taming the American wilderness in the colonial period and had gone on to fight alongside Washington in the War of Independence; some of that contribution is reflected in his American novel, *The Wilderness, or The Youthful Days of Washington* (1823). Other novels such *The O'Halloran, or The Insurgent Chief. A Tale of the United Irishmen* (1824) or *The Hearts of Steel. An Irish Historical Tale of the Last Century* (1825), engaging with recent Irish history (and subsequent emigration to America) in the even-handed manner pioneered by Sir Walter Scott's treatment of Scottish history in *Waverley* (1814), are set in the north of Ireland, with detailed reference to the topography of the north Antrim coast.

More or less indignant reaction to racial preconception animates McHenry's fiction, as it animates many subsequent Irish fictions. His contemporary, the novelist Sydney Owenson (Lady Morgan), had helped to perpetuate the Irish stereotype of Celtic conviviality, Catholicism, Milesian fancy and timeless – not to say ahistorical – ardour and generosity of spirit, noting in *The Wild Irish Girl* (1806) that this 'genuine Irish character' gradually disappeared as one travelled up into the north of Ireland, which she effectively acknowledged as a separate region. The already widespread stage-Irish perception of the Irishman at home and abroad as warm-hearted, illogical, romantic and feckless could not accommodate northern Irishmen such as McHenry himself, Presbyterian, Scots-descended, resourceful, grimly industrious and uncompromising, perhaps a little dour, who in the course of the eighteenth century had settled in Pennsylvania and points south and west, and had toiled and fought to settle and secure an independent United States.

A different kind of history and a different kind of reaction can be found in the work of the Banim brothers. *The Boyne Water* (1826), perhaps their best historical novel, reacted against sectarian triumphalism stemming from the conflicts of the seventeenth century and incorporated distinctive northern scenes and Scots-descended northern Protestants in a narrative which attempted to encompass the whole of Ireland and its different peoples and traditions. But this specificity was unusual. Even though William Carleton grew up in Co. Tyrone, in the heart of rural Ulster, he usually tried in his *Traits and Stories of the Irish Peasantry* (1830–3) and in his novels to give a generically Irish, rather than local or regional, quality to dialect and subject matter alike. It was not until the early twentieth century that the twin triumphs of (mainly) Catholic nationalism and rural-minded Celtic revivalism confirmed a general sense of (mainly) Protestant and partly urban and industrial north-east Ulster as a place apart, owing more culturally to English and lowland Scottish influences, and to Protestant traditions, than to resurgent Celtic Catholicism.

This sometimes truculent awareness stimulated regional consciousness and the production and consumption of regional writing, both anticipating and later helping to rationalise the non-inclusion of six northern counties in the new Irish Free State in 1922. The new arrangement was formally expressed in the establishment of a separate regional parliament and administration in Belfast, still within the United Kingdom, which was eventually redescribed as the United Kingdom of Great Britain and Northern Ireland.

Ulster regionalism

The process of reaction to emergent Catholic nationalism and the Literary Revival, and the literary exploration of other identities and concerns in Ulster, characteristically involved Protestant clergymen, their relations and their congregations. As an alternative to embracing the newly and aggressively articulated 'Irish Ireland', the sense of special connection with Presbyterian Scotland (or North Britain) as motherland for Irish Presbyterians was often emphasised. Moreover, the traditions of rural life in much of the region were English-speaking rather than Irish-speaking, so for local writers the idiom and atmosphere of Lady Gregory's Kiltartan, in the Irish-speaking far west, were usually less appropriate than English or Scottish literary models. Daughter and wife of English Unitarian ministers, Elizabeth Gaskell had developed social sympathies and a sense of specific communities in her novels and stories as a consequence of her own and her husband's pastoral experience, and similar claims could be made for several Ulster writers. Agnes Romilly White (1872–1945) was the daughter of a Church of Ireland Rector who ministered in Dundonald, just outside Belfast, from 1890 to 1912. Vivid recollections of the Dundonald years and sensitive pastoral awareness of poverty and bereavement, as well as of the human comedy, lie behind her novels of village life near the city, *Gape Row* (1934) and the more closely plotted *Mrs Murphy Buries the Hatchet* (1936).

J. M. Barrie's *Auld Licht Idylls* (1888) and other productions of the so-called 'Kailyard' school of Scottish writers, accused by their critics of seeing life through the window of a Presbyterian manse, had provided a model for sketches of Ulster Presbyterian life such as Archibald McIlroy's *The Auld Meetin' Hoose Green* (Belfast, 1898), based on his native Ballyclare, in Co. Antrim, and, rather later, *Carragloon: Tales of our Townland* (1935) by the Presbyterian minister and naturalist W. R. Megaw. The Tyrone minister W. F. Marshall (1888–1959) was more ambitious in his historical novel, *Planted by a River* (1948). Set in rural Tyrone in the early eighteenth century, a peaceful era but within living memory of the seige of Derry in 1689, it responds to the nationalist and nativist legend of dispossession and oppression on the land by presenting Psalm-singing Presbyterian settlers (or 'planters') as patiently improving previously uncultivated land. The protagonist's grandfather had come as a stranger from Ayrshire into that part of Ireland, dominated by the rampart of the Sperrin mountains and hills glowing with whin blossom, but now, two generations later, there is an acquired sense of belonging to this unchanging landscape: 'This was my country.'[3] The title recalls the first Psalm, Scottish metrical version ('He shall be like a tree that hath / Been planted by a river'), describing the blessedness of the godly, and serves as a reminder of perceived connections between the religious confidence in different places of the Jewish people of the Old Testament and that of Scots-descended Presbyterians 'planted' in Ulster.

The Ulster novelist Forrest Reid (1875–1947), great-nephew of the Presbyterian historian James Seaton Reid, born into the business world of Belfast, reacted against his characteristic northern Protestant background but not to the extent of espousing Celtic revivalism. He owed much more to the writing of friends in England, such as Walter de la Mare, and to nineteenth-century French literature, than to Fenianism or Young Ireland. His own distinctive cult of youth and romantic reverie in novels such as *Peter Waring* (1937) and *Young Tom* (1944) went with a long-cultivated aestheticism which issued in a superb, very English essay in Victorian art appreciation, *Illustrators of the Sixties* (1928), and a volume of prose translations from the Greek Anthology, eventually published in 1943. The neo-Paganism of this collection and of his outlook more generally invites comparison not with Yeats, but with the Edwardian cult of Pan, illustrated in 'The Story of a Panic' (1902), an early short story by his friend E. M. Forster, or Kenneth Grahame's *The Wind in the Willows* (1908).

The Ulster dramatist and novelist St John Ervine (1883–1971), a realist where Reid was more of a fantasist, stayed closer to his northern roots. Born in Belfast but early exposed to the London-based Fabian socialism of Wells and Shaw, from which he always claimed he had derived his higher education, he wrote for Dublin's Abbey Theatre successful, specifically Ulster plays such as *Mixed Marriage* (1911) and *John Ferguson* (1915). A cantankerous Ulster unionist in later life, he started out as a moderate nationalist convinced that the business-like ethos of urban Ulster could contribute significantly to an independent Ireland. But he was ambivalent about his native place. His novel *Mrs Martin's Man* (1914), originally written as another Ulster play for the Abbey but rejected by Yeats, draws on childhood memories of his redoubtable shopkeeper grandmother and the austere self-reliant industry characteristic of lower middle-class life in strongly Protestant east Belfast and north Down. Disciplined by the residual dramatic structure, the evocation is precise but unsentimental. Mrs Martin's absentee husband is sullen and irresponsible, but he is shown to have had reasons for wanting to escape: the peace and frugal comfort of home, and his wife's calm and stoical resilience, have to be balanced against the stifling respectability, sanctimonious humbug and bigotry of the locality. The same congenial, but often also narrow and self-important, world is invoked in some of his later novels, such as *The Foolish Lovers* (1920) and *The Wayward Man* (1927); both of these use flawed, quasi-autobiographical personae to explore the Wellsian theme of half-foolish longing to escape from the limitations of provincialism, shops and shopkeepers, tempered by loneliness and the attractiveness of the familiar. Ervine's refusal in his fiction (if not always in his plays or his journalism) to idealise ordinary and often difficult lives in obscure places, or to relapse into sentimental regional idyll, and his tendency to present real places under transparent pseudo-nyms ('Ballyards' for 'Newtownards', 'Millreagh' as a conflation of Millisle and nearby Donaghadee), recall the 'Wessex' novels of his friend Thomas Hardy, a model for Ervine as for subsequent Ulster novelists. Hardy's song 'Donaghadee' (in *Human Shows*, 1925) prompted a letter from Ervine about the meaning and pronunciation of the name.

There were other connections between English and Ulster regionalism and regionalists. To take an early example, Shan Bullock (1865–1935) wrote austere narratives of Co. Fermanagh country life, unassisted by any obviously benign providence, which revisit several of Hardy's recurrent themes from an Ulster perspective. Urbanisation and the late nineteenth-century agricultural depression in England had adversely affected country life, as depicted in Hardy's regional novels, and this had its counterpart in the perennial problem of Irish land, felt all the more acutely at the end of the nineteenth century because of the perceived inadequacy of successive reforms, beginning with Gladstone's Land Act of 1870. Rural Ulster, with a better history of landlord and tenant relations than elsewhere in Ireland, had maintained a modest prosperity, but this did not extend across the whole province. Fermanagh in the far west had been particularly badly affected by the Famine and its aftermath, and the decline of traditional industries, and the lure of industrial Belfast and the emigrant ship, precipitated severe rural depopulation. Bullock's father was steward to the Earl of Erne and later a tenant farmer at Killynick on the southern shore of Lough Erne, so he was fully aware of the problems from childhood. The increasingly unsatisfactory economics of life on the poorish land around Lough Erne, despite the magnificence of lake and mountain scenery, gave rise to unsentimental narratives such as *By Thrasna River* (1895), recounting the difficult courtship of the inarticulate Wee James Trotter, a small hill farmer; *Dan the Dollar* (1906), in which the money from America that will change everything does not last; and *The Loughsiders* (1924). In this last novel the central character, Richard Jebb, is a coldly calculating middle-aged farmer who craftily secures a farm by marrying a widow; but he is a realist rather than a rascal and is treated with some sympathy. He speaks for the cramped lives of all his neighbours when he says to an old friend, with characteristically understated mildness, 'Don't ye ever feel, Mary, that God could be a trifle more generous to ye without much of a struggle?'[4]

The generosity of the Almighty is more strenuously challenged in Hardy, whose anti-pastoral realism was combined in his later novels with a mounting impatience with the institutional church and an irascibly liberal, progressive attitude towards unconventional sexuality. Sam Hanna Bell (1909–90) showed some sympathy with this point of view in his bleakly humane novel, *December Bride*. Published in 1951 with an epigraph taken from one of Hardy's poems, this was subsequently adapted for the stage (1955) and successfully filmed by Thaddaeus O'Sullivan in 1990. Set in a remote farming community on the shores of Strangford Lough in Co. Down and based on a true story, it presents us with the sturdily independent servant Sarah Gomartin. Despite the conventional outrage of the minister, an unhappily married man who is himself guiltily attracted to her, Sarah continues to live with two bachelor brothers after their widower father's death, bears a son which either of them might have fathered and eventually, late in life, marries one of the brothers, but reluctantly and only because her own daughter's marriage is in prospect. Hardy's Tess in *Tess of the d'Urbervilles*, mother of an illegitimate child, is coat-trailingly described as a 'pure woman' who had broken none of nature's laws, and it is implied that a similar claim can be made for Sarah Gomartin. She is scathing about making any compromise with public opinion, courageously telling the minister that marrying one of the brothers for the sake of appearances would be mere hypocrisy, 'to bend and contrive things so that all would be smooth from the outside, like the way a lazy workman finishes a creel'.[5] But the situation is not romanticised and she is hardly a romantic heroine: even in her love she is reserved, passionless and undemonstrative, and she is capable of sectarian spite against a Catholic neighbour.

Bell was a pioneering features producer (mainly for radio) with the Northern Ireland region of the BBC, an underestimated influence on the development of Ulster writing, and was responsible for numerous outside broadcasts and programmes even-handedly investigating the varied customs and traditions of the region, both Catholic and Protestant. Politically a man of the left, less comfortable than Marshall or Ervine with the plantation of Ulster and then the growth of aggressively Protestant industrial and commercial Belfast from the late eighteenth century, he sharply interrogated both processes in his acerbic historical novels, *Across the Narrow Seas* (1987) and *A Man Flourishing* (1973).

Maurice Leitch (b.1933), who also worked for the BBC as a producer in Belfast and London, was equally uncomfortable with the sectarian heritage of his region. Born in Muckamore, Co. Antrim, he had worked as a teacher and was sensitive to the undercurrents of power and religious prejudice in small places. One of his most effective earlier novels, set in south Antrim, is *The Liberty Lad* (1965), with a well-intentioned, late-maturing schoolteacher protagonist. The story juxtaposes threatened factory closure and a corrupt unionist politician. In some ways, Leitch anticipates the 'dirty realism' associated with southern Irish writers of the 1990s, such as Dermot Bolger and Roddy Doyle. Even before the outbreak of the Ulster Troubles, the subject of later Leitch novels such as *Silver's City* (1981), Leitch had sensed and conveyed terminal decay, sullen hatred and sour futility in his region. This is explored in *Poor Lazarus* (1969), which is set in 1967 in the tense border area of south Armagh and Monaghan, where the IRA border campaign of the 1950s is a raw and recent memory. The two central characters – the Derry-born Canadian film-producer Quigley, who needs to make a film about the locality, and the disturbed, unhappily married, wilfully unsuccessful shopkeeper Yarr, the local man who is showing him round – are both in a sense burnt-out cases borrowing some semblance of vitality from each other, neither of them really knowing where to start or what they are looking for. The question of what to make of it all is obviously bigger than either of them. Narrative point of view is managed with some technical virtuosity so that it oscillates between Yarr and Quigley's diary. Recurring themes are the withering of dreams and the emptiness of local life, at best shallow performances represented by a debased sexuality and a series of camera-friendly set pieces in which Quigley might be interested, such as a dance, a brutal cockfight and an

Orange meeting. The eventually suicidal paranoia of Yarr, a Protestant in a mainly Catholic area, does duty for larger insecurities and the surreal madness of his time and place.

The innocent yet instructive outsider's perception represented by the Irish-Canadian film-maker Quigley has a parallel in *Nothing Happens in Carmincross* (1985) by the Tyrone novelist and broadcaster Benedict Kiely (b.1919), the culmination of forty years of novel-writing. In this novel Mervyn Kavanagh, an Irish-American, comes back to his native rural Ulster for a family wedding. Attentive, like Kiely himself, to oral tradition, ballad and folk tale, Kavanagh develops through exposure to new sights and scenes and endless talk an ever-widening and ever-lengthening consciousness of the multiple contexts of terrorism – Catholic and Protestant – and indigenous political violence. Nothing, and yet everything, happens in Carmincross, at least in the mind. Local hatreds are linked with English, American and European wars and with Irish writings ranging from the Book of Kells, Sydney Owenson, Wolfe Tone and Thomas Davis to James Joyce and beyond. Kiely's richly, even oppressively allusive sense of cultural complexity and the problem of how to write about troubled (Northern) Ireland is honed by his own earlier critical and scholarly encounters with the fiction of William Carleton (*Poor Scholar*, 1948) and more recent Irish novelists (*Modern Irish Fiction*, 1950).

Joseph Tomelty (1911–95), yet another Ulster writer associated with broadcasting, a dramatist and author of a long-running local radio serial, *The McCooeys* (1947–54), had had first-hand experience of yet another community or subregion in Northern Ireland, the world of seafarers and small farmers around Portaferry, Co. Down, where he was born. *Red is the Port Light* (1948) is a grim but effective novel with debts to Conrad and perhaps Dickens, as well as Hardy. The bleak melodrama of the story, in which a young shipwrecked sailor, alone in the world, impulsively marries his skipper's strange widow only to find he has made a dreadful mistake which leads him to murder, is alleviated by the humane portrait of an elderly retired seafaring couple, one a Catholic, one a Protestant, unobtrusively devoted to each other, still living in the beached hull of their boat, a little like the Peggotty family in *David Copperfield*.

There is less melodrama and a more developed sympathy for the sometimes difficult lives of Northern Catholics in the fiction of Michael McLaverty (1904–92), a schoolteacher like the younger Maurice Leitch, gifted with imaginative sympathy and insight into the developing awareness, economic and social insecurities, and restricted family circumstances of young people and their all-too-human teachers. The sights and sounds of children playing, symbol of hope and continuing life, bring both *Lost*

Fields (1942) and *School for Hope* (1954) to muted yet moving conclusions. Born in Monaghan, McLaverty lived for a time on Rathlin Island, Co. Antrim, but moved to the city of Belfast when still a child. The age-old tension between country and city is a recurring theme in his quiet, authorially unobtrusive fiction, beginning with the semi-autobiographical *Call my Brother Back* (1939), which presents a child's vision of traditional life on Rathlin in sharp contrast with violent modern life in sectarian Belfast in 1922. In *Lost Fields*, Peter Griffin recklessly steals a bicycle in Belfast so he can escape for a time to his grandmother in the country. But if life is cramped and money short in the city, the Ulster countryside is no paradise either. After much debate, the Griffin family move back to the country at the end of the novel: 'We haven't much', says Johnny to Kate. 'We'll always be living from hand to mouth – yet we'll not starve.'[6] Escape is not always in the direction of the countryside: in *Truth in the Night* (1952), Rathlin is beautiful enough, but life is hard and the Craigs soon leave it for Belfast. Others would like to follow them. But though the novel ends with the death of an unhappy woman, when her coffin is taken back from the mainland to Rathlin it is a kind of ultimate homecoming. McLaverty, used as a source by the most recent historian of Catholic Ulster,[7] can be variously presented as articulating the uncomfortable Catholic sense of belonging in urban Ulster, as a moralist in the grand European tradition stemming from Chekhov, or as a specifically Catholic moralist in the manner of Mauriac, but all this is in a sense to minimise his humane and exact perception of ordinary life in the ordinary places of Northern Ireland.

Tomelty and McLaverty were country-born Catholics who had moved to the city. By contrast, the novelist Brian Moore (1921–99) was born into the Belfast Catholic middle class, a background reflected in the mingled realism and nightmare of some of his early novels. *The Lonely Passion of Judith Hearne* (1955, originally published as *Judith Hearne*) is a harrowing study of shabby gentility juxtaposed with the more comfortable home life Moore himself had enjoyed. Religion offers no consolation, and the Catholic God seems appallingly indifferent to a lonely and impoverished spinster as she descends into dipsomania and insanity. *The Emperor of Ice-Cream* (1965) is a coming-of-age novel set among the air raids of wartime Belfast, drawing on the author's youthful experience of this bizarre interlude and sensitive to the ambivalent feelings of Catholic nationalists involved willy-nilly in Britain's war with Germany. *The Feast of Lupercal* (1957, reprinted in 1965 as *A Moment of Love*), uncomfortably juxtaposing sex and sadistic violence, probably caricatures Moore's own experience of a repressive Catholic school in Belfast, but the protagonist is not a schoolboy:

he is a lonely master, a former pupil of the school, who still has to come to terms with his own sexual nature.

Region and realism

The loneliness of many of Moore's urban protagonists, like the loneliness of Yarr in Leitch's border novel *Poor Lazarus*, can be paralleled in rural fictions north and south. Country life in Ireland, often harsh and poverty-stricken, could be all the more desolate and lonely if there were a semi-official expectation that it should be warmly communal and spiritually rewarding. As late as 1943, Eamon de Valera's famous St Patrick's Day broadcast was still singing the praises of cosy homesteads and country firesides in the Ireland of his dreams. The writing of the Irish Literary Revival had privileged and intermittently idealised country life and country people, particularly Irish-speakers. But this produced complex reactions in the theatre of the so-called Cork realists such as Lennox Robinson and T. C. Murray, in the sour yet sometimes visionary poetry of Patrick Kavanagh and in works of fiction such as Kavanagh's partly autobiographical *Tarry Flynn* (1948), which draws on the author's ambivalent sense of the Monaghan farm from which he had eventually escaped, exploring daydreams in stony fields, sensing beauty and magic in among violence and sterility.

The sense of rural community and tradition identified in Carleton's *Traits and Stories of the Irish Peasantry* and later in Charles Kickham's uncritically admired *Knocknagow, or The Homes of Tipperary* (1879) – complicated rather than repudiated in Kavanagh – could turn sour and oppressive, isolating and alienating sensitive and talented individuals. Perhaps the most extreme and controversial example is Brinsley MacNamara's scathing denunciation of rural life in the ugly village of Garradrimna (based on his native Delvin in Co.Westmeath) in *The Valley of the Squinting Windows* (1918), an Irish parallel to the Scottish writer George Douglas Brown's savagely anti-Kailyard *House of the Green Shutters* (1901). Undeterred by local hostility, MacNamara (b. John Weldon, 1890–1963) went on to write *The Clanking of Chains* (1919), in which the idealistic hero, who resembles Robert Emmet (a role he plays in a local dramatic production), is defeated and driven away by the hopeless narrowness and time-serving of his community.

But this iconoclasm produced its own counter-reaction, an often self-deluding rural self-image influenced by post-Treaty wish-fulfilment. Padraic Colum's rather unsatisfactory late novel *The Flying Swans* (1957), a partly symbolic fable of identity, dispossession and return as it affects Ulick

O'Rehill, son of a decayed Catholic gentry family, in effect ignores contemporary Ireland altogether. In Celtic revivalist fashion it draws on the vivid stories of rural life and the open road which Colum had heard in childhood more than sixty years before in the Longford workhouse where his father was manager (master).

Readers of the entertaining but undemanding romantic fictions of Maurice Walsh, such as *Green Rushes* (1935) and *Thomasheen James, Man of No Work* (1941), were removed considerably further from Irish realities by John Ford's celebrated film *The Quiet Man* (1952), based on one of the stories incorporated in *Green Rushes*. There is a parallel in the roseate vision of Ireland conveyed in the Harvard sociologist Conrad Arensberg's *The Irish Countryman* (1937), a profoundly flawed anthropological study of west Clare, presenting a timelessly stable harmonious community. This naive and selective construction, blithely ignoring economic change and very high emigration rates, has been savagely attacked by modern historians such as Joseph Lee.[8]

Bryan MacMahon's cultural-nationalist idyll of a Kerry village, *Children of the Rainbow* (1952), is similarly impervious to historical realities. The scholar-critic Augustine Martin has suggested that, in his early work, the contemporary poet Brendan Kennelly tried to write about his birthplace in rural Kerry only to find it already crowded with characters from MacMahon, Walsh and others, so he felt driven back to iconoclastic satire in his grim allegorical novel *The Crooked Cross* (1963).[9]

Region and reaction

This complex process of reactions and counter-reactions is characteristic of twentieth-century Irish fiction more generally. It happened not only in MacMahon's Kerry, and in Dublin, where one might expect it, but in Cork. The Cork writer Daniel Corkery (1878–1964), charismatic teacher and Irish language enthusiast, was a dramatist, novelist and writer of short stories, though he is remembered now chiefly for *The Hidden Ireland* (1924), his influential study of the Gaelic poetry of eighteenth-century Munster, and his polemical *Synge and Anglo-Irish Literature* (1931). He was the paradigmatic 'Irish Ireland' cultural nationalist, convinced that Catholicism, the land and the Irish language were integral parts of nationality, who profoundly influenced – and provoked – at least two other writer-patriots in the Cork area, Sean O'Faolain and Frank O'Connor. Corkery's only novel, *The Threshold of Quiet* (1917), is sombre and muted, reacting against both the stage-Irish boisterousness of nineteenth-century Anglo-Irish fictions and the glamour of the Anglo-Irish Literary Revival. It contrasts the babble of the marketplace with the stillness of the hills above Cork, and seeks to explore the hidden bleakness of quiet lives confronted by the disturbing forces of encroaching modernity. Thoreau's assertion (in *Walden*, 1854) that 'the mass of men lead lives of quiet desperation' is invoked as an alternative perspective to the superficial impressions of bustling life in Cork as registered by the tourist.

The call of the cloister or the priesthood had already been presented as a problem rather than any kind of a solution in the early fictions of George Moore and James Joyce. This theme was to continue in raw, angry novels such as *Vocations* (1921), the ex-priest Gerald O'Donovan's savage on-slaught on the complex personal, social and economic pressures distorting the call to the religious life in Ireland, including emotional disaster and self-deception, social snobbery in mothers and daughters, hypocritical self-seeking and institutional avarice. Yet Corkery ends *The Threshold of Quiet* on a very Catholic note of resignation, as Lily Bresnan enters a convent and the rather ineffectual protagonist Martin Cloyne, who loves her, eventually finds himself able to accept it.

Despite a sophisticated recent attempt to rehabilitate Corkery as ideo-logically reputable and a site of significant conflicts,[10] it is tempting to dis-miss him as backward-looking and old-fashioned even in his own time. The scrupulous, quiet manner of his novel and his short stories was eventu-ally emulated by the Ulster Catholic writer Michael McLaverty, but Cork writers who had been his friends and disciples were less impressed. How-ever, this coolness was attributable to revulsion from Corkery the ideologue rather than Corkery the artist.

The cultural polemicist in Corkery was horrified when the end of the Civil War brought a harsh reaction against romantic nationalism in literature as well as in life. New writers were more disposed to emphasise the violence and the horror of the struggle than the national and cultural-nationalist ideals that had been at stake. In talks and lectures and an unpublished essay of 1927 entitled 'The Literature of Collapse', he struck back at what he saw as a literature of misrepresentation, and particularly attacked the early dramas of Sean O'Casey and the fiction of Liam O'Flaherty as destruc-tive betrayals of their country.[11] O'Flaherty, and Corkery's own protégés Sean O'Faolain and Frank O'Connor, had certainly not found peace or Catholic quiet through cultural nationalism or participation in armed struggle.

Liam O'Flaherty (1896–1984) had in fact come to believe in an amoral Social Darwinism rather than any kind of divine or national destiny. His uncomfortable, jagged, often melodramatic narratives of psychological ex-tremity and post-traumatic shock, notably *Thy Neighbour's Wife* (1923), about a despairing priest in the grip of sexual passion, *Black Soul* (1924) and *The Informer* (1925), explore pathological conditions and reflect his own bruising experiences as sometime student for the priesthood and then severely traumatised soldier in the Great War and the Irish Civil War. All this left him a more or less alienated wanderer, brooding and observing on the Aran Islands (where he was born), in Dublin and in the wider world. If anything at all was to emerge from the years of violence and catastrophe in Europe and in Ireland, O'Flaherty thought it might be a bleak new world stripped at last of humanitarian illusions.

While O'Faolain (b. John Whelan, 1900–91) and O'Connor (b. Michael O'Donovan, 1903–66) were masters of the short story, rather than the novel, and established themselves as writers with their short fiction, O'Faolain tried hard to give vent to some of his complex angers through the novel form. His first attempt was *A Nest of Simple Folk* (1933), the story of the English- and Irish-descended Leo Foxe-Donnell. Incorporating an unillusioned overview of Irish social evolution and a national cause that gradually seems to lose its way, it begins in 1854, soon after the death of Daniel O'Connell (the Liberator), and carries through to the Easter Rising in 1916, moving as so many Irish people did at that period from country-side to small town to city. Religion, land and nationalism may have been major forces in Irish literature for purists such as Corkery, but they provide little comfort in this narrative. Self-consciously anti-romantic, despite moments of freedom and hope, it begins with sodden fields and ends in madness and fear, and the faint crackling of rifle fire.

A Nest of Simple Folk cannot quite sustain its burden of despondent history. O'Faolain was always more assured in handling particular scenes and tense moments than in shaping an extended narrative. But in his next novel, *Bird Alone* (1936), he managed to articulate a devastating attack on Irish political bankruptcy and Catholic attitudes to sexuality and militant nationalism. The bitter, controversial, ill-proportioned narrative, intended as an Irish version of Hawthorne's *Scarlet Letter* in its assault on life-denying sexual puritanism, is set just after the fall of Charles Stewart Parnell in 1891, though it also draws on O'Faolain's childhood in Cork a gener-ation later. The increasingly isolated protagonist Corny Crone, resentful of a self-serving father who is 'miserable with piety', has more respect for his grandfather's undying hostility to the Catholic Church, the church of his baptism, which had denied him the sacraments for being a Fenian. O'Faolain's third novel, *Come Back to Erin* (1940), the title an ironic reference to a sentimental Irish song, describes how one of the last of the old IRA gunmen on the run escapes to America, only to find himself more a stranger than a hero in the sentimental Irish-American community. He is further alienated by the rather joyless Catholic piety of his only outwardly successful brother, an ambiguous representative of the (Irish-)American Dream.

A different kind of discontent surfaces in the satirical fictions of Eimar O'Duffy (1893–1935) and Mervyn Wall (b. Eugene Welply, 1908–97). If realism includes a deliberately anti-romantic attentiveness to actual material circumstances, then O'Duffy and Wall can count as realists, even if they often purported to be fantasists. By the 1920s, institutionalised Catholic nationalism had issued in a conservatively Catholic bourgeois state, saddled for various reasons with a stagnant rural economy and high rates of emigration. Sentimental invocations of past national glories when Ireland was the land of legendary Celtic warriors, or, a little later, saints and scholars, were natural targets for the satirists, romantic fantasies which tempted them to alternative fantasies. O'Duffy's disillusionment with contemporary Irish society, futile party politics and malfunctioning capitalism encouraged him to elaborate dystopian extravaganzas. He gives the legendary Cuchulain a son, Cuanduine, and in the first of his Cuanduine trilogy, *King Goshawk and the Birds* (1926), he lampoons an international magnate who has found a way of charging for birdsong. *The Spacious Adventures of the Man in the Street* (1928) presents a back-to-front world in which class distinction and the economics of self-interest are unknown and food, not sex as in Catholic Ireland, is the great unmentionable. He drives lorries across imagined landscapes: chapters on 'The Night Journey' or 'The Gathering of the Twilight Host', which appear to be versions of Irish mythic narratives, turn out to be much more like contemporary narratives of travel or military conflict in Ireland. In some ways, O'Duffy anticipates Flann O'Brien's more complex fantasies, which incorporate elements of traditional Irish narratives such as the Sweeney story in *At Swim-Two-Birds* (1939) and tales of the otherworld in *The Third Policeman* (1940, published 1967), to challenge not just familiar Irish narrative types but conventional literary constructions of time, character and fictional narrative itself.

In *The Unfortunate Fursey* (1946), followed by *The Return of Fursey* (1948), Mervyn Wall revisits the great medieval sites of Clonmacnoise and Cashel in the Irish midlands, but not to venerate them. Fursey is a harmless monk at Clonmacnoise who has the misfortune to become the unwitting ally of the Devil and 'the boys', his attendant demons. Fursey is sent away and then becomes a kind of involuntary innocent abroad, encountering the sharp material discomforts usually edited out of the legendary Ireland of saints and scholars. The action is rather episodic, but with some splendid moments. The Devil gets some very good lines, assuming the autocratic Bishop Flanagan will go to hell as a matter of course and will then inevitably complain about the nudity of the damned, trying to alter the machinery of creation there as he does in this world. He expects Hell will change for the worse until it resembles the Annual General Meeting of the Catholic Truth Society. The ferocious Father Furiosus robustly argues that specifically Irish demons are much superior to the foreign brand, upright, pure and famed for their chastity. While the satire on Catholic Puritanism seems almost timeless, its immediate cause is the government Committee on Evil Literature of 1926, leading to the establishment, under pressure from Catholic laymen, of the Irish Censorship Board in 1929. This was an enduring source of aggravation to realist writers, who registered their protest in works such as Liam O'Flaherty's *The Puritan* (1932).

Something of this inflamed anti-Puritan animus is found in Wall's later work, notably *No Trophies Raise* (1956). This deals with mundane lives in an apparently mundane, realist manner: it is a black comedy of contemporary life, variously poking fun at crass commercialism, the 'crime' of injuring public morals by kissing a woman in public, and the quasi-masonic Catholic secret society, the Warriors of the Cross, based on the Knights of Columbanus. Drawing irreverently on his own experience of the Irish civil service, Wall imagines a minister and amateur philosopher who greatly admires the thought of Albert Thomas Hand but thinks he is a German, not realising he earns his living as an obscure unpromoted clerk in his own department. The novel lurches to a tragicomic conclusion with the death of Hand at a farcical Philosophers' Convention in Killarney, designed to boost the tourist trade.

Literary protest against the social and economic status quo has usually been more sombre. Perceived poverty and repression, and the frustrations and narrowness of rural life, give a controversial and polemical edge to the courageous earlier fictions of Edna O'Brien (b. 1930) and John McGahern (1934–2006). If hereditary Puritanism and patriarchal oppression of women delayed the onset of sexual liberation in Ireland, the city encountered it sooner than the countryside and attractively wicked London was not too far away, a place of liberty and licence as well as of economic opportunity. The process of movement from the country to the apparent freedoms and excitements of Dublin, and the dangerous new horizons of London, is traced with a new frankness, with compassion as well as irony, in Edna O'Brien's early trilogy *The Country Girls* (1960), *The Lonely Girl* (1962) and *Girls in their Married Bliss* (1963), all of which were banned under the Irish Censorship of Publications Act.

McGahern's *The Dark* (1965), also banned, cost the author his job as a schoolteacher in rural Ireland. A coming-of-age novel and a study of awakening sexuality, spare and understated like all of McGahern's best work, it is also an uncomfortable indictment of the patriarchal family and an indication of how not to bring up a child in Catholic Ireland. The widower father, struggling on a poor farm, tyrannises and alienates his children, even though he needs their emotional support. Many of McGahern's father figures, in this and later novels, are domineering yet ultimately inadequate. By the end of *The Dark* the bullying father, sentimental and self-deluding, has found a way of accepting the otherness of his son as an adult. There is a developing sense in McGahern that Ireland itself needs to come of age, to pass on at last from a repressive past and the violent legacy of the War of Independence. Those such as Sergeant Reegan, in *The Barracks* (1963), a decent, disgruntled policeman with a dying wife he loves but cannot reach or help, and the ailing Moran in *Amongst Women* (1990), were heroes in that earlier time. But by the more outward-looking 1970s, things had changed. *Amongst Women* explores the restrictions and complexity of a post-heroic present characterised by migration to England. The increasing independence of the next generation, particularly its women, educated and competent, promises a different and perhaps a better future.

NOTES

1. Cairns Craig, 'Scotland and the Regional Novel', in K. D. M. Snell (ed.), *The Regional Novel in Britain and Ireland, 1800–1990* (Cambridge: Cambridge University Press, 1998), p. 221.
2. Joe Cleary, *Literature, Partition and the Nation State: Culture and Conflict in Ireland, Israel and Palestine* (Cambridge: Cambridge University Press, 2002), p. 78.
3. W. F. Marshall, *Planted by a River* (Belfast: William Mullan & Son, 1948), p. 249.
4. Shan Bullock, *The Loughsiders* (London: Harrap, 1924), p. 10.
5. Sam Hanna Bell, *December Bride* (1951; Belfast: Blackstaff Press, 1974), p. 135.
6. Michael McLaverty, *Lost Fields* (1942; Dublin: Poolbeg Press, 1980), p. 201.
7. Marianne Elliott, *The Catholics of Ulster* (London: Allen Lane, 2000), pp. 375–6.
8. J. J. Lee, *Ireland 1912–1985: Politics and Society* (Cambridge: Cambridge University Press, 1989), p. 651.
9. Augustine Martin, 'Technique and Territory in Brendan Kennelly's Early Work', in Richard Pine (ed.), *Dark Fathers into Light: Brendan Kennelly* (Newcastle upon Tyne: Bloodaxe Books, 1994), pp. 40–1.
10. Paul Delaney, 'Becoming National: Daniel Corkery and the Reterritorialised Subject', in Aaron Kelly and Alan A. Gillis (eds.), *Critical Ireland: New Essays in Literature and Culture* (Dublin: Four Courts Press, 2001).
11. See Patrick Maume, *'Life that is Exile': Daniel Corkery and the Search for Irish Ireland* (Belfast: Institute of Irish Studies, 1993), pp. 97–100.

GUIDE TO FURTHER READING

Acheson, James (ed.). *The British and Irish Novel since 1960*. Basingstoke: Macmillan, 1991.

Cahalan, James M. *The Irish Novel: A Critical History*. Dublin: Gill & Macmillan, 1988.

Cronin, John. *Irish Fiction 1900–1940*. Belfast: Appletree Press, 1992.

Foster, John Wilson. *Fictions of the Irish Literary Revival: A Changeling Art*. Syracuse, NY: Syracuse University Press, 1987.

Foster, John Wilson. *Forces and Themes in Ulster Fiction*. Dublin: Gill & Macmillan, 1974.

Herr, Cheryl. *Critical Regionalism and Cultural Studies: From Ireland to the American Midwest*. Gainesville: University of Florida Press, 1996.

Snell, K. D. M. (ed.). *The Regional Novel in Britain and Ireland, 1800–1990*. Cambridge: Cambridge University Press, 1998.

Vance, Norman. *Irish Literature since 1800*. Harlow: Longman, 2002.

9

ALAN TITLEY

The novel in Irish

The Gaelic Revival

The novel came late in Irish.[1] Despite an unbroken literary tradition that predates the arrival of literacy and Christianity, the fortunes of history decided that secular prose composition for the ordinary reader would be much attenuated. While the major world languages were developing the novel for the growing literate public in the eighteenth and nineteenth centuries, the Irish language was retreating both socially and geographically. There may have been more Irish speakers than ever before on the cusp of the Great Famine in 1845, but they were almost exclusively poor and unlettered. Had somebody written a novel in Irish at that time, its readership would have been confined to a small coterie of scholars (many of whom were learners), some members of the new Catholic middle class – a class that in large measure was trying to forget the language as quickly as it could – and whatever scribes remained, who would have looked down upon it as a poor substitution for the traditional literature. We can be sure that it never entered the head of William Carleton, a native speaker of Irish, to write in his native tongue.

The change came about with the return of the native as part of the cultural revival, which is conventionally dated to the 1880s. When *Irisleabhar na Gaedhilge* (*The Gaelic Journal*) was first published in 1882 it had as its express policy the cultivation of a modern literature in the Irish language. This also, interestingly, was one of the main aims of *Conradh na Gaeilge* (*The Gaelic League*) when it was founded eleven years later. While this may be seen as the reverse of what Samuel Ferguson, Standish James O'Grady and, to a lesser extent, James Clarence Mangan were doing – that is, 'getting Irish literature into the English tongue' (as it was put in the title of Stopford A. Brooke's lecture to the Irish Literature Society in London in 1893)[2] – it was also part of that belief which put the creative literary mind at the centre of a national culture. If colonialism believes that its ways and writings are superior to the natives', then the anti-colonialist will necessarily write back to contradict.

What is generally called 'The Gaelic Revival' was much more complicated than this. It was conservative in so far as it was attempting to 'conserve' the language and its culture, but it was revolutionary in so far as it was attempting to create a new society as 'a rational continuation of the past', in Douglas Hyde's telling phrase.[3] It was energising and uplifting in that it gave dignity to people whose language had been despised for generations as a peasant patois, but it was enervating and constricting when it gave a too prescriptive and one-dimensional account of its imagined past and hoped-for future. These tensions and contradictions become the stuff of the new literature, and in particular the novel.

The struggle between the 'modernists' and the 'traditionalists' took root at the beginning. The very first novel in Irish is acknowledged to be *Séadna*[4] (1904) by Peadar Ua Laoghaire (Peter O'Leary) (1839–1920),[5] initially serialised in a journal and later in a weekly newspaper between 1894 and 1901, before it was published in final book form. On the surface, it appears to be an elaboration of the folk tale in which a man sells his soul to the devil in return for prosperity, the Faust story implanted in the Irish countryside. Indeed, the story is deliberately given a folk-scaffolding, as if the Irish reader could not cleanly break from the oral tradition without the comfortable chatter of the women around the fireside, one of whom is the narrator. But the main character, Séadna himself, is far more complicated than any folk hero or villain. At the beginning of the narrative he is no more than a simple, certainly very innocent shoemaker, struggling to make ends meet, but by the end he is made wise in the ways of this world and of the next by his encounters with the black stranger, who we come to learn is the devil. Although we must always suppose that good will overcome evil throughout the story, especially as O'Leary himself was a priest with very unyielding nineteenth-century post-Tridentine infallible views, the slow development of the plot leads to a final tension which is explosive, despite its inevitability. More remarkably, Séadna is not always likeable. His initial stupidity, his cruelty to his neighbours and his indifference to the woman who loves him do not always overcome in our eyes his growing independence of spirit and his occasional despair. But as often in Irish writing, it is the style which is the ultimate triumph, the language itself which is the occasion and source of the art.

The novel is often seen as that art form which, alas, tells a story, as E. M. Forster admitted in *Aspects of the Novel* (1924), but may also plumb the depths and caverns of the human spirit. Its strength is the circumventing of the artifice, which is the glory of the poem and the verse drama. There are, undoubtedly, Irish novels which go straight for the story and, with luck and some skill, give us memorable characterisation. But one hallmark of the novels discussed in this chapter is their concern with the language itself, not just as something that does the business, but as a real and palpable presence. In the Irish novel, the words on the page speak often more loudly than those in the mouths of the characters or in the flow of the narrative.

There were, and are, very good reasons for this. Irish prose had been frozen in a high discursive form since the seventeenth century. Narrative consisted of stylised romantic tales or impoverished folk stories. There were a few inchoate attempts to escape from the armature of the romantic tale in the eighteenth century, such as *Stair Éamuinn Uí Chléire* [6] (*The Adventures of Edward Cleary*) by Seán Ó Neachtain (?1650–1729), but despite its humour and burlesque, this work doesn't quite get across the moat from the medieval romance. At the end of the nineteenth century, there were no models of ordinary decent prose for the novelist to follow. It was as if in English the only signposts in the modern age were going to be a cross between John Milton's *Areopagetica* and the prose of Thomas Cranmer. The writer of Irish had more than two hundred years of desert to cross, with only the chatter of his neighbours in his ears as guidance. Most writers in this first generation of the Revival had never read a book in Irish until they reached adulthood. It was this fashioning anew that gave literature in Irish its particular flavour: the fact that every novelist had not only to create a story and people it with characters, but had also to 'create' the language itself.

O'Leary was well aware of this, as his letters, public statements and literary rows demonstrate. He was deliberately writing a book which would show that ordinary speech, if artistically wrought and lovingly crafted, could be the vehicle of significant literature. He was also writing for learners of the language and for young people, which meant that his style was clear, uncluttered and pungent. *Séadna* became a classic, largely because of its style, and became a standard text for schools in an abbreviated form for more than half a century. Inevitably, O'Leary's dominance and his unremitting ultramontane puritanism in all of his prolific writings invited a reaction.

If there was to be an opposite of O'Leary, it was Pádraic Ó Conaire (1882–1928). Both were native Irish speakers, like most writers of this period, but while O'Leary followed a trajectory which took him from a small rural household to the seminary of Maynooth, the priesthood and some eminence within the church, Ó Conaire was one of the very few native speakers to have been born and raised in a city where Irish was still spoken; he was schooled in the underworld of the Galway docks and lived his intellectual life through the great writers of the nineteenth century,

including Balzac, Dickens and Dostoevsky. There is a sense in which
Ó Conaire wanted to be a writer, and not just an *Irish* writer, although
the distinction is ultimately false. He was less beholden to style than most
of his contemporaries and had a vision of life which was entirely his own.
This vision was bleak and pessimistic, and occasionally grotesque. He was,
however, true to it. He lived the life of his characters and demonstrated
that his practice followed his imagination rather than his own biography,
with his fictional people being mere versions of those he had known.

His most successful novel is *Deoraíocht* (1910).[7] It recounts how a kind
of picaresque character flees Ireland for London, loses an arm and a leg in
an accident, and finds a job as a freak in a downmarket exploitative circus
run by a 'weirdo' just as unlikely as himself. The plot, such as it is, is bizarre
and depends on a series of coincidences of which even music-hall comedy
would be ashamed. Gods jump out of machines precisely when they are
expected. The characters are gross, both physically and metaphorically. The
ending makes us wonder at the audacity of the author and how he thought
he would get away with it. And yet the whole throbs with a life of its own,
beyond all the rules and conventions. Although it can be read entirely
realistically, with some allowance for the magic elasticity of the plot, it is
much more a symbolic rendering of the fate of the Irish in exile than a
documentary telling. They are cut adrift from the homeland which expected
them to conform and thrown into a whirligig of uncertainty in which
anything can happen, and does. The home characters are dull, pious and
calculating; the exiled are mad, wounded and unpredictable. His gift is
that he creates a mental map of his own making, a clime in which his off-
beam and nutty characters are completely natural. Ó Conaire eschewed all
those literary debates over whether Irish could be used as a medium for
urban speech, or if people who spoke English in reality could be shown
to have Irish coming out of their mouths, or whether there was an appropriate subject matter for the novel in Irish. Although he wrote a large body
of journalism and of literary criticism, they did not impinge on his writing
of novels or stories. Unfortunately, he lived the life of his imagination and
died penniless on a Dublin street at the age of forty-six, in the early years of
the new Irish Free State. If people thought that writers in Irish were going
to be cosseted and privileged in the new dispensation, he was its living
and dying antithesis.

Séamas Ó Grianna

One of the results of the Gaelic Revival was the 'discovery' of Irish-speaking
areas and life therein. There was a 'romantic' dividend to be gained from

this discovery, although the reality was never very pleasant. There was also the realisation that these Irish-speaking communities, known collectively as the Gaeltacht, differed significantly in dialect from place to place. The main Gaeltacht areas were in north-west Ulster with its clipped speech, in west Galway with vowels as long as the winter night, and in south-west Munster with clamping consonants, along with significant pockets elsewhere in these provinces; as a community language with hope of passage to the next generation, Irish had been melted away in most of Leinster by the time of the Revival. Since Irish had not been a standardised language since the seventeenth century, these dialects were given their head in the new awakening. Consequently, it was not only the language itself that took on major importance, but its particular regional form. Literary merit was often measured by the proximity of the writer's origin to the reader's place of birth, rather than by any other yardstick. Thus, Peter O'Leary's *Séadna* was more widely read in the south of the country than in the north, and Pádraic Ó Conaire was mainly championed west of the Shannon, even if he should have been universal in his appeal. It was not possible to read an Irish text without some kind of awareness of how it sounded. Dialect, also, became an arbiter of literary excellence.

Séamas Ó Grianna (1889–1969), writing under the pen name of 'Máire', became the most popular Ulster author of his generation. He chose a pen name as pseudonyms were common to Irish writers at the time, and the pen name usually said something about the character of the writer. His mother's name was Máire, but he may also have chosen it to give a sense of homeliness to his writing. Interestingly, some of his early stories are narrated as if a local women called Máire were really speaking. Born into a family steeped in local story-telling and music tradition in north-west Donegal, he received the kind of formal and informal education of his time and place. Hired as a farmhand in the flat lands of east Donegal and later working in the bothies of Scotland, he garnered enough experience to pack into his novels and short stories for the rest of his life. He wrote ten of these novels and more than a hundred stories, as well as two volumes of autobiography, books of local lore, essays, translations and voluminous journalism. Although acerbic and bitter in his literary feuds with other writers, his novels tell of an idyllic Gaeltacht in the Rosses, where life was hard and where disappointment grew from the inevitable blows of cruel fate, rather than in any evil which might lurk among the sand dunes. He was cynical about human relations, but failure arrived not because of nasty brutish people, but because of pettiness and smallmindedness and the calculations of people who had a lot to lose and not a great deal to gain. His is one of the truest depictions of rural Ireland in the second half of the nineteenth century – for he seems to write of a time roughly a generation before he was born – where life is bitter and harsh, and one's horizon doesn't stretch beyond the waves of Tory Island. Ambition is withered in the bud and true love is crushed between the grind of the quernstone and the Gorbals of Glasgow.

His most celebrated novel is *Caisleáin Óir* (*Golden Castles*) (1924). This was published less than two years after the winning of the Irish Free State, and might have been expected to sing some of the glories of the revolution. His first novel *Mo Dhá Róisín* (*My Two Róisíns*) (1921) had appeared at the height of the war of independence and had featured a feminine hero out of Walter Scott who would not deign to marry until her country was free; accounts differ as to whether she is still a spinster or not. But the shine had gone off the sun at the end of the rainbow in *Caisleáin Óir*, long before Frank O'Connor and Sean O'Faolain themselves had become disillusioned. From a social perspective, this is an accurate and telling account. Love is thwarted by the exigencies of material deprivation, whereby Irish rural youth had to emigrate in order to make a normal living. The English-language Donegal novels of Patrick McGill (1889–1960) tell of a similar experience of emigration and disillusionment from out of the same rural hole of despair, but his ideology inclines him towards rhetoric and bombast in the public sphere, while Ó Grianna documents without penetrating the political or social causes of his people's distress. Ó Grianna's fiction may well be the greatest 'con job' in modern Irish literature, creating a world which only ever existed in the sentimental memory of the exile, but which yet was accurate in social nuance and detail. While Joyce claimed that the Dublin of his youth could be recreated from the pages of *Ulysses* (1922), it would not be inaccurate to suppose that the Rosses of the second half of the nineteenth century could be recreated from Ó Grianna's stories and novels. Certainly, the language was inerrantly recorded. As rich and as idiomatic as O'Leary's, it provided Ulster native speakers with a world that was instantly recognisable, and learners of the language from the north with an idiom that was readily attainable in a time and place. This was no small revolution. Irish speakers had never seen their own language, as they understood it, set down in print and given the status accorded to Englishes everywhere. More than that, his stories recorded the common experience of his people in such a way that they could understand it without the intercession of other literary forms. North-west Donegal is alive to us in a way in which, for example, Longford, East Offaly or North Wexford can never be. One of the greatest things a writer can do is to create his own world, and Séamas Ó Grianna succeeded in doing this for several generations of readers who, particularly in the north of Ireland, waited with baited pennies for his next book.

Any description of *Caisleáin Óir* would be madly reductive, although it follows a pattern inscribed in most of its author's fictions. He/she falls in love with her/him; there is no money; he/she emigrates to America/Scotland; he/she falls in love with someone else, or goes on the booze, or remains transfixed by love without ever thinking of returning. Its ending is one of the saddest in fiction, not just sad in the sense of describing arrested and tramelled love, but sad that a talented writer should expect us to believe that people in their dotage still thought that their erstwhile young lass or buck hadn't grown old and decrepit with the years. His stories never have a happy ending and never can. Fate conquers all and fate is resolutely an ill wind. His novels and stories continued to be published into the 1960s, although there is general agreement that his earlier work was his best. If the novel is the art form which shows man as a member of society and the pressures of that society on him, then Séamas Ó Grianna's are the best examples we have.

Irish and Anglo-Irish literatures

Publishing in Irish was always a hazardous business. The small readership did not guarantee fat profits, and while the Gaelic League produced many worthwhile books in the first twenty years of the century, these were mainly thin, cheap and unattractive. Consequently, within five years of independence, the new state set about the establishment of a publishing operation which became known as *An Gúm*. Its remit was to produce new books of all kinds for the expected growing literate public in Irish. It was part of the state's commitment to the culture which had fuelled its begetting, as was its support for other worthwhile projects, including the Abbey Theatre. *An Gúm* provided money, sustenance and support for many Irish writers when none would have been forthcoming from other sources; nonetheless, some of its best authors never ceased in finding it mean-spirited and parsimonious. It did, however, succeed in publishing the most significant fiction from the late twenties to the early forties. Equally important, it set up a scheme of translations which simultaneously allowed writers to earn money, to learn their craft and to train readers in the practice of engaging with prose fictions of reasonable length. Many authors cut their teeth in the hackwork of translation, although at its best the scheme produced work of real beauty and lasting value. Translators initially had a penchant for re-working classics of Anglo-Irish fiction, including novels by Canon Sheehan, Charles J. Kickham and William Carleton. They later graduated to more challenging works by Dickens, Daudet, Tolstoy, Conrad and Carlo Collodi. There is now a corpus of world classics rendered in natural idiomatic Irish, which filled a gap that would not have been there if it had not been for the drought of the eighteenth and nineteenth centuries.

Apart from its language, literature in Irish and in English in the first two decades of the twentieth century were driven by different projects. Literature in Irish tended towards the normal, the natural, the commonplace, whereas literature in English leaned towards the mythic, the heroic, the fantastic. When O'Connor, O'Faolain and Liam O'Flaherty returned Irish literature to this earth after the airy flights of the Celtic Revival, prose fiction in Irish was already rooted in the social and in the realistic. An author such as Éamonn Mac Giolla Iasachta (Edward McLysaght, 1887–1986) produced two weighty novels, *Cúrsaí Thomáis* (*Tom's Affairs*) (1927) and *Toil Dé* (*The Will of God*) (1934),[8] which were as detailed and as minutely documented as the dourest realist could expect. The first chronicles farm life in a quiet unhurried way, while the second wrestled with the still-vexed question of the civil war. They were sensitive reflections on Irish society, showing a breadth of class concerns and a sweep of characters which had been missing from the narrowly focussed novels of the rural poor which were then current.[9]

The Gaeltacht autobiography

The rural poor resided in the Gaeltacht, or Irish-speaking areas. The Gaeltacht, although a real place inhabited by real people in real poverty, also became a place of the mind for urban Irish speakers. It symbolised both a lost world and a world of possibilities. There was an inevitable confusion between the linguistic purity of the Gaeltacht and the kind of life that was lived there, which further reinforced the stereotype of the Irish speaker as an island-dweller on the edge of the known world. Despite all the attempts to create a new modern literature, the books which satisfied the quest for the purest language and for an unsullied society melded in a series of autobiographies, the most famous of which were composed on the Blasket Islands in the 1920s and 1930s. Although there is no way in which we can call *An tOileánach* (*The Islandman*) (1929) by Tomás Ó Criomhthain (Tomás Ó Crohan, 1856–1937) a novel,[10] it was the first begetter of a number of autobiographies which might better be described as novels of growing up, as much for their invention as for their form. The most remarkable of these is *Fiche Blian ag Fás* (*Twenty Years A-Growing*) (1933) by Muiris Ó Súilleabháin (Maurice O'Sullivan, 1904–50), which describes his youth on the great Blasket Island with love, affection, humour and precocious geniality.[11] This cult of the autobiography teetering towards the novel has its culmination in *Mo Bhealach Féin* (*My Own Way*) (1940) by Seosamh Mac Grianna (1901–90), which champions the personal dream over communal conformity.

Mac Grianna was the younger brother of Séamas Ó Grianna, despite the slightly different surname. Having written some short stories and some unsuccessful novels, he set about his artistic apologia, which he cast in the form of an autobiography. There is little contiguity, however, between the standard autobiography and *Mo Bhealach Féin*. He eschews any description of his childhood and education, but rather plunges into the dingy world of backstreet Dublin where he creates a character that bears some resemblance to himself. The best part of his narrative displays a mind at war with the world, acting the part of the superior artist but ultimately suffering for it. When the city becomes too stultifying, he steals a small boat with the intention of rowing across to Wales. Later, he walks that country from south to north, living the life of a tramp, part medieval hero, part down-and-out wastrel. He wrote a more conventional novel around the same time, entitled *An Druma Mór* (*The Big Drum*), but it was not published until 1969 because it was too politically sensitive and the event on which it was based was still a live issue. It was felt at the time that many characters on which the book was based could be recognised. Given the passion of his other work, a novel about the intrusion of national politics into a small rural community, written with sympathy and understanding for all sides, is quite surprising. A central feature of the novel is the growth of physical-force nationalism in a local townland which had been used to a more gentle form of political expression before this. It may have been that Mac Grianna never really discovered what kind of writer he was or that his talent failed to meet exactly the subject which suited his voice. An unfinished novel, *Dá mBíodh Ruball ar an Éan* (*If the Bird Had a Tail*) (1940), showed extraordinary linguistic virtuosity and originality, but his health broke down before he could finish it.

If the Gaeltacht autobiography was seen as the dominant prose art form for nearly a generation, it met its nemesis in a hilarious send-up, *An Béal Bocht* (*The Poor Mouth*) (1941) by Myles na gCopaleen.[12] Myles na gCopaleen was the pen name of Brian Ó Nualláin (1911–66), or Brian O'Nolan, also known as Flann O'Brien, already the author of *At Swim-Two-Birds* (1939). Like most of our authors, he was a native Irish speaker, albeit not from the traditional Gaeltacht. He learned his English largely through books and had read the better part of Irish literature in both languages before he eventually went to school at the age of eleven. This anarchic and wayward education must have contributed to his wry and individual outlook. He wrote *An Béal Bocht* in a swift rush of a single week, as a mark of respect, he tells us, to *An tOileánach*. It was much more than this, of course. It was a parody of just about every Gaeltacht autobiography that had ever been, perhaps as many as twenty at this time, and a satire on the pieties of the Irish language movement. He creates a Gaeltacht area where it always rains, where the Aran Islands can be seen out of one window and the Blaskets out of another, where pigs are too fat to get out through the door of the house, where people dance until they drop, and where the best Irish is that which is entirely unintelligible.

Even though it can be read just as a hilarious romp through the western seaboard, *An Béal Bocht* is also interwoven with palimpsestic layers of reference to phrases, idioms, jokes, happenings and adventures in modern and in older Irish literature. This throwaway intertextuality innervates the story below the surface satire.[13] A classic scene in many of these autobiographies is when the author goes to school and is given an English name. When the hero of *An Béal Bocht* goes to school he is given the name 'Jams O'Donnell', a direct echo of the experience recounted in *Scéal Hiúdaí Sheáinín (Hughie John's Story)* (1940) by Eoghan Ó Dómhnaill (1908–66). But *An Béal Bocht* is ultimately singular. It marks the end of a period of veneration of the native speaker in his time and location, a veneration originally fuelled by the discovery of a world hitherto hidden to the greater public, to historians and to common discourse. Although Tomás Ó Criomhthain was one of the most unromantic and flintily unadorning of writers, it did not prevent other novelists and autobiographers from inventing a Gaeltacht world which the new urban reader wished to have existed.

Máirtín Ó Cadhain

Perhaps the reaction was coming anyway. Arguably, the finest writer of prose in Irish in the twentieth century was Máirtín Ó Cadhain (1906–70). He started experimenting with the short story as most apprentice writers do, but almost unbidden produced the finest novel in Irish, and certainly one of the best in either language, shortly after his release from the Curragh Internment Camp during the Second World War. He was interned as a member of the IRA and received an education there amongst the other prisoners which he claimed was better than any university. *Cré na Cille (Graveyard Clay)* (1949) is deceptively simple, but it is set in a graveyard where all the characters are dead and continue to gabble to one another about the pettiest matter of life in the upperworld as if nothing had changed. This static structure seems inevitably constricting, but was probably chosen by Ó Cadhain to avoid all the extraneous description of houses, fields, people and daily comings and goings, in order to allow him to indulge his enormous talent in recording and inventing the speech of his people.

The celebrated opening of *Cré na Cille* finds Caitríona Pháidín, the main character of the novel if such there is, 'awakening' in her grave and wondering where she is:

> Ní mé an ar Áit an Phúint nó na Cúig Déag atá mé curtha? . . . Now I wonder if it is in the pound plot or in the fifteen shilling plot they have me buried. They went to the devil entirely if it's in the ten shilling place they threw me after all the warnings I gave them. The morning of the day I died I called Pádraig up from the kitchen. 'Will you do me a favour, Pádraig, asthore' says I. 'Bury me in the pound plot. The pound plot. Some of us are laid in the ten shilling part, but if they are itself . . . '[14]

This translation is rendered in a form of Hiberno-English which, for all its attempts at idiomatic accuracy, gives the impression of a kind of Synge-speak. One of the glories of the book is, however, that this speech is entirely natural, the common currency of everyday chatter and carries no hint or whiff of being exotic, odd or romantic. On the other hand, to translate it into standard English would lose some of the flavour of inventiveness and word-fencing which was part of the craft of speech as practised by Gaeltacht people and which was raised to a higher art by Máirtín Ó Cadhain. *Cré na Cille* is nothing but talk. But it is talk which reveals a complete community and exposes a whole world. People complain and moan and fight and backbite and gossip and curse and vilify one another from the depth of the grave for more than three hundred pages, without a great deal of subtlety. Their interests are the interests of most people: who will marry whom, how your man got your woman, who is going to die soon, what will be in the next will, who said what to whom or didn't say, what the other one will say when she hears about it, how much land a man needs to be better than the next one – the entire petty world of unpleasant peasants set forth before us in raw slabs. But it is also hilarious, as the pit is when seen from above.

One collection of Ó Cadhain's short stories was titled *Idir Shúgradh is Dáiríre* (1939), which might be translated as *Both Fun and Seriousness*. He once claimed that this was characteristic of the Irish, that humour should intermix with the most solemn when it was least expected. He instanced how his father at his wedding, while all were drinking, dancing, singing and carousing, fell on his knees in the middle of the floor to say the rosary. *Cré na Cille* inhabits the same world of people being entirely humourless in the small things and bursting into hilarity when greater seriousness calls. It is a novel in which everybody is dead, but the talk is most alive; where nothing happens, but a community pulls itself apart; it is a novel that should be as silent as the grave, but is screaming with the sounds of sourness; that is entirely unrealistic, yet gives us the truest picture of a small rural community that we will ever have.

Cré na Cille became a legend within a few years. It was read in Gaeltacht communities where no book had penetrated before, it was the subject of debate in fields at harvest time, chunks of it were learned off by heart and quoted, it was mentioned in debates in the Dáil, its phrases and idioms have entered the language, it has been adapted for stage and radio, and been the subject of more critical commentary than any other Irish novel. And yet it was one of the earliest of Ó Cadhain's works. He wrote two other substantial novels or prose fictions: *Athnuachan* (*Renewal*) (1995) and *Barbed Wire* (2002), but they were not published for artistic and legal reasons until long after his death. While he concentrated on the short story, he also wrote novellas which were among his finest achievements. *An Eochair* (*The Key*) (1967) is a vicious satire on the bureaucracy of the civil service, in which a minor official dies of thirst and hunger in a government office because the red tape which might save him cannot be cut through in time. It is not a new idea, but he handles it with a prodigious use of language, using his own native dialect, new official jargon, bits of nursery rhymes, echoes from the catechism and necessary slapstick to create a sense of mayhem where nothing rules, only madness. His death in 1970 left a gap in prose fiction which was difficult to fill, as he had been a commanding presence and a touchstone of excellence for a quarter of a century.

Fiction of the 1960s

It is true that the 1960s experienced a significant revival. The first novels of Diarmaid Ó Súilleabháin (1932–85), Eoghan Ó Tuairisc (Eugene Watters, 1919–82) and Breandán Ó Doibhlin (b. 1931) appeared in that decade. Although each one of them was very significant, none of them achieved the popularity of Ó Cadhain, as they were each consciously 'literary' in their own way. They were ambitious in form, in subject and in language. Ó Doibhlin's *Néal Maidne agus Tine Oíche* (*Morning Cloud and Night Fire*) (1964) is consciously biblical in style and allegorical in manner, but the ordinary reader required some of Ó Doibhlin's own erudition and range of reference to travel beyond its foothills. Ó Súilleabháin started with a fairly conventional historical novel, *Dianmhuilte Dé* (*The Hard Mills of God*) (1964), but moved on to works of more social and personal comment, particularly *Caoin Tú Féin* (*Weep for Yourself*) (1967) and *An Uain Bheo*

(*The Time Alive*) (1968). These latter novels tackle urban life, marriage breakdown and mental disintegration, as well as taking some savage swipes at the new Ireland of the horsey set, with their money and pretensions. His target was the new Catholic middle class occupying the places of their former colonial masters, and they came easily into his sights. Even though most readers of Irish novels were educated urban dwellers anyway, not unlike readers in other languages, this urban milieu, although not absent, had never been the central concern of the Irish novel. Ó Súilleabháin caught the pulse of the time, and for a while it seemed as if he might be the successor to Ó Cadhain.

Eoghan Ó Tuairisc's *l'Attaque* (1962) went in a different direction entirely. Historical fiction in Irish had been for the most part heroic and romantic, which one might expect in a language celebrating a victory of sorts after the defeat of centuries. *L'Attaque* makes no such gestures. It deals narrowly with the French support for the Irish revolution in Co. Mayo in 1798, much as Thomas Flanagan did in *The Year of the French* (1979) some time later. Ó Tuairisc focusses on one 'typical' man caught up in the wonder and excitement of the time. Although newly married, he takes his pike from the thatch and follows his leaders when the call comes. The initial enthusiasm gives way to the grim reality of sleeping rough, hunger, rain, bellicose officers, frightened boys, long marching through bog and mucky hillside. Ó Tuairisc is brilliant in his close and tight descriptions of sound and smell. He describes coldly the reality of a military campaign and documents without comment the motivations of the protagonists. He is equally unromantic in his descriptions of battle scenes, as bloody and uncompromising as the most gory of films can deliver. For what it is worth, his hero dies an inconsequential death in the heat of the battle without glory, without honour, without any great deed.

And yet, as with much Irish fiction, it is the style that is the main victor. It is as if he had created a new language out of the best of folk poetry and the vocabulary of sensile reality. We read pages of his work as we would read a lyric poem. But precisely because the novel is not a lyric poem, this same approach did not work as well in his next novel, *Dé Luain* (*Monday*)[15] (1966), which is a kind of documentary homage to and reconstruction of the rebellion of 1916. Despite its beauty and craft it lacks the tension and narrative, even the crude simplicity of story, to make it an entirely successful novel. An interest in the linkage of the private and the public, particularly the great military events of our time and the small lives that we live, marks much of Ó Tuairisc's writings, which may also be seen in his long poems *Aifreann na Marbh* (*The Mass of the Dead*) and, writing as Eugene Watters, *The Weekend of Dermot and Grace*.

Breandán Ó hEithir

Breandán Ó hEithir (1930–90), nephew of Liam O'Flaherty and also from the Aran Islands, had been writing as a sharp, witty and often acerbic print, radio and television journalist for more than twenty years before he wrote his first novel. *Lig Sinn i gCathú* (1976) had already won an *Oireachtas* prize and was awaited with unblown trumpets for months before it was published.[16] It was entirely unusual in being the only novel in Irish ever to reach the top of the national bestselling lists, proving that there was a large passive pool of readers for fiction in the language. Part of this success was due to 'hype', part of it to the popularity of the author as a public personality, and part of it to the rollicking narrative which included all the ingredients of a good read – sex, politics, booze and the adventures of a loveable rogue.

Ó hEithir focussed his narrative on the weekend of the declaration of the Republic, at Easter 1949, when a young student throws off the shackles of pious puritanism and the country establishes itself independently anew. While the symmetry of the Easter resurrection and the narrator's human salvation through his first sexual encounter is a bit obvious, and the symbolism unsubtle, the narrative whips along, the characters are deliciously off-centre and the book throbs with a truth to time and place and persons which cannot be denied. Ironically, his second novel, *Sionnach ar mo Dhuán* (*A Fox on My Hook*) (1988), which is a far more ambitious, ambiguous, layered, haunting novel of coming of age, was less well received. There may have been a sense in which the Irish reading public were quite unused to the long, engaging, intelligent read, prescinding entirely from bizarre or experimental works. Little else can explain the neglect of *Deoraithe* (*Exiles*) (1986), a novel by Dónall Mac Amhlaigh (1926–89), which epically tells the story of a whole generation of Irish workers in England and which comprehensively relates their fate in such a way that no other novel or film does.

Contemporary fiction in Irish

Since the first prose fictions which we can properly call novels (about a hundred years ago), there have been in the region of two hundred novels published in Irish.[17] This does not include novels for children, for learners or for young people. For example, Cathal Ó Sándair (1922–96) wrote more than one hundred novels for children between the 1940s and 1960s, and there has been a steady production of children's fiction from private publishers and from the state publishing company, *An Gúm*, particularly in recent decades.

There was always a division between regional publishing, or publishing directed at specific Gaeltacht regions, and writing for the more general Irish-speaking, Irish-reading or Irish-using public. For example, the novels of Pádraig Ua Maoileoin (1913–2002) or Maidhc Dainín Ó Sé (b. 1942), apart from their use on college or school courses, would have had a determinedly local readership in their native Kerry and environs. There were always particular Gaeltacht readers who bought and read books to see if they or their relations figured in them, probably with the intention of instigating a feud. Pádraig Standún (b. 1946) would test the rule, however. Working as a priest in the Connemara and Mayo Gaeltacht, he wrote a series of highly popular and accessible novels with the express intention of highlighting particular social issues. His most celebrated work is *Súil le Breith*[18] (*Waiting for Judgement*) (1983), although my Englished title hides the fact that *breith* also means 'birth'. It concerns a priest who takes in an unmarried woman and her son to live with him in a remote part of the west of Ireland, and the havoc this wreaks on the community and the local church.

The main stream of the Irish novel has always been literary, however. Written for a small educated public, although more numerous than ever before, no single work is ever likely to figure hugely in public discourse. *Cuaifeach Mo Lon Dubh Buí* (*Whirlwind My Yellow Blackbird*) (1983) by Séamas Mac Annaidh (b. 1961) made quite a stir and was the first of a trilogy by an author who was very young at the time.[19] It is a mad maelstrom of a book which he has never quite matched since. Liam Mac Cóil (b. 1955) has crafted two very intelligent novels, *An Dr Áthas* (*Dr Happiness*) (1994) and *An Claíomh Solais* (*The Sword of Light*) (1998), both of which probe our personal and public lives with clarity and imagination. *An Fear Dána* (*The Man of Art*) (1993)[20] by Alan Titley (b. 1947) is a meditation on, and a reconstruction of, the life of the thirteenth-century Irish and Scottish poet, Muireadhach Albanach Ó Dálaigh. Of contemporary novelists, Pádraig Ó Cíobháin (b. 1951) is the most prolific in the last decade. Using his native Gaeltacht idiom as his basic style, he builds castles on top of it and infests it with passages and byways, slashing his way through contemporary life with abandon – a kind of Irish Wilson Harris.

Despite their lack of fanfare, these two hundred or so novels are quite an achievement, given the neglect and underdevelopment of prose fiction in the language for several hundred years. In this light, the new literacy of the twentieth century is quite remarkable. The novelist had to contend with an untrained reading public, the tug of the folksy, the war of the dialects, the change in scripts,[21] the conventional superiority of poetry, the disdain for what is difficult, the snobbery of the clerks, asinine critical judgments[22] and literary establishment neglect. There is the also the curious dearth of women authors, for which there is simply no adequate explanation.[23] Éilís Ní Dhuibhne (b. 1954), also a bilingual writer, has written several note-worthy novels, with a definite eye on creating a reading public. Her *Cailíní Beaga Ghleann na mBláth* (*The Little Girls of the Glen of the Flowers*) (2003) deals with an experience which many Irish children encounter when they first leave home to go to a summer Irish-language college. With an unflinching gaze, the innocence of hope and youth is contrasted with the worried responsibility of the mature parent.

There are more novels in Irish being published than ever before. There were more novels produced in the nineties of the last century than in any other decade. This may partly reflect the greater ease of publication, but it is also an index of a steady readership, small but loyal. Size or quantity doesn't always matter, but it does have some relevance. The strength or goodness of the novel will bear a relationship to the situation of the language, but the most wondrous thing about the novel is that it always surprises.

NOTES

1. I use the word 'Irish' to describe the language throughout, in preference to 'Gaelic'. This is because it is more historically accurate and differentiates from the Gaelic of Scotland, which is a related but distinct language with a very different literate and novelistic tradition. It does, of course, raise difficulties with regard to a phrase like 'the Irish novel'. When I use it in this essay, it means the novel written in the Irish language.

2. Stopford A. Brooke, *The Need and Use of Getting Irish Literature into the English Tongue: An Address* (London 1895).

3. Douglas Hyde's Irish Ireland philosophy was most cogently set down in his lecture to the National Literary Society in Dublin, 25 November 1892. It was entitled 'The Necessity for De-Anglicising Ireland'. An excerpt from this lecture appears in *The Field Day Anthology of Irish Writing*, gen. ed. Seamus Deane (Derry: Field Day, 1991), vol. II, pp. 527–33.

4. Translated into English by Cyril Ó Céirín (1989). This is not the full translation, but rather an abbreviated version which was common in schools.

5. Where authors are also sometimes known by their English names, I give them in brackets. Where they are not, I give them in their recognised and original form.

6. *Stair Éamuinn Uí Chléire do réir Sheáin Uí Neachtain.* Although this was written in the eighteenth century, it did not appear in book form until 1918.

7. Translated into English by Gearailt Mac Eoin as *Exile* (Dublin, 1997).

8. Translated into English by E. O'Clery as *The Small Fields of Carrick* in 1929. Here as elsewhere, the translated title in brackets is my own. Where there is a discrepancy, I give my version of the title in an endnote. Edward MacLysaght, also Edward Lysaght, was a genealogist and a historian. He was the foremost

authority on Irish surnames during his lifetime. He also wrote several novels in English, including *The Gael* (1919).

9. Pádhraic Óg Ó Conaire, *Seóid ó'n Iarthar Órdha (A Jewel from the Golden West)* (1926) and Seán Ó Ruadháin, *Pádhraic Mháire Bhán (Fair Mary's Patrick)* (1932) are representative of a kind of sentimentality about rural life which was much in demand.

10. *An tOileánach* was translated into English by Robin Flower as *The Islandman* (London, 1934). It has also been translated into other European languages including French, Italian and Swedish.

11. The translation, *Twenty Years A-Growing* (1933), was by Moya Llewelyn Davies and George Thomson.

12. *An Béal Bocht* was translated by Patrick C. Power as *The Poor Mouth* (London, 1964).

13. The most comprehensive study of this nexus of *An Béal Bocht* with Irish literature is *Myles na Gaeilge* by Breandán Ó Conaire (Baile Átha Cliath, 1986).

14. *Cré na Cille* has not been published in a full English translation. This extract is by Eibhlín Ní Alluráin and Maitiú Ó Néill in *The Field Day Anthology of Irish Writing*, vol. III, p. 857.

15. *Dé Luain* can also mean 'day of reckoning', 'the day of judgment' or 'the last day', and has echoes of 'day of madness'. Ó Tuairisc deliberately chose this ambiguity for his title.

16. The author translated his novel under the title *Lead us into Temptation* (1978). The *Oireachtas* is an annual Irish language cultural festival, part of which includes literary competitions. These are the premier literary awards for works in Irish.

17. The most comprehensive survey of these novels is in Alan Titley, *An tÚrscéal Gaeilge* (Baile Átha Cliath, 1991). A useful study of the historical novel is Breandán Delap, *An tÚrscéal Stairiúil* (Baile Átha Cliath, 1992).

18. Translated by the author as *Lovers* (1991).

19. Mac Annaidh was only twenty-one when *Cuaifeach Mo Lon Dubh Buí* was published. He completed his trilogy with *Mo Dhá Mhicí* (1986) and *Ruball na Mickies* (1990). Apart from a short novel (1996) and a collection of short stories (1992), however, he has been strangely silent.

20. A short translated excerpt appears in *An Leabhar Mór / The Great Book of Gaelic*, eds. Malcolm Maclean and Theo Dorgan (Edinburgh, 2002).

21. Many Irish books were published in the so-called Gaelic script until the 1950s and in some cases beyond. The roman script did not become universal until the late 1960s.

22. There were many stupid contentions in Irish criticism. A notorious one was a narrow definition by some critics of what a novel is, taking their cue entirely from the nineteenth-century realist tradition. More bizarre was a contention that you could not write a realistic novel in Irish about urban life since Irish was not the language of any city. These misunderstandings derived from their lack of reading in the genre.

23. This is surprising, given female authors' prominence in poetry. Facile explanations such as that women have not the leisure to devote to long and time-consuming works is resoundly contradicted by the number of excellent female scholars such as Máirín Nic Eoin, Caoilfhionn Nic Pháidín, Angela

Bourke, Aisling Ní Dhonnchadha, Pádraigín Riggs, Gearóidín Uí Laighléis, Ríóna Ní Fhrighil, who have all produced substantial works on modern Irish literature. The reason why there are not many female novelists remains a mystery.

GUIDE TO FURTHER READING

Deane, Seamus. 'Mo Bhealach Féin', in John Jordan (ed.), *The Pleasures of Gaelic Literature*. Cork: Mercier Press, 1977.

Greene, David. *Writing in Irish Today / Scríbhneoireacht Ghaeilge an Lae Inniu*. Cork: Cultural Relations Committee of Ireland / Mercier Press, 1972.

Kiberd, Declan. '*Cré na Cille*: Ó Cadhain agus Beckett', in *Nua-Aois*. Dublin: An Cumann Liteartha, UCD, 1984.

Mac Eoin, Gearóid S. 'Twentieth Century Irish Literature', in Brian Ó Cuív (ed.), *A View of the Irish Language*. Dublin: Oifig an tSoláthair / Stationery Office, 1969.

Mhac an tSaoi, Máire. 'Writing in Modern Irish – A Benign Anachronism?', *The Southern Review* 31.3 (1995).

Nic Eoin, Máirín. *Trén bhFearann Breac: an díláithriú cultúir agus nualitríocht na Gaeilge*. Dublin: Cois Life, 2005.

Nic Eoin, Máirín. 'Le Roman en tant que forme littéraire dans le contexte d'une langue minoritaire: l'exemple irlandais', *Ecrits du Canada Français*. Montreal, 1987.

Ó Cadhain, Máirtín. *Páipéir Bhána agus Páipéir Bhreaca*. Dublin: An Clóchomhar, 1969.

Ó Cadhain, Máirtín. 'Irish Prose in the Twentieth Century', in J. E. Caerwyn Williams (ed.), *Literature in Celtic Countries*. Proceedings of the Taliesin Congress 1969. Cardiff: University of Wales Press, 1971.

Ó Conaire, Breandán. *Myles na Gaeilge: Lámhleabhar ar Shaothar Gaeilge Bhrian Ó Nualláin*. Dublin: An Clóchomhar, 1986.

Ó Doibhlin, Breandán. 'Smaointe ar Chúrsaí na Próslitríochta', in *Comhar*. Dublin: Lúnasa, 1984.

Ó Háinle, Cathal. 'An tÚrscéal nár Tháinig', in *Promhadh Pinn*. Má Nuad: An Sagart, 1978.

Ó hAnluain, Eoghan. 'The Twentieth Century: Prose and Verse', in Aodh de Blácam (ed.), *Gaelic Literature Surveyed*. Dublin: Talbot Press, 1973.

O'Leary, Philip. *The Prose Literature of the Gaelic Revival 1881–1921: Ideology and Innovation*. University Park: Pennsylvania State University Press, 1994.

O'Leary, Philip. *Gaelic Prose in the Irish Free State 1922–1939*. Dublin: University College Dublin Press, 2004.

Ó Tuama, Seán. 'The Other Tradition: Some Highlights of Modern Fiction in Irish', in Patrick Rafroidi (ed.), *The Irish Novel in Our Time*. Lille: Publications de l'Université de Lille, 1976.

Titley, Alan. 'Contemporary Irish Literature', *The Crane Bag* 5 (1981).

Titley, Alan. 'Littérature et traduction en gaélique', *Bretagne des Livres* (1996).

Titley, Alan. 'Letras d'Irlanda', *Occitans!* 75 (September–October, 1996).

10

ANN OWENS WEEKES

Women novelists, 1930s–1960s

As political trauma decreased and conditions improved slowly in the 1930s, the opportunity of higher education and the growth of a middle class increased the confidence and raised the profile of Irish women writers, after a national cultural revival in which they played a secondary role. The political rationale on all sides in the Anglo-Irish debate, while acknowledging and protesting ethnic and religious restrictions, had rested on unacknowledged gender and class restrictions which consumed or distorted many voices prior to independence. This national or political debate disappears in the work of most Irish women writers, although the related religious divide continues to be important, particularly in Northern Ireland. Ignoring divisive political debates enabled women to attend to the very distinctions and restrictions which buttressed these debates and continued to affect most women negatively. This close link between subject and writer, between the real and the fictional life, might have produced emotional or pedantic work, but the important novels of the period reflect the wisdom, detachment and humour of disciplined artists, related no doubt to the financial and educational privilege of the writers themselves. Uninterested in either the fantasies of the Irish Literary Revival or the formal experimentation of the modernists, subject matter being the locus of their attention, women novelists embraced realism, occasionally achieving poetic beauty.

Elizabeth Bowen

Demands of space naturally exclude many writers from this essay; those examined are the focus of contemporary scholarship, as well as my own choices. The first, Elizabeth Bowen (1899–1973), born in Dublin and the last owner of Bowen's Court, a 'big house' in Co. Cork, follows Anglo-Irish characters through decline and disintegration. The only child of Henry and Florence Bowen, Elizabeth, like many Anglo-Irish writers, used the trope of the only child to represent the situation of the Anglo-Irish, emotionally tied to Ireland yet dependent on England for tradition, education and employment. A writer for whom place looms large, Bowen provides intimate descriptions of rooms, houses and countryside, the visual and sensory images suggesting the close interaction of narrator and place. On the other hand, characters are viewed from a distance, their antics provoking humour, as the narrator – recorder may be a better term – perceives the farcical in even the most consequential human behaviour. The sophistication of Bowen's work is due in some part to the perfectly sustained balance of commitment to place and humorous distance from characters.

Unsurprisingly, then, Bowen assigns houses the importance of characters, particularly Danielstown, the 'big house' in *The Last September* (1929), the novel nearest her heart.[1] Danielstown hovers, an unamused observer of the 1920 'Troubles', of young Lois Farquahar's uncertain approaches to country and lover, and of the British army's attempts to subdue the countryside. Through Lois's eyes, readers become familiar with the sensuous details of gardens, tennis court, dining room, terrace and bedrooms, and the lovely ceremonies of gracious living. But, seen from the perspective of a native Irish home, the house, 'seemed to huddle its trees close in fright and amazement at the wide light lovely unloving country, the unwilling bosom whereon it was set'.[2] As the Naylors, Lois's relatives and the owners of Danielstown, protest that the 'real' Irish people love them, the house too seems shocked by the anger and determination of the natives. The deliberate blindness of the Naylors is affectionately mocked, but their situation and even the killing of Gerald Lesworth, the young British officer who loves Lois, seem of less consequence than the 'execution' of Danielstown, in which the novel culminates. Despite the traumatic political times, the novel resists both national debate and nostalgia: the demise of the society is depicted as the inevitable result of their irrelevance, the loss of the beautiful house alone seeming tragic.

Lois, the orphaned niece of the Naylors, epitomises the plight of the Anglo-Irish: sympathising with the native Irish but unable to commit to the IRA, disliking and resenting British paternalism but desiring a British lover because marriage seems the only avenue to middle-class female maturity. Employed by an agency of the British government during the Second World War, the mature Stella Rodney in *The Heat of the Day* (1949) had, like Lois, expected but failed to find dignity and purpose in marriage. In this story of spying and compromised loyalties in war-time Britain, Stella experiences British-Irish hostilities when she visits the Irish house her son has inherited. Expecting freedom from war-time restrictions in neutral Ireland, she is embarrassed to realise that the servants deprive themselves as they attempt to provide generously for her. The mockery of some English acquaintances, who picture the 'Emerald Isle' as enjoying the fat of the land, its people unaware of war, irks Stella, whereas she sympathises with old Colonel Pole, an Anglo-Irish acquaintance, who anguishes that the brave Ireland of his youth has been replaced by the neutrality of the 'rebels' now running the country.[3] Unflinchingly clear, this novel, like the previous one, commits to no side, but exposes the ambiguities and flaws in the rationales of idealists and dogmatists. Nothing is excused or accepted: the propaganda of the war-time British media is both shocking and surprisingly modern-sounding. No narratorial comment exposes or condemns the deceptions, however, as Bowen maintains comic distance, allowing the absurdities of both the perpetrators and the gullible to speak for themselves.

Lilia Danby, the wife of the manager of Montefort, the 'big house' in *A World of Love* (1955), illustrates the fate of a woman who accepted marriage as the only possibility, the unattractive, dull person she has become paralleling both the condition of the house and of the Anglo-Irish in the Republic of 1955. Elegant homes are now the property of foreigners and Montefort is presided over by the 'by-blow', the illegitimate Fred. Coerced into marriage with Fred some twenty years previously by Antonia (Fred's cousin and the owner of Montefort), Lilia suffers boredom in marriage and motherhood, and in the absence of a peer society in economically, intellectually and socially deprived provincial Ireland. Deference to the once-powerful Ascendancy is preserved only in the degraded fawning of shopkeepers, while home and family are at the mercy of sloppy servants. While Guy, Lilia's long-dead fiancé, lives imaginatively in this novel, the living characters seem less animate than nature, bleached by the dead heat of summer.

Comedy abounds, and yet a pervasive sense of loss overshadows this novel. In the early work, English characters are the source of comedy, the minutia of their conversation a particular target; here, however, the conversation of the inarticulate Fred and Lilia is sensitively reported. Transferring her focus here from young and adult women to women as wives and mothers, Bowen exposes the cruelty of the dismissal of mothers by daughters colluding with male-dominated society. Narratorial objectivity is not sacrificed but, conflating commentary on nature and characters, Bowen allows us to see the complexity of these most ordinary people. In the sated summer of their lives, Fred and Lilia attempt for the first time to speak their secrets. Nature itself seems to pause as their words peter out, their tentative moves toward communion seem, like the end of summer, more 'dissolution' than 'solution', 'a thinning-away of the hardness of many seasons, estrangement, dulledness, shame at the waste and loss'.[4] Nothing as final as resolution is reached in this diminished society, but 'survival seemed more possible now' (p. 169).

Molly Keane (M. J. Farrell)

Like her friend Elizabeth Bowen, Molly Keane (1904–96) was also a daughter of the Ascendancy, although the hunting society she frequented was little interested in the intellectual pursuits Bowen enjoyed. Keane's writing career (forged under the pen name of M. J. Farrell) was interrupted mid-term by the death of her husband, but resumed successfully and un-expectedly in the 1980s; the second stage (conducted under her own name) is discussed in chapter 3 of this volume.

Hunting features prominently in most Keane novels; the detailed, loving recreations of country, foxes, hounds, masters of hounds, excited beauti-ful girls and frightened children, all painted in brilliant colours, delight readers initially but eventually seem repetitive. Keane lingers longer and more lovingly than Bowen on the beauty of flowers, gardens, homes; dissertations on food, usually attributed to the characters, reveal this con-summate cook's pleasure in her work. Characters are also distanced by a comic perspective, as the narrator uses their own words to ridicule their class and gender prejudices. Distinctions maintained by the upper class are often brutally enforced by servants complicit in the hierarchical struc-ture. Adult guardians interfere in their wards' lives in Bowen, but never so ruthlessly as Keane's manipulative mothers, who may owe something to contemporaneous stereotyping. Politics, as murderous in Keane as in Bowen, are seen by most of Keane's upper-class characters as merely ridiculous and inconvenient.

Mad Puppetstown (1931), like several other Keane novels and *The Last September*, presents a conscious reflection of the past *as* past. Some novels are set in the 'Troubles' of early twentieth-century Ireland, but their pur-pose is not to re-vision the political struggle, rather to examine those areas neglected by a literature focussing too fixedly on national politics. Elderly unmarried ladies, beautiful domineering women, inept men and pathetic girls represent the fate of a dying Ascendancy in Keane. The elderly Aunt Dicksie is merely ignored in *Mad Puppetstown*, whereas the brutalisation of Aunt Pidgie at the hands of a servant in *Two Days in Aragon* (1941) is tolerated because the servant is invaluable. The dilapidation of Puppets-town after the war is ugly rather than nostalgic, a vision that parallels the novel's distrust of romance. Plentiful political ironies also complement the ugliness: when a Puppetstown servant attempts to protect a British soldier by lying about his route to his enemies, for example, the soldier meets his death, for he, believing all Irish to be informers, has himself lied to the servant.

The Rising Tide (1937) and *Two Days in Aragon* introduce several varieties of Keane's domineering women. Competent, or by some exception empowered financially, their scope limited by class and gender conventions, these women become petty tyrants, mercilessly enforcing the submission of vulnerable dependants. In the former novel, Lady Charlotte French-McGrath rules her husband and four daughters with demanding, dreadful precision; only her son escapes her net. Lady Charlotte believes that she loves her daughters passionately, although this love entails their unquestioning obedience. Society, servants, friends, husbands happily ignore the tyranny of beautiful women in Keane, all admiring Lady Charlotte, for example, as an extraordinary woman. Even her emotionally maimed children ignore her faults, refusing to acknowledge her destruction of their lives. Only Diana, the youngest, least conventionally pretty daughter, voices a muted dissent, but she is thirty-two before she escapes. Hardly escape, for Diana, an early example of Keane's pathetic girls, becomes embroiled with and controlled by her beautiful sister-in-law, Cynthia. As domineering as her mother-in-law, Cynthia acknowledges that she does not love her children: determined, however, not to feel ashamed of them, she forces them to hunt, often on horses of which they are rightfully fearful, justifying her actions as necessary to the children's acceptance in society. The Irish Civil War is simply a disruption of Cynthia's social life, of the visits from the enthralled British guests who find everything about the native Irish hilarious, particularly delighting in imitating the accents of servants recounting disasters.

Two Days in Aragon highlights Nan, once the nannie, now the housekeeper or manager of Aragon, who is descended, like Fred in *A World of Love*, from an extramarital union, in this case that of a Fox master of Aragon with a servant. As ruthlessly as any of Keane's controlling wives, Nan determines that no one shall blot the Fox name, the Fox lineage being her private pride. When foolish young Grania Fox transgresses gender and class boundaries in a relationship with Nan's own son, Foley, Nan determines to end both the relationship and possible pregnancy. As she often does, Keane homes in on what she presents as native repressions: while Grania awakens Foley's desire, 'the peasant in him' resents her sexual freedom, and the Catholic in him is frightened at 'his own wickedness in taking her love'.[5] Sylvia, Grania's sister, is a model of Ascendancy good behaviour and exhibits the courage that Keane often associates with such women. The burning of Aragon results from misperceptions and the death of Nan is an accident, but a brutal logic seems at work in the simultaneous destruction of Nan and her great love, Aragon. Nan's cruelty is distilled from the crimes and inhumanity of her history and is passed to her son. This novel alone of Keane's sheds a serious light on the 'Troubles': 'Tired men afraid of one another laid plans against overwhelming odds', the narrator notes, plans labelled as 'dirty ambushes and cowardly assassinations' by 'British officers who persistently refused to conduct themselves as though they were at war and in an enemy's country' (pp. 87–8). In this her darkest novel, Keane looks back to the lovely houses in fond, sad remembrance, seeing Aragon as a beautiful woman, 'still in her perfection', aware of the coming violence and the 'desertion far more tragic than any sudden ending' (pp. 94, 139).

The contemporary society of *Devoted Ladies* (1934) sets the novel apart from those discussed above. As sophisticates from London, Anglo-Irish Sylvester, American Jane and British Jessica visit Sylvester's impoverished, ageing Irish cousins, Keane pictures this society as less gracious and less interesting than the earlier one. The lesbian relationship of Jane and Jessica is presented as the stereotype of the nineteenth and early twentieth centuries, as in George Moore's *A Drama in Muslin* (1886): Jessica is an unattractive bully and the vague Jane, a dependent beauty. Similar to Keane's domineering mothers in her manipulations, Jessica, however, cannot conceal her temper or control her passion, and thus is the object of social ridicule.

Piggy, an Irish cousin, is a fully developed pathetic woman. Sad, fat and unpleasant, Piggy is usually ignored and consequently flattered and over-responsive to any attention, often welcoming even vicious ridicule. Desiring love, an emotion she cannot comprehend but attempts to purchase with gifts or services, Piggy performs one last act of service for the man she thinks she loves, sacrificing her own life as she drives herself and the 'evil' Jessica over a cliff.[6] Tragedy is avoided by the comic distance and rich metaphorical writing. And, as in all her work, Keane cuts through the veneer of good behaviour to expose the sad little charades necessary to preserve the appearance of respectability, the only superiority left to her unhappy, unattractive women.

Kathleen Coyle

Kathleen Coyle (1883–1952), born in Derry to a Catholic mother and a father secretive about his religion, moved to England in 1906 and then back to Ireland, to Dublin, in 1911, where she married, mothered two children and divorced before moving back to England, then to the Continent, and finally to the United States. She provided for her family by writing novels, but would insist that only the remarkable work, *A Flock of Birds* (1930), was artistically valuable.[7]

A Flock of Birds focusses relentlessly on the suffering of a mother, Catherine Munster, whose son is about to be executed. Although Christy Munster is sentenced to death for a political crime in an un-named city in Ireland around 1918, the novel ignores the political ideologies and violence of the time, dwelling instead on the agonies of the middle-class family members, their lives and ways of thinking shattered by unexpected tragedy. Christy's radical politics are shared only with his Catholic fiancée, Cicily, whose relationship with Christy, a matter of attraction and shared loyalties, pales nevertheless in comparison to the deep mother–son bond. While Cicily and Christy's siblings busy themselves in attempting to free Christy, Catherine sees their activities as falsely optimistic and insists that Christy not be distracted or distressed by exposure to his family's unrealistic hopes.

In her desolation, Catherine, neither Catholic nor conventionally religious, enters a church. Feeling herself made lifeless by Christy's impending death, she is drawn to an image of the sorrowing Mary bearing her dead son. In a moment of insight, Catherine recognises her sorrow as a re-enactment of Mary's and of women's over the centuries, especially in times of war. While men die as heroes, women, she understands, were always left to absorb 'the bitter, unsatisfying taste of life'.[8] Deprived of all human hope, she looks to God for strength to bear her burden. Visiting Christy subsequently, she tentatively approaches the subject of God and is rewarded by Christy's expression of belief, which allows her to conceive of reunion after death. The night before his execution, she promises Christy to kneel and pray the entire night, her body a reservoir from which he can draw spiritual, as he once drew material, sustenance. As she leaves his cell, a warden attempts to touch, perhaps to comfort, her; but the secular must not intrude on this holy communion and, like the risen Christ, she warns, 'Do not touch me' (p. 158).

Although concentrating on the mother's consciousness, the novel is also filled with nuanced vignettes of city life. The divisions between radicals and constitutionalists, Catholics and Protestants, gregarious and private persons, are carefully drawn, but all are capable of surprising words and deeds when events or human sympathy shift their patterns of perception. Class alone, Catherine realises, enables her to interrupt the prison governor with requests to see her son, whereas the poor man who visits his wife, a child-murderer, is bullied by the warden. This man's love for his wife is imaged in the bunch of nasturtiums he furtively conceals, 'a hand pushed up from earth holding the burning bright flowers', a beam of human possibility in the darkness of the prison for Catherine, and in the wreckage of war for Ireland (p. 126). Although we expect the worst of the warden, he allows man and package inside, as, Catherine thinks, he had meant to all along.

Kate O'Brien

Born to a middle-class Catholic family in Limerick, Kate O'Brien (1897–1974) presents one of the first thorough and critical portrayals of this prosperous, emerging society. She is the first writer discussed in this chapter to take a university degree, a route most subsequent writers follow. She spent some time as a journalist in England (where at a later date she was married for a brief period) and as a governess in Spain. Devoted to freedom – from authoritarian governments, and class, religious and gender prejudices – she was denied entry to her beloved Spain from 1937 to 1957, following the publication of her travel book, *Farewell Spain* (1937).

O'Brien's first novel, *Without My Cloak* (1931), reads as an origin myth for the Catholic middle class, whose patriarchal values reflect the times and are ultimately upheld, usually at the expense of women. Later novels focus more on women's ethical and emotional conflicts, and on the fragility and cost of human love. In *The Ante-Room* (1934), Agnes Mulqueen is torn between her Catholic conscience and passion for the husband of her much-loved sister. In most O'Brien novels, a wise narrator comments cynically on motives and illusions, but Agnes is accorded heroine status, her struggle presented as a deep, ultimate and tragic human conflict. In a rare moment of literary sorority, its importance emphasised by Agnes's deeply held belief in Catholic doctrines, Agnes forgoes desire, not in the interest of her own salvation but out of love for her sister. Ironically, meanwhile, the dying Mulqueen matriarch, Teresa – an unquestioning Catholic – agonises over the fate of her beloved, syphilitic, ageing son and plots for him a marriage whose inevitable childlessness militates against Catholic precepts. Teresa is successful because the nurse she entices, unlike the Mulqueens, lacks financial support and must take the meanest opportunity to survive in late nineteenth-century Ireland. Dying happily, Teresa, blessed by her priestly brother, remarks the goodness of God.

Society's insistence on the priority of family over individual, a priority upheld by church and most middle-class women, and by the Free State Constitution of 1937, remains constant in O'Brien's later novels, but the cost to individuals is emphasised. *The Land of Spices* (1941), a *Bildungsroman* set between 1904 and 1914, evokes James Joyce's *A Portrait of the Artist* (1916) but revises the genre by presenting two intertwined stories of development, suggesting the possibility of mutual human experience from which both characters can draw. O'Brien's first portrait, that of Anna Murphy, is traditional in following Anna through childhood and youth, but her second, that of the English Mother Superior in Anna's school, unconventionally traces the nun's mature development. O'Brien underscores the difficulties of female children, particularly in the matter of education. If education is a given for the self-focussed Stephen Dedalus, it is the ground on which Anna must battle her powerful grandmother, who dismisses third-level education as excessive for women. Mother Superior comes to Anna's aid and must herself battle Irish provincial prejudices against foreign languages, customs and people.

The English figures in O'Brien are, in contrast to those in Bowen and Keane, usually positive, often suggesting a broader view of life, as does the English suffragette in this novel. Similarly, in *The Last of Summer* (1943), set during the Second World War, O'Brien features those who support Irish neutrality as narrow-minded and provincial, while those with broader vision agonise over the trauma, which they see as human, not narrowly national. Illustrating the myopia that O'Brien critiques, the Irish censorship board banned *The Land of Spices* because one sentence noted, without approving or disapproving, a homosexual relationship.

Romantic love competes with, but is firmly routed by, selfish mother-love in *The Last of Summer*, as Hannah Kernahan ensures that her beloved son will not marry the girl whose father rejected Hannah. Richer and more nuanced than Keane's portraits of vicious mothers, O'Brien's Hannah is widely admired, her domination of her children seen as responsible nurturing rather than tyranny. Hannah not only believes in her right to determine her children's future, she prays zealously for divine support of her efforts. Angèle, the young woman who loves Tom Kernahan, accepts defeat rather than a marriage entailing constant unexpressed rivalry, for Tom adores his mother, whose manipulative 'love' Angèle has experienced and knows to be both ruthless and unrelenting.

Irish writers were slow to acknowledge lesbian existence; those who included lesbian characters without ridicule confined them to metaphorical corners of the text, as did George Moore and Bowen, and O'Brien herself in *Mary Lavelle* (1936). In 1958, however, in her last novel, *As Music and Splendour*, O'Brien presented the first positive extended portrait of lesbian relationships. This novel follows two Irish friends, Claire Halvey and Rose Lennane, professional divas who move from one opera season to another, usually in European cities, at the end of the nineteenth century. Claire's relationship with her lover, Luisa, is happy, filled with music, laughter and good food, wine and conversation. Like most O'Brien heroines, Claire is a thinking, committed Catholic; thus, she is fully aware and believes in the sinfulness of her decision to love Luisa, a decision that, like Agnes Mulqueen's, marks another brave commitment to human love. All commitments to love in O'Brien lead to great misery, but are also, as the narrators often note, the source of the greatest human happiness. Claire's view of her relationship with Luisa as sinful but in no way different in the eyes of God from Rose's extramarital heterosexual relationship was, in 1958, a big step in the liberation of the fictional lesbian. As always, O'Brien rejects idylls: love is as fragile and arbitrary as ever; neither Claire nor Rose finds fidelity or permanence in their relationships.

Maura Laverty

Maura Laverty (1907–66) was born to a farming family. Trained as a teacher, she, like Kate O'Brien, spent several years in Spain as a governess and journalist. When she returned to Ireland, she continued journalism, going into broadcasting; her programmes, cookery books and novels were very popular in the 1950s.

The early novel, *Never No More* (1942), is a picture of village life from a woman's perspective that we do not find in the previous writers discussed in this chapter, though the village was the locus of life for a majority of Irish people until the 1960s. Set in 1920, in a village near the Bog of Allen, this novel introduces a huge cast of colourful characters, the politics of the time barely registering in the village. The poverty of the villagers is offset by the nurture and support of those who have a little more, and by the gorgeous 'prodigality' of the bog, whose heather 'ravished every shade of blue for its cloak'.[9] Delia Scully's warm relationship with her grandmother and community is the centre of this *Bildungsroman*, in which the young woman must adjust not to society but to her difficult relationship with her mother. Delia is perceptive and more tolerant of her mother than many of the fictional daughters who would examine mother–daughter interactions in later novels. Delia understands that she angers her mother because she resembles her beloved father, who impoverished the family by gambling away his wife's earnings, and she, Delia, has inherited some of his habits. Wisely, she recognises that her mother's anger does not preclude love: the 'Deep love, but no liking' (p. 10) which exists between the mother and daughter is not a matter of virtue or lack thereof, but simply of incompatibility. Laverty rejects the literary elitism which so often ridicules middle-class endeavours: Delia recognises and admires the business skills which allow her mother to succeed and to provide for her family following her husband's death.

A later novel, *Lift Up Your Gates* (1947; published in the United States as *Liffey Lane*), the basis of a popular 1960s Irish television series, *Tolka Row*, focusses on the poverty of Dublin tenements during the Second World War. Helping her brother to deliver papers, young Chrissie Doyle is exposed to the terrible conditions of employment, housing, health and education which beset Dublin's poor. Lice, rats, disease and brutal labour she can accept, but the children's job of searching the dumps for cinders, which are then sold for a few pence in coal-rationed Dublin, almost breaks her.[10] Again, Laverty features a fraught, but not atypical, mother–daughter relationship. Barely feeding her family on a small pension and the pennies her children earn, Chrissie's mother turns on Chrissie in anger when she begs for favours. We recognise her anger as the only defence of the helpless and a disguise for the hopeless sympathy she feels for Chrissie. Despite exposing brutalising poverty, Laverty, unlike contemporary novelists of such scenes, depicts many acts of kindness. Most telling for Chrissie is the offer of a job in the convent, which saves her from the horror of rag-picking, the only 'work' open to poor girls in war-starved Dublin.

Mary Lavin

Mary Lavin (1912–96) was born to Irish immigrants in the United States; she and her mother came to live in Ireland when Mary was nine, her father returning after some years to manage a farm in Meath. Like Kate O'Brien before her, Lavin's fictional world is that of the Irish Catholic middle class. An introspective writer, she introduces characters who must create their own systems of morality, systems that accord with their emotional and ethical perceptions of the world rather than with directives of church, state or class. These characters usually clash with, and are defeated by, those who frame their own morality in line with narrow interpretations. Widowed early in life, with three small children, Lavin often features characters in similar situations, as she explores the emotional and moral behaviour of women as lovers, mothers, widows and elderly parents. An accomplished short-story writer before she turned to the novel, Lavin dismissed her own novels.[11] The stories are exemplary models of understated complexity and richness, but the novels' detailed views of family life and changing circumstances in early twentieth-century Ireland also make them worthwhile.

Unlike the pared-down stories, the novels include intrusive, sometimes directive, narratorial commentary. *The House in Clewe Street* (1945), Gabriel Galloway's *Bildungsroman*, details the boredom of small-town Irish life in the early century. Theresa Coniffe, Gabriel's aunt and guardian, exemplifies the angular distortion of Lavin's 'good' people, those who narrowly interpret and ostentatiously follow church and family duties. Theresa's malformation is in part the consequence of her lost youth: wrenched from childhood by her mother's death, Theresa became companion and business assistant to her father and mother to her two younger sisters, a fairly frequent pattern for women also featured in Janet McNeill's *Tea at Four O'Clock* (1956). The authority so willingly granted by her father is too heavy a load, forcing Theresa to forgo the youthful interactions which usually develop human understanding and sympathy. Gabriel must endure Theresa's constant supervision, a supervision she decrees necessary to prevent his following in the footsteps of his father, whose faults she unstintingly and frequently recounts. Gabriel is accorded narratorial sympathy, even as he teases the young maidservant, Onny Sorohan, with whom he runs away to Dublin. When Onny becomes pregnant and seeks an abortion, Gabriel sees her as inhuman and sinful. Her death following a back-street abortion seems a punitive resolution, an uneasy hint that her function in life was to educate and humanise Gabriel.

In contrast, *Mary O'Grady* (1950) presents the 'ideal' mother of the 1937 conservative 'Catholic' Irish Constitution, a woman who loves her husband but never so much as her children, especially, as was often the case, her male children. Despite loving her daughters, she constantly compares them unfavourably with herself, only grudgingly admitting, though not recognising, their qualities when men admire them. The O'Grady family enjoys some comfort, and their opportunities increase: the only outlet for the eldest son, for example, is emigration, while the youngest daughter of the large family has the choice of third-level education. On a different plane to Laverty's Dubliners, then, Lavin's picture is still one of poverty, the busy mother suppressing all personal expectations.

Anne Crone

Anne Crone (1915–72) was born in Dublin and educated in Belfast and Oxford. She set her three novels – *Bridie Steen* (1948), *This Pleasant Lea* (1951) and *My Heart and I* (1955) – in County Fermanagh, which, as Lord Dunsany notes in the introduction to *Bridie Steen*, she preserves as authentically and imaginatively as Hardy does Dorset, and in which she examines the consequences of bitter religious divisions in Northern Ireland.[12] Crone's characters are moulded by harsh labour conditions, as well as religious conflict: some few grow as sparse and beautiful as the cotton on the lovely bogs, but the majority shrink like distorted plants.

The eponymous Bridie Steen of the 1948 novel is the unfortunate daughter of a Catholic maid and the son of the maid's Protestant employer.

Bridie's grandmother is as manipulative and controlling as O'Brien's Hannah Kernahan. Crone does not take sides: the bitterness of Lisha Musgrave, Bridie's paternal grandmother, is matched by that of Aunt Rose Anne, her Catholic aunt. The cruelty of these women is exacerbated by the death of a lover in one case, grinding poverty in the other; Crone does not excuse their behaviour, however, for similar conditions fail to embitter other characters. Like O'Brien's Agnes Mulqueen, though less capable of analysis, Bridie is faced with an excruciating battle between emotion and conscience, as her dying grandmother, whom she has come to love, attempts to force her to 'turn', to become a Protestant. If Bridie complies, the grandmother insists that she will die happily, leaving her granddaughter the estate that would have been her father's and blessing her marriage with the cousin whom Bridie loves. Bridie's tragic death convinces her cousin that he too, though not burdened by overt prejudice, is as guilty as most of his northern peers, Protestants and Catholics, of preaching and fighting about a God of whose love they are ignorant.

Maeve Brennan

Maeve Brennan (1917–93) moved with her family in 1934 to the United States, when her father, who had taken part in the Easter Rising, was appointed Irish ambassador to the US. She remained in New York when her family returned to Ireland, and worked as a diarist for *The New Yorker*, where many of her short stories first appeared. Two volumes of short stories were eventually published and a collection of sketches from *The New Yorker*. A privileged background, beauty, intelligence and marriage with the managing editor of *The New Yorker* might seem a formula for happiness, but Brennan's life and work were both pervaded by a sense of loneliness, of homelessness, surely exacerbated by her life away from family, her husband's alcoholism and the snobbery of upper-class New York society. Her life deteriorated from loneliness to eccentricity, and finally to mental disease, before her death in 1993.

One excellent novella, *The Visitor*, which Brennan wrote in the 1940s, was unpublished in her lifetime but discovered and published in 2000. Love, revenge and homelessness – familiar Brennan themes – figure prominently as, following her mother's death, Anastasia King makes her way from France to the Dublin house of her paternal grandmother, where she had spent her first sixteen years, hoping to find a home with her only close relative. The prosperous Mrs King, now in her seventies, has no sympathy for the lonely girl and reminds her that she made her choice at sixteen, when she left Dublin, father and grandmother to live with her mother in France.

Like so many fictional mothers, Mrs King was jealously possessive of her son and made her daughter-in-law's life one of insignificance and misery, the son's siding with his apparently reasonable mother finally driving Mary King away. Uncertainty besets Anastasia, while the desire for love, inherited perhaps from her lonely mother, consumes her, but both she and reader see the grandmother's rejection as inevitable. Like many lonely people, like Brennan herself, Anastasia is a keen observer; combined with the beautifully controlled language and refusal to exaggerate, her observations lift the novella and all this writer's treatments of loneliness, as Clare Boylan remarks in her Foreword, to the level of art.[13]

Janet McNeill

Janet McNeill (b. 1907) was born in Dublin, attended school in England where the family moved in 1913, and returned with family to Ireland, to Belfast, where she worked as a journalist. Married in 1933, she devoted herself for many years to her children, writing more than twenty children's books, as well as radio plays and two opera libretti. When her children became independent, she continued her adult writing career.

McNeill's sharply humorous novels, such as *Talk to Me* (1965) and *The Small Widow* (1967), concentrate on the lives of upper-middle-class Belfast women, lives governed by adherence to the gender and class conventions of 1950s Ireland. Despite the political, religious, social and economic differences between Northern Ireland and the Republic, there were sufficient similarities between the urban middle classes in Dublin and Belfast to warrant reading McNeill's novels alongside those of middle-class women from the Republic. No other Irish writer has so clearly and consistently revealed the stark waste and despair beneath the cramped existence of these women, an existence unmitigated by illusions and made the more bitter by the women's determination to suppress any public and, if possible, private recognition of this waste. The gender dependency that decreed successful women be physically attractive and thus marriageable, that ignored women's sexual needs and that allowed widowers to turn their daughters into caretakers, is buttressed by the women's own polite, instinctive linking of sexual and class codes.

Despite their self-repressions, women in *The Maiden Dinosaur* (1964) are more at ease in female than in male company; the fact that they see their sheltered school days as the best of their lives underscores the dreary narrowness of their existence. Plain Sarah Vincent's obsession with the beautiful, demanding Helen Harris lasts from school days through to middle age, but this unstated lesbian relationship, like so many heterosexual ones, takes a particularly heavy toll on one partner. The women friends find Sarah's virginity comic and pitiable, but all the women long in vain for sensual responses from their partners. Helen thinks that Sarah couldn't possibly understand her need for passion: she remembers burning with desire while her husband offered only tenderness, weeping at his sexual failures and exulting at his small successes. Addie Pratt, whose parents' 'trade' connections had been a matter of concern in schooldays, attempts at least to awaken some response in her husband. Massaging his back, she tells him of an article on mature sexuality she has read. 'We shouldn't think it is over, should we?' she asks wistfully; Gerald replies, 'A little to the left, dear'.[14] Despite the failure of heterosexual relationships, male approval is understood to validate a woman's sexuality, a belief tragically passed to the next generation in McNeill's 1964 novel.

The neglect of women's fiction seems a fitting subject to close this essay. Towards the end of a television interview, following publication of a volume of her poetry, Sarah gets the usual question: has her background (suggesting both her class and gender) been 'a restrictive element' in her work. Despairingly, she thinks that this condescension, this implication that women are mere 'canaries pecking lightly at life' (p. 99), this dismissal of women's concerns and positions because they are women's, always wins. But Addie, Sarah's friend, interrupts, tartly announcing that the interviewer clearly believes that they should feel deprived by their comfortable middle-class backgrounds and merely literary acquaintance with 'brothels and dry-closets'. In doing so, Addie exposes as prejudice the implication that middle-class existence deprives women of meaningful emotional, intellectual and social experience, and as ignorance the dismissal of women's writing (p. 99).

Sophisticated, urbane, almost always liberal, these writers bring women to centre stage, spot-lighting them and opening a wide vista for future writers to mine. While their novels resist the experimental form and 'cutting-edge' subjects acclaimed in earlier Irish work, their disciplined, restrained expression speaks eloquently to the terrible repressions Irish women endured. Later writers would be more explicit, more experimental, but few would surpass the elegance, wit and wisdom of these predecessors.

NOTES

1. Elizabeth Bowen, preface to *The Last September* (1929; New York: Avon, 1952), p. viii.
2. Elizabeth Bowen, *The Last September*, p. 78.
3. Elizabeth Bowen, *The Heat of the Day* (New York: Jonathan Cape, 1949), p. 87.
4. Elizabeth Bowen, *A World of Love* (New York: Alfred A. Knopf, 1955), p. 168.

5. M. J. Farrell (Molly Keane), *Two Days in Aragon* (1941; London: Virago Press, 1985), p. 83.
6. M. J. Farrell (Molly Keane), *Devoted Ladies* (1934; London: Virago Press, 1984), p. 303.
7. John Cronin, *The Anglo-Irish Novel* (Belfast: Appletree, 1980), vol. II: *1900–1940*, p. 130.
8. Kathleen Coyle, *A Flock of Birds* (1930; Dublin: Wolfhound Press, 1985), p. 109.
9. Maura Laverty, *Never No More* (London: Longmans, Green & Co., 1942), pp. 46–7.
10. Maura Laverty, *Liffey Lane* (1946; New York: Longmans, Green & Co., 1947), p. 119.
11. Lavin expressed this sentiment in interview with author and elsewhere. See, for example, Marianne Koenig, 'Mary Lavin: The Novels and the Stories', *Irish University Review* 9 (Autumn 1979), 244.
12. Lord Dunsany, introduction to *Bridie Steen* (1948; London: Heinemann, 1949), p. vi.
13. Clare Boylan, foreword to *The Visitor* (2000; Dublin: New Island Books, 2001), n.p.
14. Janet McNeill, *The Maiden Dinosaur* (1964; repr. Belfast/Dublin: Blackstaff and Arlen House, 1984), p. 62.

GUIDE TO FURTHER READING

Bourke, Angela. *Maeve Brennan: Homesick at* The New Yorker. London: Jonathan Cape, 2004.
Coughlan, Patricia. 'Women and Desire in the Work of Elizabeth Bowen', in *Sex, Nation and Dissent in Irish Writing*, ed. Eibhear Walshe. Cork: Cork University Press, 2004.
Dalsimer, Adele M. *Kate O'Brien: A Critical Study*. Dublin: Gill & Macmillan, 1990.
Foster, John Wilson. 'Zoo Stories: The Novels of Janet McNeill', *Eire-Ireland* 9 (1974), 104–14.
Greacen, Robert. *Rooted in Ulster: Nine Northern Writers*. Belfast: Lagan Press, 2001.
Kelly, A. A. *Mary Lavin: Quiet Rebel*. New York: Barnes & Noble, 1980.
Lassner, Phyllis. 'The Past is a Burning Pattern: Elizabeth Bowen's *The Last September*', *Eire-Ireland* 21 (1986), 40–54.
Lee, Hermione. *Elizabeth Bowen: An Estimation*. Totowa, NJ: Barnes & Noble, 1981.
Murray, Thomas. 'Mary Lavin's World: Lovers and Strangers', *Eire-Ireland* 7 (1972), 122–31.
Walshe, Eibhear (ed.). *Ordinary People Dancing: Essays on Kate O'Brien*. Cork: Cork University Press, 1993.
Weekes, Ann Owens. 'A Trackless Road: Irish Nationalisms and Lesbian Writing', in Kathryn Kirkpatrick (ed.), *Border Crossings: Irish Women Writers and National Identities*. Tuscaloosa and London: University of Alabama Press, 2000.
Weekes, Ann Owens. *Irish Women Writers: An Uncharted Tradition*. Lexington: University of Kentucky Press, 1990.

II

TERENCE BROWN

Two post-modern novelists: Samuel Beckett and Flann O'Brien

Beckett and story

The English writer E. M. Forster admitted of the novel as a form: 'Yes – oh dear yes–the novel tells a story.'[1] It is difficult to imagine many Irish novelists so regretting story as the basis of their craft. Indeed, the novelist and playwright Thomas Kilroy has perceptively observed that that chromosome of story, the anecdote, is in the DNA of the Irish fictional tradition from at least the end of the eighteenth century. He advises, with reference to Maria Edgeworth's *Castle Rackrent* (1800):

> The distinctive characteristic of our 'first' novel, that which makes it what it is, is not so much its idea, revolutionary as that may be, as its imitation of the speaking voice engaged in the telling of a tale. The model will be exemplary for the reader who has read widely in Irish fiction: it is a voice heard over and over again, whatever its accent, a voice with a supreme confidence in its own histrionics, one that shares with its audience a shared ownership of the told tale and all that it implies: a taste for anecdote, an unshakeable belief in the value of human action, a belief that life may be adequately encapsulated into stories that require no reference, no qualifications beyond their own selves.[2]

This is certainly a voice the reader can hear loud and clear in the novels of Samuel Beckett (1906–89), though subjected there to the kind of satiric deconstruction that the weight of so settled a tradition might require. For the narrative energies of the anecdote and the told tale are pervasive in Irish fiction, in a way which can make the short story seem culturally indigenous where the novel has never quite appeared so. And the Irish novel in that context has certainly been dominated by a rich zest for story-shaped worlds. It may indeed be, as Kilroy hints, that story-telling has offered Ireland in modern times what in other cultures philosophy, theology and science have struggled to provide: a means of apprehending life's enigmatic truths and of accounting for what transpires in the world. For many Irish writers and their readers, 'life' can be 'adequately encapsulated into stories'.

This is not an idea which Beckett would have entertained. A brilliantly adept storyteller, he nonetheless lacked the kind of faith in the efficacy of narrative Kilroy suggests is 'exemplary' in the tradition. Nor was he bereft of interest in other modes of knowing such unthinking confidence implies. For Beckett employed narrative to explore problems explicitly posed by philosophic reflection, to a degree that can make him seem an anomalous figure in an Irish context. Yet it was his peculiar predilection for addressing issues of philosophic import in complex narratives which in part accounts for his remarkable achievement as a novelist.[3]

Murphy

Samuel Beckett's *Murphy* (1938) was the author's first published novel (he had published a collection of interlinked stories, *More Pricks than Kicks*, in 1934) and the first work about which he felt reasonably secure as a writer. Most of the pretentious attitudinising and passages of tedious intellectual display which had marred the earlier fictional venture (only the bleakly sardonic final page of 'Belacqua and the Lobster' in *More Pricks than Kicks* gave a full hint of future powers) had been slewed away in a text that made a succinct comedy out of philosophic matter. For in *Murphy*, Beckett, the Trinity-college scholar, explores by means of a bizarre yet strangely affecting comic narrative the implications of the Cartesian dualism his studies had encouraged him obsessively to ponder.

Murphy, in exile from Ireland and resident in London (we do not learn his given names), by his own reckoning a 'chronic emeritus',[4] is pathologically averse to work. His chief delight is to while away the hours on a rocking chair in mental separation from the world, intent as he is on loving himself. He has, however, against his will fallen in love with a London prostitute (also Irish by origin), who urges him to seek employment, lest she, Celia, will be forced back on the streets. A major part of the narrative concerns his desperate stratagems to avoid both work and Celia (despite the sexual rapture they enjoy together – 'serenade, nocturne, albada', p. 46) and his eventual employment in a lunatic asylum, The Magdalene Mental Mercyseat (the MMM). There he encounters a patient, a Mr Endon, whose near catatonic imperviousness to the world about him is symbolised in the game of chess Murphy and he play, in which Mr Endon refuses to react to any of Murphy's moves, to the point where Murphy must abandon the non-existent contest. Mr Endon seems to Murphy the ideal type, who has resolved the Cartesian conundrum of how the mind can be connected in acts of the will to the body and to the external world of other people and of objects, by retreating to the willessness of his own mind. Unable to make any contact with Mr Endon, Murphy is forced back to his rocking chair, now set up in a garret in the asylum, where he meets his death in an apparently accidental gas explosion. He is cremated and his ashes strewn among the waste matter on the floor of a London pub. In an elaborate subplot, a gallery of Irish grotesques for complicated amatory reasons are set on discovering Murphy's London whereabouts, mounting indeed an increasingly futile philosophic quest for one whose intention it is to disappear into the serene stasis of his own mind.

Murphy, it must be stressed, is no merely clever, arid novel of ideas (though it has its moments of intellectual showmanship) in which a philosophic conundrum is presented in narrative form. Rather, its power as a work of fiction derives from the way in which the implications of an idea are tested in the crucible of human feeling. The story it tells in comic mode is also a poignant one. For in the text, Celia is sketched tenderly as a victim of her own needy heart and Murphy's death represents for her the end of her hopes. Furthermore, in anticipation of a central theme of Beckett's *œuvre* as a whole, the novel is constantly alert to the dimensions and particulars of human suffering, mental and physical. In the course of a book that climaxes with Murphy's suspicious death, we hear of two suicides (that of 'the old boy', a grisly affair indeed) and bodily afflictions of one kind or another (Miss Dew has Duck's Disease, Cooper is unable to sit, while Celia's paternal grandfather Mr Willoughby Kelly can do little but sit, since he is confined to a wheelchair). In the MMM, we are afforded a glimpse of well-regulated mental and physical sadism, while the narrative voice of the book insists almost to the point of a ghastly relish that suffering is an ineluctable fact of the human condition. Of Neary's night panics, for example, the narrator grimly observes: 'he simply had this alarming conviction that every second was going to announce itself as the first of his last ten minutes or quarter of an hour on earth. The number of seconds in one dark night is a simple calculation that the curious reader will work out for himself' (p. 125). A prevailing assumption in the book is that Murphy has good reason to seek sanctuary in his mind, which pictures itself 'as a large hollow sphere, hermetically closed to the universe without' (p. 63).

Murphy is in fact trapped in a reality that can only be truly escaped by death. Although the narrator assures us that Murphy is in some sense a free agent in the novel, when the other characters are merely the narrator's puppets, the text is dominated by chronology (complicated flashbacks keep the reader alert to days and dates), by an awareness of astrological seasons and Newtonian physics, and by a sense of city districts as grid-maps of streets. Geometry is a controlling metaphor; the events of the novel compose complex patterns of echo and repetition. The effect is to suggest the vanity of human wishes in a deterministic universe, where the narrator's moods vary from bitter revulsion from the antics of his puppets to comedic satisfaction at the dark absurdity of life that occasions pity. Like Murphy's, the narrator's is a bifurcated nature, split between an intellect that indulges an allusive, cerebral style, exaggeratedly recondite in its word choice, and a sensibility open to atmospheres, locales, the pull of emotion on the heart-strings (the novel ends in an affecting scene, with Mr Kelly sending his kite into the 'pale limitless blue', p. 157). It is the self-contradictory voice of the narrator that we remember from the novel when the complexities of its philosophic purport and its structural detail begin to fade.

As text, *Murphy* retains a purchase on a recognisable social world. The residual constraints of fictional realism anchor the book in time and place, with occasionally obtrusive references to the actual conditions of newly independent Ireland suggesting, furthermore, elements of the *roman à clef* (the portrayal of the pot-poet Austin Ticklepenny is a libellous lampoon on the poet Austin Clarke). A modernist consciousness of textuality, however (Celia is introduced to us, for example, in a columnar list of characteristics and vital statistics), indicates an author at work in the wake of Joycean experiment. And Murphy as alienated outsider suffering a grotesque fate is the precursor of the indigents and tramps who people Beckett's subsequent, more radically experimental novels, in which we enter a universe of imagining that cuts loose from the social almost entirely, to reveal a blackly comic world, relentlessly apprehended in a mental and emotional space of its own. Of these, *Watt* (1953) and a trilogy of texts – *Molloy* (1951), *Malone Dies* (1951) and *The Unnamable* (1953), henceforth the Trilogy – constitute works that subject the very idea of the novel to such interrogation that the form itself can seem to undergo a terminal, post-modernist meltdown. In each of these, as in *Murphy*, philosophic issues are explored in a story-shaped world.

Watt

In one respect, *Watt* is even more than *Murphy* a work of realism, since it engages in an obsessively rational inspection of the physical world of things and data. But this is in the context of a fiction the manifest purpose of which is to display the outright lunacy of such rational ambition, which makes its passages of hyper-realism an intellectual inanity. Watt is a temporary inhabitant as servant in the house of one Mr Knott. Beginning his service on the ground floor, he graduates in time to the first, without any increase in his knowledge as to who his master really is, or of the true nature of his surroundings, which seem to be in a constant state of alteration.

Lacking absolute knowledge, partial information leaves open endless fields of possibility and alternatives that bifurcate to the point of madness. Watt's ultimate fate is residence in an institution, possibly an asylum, where he narrates his tale of Mr Knott's perplexing house to a fellow inmate.

To seek to know in Mr Knott's house is to condemn oneself to manic consideration of all the possible permutations that reality can present. And to imagine that the conditions of rational order obtain among copious alternatives, scrupulously adumbrated, is to enter a zone of the ludicrous, where certainty can be achieved only at the expense of the rational or common sense as conventionally understood. An extended riff in the novel imagines how Mr Knott manages to have a starving dog come every day at the appointed time to consume the food superfluous to Mr Knott's needs on that day. This involves the summoning into wonderful, absurd textual existence of the bizarrely numerous and physically afflicted Lynch family, whose role it is to service Mr Knott's canine requirements.

Watt subjects reason as epistemological tool to unremitting scorn. Where reason enters, alternatives proliferate with an inventive persistence that is cognate with narration. For in this text, story and the findings of reason seem to share the same status, each of them only ways of seeking to make sense of an unknowable reality. Where the prose style attempts in its reiterated subjunctives and conditionals, its untiring qualifications, to establish at least something for certain, anecdote, tale and story push their way into the text with a unsettling air of inconsequence. Characters (the Galls, father and son piano tuners, to cite but two) appear and disappear while the tangential tale of a west of Ireland research trip by a Trinity student is tied to the main narrative in whimsically tenuous fashion. Narrative is invention, the text implies, no more trustworthy than reason, for all its histrionic self-assurance.

And text itself is a contingent thing, *Watt* gives us to understand. For we are advised midway and also later on that the words we are reading are derived from the record Watt's companion Sam has made in a notebook, in their place of refuge, which in part accounts for lacunae in the text indicated by question marks and gaps. Though Sam can also seem like an omniscient narrator, Beckett himself (another Sam) enters this complicated narrative equation when in 'Addenda (1)' – there is no Addenda (2) – he advises in a footnote that 'The following precious and illuminating material should be carefully studied. Only fatigue and disgust prevented its incorporation.'[5] The novel could, this implies, have been other than it is, rendering what we have been given, disturbingly arbitrary. A sense of that contingent quality as an attribute of fiction itself is forced on the reader, who experiences the text as a highly unpredictable set of variations between almost detachable sections (though patterns are established among the four parts). In some of these, a prose of cold rational distinctions is extended to a preposterous degree. In other lengthy passages, oral discourse is fore-grounded. In a book where reason has sought to set feeling aside, these passages sometimes carry a burden of emotion (as in Arsene's 'short state-ment' of about twenty-eight pages, with its tale of housemaid Mary's peculiar eating habits and its poignant, bitterly lyrical evocation of the seasons' endless cycle).

That language which both reason and story-telling depend on is also arbitrary is a further revelation of this subversive, proleptically post-modern text. Part of Sam's problem in telling Watt's tale is that Watt has been afflicted by a curious mental state which causes him to invert what he says in highly complicated ways. Some of Sam's account of Watt's experience in Mr Knott's house is in fact therefore a translation from Watt-speak, which as Sam acknowledges at length was 'so much Irish' to him. He admits that of all he heard in Watt's private tongue, he understood 'fully one half of what won its way through [his] tympan' (p. 169).

Watt was written in English, in France, during the Second World War. The major works that were to follow in the period 1946–53, culminating in the play *Waiting for Godot* that established Beckett's international re-putation, were all written in French by the Irish author who had made Paris his home. Beckett's near bilingualism has its analogue in his multi-genre versatility. The works of this period include the three novels of the Trilogy, the first of which was translated into English by Patrick Bowles in colla-boration with Beckett, the second and third by Beckett himself. This fact of compositional and publishing history means that novels which in rami-fying narratives exhibit, as we shall see, the philosophic impotence of dis-course, themselves hover in a kind of linguistic no-man's-land, where acts of translation highlight how language is both contingent and an inescapable fate.

Beckett and French

Beckett's shift from English to French[6] in this wonderfully creative period of his writing life was accompanied by a revision of his aesthetic ambition as artist. In an oft quoted interview of the 1950s, he spoke of how he sensed at this time that literature could no longer seek the encyclopaedic totality that had governed the Joycean enterprise in fiction: 'The more Joyce knew the more he could. He's tending towards omniscience and omnipotence as an artist.' By contrast, he confessed: 'I'm working with impotence, ignor-ance. I don't think impotence has been exploited in the past. There seems to be a kind of esthetic axiom that expression is achievement – must be achievement. My little exploration is that whole zone of being that has been set aside by artists as something unusable – as something by definition incompatible with art.'[7] In other words, Beckett was prepared to accept that the less he knew, the less he could – that in consequence of epistemological despair, writing must be intimate with failure. The better to explore this 'zone of being', he turned to French, which would he felt allow him to write 'without style'.[8] For such a project involved paring language down, relieving it of the weight of centuries of familiar English usage that gave the illusion of expression as knowledgeable achievement.

Existing as if between two languages (in French the Irish proper names in the Trilogy are curiously defamiliarising, while in the English version they seem merely generic in a landscape that eschews geographic specificity), in the condition of translation as it were, the prose of the Trilogy manages to suggest a language constantly discovering its own contingency. The Trilogy seems inexorably driven to restate itself in the face of a recurrent failure, even adequately to explore failure. A result of this is to make it a perverse triumph of the deconstructive impulse which so characterised the post-modern turn in late twentieth-century culture. For in this trio of novels, story becomes the means by which a despairing philosophy of knowledge is made markedly available as a textual experience; a paradoxical experience, to be sure, of what it is like to know and feel that 'there is nothing to express, nothing with which to express, nothing from which to express, no power to express, no desire to express, together with the obligation to express'.[9]

The Trilogy

In the first novel of the Trilogy, *Molloy*, the textual status of the 'story' is established from the start. Molloy, the narrator, is in his mother's room (he presumes his mother is dead). Each week, a man supplies him with paper and gives him money for the pages he has managed to cover with words, and returns earlier work marked up with signs he does not understand. It seems (though this is not stated) we are reading the product of this strange exchange. The tale Molloy unfolds is of a mysterious quest in which the narrator, a grotesque derelict, describes how he set out to visit his mother and failed. How eventually he arrived at her room, he does not know. His journey, first by bicycle and then on crutches, involves an encounter with the police, the accidental killing of a dog, a prolonged sojourn in a lady's house in an extended passage that evokes Ulysses's enchantment on Calypso's island in the *Odyssey*, culminating in an attack on a charcoal burner in the wood where Molloy loses his way and falls into a ditch.

Throughout his 'story', Molloy reminds the reader that he is an artist of sorts, spinning a tale (like Homer, it could be said). He speaks of 'the heat of composition',[10] yet admits 'all I know is what the words know' (p. 31). Later he confesses: 'I weary of these inventions and others beckon to me. But in order to blacken a few more pages may I say I spent some time at the seaside, without incident' (p. 68). He senses that in some odd fashion his stories are telling him, as if he is possessed by narrative voices that make him their conduit. His prose style emphasises this doubt as to author- ial control of his own narration (at one point he exclaims: 'What a story, God send I don't make a balls of it', p. 77). Although the narrative is of an onward journey, sentences constantly backtrack on themselves in qualifica- tion and reservation, as though governed by uncertainty. Yet this also creates the sense of an author who aspires to punctilious word choice in a manner suggestive of post-modernist textuality, where words offer a refined exactitude only their self-conscious pastiche of literary expression would appear to warrant.

That in *Molloy* we are in fact experiencing something akin to pastiche is revealed in part 2 of the novel. Here we are alerted to the fact that in part 1 we have been immersed in what, if normal chronology had been followed by Beckett, could be read as the increasingly mysterious second part of a spy or detective story (a 'mystery' in genre terms), with hints of the boys' adventure yarn thrown in (much is made in part 2 of accoutre- ments gathered together for the task undertaken). For in part 2, we learn how Moran works for a boss named Youdi, who sends agents out on missions, such as the one that he embarks on to discover Molloy's where- abouts and report back. Part 2, apparently, is Moran's report on his fruitless quest.

The textuality of *Malone Dies* is even more pronounced than that of *Molloy*. Malone, another afflicted monologuist (he shares Molloy's disable- ment and even some of his possessions), awaits his death. To pass the time he will tell stories, writing them in pencil in an exercise book (he promises four stories but only manages one), commenting on what he has written as he goes. What he gives us is a pastiche *Bildungsroman* about a boy named Saposcat, who grows up to become a man called Macmann (son of man, no less). We are recurrently made aware both of the difficulties involved in producing this text (at one point the pencil seems to have slipped from Malone's fingers and is only recovered 'after forty-eight hours . . . of intermittent effort',)[11] and of the arbitrary quality of story itself (although Malone affects to struggle for historical accuracy about his hero). Death will be a relief from the compulsion to narrative, Malone hopes. He is also at pains to distinguish himself as author from his creation: 'Nothing is less like me than this patient, reasonable, child, struggling all alone for years to shed a little light upon himself, avid of the least gleam, a stranger to the joys of darkness' (p. 193).

However, the tale Malone tells of Saposcat and Macmann might well be his own, or that of what in Beckett's work has become, with the publication of *Malone Dies*, the typical Beckettian persona. For the child Saposcat becomes the Macmann whose career ends in a lunatic asylum, amid black comic grotesqueries of the kind that have been the stuff of Beckett's fiction since *Murphy*. Beckett himself intrudes in the text, indeed, when he has Malone long for fictional closure in death: 'Then it will all be over with the Murphys, Merciers, Molloys, Morans and Malones' (p. 236). At this juncture, the text implodes as artifice in its allusion to previous works by Beckett about which the invented Malone cannot be presumed to know. The very act of fiction is for the reader deconstructively set in question, therefore, in a way which can make the Trilogy a work subversive of literature's claims to represent reality in any way. In such an interpretation, what we have been reading, as we have followed our author's novelistic career, are narratives spun out of Beckett's head, ways of spending the time before death to be sure, but no more than that. Accordingly, it can seem entirely apt that as *Malone Dies* ends with Malone's presumed death, the narrator and his character Macmann begin to seem one and the same person. Beckett, as author, and his creations have begun to seem indistinguishable, both existing as arbitrary fabrications in a story-shaped world, in which the death of the author is implicit in the death of literature. Nor should it surprise that the final work in this trilogy of novels should bear the title that it does. For in *The Unnamable*, it is not at all certain who actually possesses the narrative voice to which we are invited to attend.

In *The Unnamable*, it is narrative itself which seems to generate the text. The text's implied author refers impatiently to his 'Murphys, Molloys and Malones',[12] a gallery of literary personae who have wasted narrative time, instead of allowing what is now merely a narrative voice, without context or setting, to achieve a real goal: 'if I could speak and yet say nothing really nothing?' (p. 303). For that would be truth in face of the lies fiction perpetrates.

The Unnamable makes that attempt to coerce language to represent its own essential impotence as a means of expression and mode of knowledge. As it does, the prose becomes more and more the voice of entrapment, as the text becomes an urgent, oppressive tirade that cannot be arrested. It seems that the more the voice of narrative tries to escape from the grotesquely, blackly comic stories (about another Beckettian persona *in extremis*) that flower rampantly even from this stony ground, as it struggles to express nothing, the more it is immured in the prison house of language. *The Unnamable* seeks to speak from the abyss of deconstructed discourse where neither writer nor text can be granted ontological authority, as if to transcend language and its arbitrary significations in some new impotent and ignorant form of utterance; but the voice presses unrelentingly on, damned by its inauthenticity, doomed to speak pointlessly of its unquenchable lust for silence.

So the Trilogy can persuasively be read as a work of deconstruction, anticipatory of a cultural turn which has been identified with the post-modern moment of the later twentieth century. Philosophy and story both find themselves subverted in its radical raid on a desired inarticulateness on the edge of all linguistic occasions. Yet to restrict its significance to the deconstructive *mise en abyme* would be, it must be said, seriously to limit to a particular cultural moment what is one of the most multivalent of twentieth-century literary masterpieces; for many other readings have found eloquent advocates. Critics have not been slow to interpret its compulsively readable pages as offering genuine, achieved insights into the human condition. There have been those, for example, who have studied the Trilogy as an interrogation of the concept of an originary, integrated selfhood, subjecting the work to an existentialist critique, while others have read it as the expression of a Schopenhauerian pessimism or of a Swiftian satiric recoil from life, both made bearable by a fundamentally comic spirit in debt to Rabelais and Sterne. Some have accounted for its hold on readers by reading the work as a searching study of Man as rational, self-conscious being in a godless, irrational world, where suffering is destiny. The bodily indignities Beckett's personae are forced to endure would make belief in a benign Christian deity, frequently referred to by the narrators, seem simply absurd.[13]

Perhaps, however, the Trilogy's capacity to hold the attention of the reader is less to do with its possible meanings or with its post-modernist subversion of meaning than with its indisputable literary power. For the Trilogy as a whole is a work of wonderfully variegated moods, shifting from lunatic comedy (at its zenith in *The Unnamable*, when Mahood is imagined leading his legless and armless existence in a jar outside a restaurant near the shambles) to a weird poetry of improbable loves (as between Moll and Macmann in *Malone Dies*). It manages, too, mesmerically to inhabit a world close to the experience of dream, in which bizarre encounters with an imagined world and with its unlikely inhabitants are poised on the edge of mythic awareness of a revelation that never quite comes. The contents of the unconscious seem available to its bleak, haunting lyricism, in what become a species of poetry that touches the depths of desire, as the prose cadences of pathos and of nostalgia are challenged by the manic exercises of a deranged reason (at its most inventively florid in the extended sucking-stones passage in *Molloy*). A distinctively Beckettian tone establishes itself over the three volumes, compact of great syntactical and semantic command with exacting rhythmic control, that engages with terminal things in a manner that induces in the reader feelings of yearning and loss. For order set at naught seems the 'message' of the work as a whole. Alienation is its predominant register; displacement, dislocation, estrangement the territories of feeling it is determined to occupy.

As the work of a sensibility imprisoned in self-exile, Beckett's Trilogy has also found a mode of interpretation in post-colonial theory. This is not just a matter of noting that the work often invokes a desolate landscape of the mind that incorporates details which suggest the constricted conditions of the putatively independent Irish Free State, nor of the way in which the experience of terminal states of feeling finds an appropriate setting in a phantom Dublin (a city beneath mountains, beside the sea, with its two canals) which haunts the text like the ghost of a lost poetics of place. It also involves reading the Trilogy – Beckett's *œuvre* indeed – as so imbricated with dispossession and self-exile as to constitute an anatomy of the post-colonial condition itself. In David Lloyd's terms, the inauthenticity that he discerns in another of Beckett's works 'is . . . the perpetual condition of the colonized: dominated, interpreted, mediated by another'.[14] So for Lloyd, 'Beckett's . . . oeuvre stands as the most exhaustive dismantling we have of the logic of identity that at every level structures and maintains the post-colonial moment' (p. 56).

Flann O'Brien: dispossession and deconstruction

A sense of what can be characterised as post-colonial dispossession and inauthenticity also permeates the ostentatiously textual novels of Beckett's near contemporary, Brian O'Nolan (1911–66), who in 1939, as Flann O'Brien, published the first of his novels employing one of his several pseudonyms.[15] That book, *At Swim-Two-Birds* (1939), can seem so dependent as a ludic work of pastiche and parody on precursor texts as to lack any truly felt life of its own, as if meaning and authority are located elsewhere. *The Third Policeman* (completed 1940, posthumously published as a work by Flann O'Brien in 1967) offers in a curiously inert prose, accompanied by footnotes of preposterous academic decorum, the first-person narrative of a man who has in fact lost his life (the emptied-out language of dispossession indeed). *The Poor Mouth*, first published in Irish as *An Béal Bocht* in 1941 and published in English in a translation by Patrick C. Power in 1973, is a blackly comic report on the living death of Irish rural deprivation, which can only be mediated in parodic terms of a generic cliché popularised in newly independent Ireland – the western island and Gaeltacht pastoral. Furthermore, each of these works, his finest achievements in the novel form, can be read as a depressed commentary on the dismal conditions of life in 1930s Ireland, in the second decade of independence. The student narrator of *At Swim-Two-Birds* inhabits a cultural world of petit-bourgeois provincial inanity. *The Third Policeman* unfolds its grim tale of crime and punishment in a hell that is indistinguishable from the Irish midlands at their most stultifying, while *The Poor Mouth* makes misery and complaint in an exiguous setting an endogenous affliction of the Irish soul.

The English language cannot be taken for granted as a medium of communication in these texts. The narrator of *At Swim-Two-Birds* composes his narrative of seedy student life in an English that reads as if it had already achieved the condition of a dead language like Latin, oddly punctilious and formal.[16] From one of the book's interpolations that parody the weird 'translationese' through which Gaelic saga literature had been mediated since the nineteenth century and the Irish Literary Revival, we learn that its odd title is in fact a clumsy version of the Irish *Snámh-dá-én*, as if to remind us that English is not native to the Irish ecosystem. That same landscape is evoked in *The Third Policeman* in a very 'queer' (a key word in the text) idiolect, that suggests simultaneously familiarity and disorientation; and of course, *The Poor Mouth* owes its existence to *An Béal Bocht* and achieves its satiric effects through a parody of the Gaelic syntax and vocabulary deployed by nativist purveyors of Irish pastoral. All this suggests that language in Ireland is the site where the post-colonial condition of inauthenticity and dispossession finds an ambiguous, hybrid realisation.

It would be difficult, however, to contain these intriguingly experimental works within a single critical paradigm. Another seems immediately apposite. As with Beckett, their fascination with the textual makes O'Brien's key novels candidates for a post-modernist analysis, for readings in which they can be entered as a species of anti-novel. In this reading, anecdote, story, elaborate narrative (the staples of the Irish tradition and of O'Brien's entire *œuvre*) and the genre of fiction itself can be seen as the objects of a fascinated inspection which, by revealing the techniques and protocols of fiction as they are enacted, robs them to a degree of expressive energy. When this post-modernist penchant for advertising what, in other forms of creativity, would be the taken-for-granted mechanics of an artefact is combined with a parasitic relish for parody and pastiche, then O'Brien's fiction can be seen to turn on itself in a sustained, deconstructive whimsy.

At Swim-Two-Birds

This is especially true of *At Swim-Two-Birds*. This zanily inventive text has as its presumed author a slothful University College Dublin undergraduate (there are obvious allusions to Stephen Dedalus's college milieu) who generates a manuscript about a novelist named Dermot Trellis. Trellis is at work on a novel which will display the deleterious effects of sin. The running gag of O'Brien's book is that Trellis's characters take on a life of their own when Trellis is asleep, and eventually turn revengefully upon him. Levels of presumed reality and fictionality are elaborately intertwined. Trellis impregnates one of his characters, who bears him the son who begins to write a further novel in which he describes terrible violence done on his progenitor, employing the characters his literary father had invented. These include the Pooka ('a species of human Irish devil')[17] and the Good Fairy – who together account for a good deal of the book's shape-changing brio, its magical realism – the giant Finn MacCool who, insistently and somewhat tediously (for characters and readers alike), chants from the saga legend of the mad king Sweeny, in extensive parodic interpolations into the text of high falutin' translationese, and a cast of Dubliners, with their cliché-ridden demotic, who might have stepped in pastiche from Joyce's collection of that name to reveal a genius for inconsequential dialogue that is all their own. That is when they are not recalling cow-punching days in Ringsend in the style of cowboy pot boilers. Throw in Jem Casey, the working man's Bard of Booterstown, with his banal verses, and a tasty Irish fictional stew is set to simmer.

As if this chinese-box plot structure (narrative contained within narrative) is not enough to challenge the very status story might be assumed to enjoy in Ireland, O'Brien also out-Becketts Beckett in giving his book a vertiginous textuality. Chapter 1 begins with three separate openings (there is no chapter 2) and the book finishes in the logical absurdity of two conclusions (*antepenultimate* and *ultimate*). Throughout, sections are headlined mock-sententiously – 'Biographical reminiscence, part the first' (p. 16), for example. Figures of speech are pedantically identified. Plot summaries of the action hitherto (some of them supplying new information) are provided and cross-referenced. Passages from the public press are cited as such, while the narrator has recourse at various points to a multi-volume *Conspectus of the Arts and Natural Sciences*, which surprisingly contains a biographical entry on Dermot Trellis, as well as the scarcely relevant matter the narrator chooses periodically to cite at confusing, if entertaining, length. The reader is constantly challenged as to point of view at any given stage in this interlacing of story (the interlacing recalls a Celtic illuminated manuscript) with self-referring textuality. The novel as novel, as genre, scarcely survives the book's bravura display of subversive high spirits.

The Third Policeman

The Third Policeman also functions in certain respects as an anti-novel and post-modern text. A rum tale of envy, greed, murder and punishment, the book offers an unreliable narrator of a very special kind. He is in fact dead, but does not know it. Nor as readers do we, until close to the final page of the novel. What our narrator takes for reality, therefore, we are given to understand by the book's conclusion, is the hell to which he has been consigned in punishment for his part in the vicious murder with which the narrative began. This strange conception turns the book inside out in a troubling way; for what we take as we read to be the real world, from which the narrator steps into a fantastical zone where Nature's laws of time and space no longer seem to apply, is in fact the reality he now occupies and what he and we have taken for normality is unreal, phantasmal.

This, oddly, makes *The Third Policeman* a book to re-read, for a second reading will be different from the first to a greater degree than is customary in fiction, even of the *policier* and mystery kind. (The text shifts from a curiously deadpan prose appropriate to a hard-boiled crime novel to, in its final stages, the glooms of Gothic fiction.) On a second reading, we will notice all the indications that the narrator is dead but is unaware of this: frequent references to negative states, for example,[18] or the simple detail that he cannot remember his own name. As we read we will realise, too, that the repetition we are experiencing is also the narrator's fate, for he is condemned endlessly to re-live (re-die?) the novel's contents. We are made aware of this horrible truth by a lengthy textual repetition in which the narrator's approach to the police barracks, where so many extraordinary things transpire, is described. 'I had never seen a police station like it',[19] says the narrator on the final page, unknowingly repeating himself in apt punishment for a capital crime. He is namelessly condemned forever to that terrible first-person pronoun.

The Third Policeman, with its unreliable narrator, its disturbingly clever play on appearance and reality, its generic echoes and its key textual repetition, certainly draws attention to itself as artifice, in what we have come to recognise as the post-modern manner. The elaborate comedy of the footnotes adds to this. These concern the narrator's obsession with the lunatic theories of a savant named De Selby, among which is the belief, for which he argues with consummate logic, that the world is sausage-shaped. Perhaps, as Clissmann, has argued, his theories pertain in thematic fashion to the hell the narrator inhabits where anything is possible,[20] but, as we read, their relevance is to exhibit how text itself is subject to bizarre exchanges in this world where time and space seem malleable. In the novel, much play is made of the atomic theory which allows O'Brien to fantasise how people become their bicycles and vice versa over the years, as atoms are exchanged in the riding. We see in this novel how the presumably main text can be parasitically invaded by 'secondary' footnotes. Chapter 11 has a footnote that runs for six pages, splitting the print in two on each page, generating two narratives, where the priority of the 'main' story is set in question by a tale of academic in-fighting and skullduggery (in their way as reprehensible as the narrator's criminality). In this chapter, the footnote has become the narrative and the text a kind of footnote.

The Poor Mouth

The Poor Mouth also makes great play with literary artifice. Its narrative of outrageous Gaelic misery is presented as an edited version by Myles na gGopaleen (the pseudonym under which O'Nolan contributed a famous humorous column to *The Irish Times*) of a document written by an in-habitant of a stereotypical Gaeltacht. In the Irish version of the work, na gGopaleen represents himself as editor of a non-existent periodical, *The Day of Want*. By the time of the English translation, this has become *The Day of Doom*. Want and doom are indeed the fate of the Gael, in what is an obvious pastiche of such widely admired accounts of western Irish life as Tomás Ó Criomhthain's *An tOileánach* (1929; translated by Robin Flower and published as *The Islandman* in 1934).[21] *The Poor Mouth*, in its savage, wildly comic stories, its exaggerations of the kind of set pieces and conventions these writings deploy, brings parody to a point where it preys as a negative energy on the precursor texts, swallow-ing them up, as it were, in a form of literary cannibalism. The anti-novel here becomes a predatory thing, like the monstrous sea-cat that pursues the narrator in one ghastly episode in the book. Its import begins to seem nihilistic.

So black in fact is this book (potatoes and eternity set in grim apposition), despite the high comedy of the characters resigning themselves to the fates literature has assigned to them, that it cast its shadow over O'Nolan's other major novels; for it alerts us to how those more humorous works are also rooted in a dark vision of life. This is not to suggest, it must be stressed, that O'Brien was any kind of ambitious philosopher, employing narrative and story as Beckett had done to examine Cartesian and epistemological conun-drums until he turned to a deconstructive interrogation of the very nature of tale-telling itself in the Trilogy. Rather, O'Brien, by contrast with his contemporary, lacked the kind of radically questioning mind that made Beckett's novels a searching engagement with the mystery of human existence. In its place was a settled conviction – the product, as Anthony Cronin has a convincingly argued, of a conservative and unquestioned Thomistic Catholicism[22] – that the bleak truths about the sinful and cruel human condition were already fully available. There was nothing new under the sun, and certainly nothing new to be said about terrestrial life. Consequently, O'Brien's novels deal in futility, comic as that can be made to seem. Stories are seen to be versions of other stories in an achievement that makes pastiche a primary literary activity. Narrative ingenuity begins to seem an end in itself. And inasmuch as O'Brien's fiction has anything much to tell us, it is that life can be heartlessly savage, that sin leads to the repetitive torments of hell and that the pleasures of the text coexist with the indignities of the body and soul. For reading *The Poor Mouth*, with its physical privations and hardships, reminds us that *At Swim-Two-Birds*, for all its fanciful literary panache, is intimate with squalor, waste, bodily functions (vomiting or 'puking' are frequent) and a miasma of intellectual purposelessness. *The Poor Mouth*, with its frenetic stories of rural thievery and violence, also highlights evil as an abiding aspect of the human predicament, as perhaps the unnerving concomitant of this storyteller's indisputable success as a whimsical humorist. This we are certainly made to understand in the evacuated prose of *The Third Policeman*, as the narrator struggles to write an infernal language when 'there are no suitable words in the world to tell [his] meaning' (p. 116).

NOTES

1. E. M. Forster, *Aspects of the Novel* (1924; London: Edward Arnold, 1974), p. 17.
2. Thomas Kilroy, 'Tellers of Tales', *Times Literary Supplement*, 17 March 1972, pp. 301–2.
3. This essay concentrates on five major novels by Beckett. It does not deal with the first novel Beckett wrote in French, *Mercier et Camier* (1946, published 1970 and in English 1974), which anticipated the concerns of the Trilogy: *Molloy* (in French 1951; in English 1955), *Malone Dies* (1951; 1958) and *The Unnamable* (1953; 1959).
4. Samuel Beckett, *Murphy* (1938; London: Pan Books, 1973), p. 16.
5. Samuel Beckett, *Watt* (1953; New York: Grove; London: Evergreen, 1959), p. 247.
6. For a sensitive analysis of the significance of translation in the production of the Trilogy, see Leslie Hill, *Beckett's Fiction: In Different Worlds* (Cambridge: Cambridge University Press, 1990), pp. 40–58.

7. Lawrence Graver and Raymond Federman (eds.), 'An Interview with Beckett: 1956', in *Samuel Beckett: The Critical Heritage* (London: Routledge & Kegan Paul, 1979), p. 148.

8. Quoted in James Knowlson, *Damned to Fame: The Life of Samuel Beckett* (London: Bloomsbury, 1996), p. 357. Knowlson usefully discusses Beckett's linguistic shift.

9. Samuel Beckett, *Dramatic Works and Dialogues* (London: John Calder, 1999), p. 26.

10. Samuel Beckett, *Three Novels* (New York: Grove Press, 1965), p. 28.

11. Beckett, *Three Novels*, p. 222.

12. Beckett, *Three Novels*, p. 303.

13. For an excellent survey of the variegated critical response to Beckett's novels, see David Pattie, *The Complete Critical Guide to Samuel Beckett* (London and New York: Routledge, 2000) to which I am indebted.

14. David Lloyd, *Anomalous States: Irish Writing and the Post-Colonial Moment* (Dublin: Lilliput Press, 1993), p. 54.

15. Brian O'Nolan published two further novels, *The Hard Life* (1961) and *The Dalkey Archive* (1964). They are much inferior to those considered in this chapter, upon which his reputation as a novelist must depend.

16. Anthony Cronin makes this point in *No Laughing Matter: The Life and Times of Flann O'Brien* (London: Grafton Books, 1989), p. 106.

17. Flann O'Brien, *At Swim-Two-Birds* (1939; London: Four Square Books, 1962), p. 55.

18. As noted by Anne Clissmann, *Flann O'Brien: A Critical Introduction to his Writings* (Dublin: Gill & Macmillan, 1975), p. 173.

19. Flann O'Brien, *The Third Policeman* (1967; London: Picador, 1974), p. 172.

20. Clissmann, *Flann O'Brien*, pp. 169–70.

21. For a study of the western island as cultural myth, see John Wilson Foster, *Fictions of the Irish Literary Revival: A Changeling Art* (Dublin: Gill & Macmillan, 1987), pp. 94–113.

22. Cronin, *No Laughing Matter*, p. 106.

GUIDE TO FURTHER READING

Ackerley, C. J. *Demented Particulars: The Annotated* Murphy. Tallahassee, FL: Journal of Beckett Studies Books, 1998.

Connor, Stephen. *Samuel Beckett: Repetition, Theory and Text.* Oxford: Blackwell, 1988.

Donohue, Keith. *The Irish Anatomist: A Study of Flann O'Brien.* Dublin: Maunsel, 2002.

Hopper, Keith. *Flann O'Brien: A Portrait of the Artist as a Young Post-modernist.* Cork: Cork University Press, 1995.

Hurson, Tess and Anne Clune (eds.). *Conjuring Complexities: Essays on Flann O'Brien.* Belfast: Institute of Irish Studies, Queen's University, 1997.

Kenner, Hugh. *A Reader's Guide to Samuel Beckett.* London: Thames & Hudson, 1973.

Levy, Eric P. *Beckett and the Voice of Species.* New York: Barnes & Noble, 1980.

Miller, Lawrence. *Samuel Beckett: The Expressive Dilemma*. New York: St Martin's Press, 1992.

O'Hara, J. D. (ed.). *Twentieth-Century Interpretations of* Molloy, Malone Dies *and* The Unnamable. Englewood Cliffs, NJ: Prentice-Hall, Inc., 1970.

Pilling, John (ed.). *The Cambridge Companion to Beckett*. Cambridge: Cambridge University Press, 1994.

Pilling, John. *Beckett Before Godot: The Formative Years (1929–1946)*. Cambridge: Cambridge University Press, 1998.

12

ELIZABETH GRUBGELD

Life writing in the twentieth century

Issues of genre

The novel has always borne a close relationship with the 'literature of fact' –
history, travel writing, confession, letters and the diary – and the parallels
between fiction and life writing are similarly deep and long-standing. James
Joyce chronicles his coming of age in a third-person narration about young
Stephen Dedalus, and writers as diverse as Patrick Kavanagh, Mary Costello
and Seamus Deane offer as novels thinly disguised versions of their early
years. Calling his three-volume autobiography, *Hail and Farewell* (1911–14),
a 'novel about real people', George Moore draws attention to the blurring
of genre endemic to life writing, as does Oliver St John Gogarty when he
prefaces *As I Was Going Down Sackville Street* (1937) with the disclaimer,
'The names in this book are real, the characters fictitious.'[1] Yet while autobiographical fiction and the fictionalised autobiography both play fast and
loose with facticity, the two genres are not synonymous, and a consideration
of their differences elucidates the contributions life writing has made to the
development of prose narrative in modern Ireland.

As Philippe Lejeune has argued, autobiography cannot be decisively
distinguished from fiction by internal generic features. The difference,
Lejeune contends, lies in a pact the author establishes with the reader
through rhetorical cues: an expectation that the narrator is coterminous
with the person whose name appears on the title page and that the story
given represents the truth of that person's experience, even if certain facts
are altered to best convey it.[2] The tacit agreement between writer and
reader affirms a correspondence between the voice that speaks and the
author's name (allowing that it may itself be a rhetorical construction);
most importantly, it also affirms a correspondence between both constructs
and the human being who lived and interacted with other human beings in
place and time. Because of their overt claims to a reality outside the text,
autobiographies often conduct their own self-examinations as to the

methods and ethics of writing about people who actually lived and events that are represented as having occurred. Autobiographical narrators worry openly over the difficulties of ascertaining truth, while repeatedly raising the problem of memory and its relationship to the written narrative. They engage in self-reflexive questioning about the speaker's reliability and authority as the teller of a tale, the issue of family privacy, and the relationship of text and audience. The challenges of representing a self lead also to new narrative strategies, including complex treatments of time and perspective, the incorporation of documentary materials and other genres, and the production of prose modelled on oral discourse.

Irish life writing has always emphasised place and time, expressing the hopes, anxieties, sufferings and triumphs of the group with whom the writer feels most associated. Each text also speaks from and to a specific historical moment. Early twentieth-century autobiographers articulate the ambitions and disillusionments of the Revival period, while later writers address the aspirations and constrictions of life in the new Republic, the decline of Anglo-Ireland, and the challenges and confusions that followed the social revolution of the 1960s and the eruption of violent conflict in the North. Like its fictional counterpart, Irish life writing addresses specifically Irish concerns: nationalism and national identity, constrained economic and artistic opportunities, and the influence of religion on family roles, political ideology, and psychological and sexual maturation. While most Irish autobiography focusses on maternal figures, religious quandaries, poverty and nation, the life writing of the class known as 'Anglo-Irish' has quite different concerns, and presents its own set of generic features. Telling most often a tale of depleted fortune and influence, Anglo-Irish writers query their national and class identity through a narrative structure patterned on patrilineal descent or the history and geography of the family properties.

The Irish Revival

Until the first decades of the twentieth century, life writing in Ireland consisted chiefly of political or military memoirs, religious testimonies, family histories, private diaries, travel writings and reflections on the customs and politics of the country. Yet within the period known as the Irish Revival, autobiography turned inward to chart the development of an authorial vocation, the emergence of self from the womb of the family, and struggles with matters of religion, sexuality and nationalism that draw the narrator away from his family and toward a more cosmopolitan life, even as the childhood place arises as an imaginative wellspring. Some of its finest practitioners were keen admirers of French literature and culture, bringing to their life writing the candour of the French realist novel and the symbolist fascination with sensation and states of consciousness.

George Moore (1852–1933) begins the process in 1888 with *Confessions of a Young Man*, an assemblage of memories, fiction, art criticism, closet drama, literary pronouncements, high comedy and desperate seriousness that traces the growth of his artistic sensibility against the incongruous alternating backdrops of bohemian Montmartre and his native County Mayo during the land wars of the early 1880s. Almost twenty years later, in *Memoirs of My Dead Life* (1906), Moore again eschews chronological organisation and plot to offer a series of psychologically revealing vignettes highlighting the nature of memory. The narrator's retrospection overcomes conventional boundaries of time, often suggesting the simultaneity of different temporal spheres. Repeatedly, the realities of the mortal body deflate aspirations to love and art, and the narrator finds his present moment overcome by the vanished world of childhood, the loss of sexual vitality, the deaths of parents and the horrific vision of his own entombment in the family vault.

Soon after the first edition of *Memoirs of My Dead Life*, Moore began work on *Hail and Farewell* (1911–14), an account of his decade in Dublin (1901–11), where, as an unlikely prodigal son, he worked toward the revitalisation of a national literature. Moore's fascination and disillusionment with Ireland forms the overarching plot of this mock-heroic tour de force, and within it appear many of the motifs of Anglo-Irish autobiography: deep emotional ties to the family house, nostalgia for a more feudal world (although here self-conscious and ironic), the sense of being haunted by ancestry and a belief (again, presented with self-mocking humour) that the land itself seems inhabited by spirits. Not only does Moore raise numerous questions about the nature of the self, the origins of art and the meaning of a nation, but he also enacts the questioning through his narrative technique. His extensive use of comic parody, for example, challenges romantic notions of a pure national language or univocal aesthetic, while his verbal caricatures demonstrate the dependence of our ideas and values upon our physical bodies and material conditions. Most innovative is his manipulation of narrative time. Rather than speaking with the retrospective wisdom of the author at the point of writing, he begins with the relative ignorance of the narrator at the point at which the story starts. As the narrator moves forward through time, his perspective also changes, causing him to review his earlier positions with increasing scepticism. Even the memories of youth recounted in the first volume require reconsideration by the narrator in the subsequent volumes.

Moore was quick to draw into his novels and short stories the technical discoveries of his autobiographies. In his 1918 short story, 'Albert Nobbs', thematic concern with the ambiguity of gender comes alive through narrative confusion over gendered pronouns, and the 1921 revision of his 1905 novel *The Lake* renders the omniscient voice, like the autobiographical narrator of *Hail and Farewell*, no more knowledgeable than the protagonist, whose increasingly astute perspective on earlier events forms the new focus of the novel.

Nothing could be more unlike Moore's stylistically avant-garde autobiographies with their calculated narrative voice and open disregard for fact than the relatively unrevised outpourings of apparently sincere emotion posthumously published as the life writing of J. M. Synge (1871–1909). Despite their introspective turn, Synge's essays, diaries and autobiographical sketches express as well the anxieties of his community. Born to an evangelical Protestant family long established as clergy and landowners in County Wicklow, he describes his gradual alienation from his family's faith, politics and way of life. The story of his apostasy climaxes with the reading of a passage from Charles Darwin that undercuts the authority of his family's conviction of their significance as a chosen people formed in God's image and, unlike their Catholic neighbours, saved by grace and privileged to commune with God directly.

Very shortly after his 'de-conversion', he becomes infatuated with Ireland and in particular with the rural poor, who seemed to share his receptivity to pantheistic spirituality, strong emotions and verbal extravagance. To Synge, such qualities were inextricably joined to a vivid apprehension of death and madness, as well as the 'excitement near to pain' and the 'prolonged unsatisfied desire' he believed to be the root of art.[3] Synge's account of his movement from the worldview of his family to a cultural nationalism founded in rural Gaelic culture epitomises the stories of hundreds of other Protestant gentlemen, but its pairing of mysticism and strong emotion with insanity and evil paradoxically reaffirms the very Puritanism from which he turned away.

Like Moore and Synge, Shane Leslie (Sir John Randolph Leslie, 1885–1971) came from a family established for several hundred years in the same location, who saw their influence and fortunes diminish in the early twentieth century. The three autobiographies he published between 1916 and 1966 present yet another version of the Anglo-Irishman who converts to nationalism, although for Leslie the conversion was so thoroughgoing that he replaced Anglicanism with Catholicism, the English language with the Irish and his given name, John, with Shane. Like others of his class, Leslie believed that he had witnessed in the First World War 'the suicide of a civilisation', and he expresses both dismay at a modern sense of rootlessness and devotion to his familial estate and its wooded demesne.[4] In their surprisingly ironic, witty approach to the serious aspects of life – religion, politics, family, sexuality, death – Leslie's autobiographies also participate in a tradition of the Anglo-Irish comic autobiography dating back to the eighteenth century. In such works, the narrative of inward development underlying most nineteenth- and twentieth-century fiction and autobiography is replaced by a picaresque plot structure and a relatively static narrator who deals with the often grotesque incongruities of a fallen world. Drawing from eighteenth-century fictional models, political and religious satires, and cultural tendencies toward scepticism and detachment, Leslie's memoirs reflect on all serious matters with deflating anticlimaxes, puns and double entendres. Although distinct from the 'tragic joy' Yeats attributed to Synge and sought in himself, Leslie's comedy, like George Moore's, acknowledges the gravity of experience and the depth of the losses incurred, while simultaneously positing an unchanging self who stands up to the exigencies of life with cool reserve.

W. B. Yeats (1865–1939) rejects the fatalistic materialism of comedy to regard autobiography instead as a potent struggle between what he calls soul and self, subjective and objective, ideal and real. According to his aesthetic theories, autobiography, whether in prose or verse, must hold the two spheres in tension and out of that tension achieve the desired end. In the highest art, the struggle resolves itself in the writer's achievement of persona, or 'mask'. The writings collected in 1938 as *The Autobiography of William Butler Yeats* consider those who failed and those who succeeded in creating art out of what Yeats called the antinomies, and this partitioning may account for the harsh difference in tone and approach among sections of the text.[5] In 'Reveries over Childhood and Youth', Yeats recounts the origins of the poet through Wordsworthian evocations of people and places in the consciousness of the maturing boy. Incorporating extracts from diaries kept at the time, 'The Death of Synge' pays homage to the man Yeats saw as a genius and cultural hero, while the final section, 'The Bounty of Sweden', projects in glowing terms the dream of a fully unified culture paralleling the unified self he sought to realise through literature. But much of the rest is a caustic memoir of those who failed to achieve the vital balance, and his judgments schematically parallel the categories of personality and history outlined in *A Vision* (1925, 1937). Yeats's *Autobiography* imparts its vision of personal and cultural unity through a range of moods and approaches, replacing a linear narrative of development with portions of diary, family history, childhood recollections, philosophical speculations, literary history, cultural criticism – and its fair share of score settling.

Life writing at mid-century

Despite a paralysed economy, cultural isolation and stringent governmental censorship, Irish life writing, like Irish fiction, flourished in the decades following independence. Along with an outpouring of autobiography by those identifying themselves as Anglo-Irish, writers from the Catholic working class bring to the genre a greater realism and a more oral discourse, while turning their attention to religious conflict, the figure of the mother and the evolution of the self as a writer amid constrained opportunities. Increasingly, they also address areas of familial and sexual experience formerly thought too private for the public text.

The autobiographies of Elizabeth Bowen (1899–1973) must here be representative of the dozens written at mid-century by those who describe themselves as Anglo-Irish. Her elegies for Anglo-Ireland reflect as well the fearful years of the Second World War, when in 'the savage and austere light of a burning world', she wrote her family chronicle *Bowen's Court* (1942) as a testimony to that which had felt significant and enduring.[6] Her meditations on the different rooms of the family house are framed by a chronological design, in which each chapter bears the name of a succeeding male ancestor. However, the Anglo-Irish genealogical obsession dooms the very sense of permanence she seeks to achieve, and as a childless woman of limited means, the inheritor of a crumbling house, she anticipates the end of a history based upon familial descent and property by entitling the final chapter not 'Elizabeth' but 'Afterword'. In a gesture reaching beyond her individual story or even that of Anglo-Ireland, she presents the house as a metonym for beloved places all around the world that had been destroyed or stood in danger of being so. Correspondingly, in the 1964 revision, written after the property had been sold and the house dismantled, she avows its abiding presence as a symbol of each person's need at the worst of times to hold fast to an image of peace and continuity.

In her other life writing, *Seven Winters: Memories of a Dublin Childhood* (1942) and the pieces collected posthumously in *Pictures and Conversations* (1975), Bowen turns from the familial house and property to the inner world of the child and the figure of her mother, with whom she lived in England after her father's inherited mental disorder broke up the family. Other Anglo-Irish women either exclude their mothers from their life stories, or, like Katherine Everett (1872–1951) in *Bricks and Flowers* (1949), Constance Malleson (1895–1975) in *After Ten Years* (1931) and Enid Starkie (1897–1970) in *A Lady's Child* (1941), view them with simultaneous pity and resentment as emissaries of restricting patriarchal ideologies. Bowen, however, shared with her mother an intimate and affectionate relationship, apart from the world of familial relations and patrilineal history depicted in *Bowen's Court*. Through a sophisticated and technically complex prose style, Bowen's narrative shifts in perspective among the sensations and partial comprehensions of her childhood self, the retrospective wisdom of the adult writer and the consciousness of her mother. In both patrilineal and matrilineal narratives, Bowen sees personal life always as the paradigm of a wider culture, and the self a responsive medium afloat in the stream of family and historical life.

With a similar emphasis on the surrounding 'stream', Louis MacNeice's *The Strings are False* (1965), like his lyric poetry, defines the emergent man and writer against the gritty northern mill town of Carrickfergus, Co. Antrim, in which he grew up. The loss of his childhood world is neither regretted nor posited as a sign of cultural discontinuity, as in Yeats, Bowen and many other Anglo-Irish autobiographers and novelists. Instead, Mac-Neice (1907–63) depicts a landscape, a people and a worldview so repellent that escape seems the only desirable response. His father's isolation as an Anglican clergyman of nationalist and liberal sympathies billeted in a fiercely unionist and intolerant town, his mother's disabling depression and his brother's mental affliction he diagnoses as symptoms of a wider malaise, epitomised by 'the dull dank days between sodden haycocks and foghorns'.[7] Childhood meant 'guilt, hell fire, Good Friday, the doctor's cough, hurried lamps in the night, melancholia, mongolism, violent sectarian voices. All this sadness and conflict and attrition and frustration were set in this one acre near the smoky town' (p. 216). Many Anglo-Irish writers look to family history as a means, however uncertain, of affirming regional and national identity, and MacNeice's family history reinforces his conviction that he belonged not in Northern Ireland but in the Connemara countryside from which his parents came. 'For many years', he writes, 'I lived on a nostalgia for somewhere I had never been' (p. 217). However, his imaginative association with the west of Ireland proves insufficient, and his literary ambitions take him abroad. Yet again, autobiography echoes the Irish novel in concluding with the artist's departure to another country and way of life.

The four-volume autobiography of another Northern Anglican, Robert Harbinson (b. 1928), is better classified with the life writings of Patrick Kavanagh, Frank O'Connor or Sean O'Faolain than with those of Synge, Yeats, Bowen or MacNeice.[8] The formative influence of Catholicism is of course absent from Harbinson's work, but so are preoccupations with family history, house and property, and cultural decline. Harbinson knew no family history, owned no house and grew up in a Belfast slum, where poverty and mistrust of all institutions produced a culture of pragmatic survivalism. Unlike the Anglo-Irish autobiography, Harbinson's childhood memoirs are distinctly matrifocal; like the mothers of O'Connor, O'Faoláin, Kavanagh and, much later, Frank McCourt, 'Big Ina' is the emotional centre of the household, as well as a figure of pity and a locus of guilt for the narrator. Disappointed repeatedly by men, she is eventually deserted by her son, who proves incapable of keeping the enviable job she secures for him on the docks and who eventually emigrates to a career as an evangelist, teacher and, finally, a writer. Strangely lacking in dialogue and related in the simple past tense without overt distinctions between past self and present narrator or writer, Harbinson's narratives are episodic rather than plotted, and devoid of allusions to the act of autobiography. Perhaps because of the absence of self-referentiality, his work seems too close to fiction to be convincing as life writing.

A reader's trust may depend much less on a text's historical accuracy than on its writer's open acknowledgment of the multiple problems of memory and representation. The autobiographies of Benedict Kiely (b. 1919), for instance, disarm doubts raised by factual impossibilities and fictional features by calling on the prerogatives of a garrulous old man revisiting with a hypothetical old friend (the reader) the very place and time in which he once set many of his short stories and novels. 'But may not a septuagenarian with eight grandchildren', he asks in his 1991 *Drink to the Bird*, 'may he not, I repeat, be occasionally permitted to repeat himself? . . . [The] aged man, remembering earlier days also has to be present all the time. And if, now and then, his mind, such as it may be, leaps back and forward, then that's only to be expected.'[9] By acknowledging the digressive, incomplete and oral nature of his telling, Kiely identifies these features as stylistic choices rather than failures of sincerity or technique.

In a 1962 television address, the poet Patrick Kavanagh (1904–67) locates his failings as an autobiographer in his unwillingness to adopt either the persona of forthright confessor or that of an openly inventive teller of autobiographical tales. 'For years', he notes, 'I have tried to find a technique through which a man might reveal himself without embarrassment. There are two fairly successful examples of this technique – *Don Quixote* and Joyce's Ulysses . . . I have found that only in verse can one confess with dignity.'[10] His early work, *The Green Fool* (1938), announces itself as autobiography, but its author never seems fully comfortable with the rhetoric of sincerity that has been requisite since Rousseau's *Confessions*. In Kavanagh's retrospective judgment, it was 'a dreadful stage-Irish so-called autobiography', true to neither the tenor nor the facts of his youth.[11] He was justly proud of his novel *Tarry Flynn* (1948) as an authentic portrait of the world of his youth and an accurate index to his feelings as a young man, yet as a novel it lacks a direct and fruitful engagement with issues of memory and narrative.

Of all the writers of mid-century Ireland, Frank O'Connor (1903–66) and Sean O'Faolain (1900–91) – both raised in working-class districts of Cork during the first decades of the twentieth century and both renowned masters of the short story – most successfully negotiate autobiography's double nature. They create a sense of intimacy with the past self through the techniques of modern short fiction: complex characterisations, resonant details, authentic dialogue and an unearthing of the tragic potential of everyday occurrences worthy of Chekhov. Additionally, their probing meta-commentaries on the autobiographical act create an equal illusion of intimacy between the reader and the adult narrator (and by implication, the writer).

O'Connor's *An Only Child* (1961) displays many of the motifs common to much Irish Catholic autobiography: the suffering mother and the unreliable alcoholic father who is nevertheless himself a figure of pathos, the growth of the artist at odds with his environment, quarrels with conventional religion, conflicts between nationalism and broader allegiances, and eventual self-exile from the place of origins. He casts his story as a battle between 'two powers that were struggling for possession of my soul': the humility and quiet grace of his mother and the 'drunkenness, dirt, and violence' of his father's family.[12] Although fiercely unsentimental, *An Only Child* pays homage to Minnie O'Donovan's sense of beauty and dignity in the face of intolerable circumstances. Explaining his desire to write fiction as a desire to honour the people of his childhood, 'those who for me represented all I should ever know of God' (p. 276), O'Connor demonstrates throughout his admiration for those who artfully transform their environment, like his deaf-mute uncle whose stories in sign were 'a triumph of art over nature', something, the writer recalls 'it would take me twenty years to learn' (p. 22).

In *Vive Moi!* (1964), Sean O'Faolain tells another story of the evolution of a writer in unlikely circumstances, but this 'history of the imagination' offers even more reflection on the workings of memory and the relation of present and past selves.[13] Maintaining the self-conscious position of the adult narrator, O'Faolain charts the maturation of his perspectives toward family, religion, nationality and art through a 'slow, tentative, always instinctive, never intellectual process of growth' (p. 115). Like O'Connor and many others, O'Faolain finds himself torn between guilt-ridden sympathy for his parents' disappointments and a shrewder recognition of their limitations, as he is also torn between fervent nationalism and an attraction to the wider world. Repudiating the perspective of his younger self, he traces his gradual recognitions that his mother was less heroic than she was emotionally stunted, and that his nationalist infatuation with the west of Ireland would necessarily come in conflict with his rejection of social, intellectual and religious conformity. He tempers his pity for the injustices his parents endured by an unflinching critique of their resignation as symptomatic of a colonial mentality that would have maimed him had he not rebelled against it. Far more complex than mere disenchantment with clergy or dogma, his persistent religious enquiry proceeds from an acute need to understand the meaning of suffering, in order to understand his parents and others around him. Unlike many autobiographies of writers, *Vive Moi!* ends with a return to his origins rather than a departure, and concludes with a testament of faith in the autobiographical act as the key to what Yeats called the unity of being. The self, O'Faolain asserts, is indeed an unbroken whole, and memory the key to its discovery: 'If once the boy within us ceases to speak to the man who enfolds him, the shape of life is broken, and there is, literally, no more to be said. I think that if my life has had any shape it is this. I have gone on listening and remembering' (p. 374).

Published just a few years before *An Only Child* and *Vive Moi!*, *Borstal Boy* (1958) by Brendan Behan (1923–64) is a very different kind of book. Treating neither childhood nor the emergence of the writer, the text ignores maternal figures and focusses exclusively on male relationships at home and in the juvenile detention centres where Behan spent his adolescence. Like Robert Harbinson's autobiographies, *Borstal Boy* lacks the self-reflexive features of most modern life writing and its dramatic, condensed episodes are indistinguishable from fiction. Unlike Harbinson, however, Behan is a talented writer of dialogue and capable of subtle characterisations. The past self grows wiser in prison ways, more disillusioned with established religion, and finds his easy assumptions about the English and the Irish repeatedly challenged. The book's strength lies in Behan's exceptional ability to capture the oral discourse of many different regions and classes, while also creating a sense of the individuality of each character through the idiosyncrasies of speech.

Revised from sketches that had been gestating since the early 1940s, *Borstal Boy* is the product of a relatively sober and self-controlled period of Behan's life. Anthony Cronin's memoir of his friendship with Behan and Kavanagh reveals that such periods were very rare. More memoir than autobiography ('My subject is not myself and my doing', Cronin intones several times), *Dead as Doornails* (1976) looks back on the milieu of the male Dublin writer at mid-century. It is a world of envy and invective, prostitution of talent, despair, some laughter, extraordinary amounts of drinking, a great deal of talking and very little writing. Unlike Behan,

Cronin has only a modest talent for dialogue, but that is more than compensated for by his ability to craft strong visual images and picaresque episodes that capture the mood of young bohemians in search of adventure, alcohol or a bit of cash. Despite the liveliness of *Dead as Doornails*, its overall mood is dark, and Cronin effectively conveys the waste of a generation in such haunting tableaux as that of Brendan Behan near the end of his short life, propped stupefied and speechless against the wall of a bar, unable even to move and with the vomit of several days prior still staining his jacket and shoes. Cronin assigns to Kavanagh the part of an old warrior, the true genius of the crew who nevertheless squandered his gift through an addiction to petty quarrels and vindictive verbal assaults as damaging as his addiction to alcohol. Having settled down with a profession and a family, the narrator appears principally as the emissary of normative values contrasting with the self-immolation of his companions. If Cronin's expose of the grimmer side of these public personalities could be thought in any sense malicious, his narrator's lack of self-aggrandisement counters such suspicions. Cronin stands apart as the sole survivor – the rest, after all, are 'dead as doornails' – but his final gesture is a gracious benediction that acknowledges the courage as well as the pathos of their lives.

Contemporary Irish life writing

As the twentieth century closed, Irish writers experimented with new forms of narrative and new configurations of the self. With a handful of exceptions, like William Trevor's *Excursions in the Real World* (1994), the Anglo-Irish autobiography ceases to exist as a distinct category. Within contemporary Irish literary autobiographies, sexual identity replaces national identity as a pressing question, and religion appears less an ongoing influence than a set of discarded behavioral restrictions and attitudes. With the decline of boundaries between private and public experience and an ever-increasing focus on the isolated individual, the late twentieth century saw an unprecedented growth in the audience for autobiography. Indebted in part to the popularity of television talk shows and the personal narratives encouraged by therapeutic counselling, more commercially successful autobiographies often take a confessional turn. Other works, however, shift away from the rhetoric of sincerity implied by the confessional mode. Instead, like much contemporary fiction, such works concede a fundamental skepticism about the reliability of memory and the kind of unitary self on which Sean O'Faolain staked his faith.

The enormous commercial and critical triumph of *Angela's Ashes* (1996) by Frank McCourt (b. 1931) represents the new enthusiasm for autobiography

among American and, increasingly, Irish readers. Like *Are You Somebody?
The Accidental Memoir of a Dublin Woman* by Nuala O'Faolain (b. 1942),
which has also enjoyed great commercial success in Ireland and America
since its release in the same year, *Angela's Ashes* lays bare the secrets of
the nuclear family. McCourt divulges the particulars of his conception
and other incidents in the sexual lives of his mother and father, as well as
their astonishing ineptitude in the daily business of survival. O'Faolain also
gives us the sexual lives of her parents, but instead of material poverty,
she details the emotional poverty of what passed for a happy middle-class
family. Drawing from the same roots as popular self-help narratives, both
authors detail their desperate straits in order to tell a story of endurance
against the lives their parents provided. Formally, the two works are conventional, if very skilfully so. McCourt takes the voice of the boy he once
was, understanding little beyond what that boy would understand and
therefore never critiquing what he relates. He coaxes the reader's trust
through fictional techniques rather than a narrator's acknowledged struggle
toward a form of truth, and his dialogue sounds so authentic and the
incidents so vivid that his book's emotional immediacy is akin to that of
an engrossing realist novel. In contrast, because Nuala O'Faolain's frank
discussion of an Irish woman's experience is unprecedented, and the narrator comments so frequently on the difficult but urgent need to tell the truth –
no matter how painful or embarrassing – *Are You Somebody?* and its
sequel, *Almost There: The Onward Journey of a Dublin Woman* (2003),
invoke the reader's faith that every incident happened as told, and that
the past self, the narrator, the public figure of the author and the person
who writes are unequivocally one and the same.

As examples of a very different approach to life writing, *The Bend for
Home* (1996) by Dermot Healy (b. 1947) and *The Star Factory* (1997) by
Ciaran Carson (b. 1948) stand with the elegant, enigmatic *Company* (1980)
by Samuel Beckett (1906–89) as the most fully post-modern autobiographies to come out of Ireland in the last quarter century. Beckett strips
referential context in *Company* to a minimum, and the speaking self is
unsure of everything it affects to know or remember, even its relationship
to the 'one on his back in the dark' for whom it claims to speak.[14] Although,
unlike Beckett, Healy and Carson locate the self firmly within the family
and community, all three writers engage in a post-modern querying of the
voice that ostensibly represents the self. Accordingly, all produce radically
unfamiliar narrative forms by which to enact their enquiry.

The subject matter of Healy's *The Bend for Home* is reminiscent of
the first two books of George O'Brien's autobiographical trilogy, in that
both writers present a richly anthropological study of small-town Ireland

in the late fifties and early sixties, as seen through the eyes of a bright but often baffled adolescent boy.[15] Like Healy, O'Brien conveys the potent grip of the past over the present self and the distance that his urge to understand and explain the past has put between him and those he loved. But the resemblance stops there. In *The Bend for Home*, the identity of the remembered self is in question from the opening paragraphs, in which the narrator's story of his birth turns out to be a local tale about someone else. Another story about surviving a wild thunderstorm while fishing ends so ambiguously that it is unclear whether others present died in the boat or at some later time, prior to the writing of the book. If the former, the story would have to be a child's nightmarish fantasy rather than an actual event; if the latter, the anecdote acts as a poignant foreshadowing of the struggle with mortality that grips the book's final section. The adolescent self, the man and the older author all meet as separate entities when the narrator's mother presents him with a diary he wrote in the years following his father's death, some twenty years prior. The author then adds the fuller characterisation and dialogue of fiction to this relic of his adolescent consciousness as seen by himself as a younger man, and the text shifts into a format entitled 'A Version of a Diary 1963'. In the final section of the book, the narrator all but vanishes as a character or a commentator, appearing primarily as the caretaker and interlocutor of his elderly mother and aunt, without thoughts or actions beyond his efforts to feed, toilet, dress and deal with the anxious demands of two old women. Numb except for the part of him that stays alert to any sounds of distress from his mother's room, the narrator's selfhood lies in his role as witness to the sufferings and indignities of old age.

In Ciaran Carson's *The Star Factory*, the speaking self disappears even further from centre stage. The narrator sifts through the many contradictory narratives provided by various historical documents and relics of his youth and his city's past. Not only is the story to be drawn from such irregular evidence, but the narrator himself is less a unitary character than a consciousness whose digressions lead from one chain of associative historical narrative to another. The narrator's obsession with metaphors of memory, the simulacrums of maps and photographs (including misleading ones), and the contrary definitions and competing etymologies of words suggest that the speaker is himself a representation amid the other representations that constitute his reality. Yet to say this is not necessarily to dissolve either the self or its history. As James Olney has repeatedly argued, 'For better or worse, we all exist and only exist within the circumference of the stories we tell about ourselves: outside that circumference human beings know nothing and can know nothing.'[16] The post-modern autobiography may highlight the constructed nature of the speaking self, but it is no less stable than the identity of the reader who holds the book in her hands.

Life writing in twentieth-century Ireland has followed some of the same paths as its fiction, from the satire of George Moore to the realist techniques of Frank O'Connor, the meta-commentary of Sean O'Faolain, Benedict Kiely's guise of the town storyteller, the confessionalism of Frank McCourt and Nuala O'Faolain, and Ciaran Carson's post-modern enquiry. Yet there are continuities across the century; even the radical dispersion of the self that occurs in *The Star Factory* locates the self in the artefacts of the city that surrounds it. When, in 1942, Elizabeth Bowen said of *Bowen's Court* that 'the experience of writing this book has been cumulative: the experience of living more than my own life',[17] she spoke for nearly every Irish autobiographer in expressing the conviction that what we call the self dwells within a world of others, living or dead. It has been the achievement of Irish life writing to have articulated not only the singular life but also one shared with others in place and time.

NOTES

1. Patrick Kavanagh, *Tarry Flynn* (1948); Seamus Deane, *Reading in the Dark* (1997); Mary Costello, *Titanic Town: A Novel* (1998); Oliver St John Gogarty, *As I was Going Down Sackville Street* (1937).
2. Philippe Lejeune, 'The Autobiographical Pact', in Paul John Eakin (ed.), *On Autobiography* (Minneapolis: University of Minnesota Press, 1989), pp. 3–30. For an overview of autobiographical theory since 1970, see Sidonie Smith and Julia Watson, *Reading Autobiography: A Guide for Interpreting Life Narratives* (Minneapolis: University of Minnesota Press, 2001).
3. J. M. Synge, 'Autobiography', in *Collected Works: Prose*, ed. Alan Price (Gerrards Cross: Colin Smythe, 1982), pp. 13, 14.
4. Shane Leslie, *The End of a Chapter* (New York: Charles Scribner's Sons, 1916), p. i. See also *The Film of Memory* (1938) and *Long Shadows* (1966).
5. *The Autobiography of William Butler Yeats* includes *Reveries over Childhood and Youth*, *The Trembling of the Veil* and *Dramatis Personae*.
6. Elizabeth Bowen, *Collected Impressions* (New York: Alfred A. Knopf, 1950), p. 50.
7. Louis MacNeice, *The Strings are False: An Unfinished Autobiography* (London: Faber & Faber, 1965), p. 228.
8. Robert Harbinson Bryans's travel writings were published under the name of Robin Bryans. His autobiographies, under the name of Robert Harbinson, were *No Surrender* (1960), *Song of Erne* (1960), *Up Spake the Cabin Boy* (1961) and *The Protégé* (1963). Short stories have been collected also under the name of Robert Harbinson.
9. Benedict Kiely, *Drink to the Bird: A Memoir* (London: Methuen, 1991), p. 2. See also *The Waves Behind Us: A Memoir* (1999).

10. Patrick Kavanagh, 'Self-Portrait', in *A Poet's Country: Selected Prose*, ed. Antoinette Quinn (Dublin: Lilliput Press), p. 305.
11. Kavanagh, 'Self-Portrait', p. 306.
12. Frank O'Connor, *An Only Child* (New York: Alfred A. Knopf, 1961), p. 20. Frank O'Connor was the pseudonym of Michael O'Donovan.
13. Sean O'Faolain, *Vive Moi!* (Boston: Little, Brown and Co., 1964), p. 24.
14. Samuel Beckett, *Company* (New York: Grove, 1980), p. 7.
15. George O'Brien, *The Village of Longing* (1987) and *Dancehall Days* (1988).
16. James Olney, 'All in One Story', *Sewanee Review* 95 (1987), 134–5.
17. Elizabeth Bowen, *Bowen's Court* (New York: Alfred A. Knopf, 1942), p. 458.

GUIDE TO FURTHER READING

Coe, Richard. *When the Grass was Taller: Autobiography and the Experience of Childhood*. New Haven, NJ: Yale University Press, 1984.

Grubgeld, Elizabeth. *George Moore and the Autogenous Self: The Autobiographies and Fiction*. Syracuse, NY: Syracuse University Press, 1994.

Grubgeld, Elizabeth. *Anglo-Irish Autobiography: Class, Gender, and the Forms of Narrative*. Syracuse, NY: Syracuse University Press, 2004.

Harte, Liam. *Modern Irish Autobiography: Self, Nation and Society*. Basingstoke: Palgrave, 2005.

Kenneally, Michael. *Portraying the Self: Sean O'Casey and the Art of Autobiography*. Gerrards Cross: Colin Smythe, 1988.

Kenneally, Michael. 'The Autobiographical Imagination and Irish Literary Autobiographies', in Michael Allen and Angela Wilcox (eds.), *Critical Approaches to Anglo-Irish Literature*. Totowa, NJ: Barnes & Noble, 1989, pp. 111–31.

Napier, Taura. *Seeking a Country: Twentieth-Century Literary Autobiographies of Irish Women*. Lanham, MD: University Press of America, 2001.

Neuman, Shirley. *Some One Myth: Yeats's Autobiographical Prose*. Mountrath, Portlaoise : Dolmen, 1982.

Ormsby, Frank (ed.). *Northern Windows: An Anthology of Ulster Autobiography*. Belfast: Blackstaff, 1987.

Quinn, Antoinette. *Patrick Kavanagh: A Critical Study*. Syracuse, NY: Syracuse University Press, 1991.

13

ELMER KENNEDY-ANDREWS

The novel and the Northern Troubles

The political novel before 1969

For the Irish novelist, the usual concerns of the English novel – personal morality and relationships – have tended to be subordinated to the more pressing issues of race, religion and nationality. The early Irish novelists, Maria Edgeworth and Sydney Owenson (Lady Morgan), attempted a reconciliation between Ireland's two nations, Edgeworth through social reform and political unionism, Owenson through Ascendancy commitment to a romantic nationalist movement which, in literature, would culminate in the work of W. B.Yeats. The big house theme inaugurated by Edgeworth and Owenson (see chapter 3 above) has continued to fascinate novelists to the present day, as Jennifer Johnston's *The Captains and the Kings* (1972), *The Gates* (1973), *How Many Miles to Babylon?* (1974) and *The Old Jest* (1979) would indicate. These novels, written at the height of the Northern Troubles, offer an oblique perspective on the conflict, and the setting of the novels in the past, in the south, suggests flight from the intractable reality of contemporary Northern Protestant unionism/loyalism in 1970s Ulster.

Complementing the big house tradition was the native tradition of 'Catholic' novelists such as the Banim brothers, Gerald Griffin and William Carleton, writers who sought to bring to light the traditions and customs of the 'hidden Ireland', often pleading for their people's plight before the bar of English public opinion, and determined to advance the idea of a distinctive Irish national character. (See chapter 5 above.) The themes of their fiction – eviction, terrorism and emigration – reflect engagement with the great social and political events of the nineteenth century: the penal laws, Catholic Emancipation, Repeal of the Union, Gaelic Revival, revolution, famine. The novelists, conservatives for the most part, took a reformist rather than revolutionary stance, the great exception being the Fenian apologist Charles Kickham. However, following the death of Charles

Stewart Parnell in 1891, constitutional nationalism was gravely weakened and militant republicanism gained new ground. The Easter Rising of 1916, galvanised by Patrick Pearse's insurrectionary rhetoric propounding a heroic myth of blood sacrifice and mystical notions of Gaelic Ireland (which continued to inform much of the thinking amongst Northern militant republicans in the 1960s, 1970s, 1980s, and 1990s), was soon to be questioned, first by non-combatants such as W. B. Yeats and Sean O'Casey and then, retrospectively, by participants such as Frank O'Connor and Sean O'Faolain.

In his writings, both autobiographical and fictional, O'Connor's experiences in the Anglo-Irish War (1919–21) and Civil War (1922–3) are conveyed as a youthful rite of passage, a progression from adolescent romanticism to responsible adulthood. His stories of hostage-taking and reprisal shootings emphasise the human cost involved in the necessary political action. The romance of war is checked by realistic reaffirmation of traditional humanistic values – the sanctity of human life, the ties of family and community. Similarly, O'Faolain, whose name is closely associated with the genesis of revisionist historiography in the 1930s and 1940s, used his stories to critique the naivety of his earlier IRA involvement in the 1920s and highlight the barren fanaticism of the patriot. These narratives' repeated juxtaposition of the 'madness' of the public world of revolutionary commitment with a superior, apolitical, private world of sexual intimacy and individual fulfilment finds an echo in many recent liberal-minded novelistic treatments of the Troubles since 1969.

In addition to the modes of romance and domestic fiction, another popular form of Troubles fiction is the thriller. Novels such as Liam O'Flaherty's *The Informer* (1925) and F. L.Green's *Odd Man Out* (1946) were early demonstrations of the possibilities of the Troubles thriller. Freeing himself from the orthodoxies of 'Irish' Ireland and adopting a cosmopolitan literary perspective, O'Flaherty (1896–1984) explored the complex figure of the informer whose presence raises unsettling questions about nationhood and identity. Yet O'Flaherty's novel insists on the elemental nature of existence; his characters' motivations are to be understood in terms of primitive, instinctual forces rather than political ideology. The informer, the pathetic Gypo Nolan, is more an unwilling victim of psycho-social and mysterious metaphysical forces, over which he has no control, than an active agent in charge of his own fate. In the end, as he struggles to the church to beg forgiveness of the mother of the man on whom he had informed, Gypo's story is transformed into a mythic drama of sin and redemption. *Odd Man Out* by Green (1902–53) is another dark, expressionistic doom-laden story, carrying the message that commitment to violence is destructive of romantic love and domestic family life. Motivation is again dependent not on political issues, but on the mysterious operation of fate. This displacement of the social and historical context, the refusal to engage with the political dimension of the struggle and the resort to a 'myth of atavism'[1] to explain the violence are all common features of popular (and many 'serious') novels on the recent Troubles.

It is the sectarian nature of the contemporary conflict which complicates any simple reading of the situation in the North as an anti-imperialist struggle in which colonised Catholic natives rebel against their English masters. Sectarian conflict between Protestants and Catholics has always been a staple theme of the Ulster novel, from Carleton's stories of Ribbonmen, Whiteboys and Orangemen in the nineteenth century to modern works written in the period leading up to the outbreak of the Troubles in 1969 by established novelists such as Michael McLaverty (1904–92), Brian Moore (1921–2000) and Maurice Leitch (b. 1933). Michael McLaverty's semi-autobiographical novel, *Call My Brother Back* (1939), tells of the uprooting of the impoverished McNeill family from the traditional rural world of Rathlin Island and their relocation to Troubles-torn Belfast during the 1920s. Yet it isn't politics, but the land – and separation from the land – which most profoundly determines character. The resistance of the land to the city and the outside world is still felt in some of the novels written after 1969, but more generally it is a secularised, urbanised and increasingly post-modernised novelistic vision which tends to predominate. In Brian Moore's *The Emperor of Ice-Cream* (1965), young Gavin Burke rejects both the extreme Irish Catholic bigotry of his father and the equally obnoxious Ulster Protestantism which he encounters in the ARP (Air Raid Precaution) during the blitz on Belfast, but the ritual assertion of liberal values at the end is unconvincing and sentimental. Maurice Leitch, in *Poor Lazarus* (1969), returns to the rural world (the Armagh/Monaghan border in 1967) to explore sectarian psychology and the Ulster Protestant character. The novel's pervasive sense of stagnation implies an essentialist view of history and identity as fixed and unchangeable. While representing a courageous confrontation of the dark side of the Protestant psyche, the novel still deals in sectarian stereotypes of psycho-sexual disorder and unquestioningly recycles disabling historic myths of difference and division.

All of these pre-1969 novels, though accomplished in their own terms, nevertheless mark the limitations of a consensual, apolitical social vision supported by a conservative realist aesthetic in dealing with conflict and division.

Popular fiction

From early on, the contemporary Troubles attracted a large number of English popular thriller writers – Max Franklin (*Hennessy*, 1975), Jon Cleary (*Peter's Pence*, 1974), John de St Jorre and Brian Shakespeare (*The Patriot Game*, 1973), Gerald Seymour (*Harry's Game*, 1975; *The Glory Boys*, 1976), Jack Higgins (*The Savage Day*, 1972; *A Prayer for the Dying*, 1973) – who were often little more than cultural tourists in the Northern wasteland. Through various political and commercial constraints, including their dependence on English publishers and distributors, these novelists tended to reproduce the cultural and political views of the British establishment, thereby reinforcing the hegemonic British discourse regarding Northern Ireland. This popular fiction generally acknowledges Catholic grievance, though in a vague and general way, and takes little account of the Protestant unionist/loyalist presence. The situation in the North is commonly presented as a colonial struggle between the IRA and the British government and its 'representatives' in Ireland. The human cost of commitment to the cause is emphasised, and the moral of the story is usually that terrorism doesn't pay. Historical or political motivation is not taken seriously. The IRA man is simplified and diabolised. If not a misguided fanatic answering Pearse's call to 'blood sacrifice', he is criminalised as a racketeer or pathological killer. By merely recycling cliché and stereotype, this fiction, despite a superficial realism, throws little light on either the causes of the conflict or the psychology of the terrorist.

Sometimes it incorporates elements of the romance, in which the private, feminised realm of love and domesticity is threatened by the brutal public world of politics and violence. A popular version of the romance plot is the 'love-across-the-barricades' story elaborated by Joan Lingard in her children's novels, *The Twelfth Day of July* (1970), *Across the Barricades* (1972), *Into Exile* (1973), *A Proper Place* (1975) and *Hostages to Fortune* (1976), in which the union of the lovers from opposing communities stands for a larger social reconciliation. In this scenario, the desired liberal outcome – the 'national romance' – can work only as long as we suppress politics, forget about partition and different national and state allegiances, and accept the political and constitutional status quo in Ireland. Not surprisingly, the Northern Irish romance frequently ends in either failure or exile.[2]

Francis Stuart and Benedict Kiely

While the majority of popular Troubles thrillers have been written by English writers, the 'serious' Troubles novel (which sometimes adopts the thriller form) has been the work of indigenous writers, mostly Northerners, writing from deep down in their environment. A notable exception is Francis Stuart (1902–2000), who made his contribution from the South (though he had family connections in Co. Antrim). Stuart was a 75-year-old author with a publishing record dating back to the 1930s when his Troubles novel, *A Hole in the Head*, appeared in 1977. At the centre of the novel, and absorbing everything in it, is Stuart's ongoing drama of the self, the radical search for personal truth. The narrator, Barnaby Shane, aka H, is a writer recovering from marital failure, mental breakdown and a self-inflicted injury to the head. Barnaby comes north in search of imaginative and artistic revitalisation. Stuart's Belbury (Belfast) is figured both emblematically and apocalyptically. Belfast, the North, the Troubles, politics, the external world generally, have a primarily interior significance. Obsessed by a sense of the world's evil, Barnaby cannot condemn the terrorists: their actions are the expression of a betrayed and wounded innocence. The terrorist is a kind of artist *maudit*: '"Fulfilment denied results in violence", yes, but only when fulfilment is desired fiercely enough. Then you have the terrorist or, more rarely, the imaginative artist.'[3] Both terrorism and art express the desire for magical, frenzied transformation of a debased reality.

Stuart's comment on the contemporary predicament is aggressively individualistic, expressive of a profound suspicion of any kind of official ideology, orthodox faith or conventional moral judgment. He writes as a self-conscious romantic in his celebration of the imaginative attitude to life, in his view of the temperament of distinction threatened by the ordinary social world. The Troubles are interpreted anthropologically as a tribal war, an irruption of dark, aboriginal energy, as the novel's concluding lines imply: 'There is an Amazonian tribe that punctures the skulls of its children in the belief that the perforations give access to both good and evil spirits, thus widening the range of perception' (p. 215). In contrast to the liberal humanist denunciation of atavism, Stuart welcomes its primitive, demonic passion and elaborates a basic opposition between elemental, instinctual life on one hand, and the deformed conscience of so-called civilised society on the other.

Appearing in the same year as *A Hole in the Head*, a short novel, *Proxopera*, by another southern writer with roots in the North, Benedict Kiely (b. 1919), offers a more conventional view of the terrorist and a more recognisably realistic world. Kiely tells the story of an old man, Mr Binchey, whose house is invaded by three masked IRA men who force him to drive a live time bomb to the home of a local, fair-minded judge, while they hold the old man's family hostage. The narrative is presented largely from Binchey's perspective which, one assumes, is very close to

Kiely's own. Binchey is a respectable, middle-class schoolteacher of history, Latin and English literature, a man who prizes civilisation and who is deeply attached to place and community. From such a point of view, terrorists are simply 'animals', figures out of nightmare, the threatening 'other' who are ready to destroy all that Binchey holds most dear.

The novel begins with an elemental landscape, with Binchey's perceptions of a timeless world of nature, a legendary world presided over by the goddess of the lake. The central trope of modernity is the political violence that threatens and disrupts originary, communal ground, but cannot ultimately annihilate it. Binchey, connected like Antaeus to roots and absorbed within a female, pagan, earth-orientated rural and mythological order, is dispossessed and expelled from home. The three invaders are denied a human face – quite literally, in that they remain hidden behind their masks. Terrorist violence is taken out of a political context and treated metaphysically, as the manifestation of evil and madness. What is interesting is Kiely's reworking of the traditional nationalist trope, which understands the root of the Troubles in terms of a struggle between a mythic motherland and a historical, imperial masculinity. Kiely's novella is premised on the conservative nationalist anti-modernist mythic or epic construction of Irish history as the adulteration of a pure (Irish) essence by an alien intruder, but radically ironises the traditional narrative by making militant Irish republicanism, not the forces of British colonialism, the alien intruder. There is no attempt to analyse the motives of the terrorist; in the end, Binchey symbolically hands the whole situation over to the authorities by driving his deadly load off the road, running the dangerous new technology to ground in the mythical Gaelic bog and requiring the help of British soldiers to escape from the wreckage.

Jennifer Johnston

Commonly, women's writing about the Troubles enforces a separation between the public political world, understood as a threatening, sectarian 'masculine' domain, and a superior 'feminine' world of personal feeling and relationship. In two Troubles novels by Jennifer Johnston (b. 1930), *Shadows on our Skin* (1977) and *The Railway Station Man* (1984), the feminine sites of domestic, creative or sexual privacy are violated by the brutalising agents of the public world. In the early novel, feminine resistance involves destabilising androcentric constructions of history, questioning the relevance of male 'liberationist' projects to the lives of ordinary women. Johnston repeats O'Casey's negative treatment of politics and 'political' men, and presents similarly heroic, non-political women. Mr Logan is a shiftless, drunken braggart, his speech as full of sentimental abstraction as O'Casey's Captain Boyle's, while Mrs Logan, a Derry Juno, is the backbone of the family, the practical provider and carer, and the scourge of Mr Logan's political pretensions. Unlike Juno, Mrs Logan remains trapped; but like Juno, she places more importance on people than on ideas or ideologies. To the end, neither Mrs Logan nor Juno understands anything about political freedom or social justice. The novel's failure to imagine any alternative agency of social change to paramilitary chaos, together with its emphasis on the destructive effect of political violence on personal relationships, makes this the most pessimistic of all Johnston's novels.

The later novel, however, not only challenges male definitions and control of both public and private space, but also brings forward various forms of female self-redefinition and self-assertion. *The Railway Station Man* is concerned with the struggle of a central female character, Helen Cuffe, an artist living in seclusion in Co. Donegal, to achieve the dream of an unconditioned life, free from the controls of patriarchy, parenthood and politics, after long years of marital entrapment and in the aftermath of political violence which claims the lives of her English lover, the railway station man, Roger Hawthorne, and her son, Jack. As teller of the tale, Helen occupies a position of power. She has the authority to determine the way events are presented, and her narration emphasises her determination to reclaim freedom and subjectivity by rejecting the conventional female roles and expectations that have governed her life. Using Jack and Helen, Johnston stages the debate between bourgeois liberal humanism and militant republicanism, between the claims of personal freedom and those of political commitment. It's a one-sided debate. Jack is addicted to cliché and abstraction, she is sceptical and independent-minded. She attempts to withdraw into an autonomous realm of the free imagination and makes no apology for her ivory towerism: 'If my ivory tower, as you call it, falls down, I'll build another one.'[4] Helen espouses a romantic sense of the capacity of the imagination to redefine the oppressive, violent social world to form a new individualistic, feminine order which exists in the privileged realm of art. In this reading, *The Railway Station Man* is a typical modernist text concerned with the artistic process itself, the struggle to affirm transcendence through art.

Maurice Leitch and Bernard MacLaverty

Two other popular novels of the early 1980s, Maurice Leitch's *Silver's City* (1981) and *Cal* (1983) by Bernard MacLaverty (b. 1942), represent a more hard-bitten romantic-realist approach to the Troubles. Both concentrate on the individual who attempts, with tragic consequences, to free himself from his earlier association with terrorism and embrace the superior values of the personal life.

Silver's City paints a vivid, naturalistic picture of a sleazy Belfast underworld of loyalist drinking clubs, massage parlours, racketeering, abduction and murder. The novel is governed by the conventions of the thriller. A series of lurid events takes place against a backdrop of urban decay and desolation. Leitch takes his epigraph from St Augustine: 'The Devil hath established His cities in the North.' Silver's city ultimately belongs not to history, but to religious allegory. It is a frightening, labyrinthine underworld, a comprehensive image of desperation, malignancy and unreality. To Silver, it is 'the true terrain of nightmare'.[5] Silver, who has served ten years in prison for the murder of a Catholic, finds that he has become a loyalist hero, but he resents the way his past actions have been converted into myth. The Belfast through which he moves is no longer Silver's city; it has become the 'property' of racketeers, politicians and the mass media: 'The scripts were different these days'; he feels 'he had wandered somehow on to a set where farce was in progress' (p. 61). The sense of a destabilised and explicitly fictionalised/theatricalised reality is central to the novel: a 'resilient realism' comes under increasing pressure.[6] Sprung from the safe and predictable routines of the prison hospital, Silver figures the subject's emergence into post-modernism. Silver is aware of himself as situated within a technological modernity: 'The newspapers and television do all your thinking for you. But then I suppose it's easier to believe it's all like some prison picture you've seen. All that drama' (p. 108). *Silver's City* thus marks a shift away from earlier realist portrayals of urban alienation in Michael McLaverty or Brian Moore and prefigures more recent representations of the city as an unstable fictional terrain.

Detaching himself from the urban nightmare, from politics and ideology, and returning to nature, Silver attempts to recreate himself through love. In the end, the emissaries of the public world track him down and break in upon his private space. Silver kills for a second time in his life and faces the realisation that he has also killed his dreams of the future. The novel ends on a deeply fatalistic note: both the personal and the political life have failed – 'the city always made you pay for your dreams' (p. 181).

A similar fatalism is evident in MacLaverty's *Cal*. Like Silver, Cal is doomed on account of a rash and irreversible action in the past and, like Silver, he attempts to escape from the public world of history and politics into a private realm of love and personal fulfilment. Cal's past action – assisting at the murder of an RUC (Royal Ulster Constabulary) man – is constructed as a sin as well as a crime, and Cal looks to Marcella, the widow of the murdered policeman, for redemption in much the same way as Gypo Nolan seeks forgiveness from the mother of the man whom he had betrayed in *The Informer*; Cal's story is similarly framed within a theological language of sin and redemption, rather than an explanatory language of social and political analysis. Not only is the very idea of a love affair between the widow and the youth hard to credit, especially given the circumstances, but the presentation of the relationship tests credulity even further. Marcella is entirely a male fantasy figure; erotic, attentive, understanding, amenable, she is Cal's fairy-tale 'Sleeping Beauty'.[7]

By centring the love theme and emphasising the mood of fatalism, the novel inevitably marginalises political explanation. MacLaverty stages a number of confrontations between Cal and the novel's two IRA men, Skeffington and Crilly, always to highlight the inhumanity of Skeffington the ideologue and the barbarity of Crilly the volunteer. Cal's own involvement in paramilitarism is presented as youthful transgression, not heroic revolt. In the depiction of the material conditions of Cal's existence, MacLaverty gives full weight to the economic deprivations and religious discrimination that one might expect to be powerful forces in politicising a disaffected Northern Irish Catholic youth like Cal. Living in a Protestant estate, he feels 'excluded and isolated' (p. 9). He is beaten up by a gang of loyalist thugs, and he and his father are firebombed out of their home. Yet none of this makes militant republicanism an attractive option to Cal. He admits to being 'very anti-British' and says he 'would like to see a united Ireland' but, as he tells Skeffington, terrorism 'goes against my conscience'(p. 148).

Cal reflects the contradictions in Northern nationalism: the novel acknowledges the oppressiveness of the Northern Protestant state and Catholic indignation against it, while at the same time recoiling from the violence that sets out to overthrow the oppressor. Cal, through the mechanism of Protestant power, is produced in terms of a traditional Catholic victim psychology, a figure of guilt, impotence and masochism. At the end, in accordance with the novel's logic of fatalism, the RUC men who arrest Cal and the British soldiers who move in on the IRA cell become the instruments of an abstract fate or nemesis, their actions serving to restore and reaffirm the state authority. By displacing politics into metaphysics and treating the violence as an irruption of dark, atavistic forces, MacLaverty excuses himself from serious investigation of political motivation and may even be accused of obscuring, rather than articulating, the issues which his novel purports to deal with.[8]

Lies of silence: Moore, Madden, Deane, Duffaud

At first sight, Brian Moore's novel *Lies of Silence* (1990) might seem to address social and political matters more directly than *Cal*. The home of a middle-class Catholic couple, Moira and Michael Dillon, is invaded by a unit of masked IRA men who order Dillon to take a bomb in his car to the hotel where he works, while his wife Moira is held hostage. The significance of the title is highlighted in the following passage, which is focalised through Dillon as he contemplates the youthful terrorists who have broken into his home:

> Dillon felt anger rise within him, anger at the lies which had made this, his and Mr Harbinson's birthplace, sick with a terminal illness of bigotry and injustice, lies told over the years to poor Protestant working people about the Catholics, lies told to poor Catholic working people about the Protestants, lies from parliaments and pulpits, lies at rallies and funeral orations, and, above all, the lies of silence from those in Westminster who did not want to face the injustices of Ulster's status quo. Angry, he stared across the room at the most dangerous victims of these lies, his youthful, ignorant, murderous captors.[9]

The social and political conflicts at the heart of the Troubles are interpreted pathologically, as 'a terminal illness'. Dillon articulates the view of the apolitical, bourgeois, liberal humanist who claims to represent 'ninety per cent of the people of Ulster' (p. 69), Protestant and Catholic. It is a view that is vague and generalised in its analysis of the social causes of the 'injustices of the Ulster status quo', and remarkably clichéd in its picture of the terrorists as hate-filled, deluded 'victims of these lies'. Moore himself, we might say, is guilty of 'lies of silence' on such issues as the motivation of the IRA men, the inner life of the volunteer and the legitimacy of the hegemonic discourses of state law. He is more interested in exploring the effects of violence on individual life, the lies of silence forced upon the terrorised liberal community by paramilitary intimidation. In giving the idea of 'lies of silence' as wide an application as possible, Moore even characterises the protagonist's private life – his relationships with wife, lover, parents and in-laws – as marked by various kinds of (masculine) emotional withholding. *Lies of Silence* thus includes a critique of the masculinist cultural paradigms that are habitually applied to and pervade all aspects of life in Northern Ireland, including its political life.

Just as the phrase 'lies of silence' indicates key categories in the cultural meaning of the North in Moore's novel, so the related idea of 'hidden symptoms' is central to the novel of that name by Deirdre Madden

(b. 1960). Theresa, a student at Queen's University, Belfast, is struggling to cope with the loss of her twin brother, Francis, who was an innocent victim of a random sectarian murder two years previously. Belfast and its Troubles are directly responsible for Theresa's grievous and far-reaching sense of loss. Belfast, having cast aside its mask of 'normality' which 'had always been forced, a prosperous façade over discrimination and injustice', reveals itself as a site of Gothic horror: 'Ulster before 1969 had been sick but with hidden symptoms. Streets and streets of houses with bricked-up windows and broken fanlights, graffiti on gable walls, soldiers everywhere: Belfast was now like a madman who tears his flesh, puts straw in his hair and screams gibberish.'[10]

The Belfast of *Hidden Symptoms* is an unstable text, written over, traversed by conflicting forces, its inherent contradictions exposed after 1969 by the return of the repressed. Repression becomes a feature of narrative style, plot construction and character presentation. Nobody knows what happened to Francis; Theresa wants no one to be told about his murder for reasons which are never explained. The past, she feels, also lies 'submerged and impossible' in memory. Francis becomes an imaginary, ghostly imitation of the lost original; Theresa is aware that she can produce only distorted copies of the unknowable reality. The death of her brother stimulates her anguished awareness that the subjective world, constructed in language, is always necessarily at a remove from reality. Following his death, she feels an overwhelming sense of dispossession, loss and exclusion, of displacement into a fallen world felt to be unreal.

Situating herself at an oblique and distanced relation to the Troubles, Madden concentrates not on the violence itself, but on its aftermath, on grief and survival. The trauma experienced by her sensitive individuals is a consequence of political violence, but the insights gained by these characters have no historical or political content. Rather, the Troubles precipitate a radical post-modernist anxiety about loss and absence, and activate an anguished metaphysical longing for the fullness of self-presence. Ultimately, the novel itself, with its complex symbolism of photographs, paintings, mirrors and reflections, its ambiguities and dislocated patterning, bears a closer resemblance to dreams than to the familiar substantial reality we think we know.

In *Reading in the Dark* (1996) by Seamus Deane (b. 1940), repression, silence and hidden symptoms are the pervasive characteristics of a colonial society. Deane's novel is a powerful evocation of conditions in Catholic nationalist Derry during the years leading up to the outbreak of the Troubles. Deane's Derry is a place of darkness, emblematic of the political situation; a place full of ghosts and shadows, 'silence everywhere',[11] a place which the child-narrator describes as 'an empty space' (p. 43) echoing with the cries of the past. Uncle Eddie is the novel's absent centre. He cannot be spoken of because he is both informer and scapegoat. The child, product of a modern educational system, thinks that, through the operations of critical reason, he can dispel the fog of rumour and myth that enshrouds Uncle Eddie, and that by knowing the family's secret life, he can know himself. However, the narrator becomes as implicated as those around him in the conspiracy of silence to suppress the facts of the past.

This is a story about the process of writing a story, about the suppressions, withholdings, silences and gaps that are part of the narrative process. But this recognisably post-modern concern is given a very definite post-colonial inflection: the boy cannot speak his own history (he never earns a name in the course of the story) because this community has been dispossessed of its full identity within the nation. At the end, however, in the streets outside, the 'noise' of civil disturbance breaks the old silence of compromise and repression as a new generation makes its revolutionary presence felt. With the father's death in July 1971, the mother 'sleeps the last sleep of the old world' (p. 233). A new phase of history is intimated, new conditions in which speech may yet be possible for the narrator.

If *Reading in the Dark* is a kind of fictionalised collective autobiography – Derry's autobiography – it is also *failed* autobiography, a self-referential novel about the problematic nature of self-discovery and self-writing in colonial conditions. The effort to repossess history and identity, it may also be noted, occurs within a remarkably parochial and sectarian frame of reference. Several kinds of boundary crossing are intimated in the book – between the tangible and the ghostly, fact and legend, modernity and tradition, oral and literate culture, Co. Derry and Co. Donegal, native and colonialist influences – but the narrative never ventures into those difficult contact zones between Catholic Derry and Protestant Derry. Indeed, the latter is consigned to the dark margins of ignorance and stereotype, or to a monologically negative discourse of gerrymandering, police harassment and savagery ('those savages with their tom-toms', p. 125).

Like Deane's *Reading in the Dark*, *A Wreath upon the Dead* (1993) by Briege Duffaud also contributes to the contemporary Irish historiographical and cultural debate. Maureen Murphy wants to write a national romance based on the story of two nineteenth-century figures: one a distant relative, Cormac O'Flaherty, the other, Marianne McLeod, the daughter of a Scottish landlord, who lived in the townland of Claghan, in south Armagh, where Maureen herself has been brought up. However, Murphy finds that as the project becomes increasingly complicated by her historical research and by her personal memory and experience, she is unable to write their story.

The past, she discovers, is a web of competing, jostling narratives. There is no master narrative of the past such as realism implies, and the novel demonstrates a post-modern insistence on complexity, ambiguity, plurality, heterogeneity and discontinuity. This aestheticism undercuts any communal identification or political purpose, and Duffaud's metafictional experiment, combining a humanist individualism and a post-modern scepticism, is therefore quite different from that of the more obviously political novelists such as Deane.

Post-modern troubles

A younger generation of writers, who were born in the 1960s and grew up during the Troubles, have sought to explore new literary ground. These novelists represent a strand of self-reflexive writing which is critical of realist premises and deconstructs the usual relationships which exist between text and reader, language and reality, fiction and history. Their novels represent a stronger urban consciousness than was evident before, and they lay claim to a wider range of cultural influences, not just from the rest of Ireland and Britain, but from Europe and, most especially, America; and not just from 'high' culture, but from popular culture, including films and the mass media, as well as traditional indigenous resources.

Resurrection Man (1994) by Eoin McNamee (b. 1961) is based on Matthew Dillon's *The Shankill Butchers*, a documentary account of the loyalist killer gang which terrorised Belfast in the 1970s. McNamee takes the historical personages and actual events, and tries to explain the perverse impulses and fantastical violence that lie beneath the orderly surfaces of civilised life. The focus of McNamee's attention is Victor Kelly, a character based on the real-life gang leader Lenny Murphy. McNamee's explanation of Victor's behaviour is psychological rather than political. In the opening sketch of Victor's childhood, we see not only poverty and deprivation, but also his unhealthy relationship with his mother and the resentment he bears his silent father, who has burdened the family with a Catholic name. Without benefit of any positive example of manliness, Victor looks to popular culture to provide him with a repertoire of desirable identities, heroic images of masculinity on which he can model himself. McNamee foregrounds the intertextuality of 'real' life through pastiche of a range of popular forms and genres, including the American gangster thriller, the comic-strip, film noir and Gothic horror stories.

Both the perpetrators of violence and the newspapermen, Ryan and Coppinger, are disturbed by the unreality of the media reports. Events are converted to text, the city to the giant ordnance survey map which covers Ryan's desk and the internal street map which Victor carries about in his head. Reality becomes its unstable representation. Just as Victor recognises the mismatch between actual occurrence and representation, so he is aware of a gap or slippage between external reality and his own perception of it. The street names 'had become untrustworthy . . . they felt weighty and ponderous on his tongue, impervious syllables that yielded neither direction nor meaning'.[12] His topographical disorientation betrays a deep uncertainty about identity, about the relation between self and world, and to ward off these troubling feelings he intones the street names like a mantra.

For Victor, violence offers the possibility of full presence. Where Cal escapes into a passive and apolitical privacy, Victor asserts himself through acts of outrage and transgression. In the nightmarish world of *Resurrection Man,* murder has a salvationist glamour, an invigorating and transfiguring attraction. The newspapermen emphasise the uniqueness of these new forms of violence. In their investigations of the first knife-murder, they note that 'the root of the tongue had been severed' (p. 15). This sentence is repeated at the end of chapter 2: 'There was a certain awe in [Coppinger's] tone. There was someone out there operating in a new context. They were being lifted into unknown areas, deep pathologies . . . They both felt a silence beginning to spread from this one. They would have to rethink procedures. The root of the tongue had been severed. New languages would have to be invented' (p. 16). The 'new language' that McNamee invents is one that conveys the sheer excitement and attraction, as well as the hideousness, of the violence. The language, grounded in naturalism, gestures towards mysticism. One character notes the 'mystic zeal' in Victor's eyes; through violence, Victor searches for a transcendent, essential self, the obliteration of doubt and uncertainty. Though acknowledging the constructedness of identity and reality, McNamee's self-reflexive metafiction nevertheless fails to indicate any alternative to the cult of violence which pervades Ulster society. *Resurrection Man* itself remains trapped within the post-modern culture of the simulacrum.

In sharp contrast to McNamee's 'new language' of Belfast Gothic is the comic overthrow of dominant Troubles language and discourse by Colin Bateman (b. 1962). *Divorcing Jack* (1995) and *Cycle of Violence* (1995) are comedy thrillers, the Troubles background providing many of the ingredients of the popular thriller, while the narration is supplied by a dishevelled, hard-drinking, wise-cracking young journalist who goes under the name of Dan Starkey in *Divorcing Jack* and Kevin Miller in *Cycle of Violence*. Bateman specialises in a fiction of picturesque extremes which, like fairy tale and melodrama, simplifies the potential complexity of the world into vivid polarities of good and evil, personified by larger-than-life characters. Without psychological depth or complexity, character tends towards caricature. At the centre of the action is the self-conscious, ironic, yet largely optimistic narrator, the ultimate 'Honest Ulsterman'. Though emphatically apolitical, he is the scourge of terrorism, bigotry and hypocrisy. Starkey is a confessed unionist, but 'Unionist with a sense of humour'.[13] Both he and Miller embody a populist ideology opposed to the corrupt institutions of church, state and corporate business. If any political programme is implied in Bateman's fiction, it is one that envisions the inauguration of a new, more rational, tolerant, less atavistic society. *Divorcing Jack* is a futuristic novel that ends on an upbeat note, with the prospect of political stability following the purging of the body politic. But Bateman does not always complete the ritual process that brings about resolution. In *Cycle of Violence*, 'poetic justice' is displaced by a stronger intuition of the absurd.

Where most crime fiction provides the illusion that there is a rational explanation for the questions it raises and that we live in a basically just world, Bateman subverts these usual expectations, experimenting with open endings, ambiguous resolutions, intertextual ironies and all kinds of inventive word play. The fiction, with its jokes, puns, sardonic one-liners, extravagant similes, grotesque caricature and wild-eyed action, and sudden switchings of languages and voices, enacts a carnivalistic overthrow of 'respectable' or 'serious' modes of discourse. Bateman's linguistic playfulness and addiction to burlesque and slapstick convey a punkish (and puckish) anarchism and libertarianism, a revolutionary potential which constitutes a radically deregulated and (post-)modernised image of Protestant unionism beyond the usual stereotypes founded on imperialism, militarism, religious fundamentalism and sectarianism.

Fat Lad (1992) by Glenn Patterson (b. 1961) writes the city as part of a rapidly metamorphosing, post-modern culture, from the point of view of 26-year-old Drew Linden, a thinly veiled portrait of the artist as a young man. Returning from England to take up a position as assistant manager of a city-centre bookstore, Drew is not a little disorientated by the experience of a city redefining itself in terms of consumer capitalism. These transformations imply renewed confidence and hope for the future, but they have meant that the old reassuring landmarks and boundaries have been erased. Yet even though the reconfiguration of Belfast tends to produce an homogenised culture, the city is still haunted by the 'old politics' of tribal conflict and territorialism. Belfast, we are reminded, is an inherently unstable city. Built on 'slobland' – 'stolen land' reclaimed from the sea – it is testimony to the human struggle to create order out of chaos, to impose the structures of civilisation upon the flux of nature. Belfast epitomises 'the battle between destruction and construction'.[14] Within the contested space of the city, Patterson emphasises the variety and contradictoriness of the forces that produce a multi-textured, plural culture. Refusing to settle for any consistent, unambiguous account of events, he unfolds the story gradually through an episodic narrative that keeps looping back in time, shifting from one perspective to another.

The narrative is mainly focalised through Drew, who since childhood has been burdened by his irrational belief that he is responsible for the family's subjection to the violence of the Troubles. Returning to Belfast, he is like the goldfish swimming round and round in its bowl, unable to escape. When his sister attempts to free an actual goldfish into the larger waters of the bath, it continues to swim round and round in the small circles it had got used to in the bowl. Drew, too, despite flight to England, has been unable to swim clear of his Ulster past. But what he comes to understand through his love-making with Anna are the interminable and manifold connections that exist between him and the rest of the world: 'Vast movements of peoples were communicated in the silence of a single kiss. Borders were crossed, identities blurred. Land masses rose and fell with their bodies' (p. 249). The bomb blast with which the novel ends represents an ultimately futile attempt to coerce the swarm of heterogeneous life into reductive categories, to impose narrative closure and silence all opposition for good.

Two novels by Robert McLiam Wilson (b. 1964), *Ripley Bogle* (1989) and *Eureka Street* (1996), continue the exploration of the possibilities of post-modern, pluralist culture and identity. Ripley Bogle, situated on the margins of society, displaced from his West Belfast, Catholic, nationalist origins, reproduces a type of colonial subjectivity which is characterised by ambivalence, mimicry and hybridity, and offers a radical challenge to the identitarian politics of both nationalism and colonialism. On his first day at school, he insists on calling himself 'Ripley Irish British Bogle' in the face of coercive social forces and more straightforward categorisation. Bogle's hybrid parentage is 'part Welsh and part Irish'; hybridity makes a nonsense of wars and revolutions, a point borne in on the narrator by the thought that his maternal great-grandfather was 'having his legs and most of his testicles blown off at Passchendaele while fighting for the British nation against the German Army – while his brother (my greatgranduncle?) was having his head blown off on O'Connell Street while fighting for the Irish nation against the British Army.'[15] The first part of Bogle's narrative sees the Troubles not in political, adult terms, but from the perspective of excited childhood fascination with horror and violence. Bogle's satiric denunciation of the dominant discourses of Ireland continues through parody and pastiche, which simultaneously foreground the novel's own constructed nature. Once at Cambridge, Bogle's double vision (both Irish and English) makes him a figure of suspicion, the challenge he poses to the power and difference of authority at times pushing beyond mimicry and mockery to outright menace. Refusing to assimilate, Bogle resists the colonialist discourse as he had resisted the dominant narratives of decolonisation. He prefers to occupy a position from which he can interrogate both Englishness and Irishness. Identity remains an ever-revisable script, subject to 'revision', 'erasure', 'arbitration' (pp. 269–70) and other kinds of radical fictionality and textual play.

Eureka Street, written at the time of the second cease-fires, reflects the new mood of optimism. Violence is given its place, but not allowed to monopolise the entire narrative field. The novel is explicitly written against those reductive versions of identity and history that are easily manipulated by the ideologues. Wilson proposes instead a version of history, location and identity as a rich fabric of interweaving narratives: 'The city is a repository of narratives, of stories. Present tense, past tense or future. The city is a novel . . .'[16] Contemplating ordinary lives, Wilson's prose moves beyond irony and satire towards rhapsodic celebration, an exquisitely tender evocation of Belfast and its people 'marvellous in their beds. They are epic, these citizens, they are tender, murderable' (p. 217).

Murder comes in the form of the bomb blast, which abruptly terminates some of these life stories. Sharing Patterson's fascination with the endless interaction of human narratives, Wilson indicates how the bomb disrupts a complex, extended network of relationships in which the individual is inscribed. Through their murderous action, the bombers wish to impose their own simple, linear narrative and block the free play of history as an open-ended process of transformation.

Wilson's satire in *Eureka Street* is directed against the ideologues who 'edited or failed to mention all the complicated, pluralistic, true details' (p. 236); against a credulous America which is pictured as easy prey to the likes of Jimmy Eve and the Just Us party – thinly veiled parodies of Gerry Adams and Sinn Fein; and against the whole cultural apparatus of romantic nationalism, personified by the poet Shague Ghintoss (read Seamus Heaney?). But most of all, it is directed against all those who would presume to justify violence. In his description of the bomb blast, Wilson insists on de-politicising the atrocity and seeing it only in terms of concrete, immediate experience. For Wilson, the supreme value is the individual, not abstract causes. 'In my early years', Wilson's hero Jake says, 'I had often hoped that the future would be different. That from out of the dark mists of Ireland's past and present a new breed would arise. The New Irish. When all the old creeds and permutations would be contradicted' (p. 164). This is the novel's Eureka cry – to see that the Other can be enriching, rather than something to be distrusted or abominated or brought under control. Out of this new, post-modern humanism, a new political agenda suggests itself, for to be able to see the attractions of the Other is to escape the conventional ethnocentric pieties and open up the possibilities of a rejuvenating multi-culturalism.

As much of this fiction demonstrates, realism is still very much alive, but it is inevitably in all kinds of post-modernist trouble, having to mediate a sense of multiplicity and fragmentation. The incorporation of post-modern strategies of disruption and distancing do not proclaim the end of humanism or produce an anarchic dispersal: rather, they are the strategies for re-formulating identity, history and agency. These novelists experiment with the possibilities of remapping identity, rewriting history and reinventing the language and form of the Troubles, in some cases suggesting positive new ways of living amid breakdown and dissensus.

The novel/film interface

The thriller element of Troubles fiction has appealed to the film-maker, and films have been made of many of the novels discussed above, including the novels of the earlier Troubles, *The Informer* and *Odd Man Out*. Troubles novels have not only been taken up by Hollywood film-makers, but have contributed significantly to the current Irish film industry. The writer and film-maker Neil Jordan (b. 1950) is of particular interest as an exponent of both genres of Troubles narrative: this novelist (*The Past*, 1980; *Nightlines*, 1994) has also written and directed Troubles screenplays, namely *Angel* (*Danny Boy* in North America, 1982) and *The Crying Game* (1992). These films may, as Richard Kearney says, debunk the mythology of heroic violence which has traditionally been used to glamorise a sentimental nationalism,[17] but beyond that neither film manages to advance our understanding of the violence in the North because neither makes any attempt to examine the social and political roots of the conflict.

Angel tells the story of Danny (Stephen Rea), a saxophone player who is witness to a brutal sectarian double murder and bombing, and becomes an avenging angel intent on tracking down and killing the perpetrators of the outrage. The film sets out to denounce *all* violence, regardless of whether it is loyalist or republican. The Troubles thus become the symptom of metaphysical evil motivated by deep psychic forces that are anterior to, more fundamental than, politics and history. The film, in attempting to deny any particular political allegiance, ends up endorsing the status quo.

Nevertheless, as Jordan has commented: 'The metaphysical language in which the film speaks is a very Catholic one, to do with sin and guilt.'[18] In this respect, *Angel* resembles *Cal*: but, unlike *Cal*, the film, through its combination of a Catholic metaphysics and a magic realist style, intimates the possibility of redemption from the Ulster nightmare. Though *Angel* returns at the end to the bombed-out ballroom where it began, there is a sense of purgation and progression. Danny, miraculously saved from one policeman by the gun of another and touched by the angelic child faith-healer, re-enters the ordinary world a new man.

The Crying Game goes further in attempting to deconstruct the simplicities of identity politics. The complexities of post-colonial, post-modern identity destabilise nationalist politics, including its physical force tradition, and 'queer' the usual constructions of sexual and gender identity. Race is no longer a reliable guide to nationality; sexuality cannot be equated with gender. Jody is the most paradoxical of all the characters, and the one who has the most unsettling effect on Fergus, the traditional Irish Catholic IRA man. This British soldier taken hostage is a West Indian from Tottenham, yet the representative of British colonialism in Ireland. He is apparently prepared to have sexual relations with Jude, the IRA woman, yet is devoted to his male lover Dil. Like Jude, his name could apply to either gender. His sexuality is as indeterminate as his political and national identity. Fergus's crisis of identity involves rejection of the masculinist ethos of republican paramilitarism, a rejection motivated partly by humane feeling, partly by sexual desire. Fergus's identification with, and desire for, Jody force him to reappraise his own identity, political as well as sexual. He seeks to prove his masculinity, not any longer through post-modern guerrilla warfare, but through romance.

The film features all kinds of crossings: from the opening shot which sweeps above and across the river, to the transportation of the captured Jody across the water, to Jody's story of the frog and the scorpion crossing the river, to Fergus's crossing back to England to start a new life in London as 'Jimmy'. Fergus and Jody are linked across racial and political divisions. Dil is a 'cross-dresser' who has the body of a man and the psyche of a woman, and for whom Fergus leaves the controlling female (Jude) to embrace both masculine sameness and racial/national otherness simultaneously. Reversing the usual stereotypes, femininity, as represented by Jude, is always powerful, while masculinity tends to be negotiable and unstable. Through his relationships with Jody and then Dil, Fergus is brought to a new awareness of the fluidity and indeterminacy of identities of all kinds.

What is remarkable about *The Crying Game*, and indeed about the majority of Troubles films, whether American, British or Irish, is their construction of the Northern situation as an imperialist conflict between Britain and Ireland, rather than a sectarian conflict within Northern Ireland. In this post-colonial view, the struggle for Irish independence remains 'unfinished business' in regard to the six counties of the North which wrongly continue to remain part of the UK. To those who subscribe to the 'anti-imperialist myth', almost a million Northern Protestants can simply be 'dismissed from history' because they are 'deluded lackeys' who perversely continue to identify with British imperialist power.[19] Where unionists, and Protestants more generally, have been able to see themselves in the novels of Leitch, Patterson, Wilson, Duffaud, Bateman and Johnston, this has only rarely been the case in films and television dramas about the Troubles – Peter Smith's *No Surrender* (1985), written by Alan Bleasedale, and Graham Reid's 'Billy' plays which were written for television. More often, Protestants have been marginalised or depicted in reductive or negative terms. In Terry George's *Some Mother's Son* (1996), the only Protestants are prison officers and disruptive, loud-mouthed unionist protestors, while in Jim Sheridan's *In the Name of the Father* (1993), they appear only as RUC men; in Roger Mitchell's *Titanic Town* (1998) – from Mary Costello's 1992 autobiographical novel of that title – the Protestant community is briefly represented by a group of heavily caricatured middle-class Peace Women; in *The Crying Game* (1992) there are no Ulster Protestants at all. Similarly, Hollywood has embraced the 'anti-imperialist myth', as three films of the 1990s would illustrate – Philip Noyce's *Patriot Games* (1992), Stephen Hopkins's *Blown Away* (1994) and Alan Pakula's *The Devil's Own* (1997). British film-makers who have been attracted to Irish themes – Alan Clarke (*Contact*, 1985; *Elephant*, 1989), Mike Leigh (*Four Days in July*, 1984), Ken Loach (*Hidden Agenda*, 1990) – are generally left wing, anti-imperialist and pro-republican, and have found little to interest them in the Protestant community. The inevitable conclusion is that the Troubles film, in contrast to the Troubles novel, has made little contribution to the cultural project of envisioning new 'Northern' identities construed in terms of hybridity and transformation.

NOTES

1. The phrase is Tom Nairn's, in *The Break-Up of Britain: Crisis and Neo-Nationalism* (London: Verso, 1981). The 'myth of atavism' is the tendency of some authors and critics to see the violence in the North as irrational, rather than the result of social and political conditions.
2. See Joe Cleary, '"Fork-tongued on the Border Bit": Partition and the Politics of Form in Contemporary Narratives of the Northern Irish Conflict', *South Atlantic Quarterly* 95 (1996), 227–76.

3. Francis Stuart, *A Hole in the Head* (London: Martin, Brian & O'Keeffe, 1977), p. 185.
4. Jennifer Johnston, *The Railway Station Man* (London: Review, 1998), p. 156.
5. Maurice Leitch, *Silver's City* (London: Abacus, 1983), p. 40.
6. The phrase 'resilient realism' is from the title of John Cronin's essay, 'The Resilient Realism of Brian Moore', *Irish University Review*, special issue on Brian Moore, 18 (1988), 24–36.
7. Bernard MacLaverty, *Cal* (1983; London: Penguin, 1984), p. 124.
8. This is the view of John Hill in Luke Gibbons and John Hill (eds.), *Cinema and Ireland* (London: Croom Helm, 1987), p. 83.
9. Brian Moore, *Lies of Silence* (London: Vintage, 1992), pp. 69–70.
10. Deirdre Madden, *Hidden Symptoms* (London: Faber, 1988), pp. 13–14.
11. Seamus Deane, *Reading in the Dark* (London: Jonathan Cape, 1996), p. 43.
12. Eoin McNamee, *Resurrection Man* (London: Picador, 1994), p. 163.
13. Colin Bateman, *Divorcing Jack* (London: HarperCollins, 1995), p. 9.
14. Glenn Patterson, *Fat Lad* (London: Minerva, 1993), p. 204.
15. Robert McLiam Wilson, *Ripley Bogle* (London: Picador, 1989), p. 7.
16. Robert McLiam Wilson, *Eureka Street* (1996; London: Minerva, 1997), p. 215.
17. Richard Kearney, *Transitions: Narratives of Irish Culture* (Dublin: Wolfhound, 1988), pp. 174–83.
18. Neil Jordan, interview with Michael Open, 'Face to Face with Evil', *Film Directions* 5 (1982), 16.
19. See Nairn, *The Break-Up of Britain*, p. 231. See also Brian McIlroy's critique of Nairn's concepts of 'the myth of atavism' and 'the anti-imperialist myth' in *Shooting to Kill: Filmmaking and the 'Troubles' in Northern Ireland* (Richmond, B.C.: Steveston Press, 2001): 'In this framework the Protestants are suffering from a false consciousness. To allow this myth to work, the Protestant proletariat must be ignored, as must the fact of two diverse ethnic communities inhabiting the same land' (p. 38).

GUIDE TO FURTHER READING

Harte, Liam and Michael Parker (eds.). *Contemporary Irish Fiction: Themes, Tropes, Theories*. Basingstoke: Macmillan, 2000.
Kennedy-Andrews, Elmer. *Fiction and the Northern Ireland Troubles since 1969: (De-)Constructing the North*. Dublin: Four Courts Press, 2003.
Peach, Linden. *The Contemporary Irish Novel*. Basingstoke: Palgrave Macmillan, 2004.
Pelaschiar, Laura. *Writing the North: The Contemporary Novel in Northern Ireland*. Trieste: Edizioni Parnaso, 1998.
Smyth, Gerry. *The Novel and the Nation*. London: Pluto Press, 1997.

14

EVE PATTEN

Contemporary Irish fiction

The post-national novel

Since the mid-1980s, the rapid transformation of the Republic of Ireland's domestic and international profile has been accompanied by a heightened political engagement in Irish fiction. With a confidence bolstered by the 1990 election to the Irish presidency of a female reformist lawyer, Mary Robinson, the Irish began to face up to their position as modern Europeans who had 'not so much solved as shelved the problem of creating a liberal nationalism'.[1] Where political culture led, writers followed, and in the publishing boom of the 1990s, the Irish novel repeatedly highlighted the institutional and ideological failings of the country, tracing the halting progress of Ireland's cultural, sexual and economic evolution, and foregrounding its voices of dissent. The works categorised by critic Gerry Smyth as the 'New Irish Fiction' were distinguished by a sociological purpose, which, with a few noteworthy exceptions, bypassed philosophical abstraction. 'Less of an intellectual and more of an artisan', wrote Smyth, 'the new Irish novelist is concerned to narrate the nation as it has been and is, rather than how it should be or might have been'.[2]

From this perspective, the fiction of the contemporary period is better categorised as post-national than as post-colonial. For the most part, it remained formally conservative: beyond a prevalent social realism, its chief stylistic hallmark was a neo-Gothic idiom which signalled a haunted or traumatised Irish society and deep-seated disturbances in the national psyche. The dysfunctional family, and within it the child – abused, victimised or emotionally stunted – continued to provide staple metaphors of cultural crisis.[3] A recurrent fictional outlook, meanwhile, was retrospective. Ireland's history, and the recent past in particular, came under intense scrutiny as the testing ground of present-day cultural and political uncertainty. The revisionist controversy which engaged academic historians in the period filtered into popular consciousness through the novel, as fiction writers simultaneously began to exercise a 'robust scepticism about the pieties of Irish nationalism'[4] and geared their writing towards the subversion of official and causal narratives of the modern nation's evolution.

Irish historical fiction provides a relevant departure point, therefore, for a survey of the contemporary Irish novel. Though still attached to 'big-house' structures and the binary of dissipating Protestant aristocracy and ascendant Irish peasantry, the historical novels of the 1980s and 1990s introduced a methodological self-consciousness to the profiling of Irish historical experience, gaining impetus from revisionism's scaling down of broad national narratives towards the micro-histories obscured by summary and generalisation. The imagined past became a well-documented one, resourced with analytical skill and authentic data, even across a range of genres. *Necessary Treasons* (1985) by Maeve Kelly (b. 1930) presented a feminist exposé of seventeenth-century land struggles and religious prejudice in a story of an Irish family whose ancestral papers, brought to light in the modern civil rights era, illuminate the patriarchal oppressions tied into the concept of heritage. *Wild Geese* (2003), a historical romance by Lara Harte (b. 1975), reconstructed with documentary accuracy the merchant classes of late eighteenth-century Dublin as background to the tale of a young woman's flight to revolutionary France. And in *How to Murder a Man* (1998), Carlo Gebler (b. 1954) adapted an original nineteenth-century account of the conflict between a reforming landlord and a rural secret society as the basis for a complex and violent historical thriller.

Self-consciousness with regard to the representation of history was not, of course, a new development. J. G. Farrell and Francis Stuart, among others, had already drawn attention to the charged intersection of Irish history and fiction. But the pertinence of key contemporary Irish historical novels undoubtedly hinged on their proximity to a revisionist historiographic culture, and a *fin-de-siècle* interrogation of causality and grand narrative. This is well illustrated by one of the most accomplished historical novels of the period, *Death and Nightingales* (1998) by Eugene McCabe (b. 1930). Focussing on the small farmers and petty landowners of late nineteenth-century Ulster, McCabe unearths from the Parnellite era the rooted complexities of religion and ownership in Ireland, and illuminates the local impulses obscured by official versions of the past. The novel gestures towards allegory; the marriage of a pregnant Catholic woman from an ancient clan to a Protestant landowner produces a daughter whose hybrid identity initiates a trajectory of secret and violent misalliances. But the author refuses romantic resolution. Ireland's social composition is seen as necessarily awkward, its narratives suspect and its historical progress shaped as much by accident and coincidence as political causality.

Death and Nightingales successfully foregrounds local detail at the expense of national teleology, and the result is a purposeful inconclusiveness. Thematically, it shares an interest in the role of contingency with a second major historical novel of the period, *The Story of Lucy Gault* (2002) by William Trevor (b. 1928). Essentially a big house fiction, this too might be considered allegorical: the tale of a missing daughter and the subsequent dislocations of family, marriage and parenthood combine with the pressurised historical backdrop of Ireland during and after the War of Independence to produce a sustained comment on Irish historical sensibility. Should the tragedy of the Gault family be traced back to what was simply an accident? Or further back, to the political circumstances in which that accident occurred? What are the functions of guilt, responsibility, forgiveness and time in the processing of traumatic experiences? For the ageing Lucy Gault, playing snakes and ladders with the man who inadvertently brings about the novel's determining calamity, life becomes a means of dealing with 'how things have happened', to the extent that the spiritual, emotional and psychological management of the past is what ultimately comes to constitute 'history'. As a quiet but forceful demonstration of this point, Trevor's novel implicitly challenges the priorities of 'event-led' Irish historical narrative and gives a philosophical lead to a problematic contemporary historiography.

In a more blatant assault on the sacred cows of Irish history, several recent Irish novels have directly targeted the modern state and its unravelling historical fabric. In *Amongst Women* (1990) by John McGahern (1934–2006), the farmer Michael Moran, a bitter republican veteran of the Irish Civil War, ruthlessly visits the brutalities and outdated heroics of a bygone era on his family. Surrounded by his daughters but estranged from his sons, he slips into old age as a relic from a past which is losing its grip. A failing authoritarian, Moran mirrors symbolically the ambivalent position held in the national 'family' by former Irish president and architect of independence Eamon de Valera, enabling critics to read the novel as both a damning indictment of a patriarchal nationalism bolstered by a rigid Catholic hierarchy and as a sensitive, even sympathetic, account of traditional Irish pieties in retreat. In the resonance of this theme for a modern generation, *Amongst Women* provided a landmark in Irish fiction and confirmed, too, the capacity of the contemporary Irish novel for subtle political engagement without the abandonment of conventional narrative form and setting.

The incorporation in fiction of both emblematic and authentic historical figures produced a more overt attack on the Irish state in *The Heather Blazing* (1992), by Colm Tóibín (b. 1955). Taking its title from a rebel ballad, this novel concerns the continuing pull of historical memory in modern Ireland. In the name of his central character, Eamon Redmond, Tóibín suggests a composite allusion to Eamon de Valera and the Wexford-born MP John Redmond, a non-violent nationalist and leader of the Irish Parliamentary Party until 1918. Flashbacks to Eamon Redmond's childhood and adolescence in County Wexford in the 1940s show the extent to which his upbringing was steeped in a culture of republican commemoration and nationalist consolidation. This hinterland forms the ideological backdrop to the present day when, as a High Court Judge, his strained attempts to sustain in court the articles of the 1937 Constitution, *Bunreacht na hÉireann*, expose the divergence of contemporary Irish culture from its foundational ethos. The gap between the language of state and the reality of Irish experience is emphasised in the novel's motif of communication failure, through a series of references to aphasia, stuttering, muteness and silence. But crucially, the origin myths of the Irish state are never explicitly condemned: like McGahern, Tóibín is sensitive to the demands of the past and the nature of historical change, and the novel's guiding symbolism, depicting the Wexford coastline's slow erosion by the sea, promotes a liberal progressivism over outright renunciation.

The Heather Blazing and *Amongst Women* dominate a group of contemporary novels linked by the impulse towards revisionism and ideological realignment, and by the foregrounding of family relations as metaphoric of the national community. They are representative too, in suggesting the ascendancy of a feminine sensibility in Irish social and public life, with the masculine principles of militant nationalism, patriarchy and statism conceding to a culture of liberalism and welfare. Not surprisingly, women writers have also been prominent in addressing – though a good deal more aggressively – the gendered construction of the Irish state. *The Killeen* (1985) by Mary Leland (b. 1941), for example, offers the paradoxical position of two young women who, initially receptive to revolutionary republicanism in the wake of the 1922 Treaty, become dramatically alienated from the restrictive and militaristic ideology which ultimately shapes the reality of de Valera's Ireland in the 1930s. Set mainly in County Cork, the novel takes its title from the killeen, or in Irish *cillín*, a small graveyard customarily set aside for the burial of unbaptised babies, and – for Leland – an evocative symbol of exclusion and repression in an Irish culture driven by harsh ideological imperatives. *Fool's Sanctuary* (1987) by Jennifer Johnston (b. 1930) conveys a similar political disenchantment in the lifelong suffering of a woman haunted by her love for an executed revolutionary, while Rita, the protagonist of *Safe in the Kitchen* (1993) by Aisling Foster (b. 1949), confronts the character of de Valera directly, challenging his espousal of policy which – as the novel's punning title suggests – excluded a female contribution to the public life of the new nation and sponsored a long-term relegation of women to the sidelines of Irish history. A pastiche historical saga of Russian and Irish revolutionary intrigue, *Safe in the Kitchen* perhaps best represents a 1990s movement towards the astute exploitation of genre fiction by an Irish feminist political interest.

By the 1990s, Irish historical fiction was beginning to exhibit a discernible self-consciousness with regard to narrative realism and adopting a postmodern irreverence to traditional meta-narratives. Like Aisling Foster, several novelists of the period strategically review the key events of the century from ironic or marginal positions. *A Star Called Henry* (1999) by Roddy Doyle (b. 1958), for example, burlesques the Easter Rising and the Irish Civil War by presenting them through the accidental participation of a child of the Dublin slums, Henry Smart. Larger-than-life and sexually voracious, Smart parodies the mythical heroes of Irish legend and reduces the national story to the level of Dickensian grotesque. *At Swim, Two Boys* (2001) by Jamie O'Neill (b. 1961), similarly flirts with pastiche mode, in the story of two friends who spend the year of the 1916 Rising plotting to swim out to an island in Dublin bay to plant the Irish flag. The novel's language is freighted with deliberate echoes of Joyce, O'Casey and – as the title suggests – Flann O'Brien, its narrative peopled with caricatures of Irish revolutionaries and First World War veterans, viewed from the dislocated perspective of adolescent homosexuality. And in *Star of the Sea* (2003), Joseph O'Connor (b. 1963) revisits the Famine era from a variety of ironic tangents, weaving an elaborate play on the processes of historical and literary representation into his narrative of an emigrant voyage to America. Together, such novels convey the confidence with which a recent generation of writers, drawing on tactics of subversion and irony, has tackled not only the matter but also the *status* of Irish history, updating the historical novel – already a strong player in the Irish canon – towards a contemporary ideological non-conformism.

Country and city

The fictional emphasis on historical revision has clear affinities, too, with Ireland's ongoing political process of enquiry, manifest in the government tribunals established in the period to investigate the corruptions of previous administrations. Within this context, novelists have put particularly intense pressure on the recent past, the period from the 1950s to the 1970s, in which the contemporary literary generation grew up and in which Ireland experienced most acutely the effects of the country's failure to keep

pace with modernisation and secularisation. The conservative grip of
the Catholic Church was acknowledged, but not significantly relaxed, by
the reforms of Vatican 2 in the early 1960s. Despite projections of economic
expansionism in that decade under the new leadership of Sean Lemass, and
despite promises of an end to Irish insularity through the country's gradual
moves towards full European Economic Community membership in 1973,
there was a pervasive sense of stasis. 'If a Rip Van Winkle fell asleep in
the 1950s and woke up in the 1980s', writes critic Luke Gibbons, 'he could
be forgiven for thinking that nothing had changed in between.'[5] Yet for a
younger generation there was also cultural confusion, as traditional Ireland
began to experience, first, the inroads of popular music and media from
outside the country and, second, the belated social effects of urbanisation
following a shift in the demographic balance of country and city.

The novelist Patrick McCabe (b. 1955) has led recent Irish fiction writers
in chronicling the insecurity of this period. His writing depicts the pressures
outlined above in terms of communal crisis and individual psychosis;
his protagonists embody the repression and claustrophobia of Irish life,
and are driven by the desire to reach beyond it to alternative identities
derived from popular music, comic books, cinema and television. His novels
convey the trauma of fractured or incomplete historical transition. In *The
Dead School* (1995), headmaster Raphael Bell and schoolteacher Malachy
Dudgeon have emerged from radically different generations, and their clash
of values in a Dublin school signals the breakdown of continuity in an
Ireland caught between rigid traditionalism and cultural freefall. The novel
gains an acerbic black comedy from the juxtaposition of Bell's pietistic
liturgical refrains and nationalist iconography with the pop songs and
Hollywood films of Dudgeon's frame of reference, but its view of 1970s
Ireland is essentially dark, its macabre denouement highlighting what
is, essentially, a failure of inheritance between father figure and son.

McCabe's style has been celebrated for its anarchic Midlands vernacular
and breakneck narrative pace, both of which reinforce his representation
of ordinary life in Ireland as bizarre and malformed. His characteristic
style works to particularly vivid effect in his neo-Gothic psychodrama,
set in the late 1950s and early 1960s, *The Butcher Boy* (1992). Here, the
psychological disintegration of Francie Brady, orphaned by the suicide of
his mother and subsequent death of his alcoholic father, exposes in turn
the dysfunctionalism of an archetypal small-town community, the failings
of a sexually predatory priesthood and the obsolescence of an institutionalised nationalism. Like many of his contemporaries, such as Michael Collins
(b. 1964) in *The Life and Times of a Tea Boy* (1994), McCabe thus uses
mental illness to dramatise the enervated condition of Irishness in the

second half of the twentieth century. His writing has distinct political nuances however. In *The Butcher Boy*, as in his more recent *Call me the Breeze* (2003), the subversive excess of psychotic behaviour is linked to the Irish border region as the point at which the proximity of a politically unstable Northern Ireland ruptures the containing narratives of the Irish Republic. Even in *The Dead School*'s Dublin setting, the Northern troubles are marked with references to the IRA assassination of the British Ambassador to Ireland in 1976. The overspill of Northern violence into Southern complacency undermines the founding myths of nationalist revolution, blocking Ireland's escape from the comic-strip grotesquerie of traumatised childhood towards the integration and civility of mature national life.

While McCabe's fiction distinguished the particular neuroses of the Irish small town, several writers addressed the fate of rural Ireland within the context of a collapsing national narrative. *The Banyan Tree* (1999) by Christopher Nolan (b. 1965) details the life of a woman struggling to maintain the deserted family farm; the enigmatic *One Day as a Tiger* (1998) by Ann Haverty (b. 1959) hints at the dystopia of Irish pastoral through the symbolism of a grotesque, genetically engineered sheep; and John McGahern continued his study of an agrarian Ireland coming to terms with modernity in his elegiac novel, *That They May Face the Rising Sun* (2002). A more publicised thrust in contemporary fiction, however, was the increasing tension between rural and urban, and the fraught condition of the Irish city. Writers addressing this topic had to reckon with two prevailing myths already embedded in an Irish cultural inheritance: first, that the urban environment was a lapsed or artificial one, at odds with an idyllic, *authentic* rural Ireland and, second, that the city conversely offered freedom and sanctity to the individual on the run from Irish country and small-town oppression. The strict urban–rural polarity emphasised in both perspectives had effectively disguised at the same time the complexity of the Irish domestic landscape, where differentiations between small town and farmstead, or between inner-city affluence and peripheral working-class suburb, were in fact more accurate markers of Ireland's variegated social profile.

In filtering this material and in coping, too, with the literary archaeology of Dublin as depicted by Joyce and O'Casey, contemporary writers took on considerable baggage with this subject, but their various responses galvanised debate about transitions in Irish identity and ideology. Several novels tracked a communal narrative in the spatial and architectural growth of Dublin itself. In one of the most acclaimed of these, *The Journey Home* (1990) by Dermot Bolger (b. 1959), the protagonist Hano is the son of country-born parents who, shifted from their village to one of the new suburban estates ringing the city, set about recreating their agrarian roots in tree-planting and potato-growing. Hano's consciousness of this lost rural inheritance adds to his alienation from the old Corporation redbrick terraces of the 'real' city and from an urban centre invigoratingly free of crippling traditions but degraded at the same time by addiction, crime and political corruption. Bolger's depiction of the urban landscape is intimate and discriminating, but his outlook is bleak. An 'internal exile', disillusioned by what the nation has become, Hano eventually retreats to an old house in the woods, a rural outpost from which he prophesies on the future ruination of Dublin at the hands of corporate self-interest and international exploitation.

The Journey Home offers a particularly pessimistic view of contemporary urban Ireland. Other writers, including Roddy Doyle in Paddy Clarke Ha Ha Ha (1993), also mark the construction of Dublin's suburban estates as a rite of passage in Ireland's transition from rural innocence to urban experience, but few were as damning in their profile of the city's blighted condition. In Doyle's trilogy of novels based in the fictionalised north Dublin housing estate of Barrytown, the working-class suburb is presented, and even celebrated, as a site of cultural and social reconstruction. While acknowledging the presence of unemployment and poverty, Doyle also observes in The Snapper (1990) the pragmatic restructuring of priorities – beyond the strictures of the Church – which allows the modern family unit to incorporate without difficulty a child born outside marriage, and in The Commitments (1987) and The Van (1991), he highlights the cultural eclecticism which displaced older cultural traditions to put football, television and popular music at the heart of the home. On the periphery of the city proper, Doyle's urban landscape is seen as almost entirely disengaged from historical Dublin and detached, therefore, from the ramifications of both imperial and nationalist memory. Barrytown is a microcosm, successfully creating its own logic as a revolutionary domestic space.

Doyle's particular brand of 'dirty realism' was challenged by some readers as a patronising portrait of the Irish working class, while his narrative style in the trilogy, heavily reliant on dialogue and replete with the blasphemies and idioms of a north-side Dublin vernacular, was also seen as verging on caricature.[6] Nonetheless, his creation of Barrytown was a dramatic intervention in the literary representation of Dublin. His male characters, too, provided a statement on the shifting gender roles of a new spatial order in the 1990s city. Doyle's Jimmy Sr, father of the Rabbitte family, appears in both The Van and The Snapper as a male ego forced into realignment when the props of traditional Irish masculinity, rooted in breadwinning and patriarchy, give way to lowly service-sector jobs and a world of domesticity and childcare. This coincides with his alienation from what was, formerly, the symbolic heart of masculine status, the city centre. Safe in their largely self-sufficient housing estates, Jimmy Sr and his friend Bimbo are threatened by the pace, cost and sexual protocol of Dublin's city centre, when they travel 'into town' in *The Van*.[7] Unlike the vengeful protagonists of *Headbanger* (1996) by Hugo Hamilton (b. 1953) and *The Salesman* (1998) by Joseph O'Connor, who survive the city by adopting vigilante roles, Doyle's ordinary Irish males are depicted as vanquished players, retreating to the margins of national life.

Fiction and the feminine ethos

If a particular kind of masculinity is at odds with new urban life, a feminine ethos is welcomed, however. This is not, of course, a new concept in Irish fiction: Leopold Bloom's Dublin in *Ulysses* was essentially a female space in its fluidity and connection, a theme picked up in *The Parts* (2003), a black comedy by Keith Ridgway (b. 1965) in which six narrative voices reflect the plurality of Dublin as a home to multiple cultural and sexual identities. Key to this novel's elaborate construction is the link character of Kez, a rent boy whose pathways through the city highlight its mutable, unpredictable, yet sympathetic landscapes. In *The Fabulists* (1994) by Philip Casey (b. 1950), Mungo, the disabled and unemployed male protagonist, moves easily through Dublin's inner-city precincts because he takes on the conventionally female roles of shopping and collecting children from school. The implicit feminine usurpation of the city is reinforced by the novel's conclusion, when he joins a city-centre carnival to watch the newly appointed President, Mary Robinson, in procession through the streets. Furthermore, while male writers have emphasised the corruption of the Irish city, their female counterparts have taken on the urban landscape with confidence. The evocative art novel, *Authenticity* (2002) by Deirdre Madden (b. 1960), *The Courtship Gift* (2000) by Julie Parsons (b. 1951) and Jennifer Johnston's *This is Not a Novel* (2002) all indulge in specific and romantic topographies of Dublin city's south side. The female reclamation of the city has also been heralded at a popular level in the so-called 'city-girl' novels and novel sequences of the period from authors such as Patricia Scanlan (b. 1958) and Sheila O'Flanagan (b. 1959), which frequently feature independent young Irish women detaching themselves from traditional family structures in order to access and enjoy the social and consumerist cityscape of 'Celtic Tiger' Dublin.

This apparent divergence in masculine/feminine treatments of the Irish city in fiction is clearly linked to the revision of gender roles within historical nationalism. In novels like *The Journey Home*, a betrayed national dream coalesces with Dublin as post-nationalist nightmare. But while hinting that a feminine ethos can reclaim the urban centre, the contemporary novel has stopped short of depicting an Ireland of sexual equality. Indeed, much of the fiction of the last two decades has been dedicated to the highlighting of Irish women's continued subjugation, dovetailing in the 1980s and early 1990s with a vociferous feminist project and a series of legislative campaigns in the key areas of divorce and abortion law. In 1983, a referendum confirmed Ireland's ban on abortion; and, in 1986, the defeat of the government's referendum on divorce – eventually legalised a decade later – revealed the extent of the country's religious conservatism with regard to marriage and Irish family life. Despite the liberalising of sexual attitudes and the relaxing of restrictions on contraception, the position of women in Irish society and culture was still recognised as one of entrenched subordination.

Meanwhile, the increased visibility of women in public life brought the subjects of marriage, sexuality and family life to the forefront of public consciousness. The media played a central role in exposing what had hitherto been relegated to the private sphere, and the foundation of the Irish feminist publishing house Attic Press in 1984 offered encouragement to new writers previously marginalised by a publishing arena deemed to be male-dominated and patriarchal. The adverse response to the 1991 *Field Day Anthology of Irish Writing*, meanwhile, which was charged with the exclusion of women writers from its pages and female editors from its staff, instigated a literary campaign for recognition which culminated in the 2003 publication of two more volumes, devoted exclusively to women's writing and culture.

In fiction, the impact of women writing is marked in narrative modes geared to the representation of an abused subjectivity. Several authors use autobiographical or *Bildungsroman* constructions to depict the individual as the victim of serial political, religious and cultural restrictions in Ireland. *Stars in the Daytime* (1987) by Evelyn Conlon (b. 1952) tells the story of Rose, whose childhood, adolescence and life as an unmarried mother expose in turn the hypocrisy of a patriarchal Catholic society to an extent that leaves her, literally, retching in disgust. In *Another Alice* (1996), Lia Mills (b. 1957) employs a psychoanalytical framework to present a woman whose repressed memories of sexual abuse by her father have resulted in a malformed identity, a split between unpalatable reality and dream world which suggestively parallels the schizophrenia of the nation itself. In *The Maid's Tale* (1994) by Kathleen Ferguson (b. 1958), a woman from a violent family background, raised in an orphanage, details a life of servitude and abuse at the hands of her employer, a Catholic priest. This novel's vivid and colloquial first-person narrative similarly aligns an individual journey from victimised dependency to hesitant liberation with a national trajectory; that of Ireland's changing relationship with the institutions of Catholicism from the later 1950s to the present day. And Roddy Doyle's *The Woman Who Walked into Doors* (1996) has been well received as a male writer's attempt to imagine the complex inner life of a woman routinely beaten by her husband.

From the mid 1980s onwards, the prevalence of first-person and rites-of-passage narratives projecting the plight of female protagonists amounted to a sustained fictional campaign of self-assertion. The novel has been a means by which a marginalised female voice claimed authority in response to the ingrained misogyny of Irish life. The position of women is closely linked, however, to the representation of related issues concerning the Irish family. Enshrined by the constitution of the Irish Republic, the family is repeatedly shown in fiction as embittered, disordered and in flux. Particularly resonant have been the 'incest narratives' employed by several women writers to convey the extent of Irish family dysfunctionalism.[8] Mill's *Another Alice* signified the depth of disturbance in the Irish psyche generally, while Jennifer Johnston's *The Invisible Worm* (1991) depicted incest at the heart of a modern big house, linking the corruption of a family to the corruption of a social caste and layering sexual malformation on to existing fictional tropes of ascendancy dissipation and decline. More controversially, Edna O'Brien (b. 1932) drew on the infamous 1992 'X' case – in which a young rape victim was denied the right to travel to England for a termination – as the basis for *Down by the River* (1996). In this novel, the rhetoric of anti-abortion campaigners becomes a shrill refrain, increasingly distanced from the trauma of a girl sexually abused by her widowed father. Though criticised by some readers as exploitative, the novel was nonetheless a significant intervention in public debate and remains one of the most disconcerting commentaries of the period.

Sex and society

The rupturing of the family as presented in the recent Irish novel enacts the violence of contemporary sexual and reproductive politics on the abstractions of the Republic of Ireland Constitution and all it stood for. The fictional dismembering of the body of the family, as it were, indicates a state at odds with itself, riven with discrepancies and misfit traditions. Now, alongside a traditional symbolism of father–son conflict, sustained in novels such as Dermot Bolger's *The Valparaiso Voyage* (2001), have emerged images of a deeper crisis in the failure of mother–child connections. The living mothers of Jennifer Johnston's fiction are voracious and unsatisfied; the dead mothers of Patrick McCabe's novels leave behind warped offspring with dangerous Freudian mother-fixations. Mothers are missing, as in Dermot Bolger's *A Second Life* (1994), or simply and painfully silent as in Roddy Doyle's *Barrytown Trilogy*.

Two novels in particular elevated this trope towards philosophical and political readings of national deformity. *Mother of Pearl* (1996), a post-modern Gothic allegory by Mary Morrissy (b. 1957) presents a quasi-biblical tale of two mothers battling for possession over a child, in a narrative which relentlessly and painfully interrogates concepts of 'biological', 'natural' and 'adoptive' parenthood. And in *What Are You Like?* (2000) by Anne Enright (b. 1962), a mother's death in childbirth results in twin sisters growing up apart on either side of the Irish sea, unaware of each other's existence yet constantly troubled by misrecognitions and shadows. Like Morrissy, Enright plays on the terms of personal relationships so that concepts of coupling, progeny and sisterhood operate towards an ironic mapping of family politics back on to the canvas of the nation. Both novels stand out as subtle contemporary observations on the nature of separatism and the skewed identity politics of modern Ireland.

In the fiction of the 1960s and 1970s, the representation of sex was more often than not a token of dissent from a repressive cultural and religious hierarchy. Since the mid-1980s, however, the treatment of sexual relationships has become more explicit and, in a rich school of gay fiction in particular, more disruptive. Critics have noted that even before the decriminalisation of homosexuality in the Republic of Ireland in 1993, the expanded borders of sexual identity provided a metaphor for the collapsing parameters of 'Irishness' itself, with plurality and diversity replacing an obsolete cultural homogeneity.[9] Rejecting, too, the coded allusions of previous generations, fiction writers have been uninhibited in their depictions of sexual activity. The writing of Emma Donoghue (b. 1969) offers graphic exploration of the sexual act as a means of subverting the sexual conservatism of Irish society. Her novel of awakening, *Stir-Fry* (1994), mirrors the rural/urban movement of Edna O'Brien's *The Country Girls* (1960), but sees its country-born protagonist bypassing heterosexual romance for the intriguing lesbian subculture of her new flatmates in the city. In Donoghue's more structurally ambitious *Hood* (1995), the central character mourns the death of her lesbian lover in a sequence of flashbacks and dream visions, some of which incorporate explicit sexual scenes, challenging through candid reference to genital imagery the silencing of a lesbian presence within 'normal' Irish life.

In male homosexual writing, the conventional coming-of-age narrative is successfully appropriated in novels such as *When Love Comes to Town* (1993) by Tom Lennon, which presents a gay middle-class Dublin teenager attempting to construct, through a combination of subterfuge and fantasy, a lifestyle viable within the cultural and religious discriminations of Irish society. Keith Ridgway's *The Long Falling* (1998) and sections of *The Parts* (2003) also explore the accommodation of homosexuality within contemporary life. In each case, Irish society as a whole comes to seem erratic and abnormal from the perspective of its homosexual contingent, and in this respect gay fiction has contributed fully to a mainstream novelistic process of social critique and revision. The outstanding novel in this context is Colm Tóibín's *The Blackwater Lightship* (1999), in which a man dying of Aids is brought home to a traditional family and its house on the crumbling Irish coast. The effect of Declan's illness on three estranged generations – his sister, mother and grandmother – is to force them into a process of acknowledgment and re-engagement. Meanwhile, the flashing signals from the offshore lighthouses symbolise their options, of change on the one hand, and stasis on the other.

Metafiction

It might be argued that the emphasis on thematic treatments of social issues has restricted formal experimentation in the Irish novel, endorsing a realist conformity which obscures any relation to the non-realist antecedence of James Stephens or Flann O'Brien. In fact, several novelists continue to exploit non-realist or metafictional devices in their work. Aside from the macabre neo-Gothic of Patrick McCabe, *A Goat's Song* (1994) by Dermot Healy (b. 1947) introduces episodes drawn from Irish mythology into a story of emotional and political breakdown. A hinterland of sectarian violence and North–South friction is filtered into the narrative through the alcohol-fuelled dreams and hallucinatory memory sequences of its central character, in a subtle composition which disturbs rather than challenges a realist veneer. Patrick McGinley (b. 1937) has written several novels, including *Bogmail* (1978), *Goosefoot* (1983) and *The Trick of the Ga Bolga* (1985), which appropriate aspects of Irish folk tale to produce a contemporary hyperrealism. The futurist novel *The Bray House* (1990), by Eilís Ní Dhuibhne (b. 1954), brings science fiction into collaboration with feminist speculation, depicting a group of Swedish scientists and their attempt to document the extinct civilisation of a post-nuclear Ireland. Finally, Anne Enright continues to push the boundaries of a conventional Irish narrative realism with tactics ranging from a subversive magic realism in *The Wig My Father Wore* (1995) to the full-blown baroque stylistic extravagance of *The Pleasure of Eliza Lynch* (2002).

Metafictional and philosophical writing in Ireland continues to be dominated, however, by John Banville (b. 1945). Since the mid 1980s, Banville's fiction has continued its analysis of alternative languages and structures of perception. Following the acclaimed early eighties 'scientific tetralogy' – *Doctor Copernicus* (1976), *Kepler* (1981), *The Newton Letter* (1982), *Mefisto* (1986) – which featured the lives of mathematicians and astronomers, he produced a trilogy of novels based on motifs of art and painting, and which foregrounded concepts of representation and truth: *The Book of Evidence* (1989), *Ghosts* (1993) and *Athena* (1995). *The Book of Evidence*, inspired by a real-life incident in Ireland, presents the prison memoir of Freddie Montgomery, on trial for the brutal murder of a servant who interrupted his plan to steal a painting. In its gaps and inconsistencies, this memoir collapses the security of individual identity and, simultaneously, the truth-claims of all narrative. Montgomery's struggle with the inadequacies of language and imagination are pursued in *Ghosts* and in *Athena*.

In 1997, Banville brought his interest in these subjects to *The Untouchable*, a novel loosely based on the life of the Royal art curator and Cambridge double agent Anthony Blunt. Here, through the fractured personality of his protagonist Victor Maskell, the author teases out a series of ironic correspondences between political treason, marital infidelity and sexual ambiguity. The novel foregrounds Banville's enduring interest in the construction of selfhood, a topic pursued and expanded in the more recent *Eclipse* (2000) and its sequel, *Shroud* (2002). The development of Maskell's Anglo-Irish background illustrates at the same time Banville's characteristically tangential approach to Irish material. While the philosophical and cerebral character of his work has led many to regard his true affiliations as continental, his continued deployment of Irish landscapes and figures, together with his indulgence in a post-modern Gothic, confirm his strong affiliations to a national canon.

The novel of elsewhere

The concept of Banville's 'European' trajectory raises the larger question, however, of the expanding borders of contemporary Irish fiction and the growing school of novels situated outside Ireland itself. The Irish fiction of elsewhere, as it might be termed, obviously includes the category of emigration novels tracing a traditional Irish route to Britain. Joseph O'Connor's *Cowboys and Indians* (1991), James Ryan's *Home from England* (1995) and *Felicia's Journey* (1994), William Trevor's poignant study of Anglo-Irish relations as portrayed through the fate of a pregnant Irish girl crossing the sea to seek her English lover, are all notable variants on this theme. Several works set or partly set in mainland Europe, meanwhile, pursue the mediation of Irishness through alternative continental landscapes, including Italy in Deirdre Madden's *Remembering Light and Stone* (1992), Spain in Colm Tóibín's *The South* (1990), and Eastern Europe in *A Farewell to Prague* (1995) by Desmond Hogan (b. 1950). Perhaps most intriguing in this period have been novels which confront the historical and political experiences of other countries in implicit reflections of themes closer to home. *The Catastrophist* (1997) by Ronan Bennett (b. 1956) updates Graham Greene in a perceptive story of an Irish writer witnessing the 1960 revolution in the Congo, while in his elegant, understated trilogy of *Surrogate City* (1990), *The Last Shot* (1991) and *The Love Test* (1995), Hugo Hamilton (b. 1953) refracts familiar Irish preoccupations of memory, guilt and responsibility through the lens of Germany's wartime and post-war transitions.

The Irish novel's extension beyond national boundaries has come to be most heavily inflected, however, by a diaspora-led fiction, based in the United States and incorporating the work of younger novelists such as Dublin-born Emer Martin (b. 1968), whose *Breakfast in Babylon* (1995) and *More Bread or I'll Appear* (1999) feature contemporary Irish emigrants on picaresque tours of Europe and America respectively. Originally from County Limerick, Michael Collins has turned, in his recent works, *The Keepers of Truth* (2000) and *The Resurrectionists* (2002), to the dark underbelly of small-town Midwest America. Dominating this intersectional territory is Colum McCann (b. 1965), whose fiction is most recognisably that of a young Irish America. Following up the transatlantic connections which shaped his moving novel of family and memory, *Songdogs* (1995), he produced *This Side of Brightness* (1998), a documentary fiction of the men who built the river tunnels under New York and an elaborate historical study of the effects of racial, social and geographical displacement. Embedded in a traditional story-telling which gestures to his Irish roots, his poised descriptions and composed narrative voice suggest at the same time an American literary inheritance of Steinbeck and Hemingway, and his writing as a whole marks the turning point at which the horizons of a literary Irishness are being radically redrawn and expanded.

While it may not have constituted the critical counter-tradition of Joyce, Beckett and Flann O'Brien, the contemporary generation has nonetheless broken ground in forwarding the plurality of modern Ireland and in capitalising on voices of dissent, disillusionment and diaspora to narrate the multiple personalities of the present-day nation. The rupturing of an Irish national consensus has been two-way, of course, and in the wake of decades of emigration, it remains to be seen how the new immigrant communities recently settled in Ireland will change the profile of fictional narrative. 'How will the Irish subaltern "Other"', as one critic has put it, 'eventually cope with racial and ethnic Otherness within its own borders?'[10] This is perhaps the point at which a distinct post-colonial Irish fiction will emerge. In the meantime, the Irish novel of the contemporary period must be defined by its pursuit of a post-national ethos, its commitment to reviewing the difficult terms on which the various identities of modern Ireland have been negotiated.

NOTES

1. Declan Kiberd, *Inventing Ireland: The Literature of the Modern Nation* (London: Vintage, 1996), p. 578.
2. Gerry Smyth, *The Novel and the Nation: Studies in the New Irish Fiction* (London: Pluto, 1997), p. 177.
3. For a psychoanalysis of the 'child' as representative of Ireland in modern Irish writing, see Richard Haslam, '"A Race Bashed in the Face": Imagining Ireland as a Damaged Child', *Jouvert: A Journal of Postcolonial Studies* 4 (1999). See http://social.chass.ncsu.edu/jouvert.
4. See Roy Foster, 'We are All Revisionists Now', *Irish Review* 1 (1986), 1–5.
5. Luke Gibbons, *Transformations in Irish Culture* (Cork: Cork University Press in association with Field Day, 1996), p. 83.
6. See the discussion of Doyle and other writers by Shaun Richards, 'Northside Realism and the Twilight's Last Gleaming', *Irish Studies Review* 2 (1992), 18–20.
7. This point is developed by Gerry Smyth, 'The Right to the City: Re-presentation of Dublin in Contemporary Irish Fiction', in Liam Harte and Michael Parker (eds.), *Contemporary Irish Fiction: Themes, Tropes, Theories* (London: Macmillan, 2000).
8. See Christine St Peter's discussion of contemporary Irish incest narratives in *Changing Ireland: Strategies in Contemporary Women's Fiction* (London: Macmillan, 2000), p. 49.
9. In his editorial introduction, Éibhear Walshe makes this point in his discussion of the relationship between homosexuality and the gender hierarchies implicit within colonialism: *Sex, Nation and Dissent in Irish Writing* (Cork: Cork University Press, 1997).
10. Jennifer Jeffers, *The Irish Novel at the End of the Century: Gender, Bodies, Power* (London: Palgrave, 2002), p. 179.

GUIDE TO FURTHER READING

Cahalan, James. *The Irish Novel: A Critical History.* Dublin: Gill Macmillan, 1988.
Imhof, Rudiger. *The Modern Irish Novel: Irish Novelists after 1945.* Dublin: Wolfhound, 2002.

Kearney, Richard. *Postnationalist Ireland: Politics, Culture, Philosophy.* London: Routledge, 1997.

Kirby, Peader, Luke Gibbons and Michael Cronin (eds.). *Reinventing Ireland: Culture, Society and the Global Economy.* London: Pluto, 2003.

Peach, Linden. *The Contemporary Irish Novel: Critical Readings.* Basingstoke: Palgrave Macmillan, 2004.

Ryan, Ray (ed.). *Writing in the Irish Republic: Literature, Culture, Politics, 1949–1999.* Basingstoke: Macmillan, 2000.

INDEX

CAMBRIDGE COMPANIONS TO LITERATURE

CAMBRIDGE COMPANIONS TO CULTURE